W9-BQL-273

THE RISE
OF THE POLISH
MONARCHY

Winner of the Kosciuszko Foundation
Doctoral Dissertation Award for 1971

THE RISE
OF THE POLISH
MONARCHY

PIAST POLAND IN EAST CENTRAL
EUROPE, 1320–1370

PAUL W. KNOLL

The University of Chicago Press
Chicago and London

The University of Chicago Press, Chicago 60637
The University of Chicago Press, Ltd., London
© 1972 by The University of Chicago
All rights reserved. Published 1972
Printed in the United States of America
International Standard Book Number: 0–226–44826–6
Library of Congress Catalog Card Number: 77–187155

FOR SUE

CONTENTS

PREFACE

This book is both a study in Polish history and an analysis of one aspect of the history of east central Europe in the fourteenth century seen, as it were, from Cracow. It is not an attempt to write a complete history of the reigns of Władysław Łokietek and Casimir the Great; instead it focuses upon the re-emergence of the Polish state as a factor in the affairs of the region, and traces, in a roughly chronological manner, the role which Łokietek and Casimir gave Poland in this area and era.

Just as there developed in western Europe in the late Middle Ages a system of states in which the individual members carried out increasingly coherent policies toward one another; so also in east central Europe the great dynasties of the late Middle Ages were increasingly identified with political entities which formed an identifiable system of states. I have chosen to trace a part of this process with the Piasts in Poland because of the character and personality of the two rulers and because, of all the dynasties in this area, only the Piasts can be said to have had any kind of national base. These factors lend a unique character to the topic.

Because the historical material treated in this book is somewhat unfamiliar outside of east central Europe, I have chosen to be rather fuller in documentation, both to original sources and to secondary literature, than might otherwise have been warranted. I hope thereby to support my text so that others may follow me into this fascinating period. At the same time I hope to provide a glimpse of the impressive historiographical foundations upon which any contemporary historian rests his work.

One of the favorite images of medieval man was that expressed by Bernard of Chartres, who, according to John of Salisbury, "Used to say that we were like dwarfs seated on the shoulders of giants. If we see more and further than they, it is not due to our own clear eyes or tall bodies, but because we are raised on high and upborn by their gigantic bigness."

When I first began the study of medieval Polish history, I thought I should never see anything! Only because of many modern giants—teachers, family, friends, and historians of the past and present in Poland and elsewhere—does this present book possess any merit. I alone am responsible for its weaknesses. For the American of non-Polish background particularly, the wealth of the Polish historiographical tradition constitutes an immense debt and a foundation upon which to build. I have tried in the Introduction below to indicate the character of these riches as they apply to the topic of this book. Other giants of particular importance upon whose shoulders I have willingly stood are the late Kenneth Scott Latourette of Yale, whose unfailing interest in me as youth and adult meant more than he ever knew; S. Harrison Thomson, professor emeritus of the University of Colorado, who first led me into central Europe and who has since been my most influential mentor; the late Professor Tadeusz Manteuffel and Professor Aleksander Gieysztor of the University of Warsaw, and Docent Jerzy Zathey of the Biblioteka Jagiellońska in Cracow, each of whom greatly facilitated my research in Poland. I regret greatly never having met personally Professor Zdzisław Kaczmarczyk of Poznań, whose studies of Casimir, more than any other modern works, have left their imprint upon this book. Former colleagues at Purdue University in the history department's faculty seminar and present colleagues at the University of Southern California have patiently borne with me and provided needed intellectual stimulation and criticism. I should also like to thank Purdue Research Foundation, the American Council of Learned Societies, and the American Philosophical Society for their willingness to support financially my research in what is considered in the United States a rather esoteric subject. The University of Southern California has also contributed generous financial support toward the publication of this book. Mrs. Doug Hall and Mrs. Jerry Hintz successfully deciphered an illegible hand and transformed it into clean copy. The debt which I owe my wife, while including that for which spouses are usually thanked in prefaces, is in addition a profoundly personal one.

ABBREVIATIONS

A.G.Z.	*Akta grodzkie i ziemskie*
Annales eccl.	*Annales ecclesiastici* . . ., compiled by Baronius, Raynaldus, and Laderchius
C.D.Mor.	*Codex diplomaticus et epistolaris Moraviae*
C.D.M.P.	*Codex diplomaticus Majoris Poloniae*
C.D.P.M.	*Codex diplomaticus Poloniae Minoris*
C.D.Pol.	*Codex diplomaticus Poloniae*
C.D.Pr.	*Codex diplomaticus Prussicus*
Dogiel, *Codex*	M. Dogiel, ed., *Codex diplomaticus regni Poloniae*
Font. rer. Aust.	*Fontes rerum Austriacarum: Scriptores*
Font. rer. Boh.	*Fontes rerum Bohemicarum*
Font. rer. Germ.	*Fontes rerum Germanicarum*
Długosz, *Historia*	Johannes Długosz, *Historia Polonica*, in *Opera Omnia*
K.H.	*Kwartalnik Historyczny*
Lites	*Lites ac res gestae inter Polonos Ordinemque Cruciferorum, editio altera*
Ludewig, *Reliquiae*	J. P. Ludewig, *Reliquiae manuscriptorum*
M.G.H. SS.	*Monumenta Germaniae Historica, Scriptores*
M.G.H. SS., n.S.	*Monumenta Germaniae Historica, Scriptores rerum Germanicarum, nova Series*
Mon. Hist. Boem.	*Monumenta Historica Boemiae*
M.P.H.	*Monumenta Poloniae Historica*
M.P.V.	*Monumenta Poloniae Vaticana*
P.H.	*Przegląd Historyczny*
Pol. Słow. Biog.	*Polski Słownik biograficzny*
Pr. U.B.	*Preussische Urkundenbuch*
R.A.U.	*Rozprawy Akademii Umiejętności: wydział historyczno-filozoficzny*
S.A.U.	*Sprawozdanie Akademii Umiejętności: wydział historyczno-filozoficzny*
SS. rer. Aust.	*Scriptores rerum Austriacarum*
SS. rer. Boh.	*Scriptores rerum Bohemicarum*
SS. rer. Pr.	*Scriptores rerum Prussicarum*
Theiner, *Mon. Hung.*	A. Theiner, ed., *Vetera Monumenta historica Hungariam*
Theiner, *Mon. Pol.*	A. Theiner, ed., *Vetera Monumenta Poloniae*

INTRODUCTION
THE CONTEXT
OF POLISH HISTORY

There is, to the central European, an immediacy about history which gives him a deep appreciation of the past. Particularly in smaller countries whose halcyon days of greatness have long since fallen victim to the realities of great-power rivalries, past glories become an inspiration for an uncertain existence. This is not to say that only a few in the human community have an historical sense. Rather, it is to affirm that some depend more than others upon the past for strength in the present.

One period from which the Pole often renews his national pride is the last years of the Piast dynasty. This was a time when the century-long division into petty principalities was ended and the reunited kingdom emerged as an important power in east central Europe. Moreover, this was a time when the native Piast family led the nation, while other peoples were ruled by foreign dynasties. The reigns of Władysław Łokietek (1320–33) and his son Casimir (1333–70), the only Polish monarch to be called Great, provided the foundations upon which the later Jagiellonian dynasty rested. This book is a study of the role which Poland played in east central Europe in these years.

Three factors which shaped and guided early Polish history should be kept in mind as background to this topic: the medieval Latin Church, geography, and the Piast dynasty. The introduction of Christianity ranks with the dynastic and, later, national union with Lithuania as one of the two most important events in Polish history before the partitions. Duke Mieszko I, who had been recognized in 963 by Emperor Otto I as his *amicus*, accepted a Czech bride in 965 and was soon baptized. The fact that he chose, along with his subjects, Latin and not Orthodox Christianity forever bound Poland to the West. That he received his Christianity from Bohemia and not the empire reflected his recognition of the dangers of Germanization. Further, to protect and preserve the Slavic integrity of the state he ruled, he gave all his territory into the hands of the Holy See, making the territory part of the *patrimonium Petri*, and placed Poland under papal protection. This grant was renewed in the thirteenth century by Leszek the White.[1] Poland's ties with the West and the papacy enabled the kingdom to draw upon the West for the enrichment of its own native culture and for protection against its more powerful neighbors. The closeness of Poland's ties to the church is shown by the vigor with which the decrees of the Fourth Lateran Council (1215) were implemented in the kingdom, and by the continued support which the papacy granted the several rulers of Poland, including Władysław Łokietek and Casimir. In addition, the ecclesiastical unity within the kingdom under the archbishop of Gniezno facilitated many policies of Polish rulers and gave rise to a partnership between priest and prince which dominated the last half of the thirteenth century.

Geographical considerations have sometimes been overemphasized as factors influencing the development of a nation or state, and one cannot view everything in Polish history as the result of geography. But the features of the physical environment have nevertheless played a certain role.[2] Particularly in the Middle Ages, these features provided conditions of both protection and exposure. Except for rivers, which have not historically been effective defenses, Poland has no natural boundaries on the east and west. The state lies about midway on the great northern European plain which stretches from the Lowlands to the Ural Mountains (which are themselves not a major barrier). It has thus lain open to invasion by aggressive neighbors, while at the same time it has been able to move west or east as conditions warranted. This lack of natural protection forced medieval Polish rulers to pay particular attention to the rise and fall of political units to the west and east. During the thirteenth and fourteenth centuries, Poland had to deal with the expansionist tendencies of the rulers of Brandenburg and protect itself from the raids and invasions of Lithuanians and Tatars. To the north and south, Poland had more protection. The Baltic, which Mieszko I claimed as his border, was a formidable obstacle to invasion; but the kingdom nevertheless had to face a dangerous adversary in the north. In 1226 the Knights of the Teutonic Order were invited to aid a Mazovian duke in

1. The thorny topic of this donation is most conveniently treated in English by Francis Dvornik, *The Making of Central and Eastern Europe* (London, 1949), pp. 315–18. For more recent work, see the comments, with further bibliographical suggestions, of Henryk Łowmiański, "Les recherches sur l'histoire du moyen âge jusqu'à la fin du XVe s. au cours vingt années de la République Populaire de Pologne," in *La Pologne au XIIe Congrès International des sciences historiques à Vienne* (Warsaw, 1965), p. 177 and n. 71.

2. For the geography of Poland, physical, human, and economic, see R. H. Osborne, *East Central Europe, An Introductory Geography* (New York, 1967), pp. 227–82. An historical approach to Polish geography is provided by Norman J. G. Pounds, *Poland between East and West* (New York, 1964). A very useful Polish handbook is Stanisław Arnold, *Geografia historyczna Polski* (Warsaw, 1951).

subjugating the Prussians. When this task was finished, the Order settled permanently in Chełmno and Prussia, and carved out an *Ordensstaat*, which in the following century threatened the very existence of the Piast state. To the south, Poland was well protected by the mountains which girdle Bohemia and by the great wall of the Carpathians. The passes in these natural barriers, however, allowed both armies and more subtle influences to flow onto Polish territory. With the Czechs and their German rulers in the fourteenth century, Poland frequently had conflict; in the Magyars and their Angevin rulers, the Piasts found a traditional ally against Bohemia and threats from the east.

The historic ruling family in Poland was called Piast, although scholars are uncertain whether this word was originally a title, connoting something similar to the Mayor of the Palace of Frankish history, or the name of the founder of the dynasty, traditionally supposed to have been a simple peasant.[3] Various branches of this family ruled in Mazovia and Silesia throughout the Middle Ages, and in the kingdom proper until 1370. The significance of this dynasty is best demonstrated by the political events of the late twelfth and thirteenth centuries, when the unity which Poland had found under the early Piasts was almost irrevocably lost. Because the Poles failed to accept primogeniture, the kingdom nearly suffered the fate of the Kievan state. For a century and more, the land was divided into a number of independent principalities which vied unsuccessfully with one another for supremacy. Despite this political fragmentation, it was clearly recognized that all princes were members of the Piast family. This bond, combined with ecclesiastical unity under the archbishop of Gniezno, ultimately provided the basis for the reunion of the land and the restoration of the *regnum Poloniae*.

In addition to these background factors, certain other elements will play a major role in the narrative which follows. Through the last half-century of Piast rule in Poland a certain tension between the western and eastern interests of the state becomes increasingly apparent. For Władysław Łokietek the reunion of the kingdom was of paramount concern; this necessitated an overwhelming concentration upon relations with the Teutonic Knights, Brandenburg, and Bohemia. It was his task to protect Poland from the aggressive interests of these western neighbors, while at the same time attempting to recover lost territories, particularly Silesia and Pomorze. He utilized diplomacy when necessary, but relied more upon direct military action. Eastern concerns were decisively subordinate to the role which Poland played in the west. This was all the more true because the state's chief allies were there. From the papacy Łokietek (and Casimir after him) received material and moral support, though both monarchs contravened papal policy when they believed it to be opposed to Poland's best

---

3. The legendary antecedents of this dynasty are discussed by Kazimierz Ślaski, *Wątki historyczne w podaniach o początkach Polski* (Poznań, 1968), pp. 69–83.

interests. From Hungary both monarchs received financial and military support, and increasingly these two kingdoms were drawn closer together.

There was to be no break with the preceding period during Casimir's reign, but the greatest Piast relied more upon diplomacy and was more insistent about pursuing a peaceful policy than his father. But this statement, while true enough, will be observed to require two major qualifications. First, there was significant recourse to military means by Casimir, particularly in the middle period of his reign, for he did not hesitate to prosecute war vigorously when it served his ends; and second, the pacific policy, reflected in the west in the cession of Pomorze and Silesia, was highly pragmatic. Casimir followed the policy because it served the needs of the kingdom at the time and because he was unable to do otherwise. His recurring returns to the problem of these lost territories will suggest that he would gladly wage war if he felt his efforts would be justified by that over-whelming criterion of propriety: success. By diplomacy and war Casimir was to succeed in stabilizing a western frontier whose prior mutability contrasts sharply with its relative permanence in the four centuries following Casimir's reign.

That this border and affairs in the west were not to remain, as they had been during Łokietek's and Casimir's reigns, the focus of Polish attention was due in large measure to Casimir's own conquests in the east. These territorial acquisi-tions became in later centuries great opportunities for Polish expansion, both political and economic, and gradually the kingdom came to look eastward. But, as will be shown, this was not the interest of Casimir. His apparent un-willingness to commit Poland to an expansionist drive beyond Ruthenia and his constant concern for Silesia and Pomorze will suggest that he did not turn to the east to compensate for losses elsewhere. Rather, in the decade that it took him to stabilize Polish interests after the death of his father, Casimir was in-creasingly drawn to the east as a potential means of strengthening the *regnum* sufficiently to recover lands in the west. Thus, although affairs in the east demand ever more extensive attention in the middle chapters of this book, they will be best understood in the light of Poland's western interests.

Another important element which enriches the history of the region with which this book deals is the interplay between dynastic and national con-siderations. Although it is sometimes difficult to separate these various char-acteristics, in some instances one or the other will be observed to predominate. For example, Łokietek's and Casimir's dealings with the Angevin dynasty in Hungary, Casimir's efforts at a fruitful marriage, and his plans for his grandson Kaźko of Szczecin were peculiarly dynastic. But the attempts of these monarchs to recover Silesia and Pomorze, as well as their hostility to the Knights of the Teutonic Order, equally reflect a national consciousness that was becoming ever more evident throughout Europe. It may also be possible to add an ideological consideration to the already subtle shadings of intent and motive: Casimir's dealings in the east and his campaigns there eventually came to resemble a crusade or mission in which Poland was pursuing the larger interests of Christendom as well as its own territorial concerns. While the concept of Poland as a bulwark of Christendom (*antemurale Christianitatis*) was hardly fully developed in the fourteenth century, its essential elements emerged during Casimir's reign: Poland was beginning to regard itself, and to be regarded by others, as a borderland of Western, Latin civilization.

The growth of a regional system of states of which Poland was an integral part is yet another important theme of the following pages. At the beginning of our period, Łokietek could scarcely be counted an equal partner with the other rulers of the region. The successive Grand Masters of the Teutonic Order and the heads of the Wittelsbach, Luxemburg, and Angevin dynasties were all in a stronger position than he. Four and one half decades later, Poland had become an ally to be sought and an enemy to be avoided, and Casimir was in every respect a peer of the other leaders of the region. In addition, the influence which Poland exercised upon the emergence of the Lithuanian state in the east conditioned the role which this new element in the regional system was to play. These developments were to contribute greatly to the future history of the Polish state itself and to the complex character of the later history of the region.

Finally, it should be pointed out that such factors as internal rivalries, alliances, and administrative consolidation, while they are not central to the subject of this book, do nevertheless have an influence. An attempt has been made to indicate their role.

Though no one has attempted to delineate the whole of Poland's role in east central Europe under the last Piasts, the period is one that has been frequently written about. This historiographical tradition which we inherit is worth examining. In so doing, a portion of the riches referred to above in the Preface will be revealed; at the same time the strengths and weaknesses of this tradition can be noted.[4]

The medieval tradition in Poland can boast of two major works which bear upon the fourteenth century, the *Chronicon Polonorum* of Janko of Czarnków,[5] and

---

4. I exclude here all Western contributions and concentrate upon the Polish heritage. Few Western scholars have written upon medieval Polish history, but three exceptions are worth noting. In the nineteenth century, Jacob Caro undertook to continue the *Geschichte Polens* begun in 1840 by Richard Röpell. Caro published volume II, which covered the period from 1300 to 1386, in Gotha in 1863. By 1888 he had added another three volumes to bring the story to 1506. Despite its age, this history has not yet been superseded in the West. The French scholar Pierre David is the author of an indispensable study of the sources, *Les sources de l'histoire de Pologne à l'époque des Piasts, 963–1386* (Paris, 1934). Recently the German historian Gotthold Rhode has begun, with his *Die Ostgrenze Polens, Politische Entwicklung, kulturelle Bedeutung und geistige Auswirkung*, volume I: *Im Mittelalter bis zum Jahre 1401* (Cologne and Graz, 1955), a major study of Poland's eastern policy and its effect upon the kingdom.

5. *M.P.H.*, II, 619–756. For analyses of his work see *M.P.H.*, II, 601–618; Ludwik Kubala, "Jan Czarnkowski i jego kronika," *Biblioteka Warszawska*, XXXI (1871), iii, 348–65, iv, 59–75; Wanda Moszczeńska, "O interpretację Janka z Czarnkowa," *K.H.*, XL (1926), 400–408;

the *Historia Polonica libri XII* of Johannes Długosz.[6] The former was written by Casimir's vice-chancellor, who later became deeply involved in the political maneuverings during the reign of Louis of Anjou. His treatment of Casimir is very favorable, for part of his purpose in the work was to contrast the peace, stability, and justice of the rule of the last Piast with the years from 1370 to 1382, when "at the time of this king there was to be found neither stability nor justice in the kingdom of Poland."[7] Janko's work is uneven for Casimir's period. It is episodic and highly compressed. But as a narrative, it goes far beyond the annalistic approach of his contemporaries and may be legitimately regarded as a literary and historical document of the highest value.

The work of Długosz, who was a canon in Cracow and an informal advisor to the monarch and cardinals in his day, was modeled in part upon the *Decades* of Livy and is possessed of a breadth of vision unmatched by any other medieval Polish author and by few in western Europe.[8] The quality of Długosz's work is high, for he gathered his sources widely, took into account factors of cause and effect, and attempted to utilize nonliterary sources. Only when he dealt with matters relating to Polish-German (particularly Polish-Teutonic Order) affairs does one find his customary balance missing.[9] Długosz's view of the period treated in this book was highly influential upon succeeding historians. According to him, the reunification of the kingdom was largely Łokietek's work, as was the defense of Poland against the naked aggression of the Luxemburgers and Knights. Casimir in turn attempted to recover the lost territories while providing, internally, the peace, stability, and justice which Janko had earlier admired.

These ideas were further elaborated by two sixteenth-century authors,

---

Józef Sieradzki, "Sprawa Janka z Czarnkowa i jego utwór." *Studia Źródłoznawcze*, IV (1959), 33–57; and Jan Dąbrowski, *Dawne Dziejopisarstwo Polskie* (Wrocław, Warsaw, and Cracow, 1964), pp. 140–63.

6. In *Opera Omnia*, edited by A. Przezdziecki, 14 vol. (Cracow, 1863–87), vols. X-XIV. For analyses of his work, see Heinrich Zeissberg, *Die polnische Geschichtsschreibung des Mittelalters* (Leipzig, 1873), pp. 197–343; A. Semkowicz, *Krytyczny rozbiór Dziejów polskich Jana Długosza (do roku 1384)* (Cracow, 1887); Wanda Semkowicz-Zarembina, *Powstanie i dzieje autografu Annalium Jana Długosza* (Cracow, 1952); and Dąbrowski, *Dziejopisarstwo Polskie*, pp. 189–240.

7. *M.P.H.*, II, 721.

8. "Dlugossius multis operis sui locis Titi Livii, rerum Romanarum scriptoris, scribendi modum, pugnarum descriptiones et similia secutus est." Explanatory note to Długosz's *Litterae dedicatoriae* in the new edition of Długosz now being prepared: *Annales seu Cronicae incliti regni Poloniae opera venerabilis domini Joannis Dlugossii* . . . (Warsaw, 1964–), I, 329. Długosz himself wrote (*Annales*, I, 62), "Si quis vero ob id me carpendum putet, quod non solum Polonorum res gestas perscripserim sed eciam Bohemorum, Hungarorum, Ruthenorum, Pruthenorum, Saxonum, Lythwanorum, Romanorum insuper pontificum atque imperatorum et regum, a multis ignoratas attingerim, sciat me consulto et veritatis facibus cognoscende impulsum necessitate id egisse."

9. His anti-German feeling (which is of course perfectly understandable, since we are long past the time of any positive Polish-German interaction) was partly responsible for his collection of the documents relating to the Polish-Order legal processes of 1320–21, 1339, and 1412. His collection became the basis for the printed versions of the *Lites*.

Marcin Kromer[10] and Maciej Stryjkowski.[11] In their works, Łokietek was greatly overshadowed by his son, and they are explicit in designating the latter as Casimirus Magnus. But their histories, despite their humanistic orientation, are little more than annalistic treatments and do not even approach the high level of Długosz, the source upon which they so heavily depend. This same judgment may be made of the writers of the seventeenth and early eighteenth centuries, for in these years little attention was directed toward the Piast era. This situation was changed radically by the appearance of the historical writing of Bishop Adam Naruszewicz.

Naruszewicz (1733–96) marks the beginning of modern Polish historiography.[12] His magnum opus, for which he collected 230 volumes of notes, was his *Historya Narodu Polskiego od początku chrześcijaństwa*; it was never completed, for death interrupted the bishop's work after he reached the personal union of Poland and Lithuania of 1386. His ideal was to present the facts of Polish history honestly, impartially, and accurately. There is much documentary material included in his work, and it sometimes appears on first glance to be merely a commentary upon the sources. Closer examination reveals it to be much more, for Naruszewicz attempted to identify factors of cause and effect and to include both economic and cultural considerations as well as political narrative.[13] Very much a man of his time, he was influenced by the events of Poland's Enlightenment and the partitions. When he dealt with questions of Poland's reunification under Łokietek and the beginning of her international prestige under Casimir, he saw the greatest contributions of these monarchs in the strengthening of royal power over the aristocracy and their valiant struggle against the aggressions of foreign powers. His synthesis was the first of two in the partition and postpartition period, and has, in its emphasis upon a strong central authority and vigorous foreign policy, a certain pragmatic cast.

The second synthesis was the work of Joachim Lelewel and stands more in the romantic tradition. Lelewel (1786–1861) was a many-faceted genius—historian, patriot, numismatist, bibliographer—who fully deserved the honor bestowed

10. *Martini Cromeri De origine et rebus gestis Polonorum libri XXX* (Basel, 1555). There is a fine Polish edition under the title *Kronika Polska* (Warsaw, 1767). See also Ludwik Finkel, "Marcin Kromer, Historyk polski XVI wieku. Rozbiór krytyczny," *R.A.U.*, XVI (1883), 302–508.

11. The best edition is Maciej Stryjkowski, *Kronika Polska, litewska, zmudzka i wszystkiej Rusi*, 2 vols. (Warsaw, 1846). In these volumes see the introductory analyses of Mikołaj Malinowski, "Wiadomość o życiu i pismach Macieja Stryjkowskiego" (I, 1–30) and Ignacy Daniłowicz, "Wiadomość o właściwych litewskich latopiscach" (I, 31–63).

12. Biographical information on Naruszewicz may be found in Piotr Chmielowski's article in *Wielka Encyklopedia Powszechna Ilustrowana*, series 2, pts. i-ii (Warsaw, 1903), pp. 234–37. The best study of Naruszewicz's work is Neomisia Rutkowska, *Bishop A. Naruszewicz and His History of the Polish Nation. A Critical Study* (Washington, D.C., 1941). A later historian, Joachim Lelewel (see below) also has some important insights on Naruszewicz. See his "Porównanie Karamzina z Naruszewiczem," in *Polska, dzieje i rzeczy jej rozpatrywane* (Poznań, 1851–68), XVIII, 199–319.

13. See Bernard Ziffer, *Poland, History and Historians, Three Bibliographical Essays* (New York, 1952), p. 15, who analyzes Naruszewicz's *Memorjał względem pisania historji narodowej*.

upon him in 1858 by the *Societé Numismatique Belge*: a medal inscribed *Inter eruditissimos orbis terrarum princeps*.[14] His views on the era of Łokietek (who was a special favorite) and Casimir mark the first break with previous tradition. In 1822, at the end of his first year as professor at the University of Vilno, Lelewel delivered an address upon Łokietek's time in which he argued that the reunion of the country and the successful path it pursued in relations with other powers was the common work of monarch and nation: the rulers and the people of the kingdom had shared equally.[15] He never in any way minimized the accomplishments of Łokietek and Casimir, but as a romantic he saw freedom of the individual, of society, and of the nation as the basis for the political liberalism he advocated. The soundest element upon which this freedom may be founded is the gentry, or—since in later years the gentry was also permeated by abuses—more generally the people. In fact, Lelewel once argued that the full freedom of the nation could come only "through the people's rule, political equality, representative authorities, responsibility of officials directly to the nation, from the lowest to those holding highest office."[16] This spirit, in varying degrees, colors all of his work.

The mid-nineteenth century in Polish historiography is dominated by the figure of yet another romantic, Karol Szajnocha (1818–68). Besides Lelewel, the two most important intellectual influences upon him were the Western historians Macaulay and Thierry.[17] Szajnocha saw the struggle for reunion under Łokietek as a coalition between the future king and the nobility against the clergy.[18] This same understanding is at the root of his study of Casimir, in which he sees the nobility as the driving force with the king in pursuing Poland's place in central Europe. Because of this anticlerical tinge, Szajnocha is, despite his other "bourgeois" tendencies, relatively sympathetically treated in contemporary Poland.

14. Lelewel's production and the literature upon him is voluminous. His most important works were collected in twenty volumes and published in Poznan under the title *Polska, dzieje i rzeczy jej rozpatrywane* (1851–68). They are now being reissued in a handsome edition in Poland, where he is correctly recognized as a great scholar and regarded, with perhaps less validity, as a proto-Marxist hero (see Jan Baszkiewicz, *Powstanie zjednoczonego państwa polskiego [na przełomie, XIII i XIV w.]* [Warsaw, 1954], p. 8). Good analyses are given by Tadeusz Korzon, "Pogląd na działalność J. Lelewela," *K.H.*, XI (1897), 257–309; Helena Wieckowska, "Wstęp," in *Joachim Lelewel, Wybór pism historycznych* (Wrocław, 1950), pp. iii–lix; M.H. Serejski, "Wstęp," in *Joachim Lelewel, Wybór pism politycznych* (Warsaw, 1954), pp. v–xlix; and William J. Rose, "Lelewel as Historian," *Slavonic Review*, XV (1936), 649–62.

15. "Ocalenie Polski za króla Łokietka," in *Polska, dzieje i rzeczy jej*, XI, 239–259.

16. Quoted by Ziffer, *Poland, History and Historians*, p. 18.

17. Władysław Smolenski, *Szkoły historyczne w Polsce*, 4th ed. (Wrocław, 1952), pp. 69 f. On Szajnocha, see Ludwik Finkel, "Karol Szajnocha. Próba ujęcia syntezy i genezy poglądów historjograficznych wielkiego pisarza," *Ziemia Czerwieńska*, I (1935), 1–17; and Wiktor Hahn, "Karol Szajnocha jako autor dramatyczny. W 80-rocznicę śmierci 1868–1948," *Roczniki Zakładu Narodowego im. Ossolińskich*, III (1948), 471–528.

18. See Szajnocha, *Odrodzenie się Polski za Władysława Łokietka*, in *Pisma* (Cracow, 1887), I, 285 ff. His study *Wiek Kazimierza Wielkiego* is in *Szkice historyczne* (Lwów, 1854).

The course of Polish historiography in the second half of the nineteenth century was less clearly defined than before. Two trends, among many, are particularly relevant for this study. One was the increasing technical competence of Polish historians; the other, the disappearance of all romantic tendencies and the emergence of a stark realism (or even pessimism) about the Polish past, especially the partition period.[19]

The transformation of the Scientific Society of Cracow in 1872 into the Polska Akademia Umiejętności and the foundation fourteen years later of the Polish Historical Society in Lwów marked the beginning of a renaissance in Polish historiography. From the former came an avalanche of edited documents, including the nineteen-volume *Monumenta Medii Aevi historica res gestas Poloniae illustrantia* and the completion of the six-volume *Monumenta Poloniae Historica*. These two sets, taken together, provided well-edited sources on the basis of which a series of brilliant monographs and stimulating syntheses were written in the following decades. Many of these appeared in the *Transactions* of the philosophical-historical section of the Academy. In the meantime, in Lwów, the *Kwartalnik historyczny* was soon recognized as an outstanding historical journal, and scarcely an issue appeared without some important study on the fourteenth century.[20] The late nineteenth and early twentieth century also saw the blossoming of local historiography, with the founding of local historical societies and groups of "friends of learning" in all fields, including history; Poznań (1857), Toruń (1875), Cracow (1896), Płock and Warsaw (1907) had such groups. This historical interest on the local and national levels was responsible for many works which have been fundamental to this book.

The emergence of realism and pessimism in Polish historiography is most clearly seen in what came to be known as the Cracow school. The most active figure there in the study of the Polish Middle Ages was Józef Szujski, whose *Historia Polski treściwie opowiedzianej ksiąg dwanaście* touched especially on the fourteenth century.[21] Szujski saw Łokietek as a kind of popular hero, not

---

19. Two works are highly recommended for following this latter development: Ziffer, *Poland, History and Historians*, pp. 19–24; and, in more detail, Smolenski, *Szkoły historyczne*.

20. On the *Polska Akademia Umiejętności*, see Stanisław Kutrzeba, *Polska Akademia Umiejętności 1872–1937* (Cracow, 1938); and Jan Hulewicz, *Polska Akademia Umiejętności 1873–1948, Zarys dziejów* (Cracow, 1948). For the Polish historical society, see "Jubileusz 50-lecia P.T.H. i Kwartalnika Historycznego," *K.H.*, LI (1937), 643–53; and the comprehensive collective work *Polskie Towarzystwo Historyczne 1886–1956. Księga pamiątkowa z okazji Zjazdu Jubileuszowego PTH w Warszawie 19–21 X 1956*, ed. Stanisław Herbst and Irena Pietrzak-Pawłowska (Warsaw, 1958).

21. Published in Warsaw in 1889. Szujski was born in 1835 and died at the age of forty-eight after a distinguished career in the Chair of Polish History at the University of Cracow. In addition to his historical works, he is also noted for his poems and historical dramas. See Jan Adamus, "O syntezach historycznych Szujskiego. Szkic z dziejów polskiej myśli historycznej," in *Studia historyczne ku czci Stanisława Kutrzeby* (Cracow, 1938), II, 1–27; and Zofia Libiszowska, "Tendencje społeczne i polityczne dramatów Jozefa Szujskiego," *Prace Polonistyczne*, X (1952), 285–301.

unlike Kościuszko, and regarded his military activity as an introduction to the more broadly based diplomacy of Casimir. In his work he also pointed out the great economic progress which Poland had made in the thirteenth century and the way in which this was confirmed by the last two Piasts. At the same time, he emphasized the importance of the monarchic ideal, which he felt to be the key to an understanding of this period. This attitude foreshadowed a growing conservatism that found expression in Szujski's last years in an intolerant clericalism which unfortunately characterized much of the Cracow school.

Although he devoted his attention largely to more recent periods, Michał Bobrzyński (1849–1935), as the chief representative of the Cracow school, deserves to be mentioned here. His most famous synthetic work, and one for which he was bitterly attacked from all sides, was his *Dzieje Polski w zarysie*.[22] One of the criticisms was against his positive evaluation of the period of Czech rule in Poland and his seeming deemphasis of the significance of Casimir's diplomacy. This attitude appeared to some as a kind of false cosmopolitanism which justified foreign rule in Poland. But this was not the real heart of Bobrzyński's understanding of Polish history. It was his contention that inefficient government and internal anarchy were responsible for most of Poland's historic woes; and that a strong government, centered in the monarch, was the basis upon which national greatness was built. In this respect he gave high marks to Łokietek and Casimir, for both represented the absolute power of the state.

The grand syntheses which have been described to this point were important and stimulating, but they too often rested upon somewhat narrow scholarly foundations. This was particularly true when the period under consideration was the fourteenth century, where the extent of primary investigations was very limited. As a result, since the end of the nineteenth century, Polish scholarship has tended to concentrate upon "micrographic"[23] efforts which substantially broadened the aforementioned foundations. But only three syntheses have been attempted in this century for the medieval period. In the remainder of this introduction, we will point out some of the more significant "micrographers" and monographic scholars, then examine the contribution of the syntheses.

Both Władysław Abraham (1860–1941) and Jan Ptaśnik (1876–1930) contributed major studies of the ecclesiastical history of this period. The former's *Powstanie organizacji kościoła łacińskiego na Rusi*, of which only volume 1 appeared (Lwów, 1904), and the latter's brilliant study "Denar świętego Piotra obrońcą

---

22. Bobrzyński is also the author of "Bunt wójta krakowskiego Alberta z r. 1311," *Biblioteka Warszawska*, XXXVII, pt. iii (1877), 329–48. For two views on him and his work, see Stanisław Estreicher's biographical article in *Pol. Słow. Biog.*, II, 165–68; and Stefan Kieniewicz, "Tło historyczne 'Dziejów Polski' M. Bobrzyńskiego," *P.H.*, XXXVII (1947), 343–56.

23. Originally, I believe, the word is Oskar Halecki's. See his stimulating analysis of Polish scholarship as of the late 1920s: "Potrzeby nauki polskiej w dziedzinie historji," *Nauka Polska*, X (1929), 259–65. This article appeared as part of a general survey of the state of Polish scholarship in all fields after ten years of independence.

jedności politycznej i kościelnej w Polsce," each emphasized the importance of the church in the fourteenth century, both internally and in relation to the rulers with whom the Piasts dealt. While such a point of view was hardly a new departure, never before had such impeccable scholarship been brought to bear on it.

Another approach which received a great deal of attention in the prewar period was the question of constitutional history. Beginning with the publication in 1906 of the first volume of Stanisław Kutrzeba's *Historja ustroju Polski*,[24] most of the important scholars in Poland were involved in a very high-level polemic: Stanisław Kętrzyński, Stanisław Krzyżanowski, M. Łodyński, and especially Oswald Marjan Balzer (1858–1933).[25]

Balzer had already distinguished himself as the author of the still unsurpassed handbook, *Genealogia Piastów* (Cracow, 1895), and for some years had been working on the question of the nature of the Polish constitution. With his "uncommonly acute mind and phenomenal memory . . . extreme diligence and an ability to concentrate,"[26] Balzer was well fitted to do just this. On the basis of his other works and the polemic with Kutrzeba, he published his magisterial three-volume *Królestwo Polskie, 1295–1370* (Lwów, 1919–20). Though he intended this to be merely preliminary to a history of the legal institutions and the constitution of Poland, it stands as the supreme achievement of a career without parallel in the history of Polish scholarship.[27] Balzer's view of this period is not a balanced one, for it is broadly constitutional. His study is essentially an analysis of the concepts of the *regnum Poloniae* and the *corona regni Poloniae*. His view of the unification of Poland under Łokietek is one that emphasizes the coalescence of a variety of factors around the concept of the *regnum* personified in Łokietek; during Casimir's time, in this view, there was a further development so that the *corona* became the personification of an organically unified state. This somewhat abstract approach was particularly weak when Balzer turned to the question of how the *regnum* or the *corona* interacted with other states.

During the interwar period, the question of Polish foreign policy in the

---

24. Kutrzeba (1876–1946) was long recognized as one of the deans of Polish medievalists, and the *Studia historyczne*, 2 vol. (1938) in his honor is a model of what a *Festschrift* should be. Analyses of his work are given by Dąbrowski. "Stanisław Kutrzeba," *Nowa Polska*, VI (1946), 185–92; and Baszkiewicz, "Poglądy Stanisława Kutrzeby na państwo," *Państwo i Prawo*, V (1950), x, 60–75.

25. Balzer's articles questioning Kutrzeba are in *K.H.*, XX (1906), 1–57, and 397–441; XXI (1907), 1–58, and 193–291. Kutrzeba's responses are in *K.H.*, XX (1906), 581–626, and XXI (1907), 375–402.

26. Ziffer, *Poland, History and Historians*, p. 28. Ziffer was a student of Balzer's at Lwów.

27. See *Pol. Słow. Biog.*, I, 245–48; *Pamięci Oswalda Balzera, Przemówienia na uroczystej Akademji urządzonej staraniem Towarzystwa Naukowego 22 Stycznia 1934* (Lwów, 1934). Postwar Poland has not yet seen a major assessment of Balzer, although much of Baszkiewicz, *Powstanie zjednoczonego państwa*, is written with an eye upon Balzer and challenges many of his theses.

fourteenth century received considerable attention, though there was no comprehensive study. Stanisław Zajączkowski's *Polska a Zakon Krzyżacki w ostatnich latach Władysława Łokietka* (Lwów, 1929), emphasized the German threat to the newly reconstituted Polish state, while his "Polska a Wittelsbachowie w pierwszej połowie XIV wieku" concentrated upon Brandenburg. The postwar problems of Silesia also influenced the decision to publish the excellent three-volume *Historia Śląska od najdawniejszych czasów do roku 1400* (Cracow, 1933–39). Relations with Hungary were the subject of Jan Dąbrowski's *Ostatnie lata Ludwika Wielkiego 1370–1382* (Cracow, 1918), which continued his earlier interest in this area shown in the long article "Elżbieta Łokietkówna" (1916). The question of Poland's expansion into Ruthenia was treated by the youthful work of Henryk Paszkiewicz, *Polityka Ruska Kazimierza Wielkiego* (Warsaw, 1925). Oskar Halecki's outstanding *Dzieje Unii jagiellońskiej* (two volumes, Cracow, 1919–20) dealt not only with the union itself but also with its historical background.

Today, in the Polish People's Republic, the names of Jan Baszkiewicz and Zdzisław Kaczmarczyk are inseparably connected with the period of the last Piasts. Baszkiewicz's rigidly Marxist study, *Powstanie zjednoczonego państwa polskiego na przełomie XIII i XIV wieku*, was published in 1954. In it he analyzes all of the forces at work in the early fourteenth century, with special attention to the role of Poland's neighbors as catalytic agents in the reunification. An indication of how this author's views may have changed in the past fifteen years comes in the more flexible approach taken in his recent short biography of Łokietek.[28] Already before the war, Professor Kaczmarczyk of Poznań had published the first volume of a study of the political organization of Poland in Casimir's time. The second volume on the church and culture followed shortly after the war, and a sound but popular biography was published in 1948.[29] Since that time, he has devoted three further efforts to the reign of Casimir: a study, with Stefan Weyman, of the king's military reforms; an updated biography in honor of the six-hundredth anniversary of the University of Cracow; and a short biographical sketch in the Polish biographical dictionary.[30] The sum total of these moderate and balanced works is to present us with a more complete picture of Casimir's Poland, with emphasis upon internal affairs.

The first of three twentieth-century syntheses was the *Historia polityczna Polski*, which was sponsored by the Polska Akademia Umiejętności as a presentation of the cultural, historical, and economic background of the new Poland

28. See my review of this book, *Polska Czasów Łokietka* (Warsaw, 1968), in *The Polish Review*, XV, pt. iii (Summer 1970), 83–84.

29. Zdzisław Kaczmarczyk, *Monarchia Kazimierza Wielkiego*, 2 vols. (Poznań, 1939–46), and *Kazimierz Wielki (1333–1370)* (Warsaw, 1948).

30. Kaczmarczyk and Stefan Weyman, *Reformy wojskowe i organizacja siły zbrojnej za Kazimierza Wielkiego* (Warsaw, 1958); *Polska czasów Kazimierza Wielkiego* (Cracow, 1964); and *Pol. Słow. Biog.*, XII, 264–69.

after Versailles. The two sections which bear upon the fourteenth century were written by Stanisław Zachorowski and Oskar Halecki.[31] They are competent and well written, but break no new ground. Politics, the clergy, and the church play important roles in both sections, and few interpretive judgments are proffered. Much the same description might be given of the *Dzieje Polski średniowieczne* with sections on Łokietek and Casimir written by Zachorowski and Dąbrowski.[32] Designed for the advanced history student in the university, this work possesses all of the strengths and weaknesses of a textbook; it has coverage, balance, and proportion, and it is solid and unexciting.

The new *Historia Polski* of the Polish Academy of Sciences is a very different kind of synthesis. It is exciting, stimulating, and frequently infuriating. Work on it was begun soon after the first methodological congress of Polish historians in the winter of 1951–52. Within four years a trial edition was ready which reflected the restructuring of Polish historical science under the leadership of Marxist-Leninist-Stalinist thought. This trial edition, or *makieta*, was subjected to criticism for a time, revised, expanded, and in 1958 the first volume was published. The early sections, which include the fourteenth century, suffer from rigid periodization and compartmentalization, and the heavy hand of ideology is still apparent. Still, it provides old data in new combinations and summarizes the results of much sophisticated scholarship.[33] Few Western historians would want to rely on it exclusively; no Western historian can afford to ignore it. Whatever its weaknesses, it is the best introduction to this period.

31. Zachorowski, "Wiek XIII i panowanie Władysława Łokietka," *Encyklopedya Polska*, V, i (Warsaw, Lublin, Łódź, and Cracow, 1920), 134–309. This was a posthumously published work, since Professor Zachorowski died in 1918. Halecki, "Kazimierz Wielki, 1333–1370," *Encyk. Pol.*, V, pt. i, 310–409.

32. Roman Grodecki, Stanisław Zachorowski, and Jan Dąbrowski, *Dzieje Polski średniowiecznej*, 2 vols. (Cracow, 1926).

33. The best treatment of the new *Historia Polski* is the chapter by W. M. Drzewieniecki, "The New *Historia Polski*," in D. S. Wandycz, ed., *Studies in Polish Civilization* (New York, n.d. [1971?]), pp. 176–96.

1
RESTAURATIO REGNI

Władysław Łokietek was over seventy when he died early in March, 1333, in the royal castle of Cracow's Wawel Hill.[1] His death, though not wholly unexpected (he died "after much suffering") may well have seemed inopportune. His last years had been clouded by the invasions of aggressively hostile neighbors and the deterioration of the internal administration; these factors, combined with the relative youth and inexperience of his son and heir Casimir, made the future for the newly reestablished kingdom seem uncertain indeed. In actuality, however, these are only superficial impressions. Beneath them lay a firm foundation of unity and stability which had been partially revealed during the reign of Łokietek and which Casimir utilized to provide the basis for Poland's future greatness. The successes of the son were an extension of the achievements of the father, and the last half-century before the extinction of the Piast dynasty, though divided into two reigns, nevertheless constitutes a whole.

The Poland into which Łokietek ("the Short") was born was not a state but a collection of territorially fragmented principalities. After the death of Bolesław the Wrymouth in 1138 the ancient *regnum Poloniae* had been divided among the sons of Bolesław and their descendants in turn. As a result, for a century and more political localism and regional particularism had made steady inroads. The princes of this period developed a narrowness of outlook and a concentration upon petty dynastic advancement which in later years seriously retarded the process of reunification.

1. "In castro Cracoviensi. . . ." Janko of Czarnków, *Chronicon Polonorum*, in *M.P.H.*, II, 619. The date of death is variously given. Janko says March 12; Wigand of Marburg, *Chronica nova Prutenica*, in *SS. rer. Pr.*, II, 480, indicates February 28; but the most widely accepted date is March 2, given by *Rocznik małopolski*, in *M.P.H.*, III, 196, and Długosz, *Historia*, III, 159.

Despite this political disintegration, the development of Poland had not come to a halt. The church had in the early thirteenth century purified and strengthened itself; the intellectual life of the land had shown more openness to Italian and French, as well as German, influences; and the economic and social evolution of the former kingdom had proceeded apace. Both centrifugal and centripetal forces thus existed and vied inconclusively for ascendancy in Poland. During the lifetime of Łokietek the latter forces won out; by identifying himself with them, the future king emerged as the restorer of the kingdom.[2]

Władysław Łokietek, grandson of Duke Conrad of Mazovia and direct descendant of King Casimir the Just (*reg.* 1177–94), was born into the Kujavian branch of the Piast family sometime between March 3, 1260, and January 19, 1261.[3] When his father, Duke Casimir of Kujavia and Łęczyca, died in 1267, Łokietek's older half-brother, Leszek the Black, inherited Sieradz and Łęczyca, while another half-brother, Ziemomysł, obtained northern Kujavia together with the important city of Inowrocław. Łokietek and his two brothers received southern Kujavia together with Brześć and the region of Dobrzyń. In this microcosm of the territorially fractionalized Polish state, Łokietek's interests were zealously protected by his mother, Eufrozyna. For example, in a jurisdictional dispute with the Knights of the Teutonic Order in 1273 she spoke in his behalf.[4] Łokietek did act in his own right two years later,[5] but it was only after the death without heir of Leszek the Black on September 10, 1288, that Łokietek became able to act independently.

Upon his half-brother's death, Łokietek received only the territory of Sieradz, for the greater share of the inheritance—including the city of Cracow —went to Duke Henry IV Probus of Wrocław.[6] This young prince is in some respects one of the more appealing figures of the late thirteenth century. He was well educated, having been brought up at the court of King Přemysl Otakar II of Bohemia, one of the greatest statesmen-warriors of the Middle Ages. In addition Henry was a diplomat and statesman himself, rather than a mere soldier, and had a breadth of vision which elevated him above the narrow

2. Brief treatments of this period in English may be found in *The Cambridge History of Poland*, ed. W. F. Reddaway, et al., 2 vols. (Cambridge, 1941–50), I, 43–59, 85–107; and Oscar Halecki, *A History of Poland* (reprinted, New York, 1966), pp. 41–50. A recent shorter account by Gotthold Rhode, *Geschichte Polens, Ein Überblick* (Darmstadt, 1966), pp. 41–59 is very good. The standard treatment in Polish is now the *Historia Polski*, general editor Tadeusz Manteuffel, vol. I, *do roku 1764*, in three parts, ed. Henryk Łowmiański (Warsaw, 1958–61), pt. i, pp. 250–367. Because the major portion of his book is still the most important synthesis of Polish history in the period of re-unification, a good introduction to this era of division is Jan Baszkiewicz, *Powstanie zjednoczonego państwa polskiego (na przełomie XIII i XIV w.)* (Warsaw, 1954), pp. 27–39.

3. See Oswald Balzer, *Genealogia Piastów* (Cracow, 1895), pp. 10, 339–40, for the sources.

4. *C.D.M.P.*, I, # 450.

5. *Cod. Dipl. Pol.*, I, 56.

6. The basis for this inheritance rested upon an earlier agreement between four of the most important Polish princes. See Balzer, *Królestwo Polskie 1295–1370*, 3 vols. (Lwów, 1919–20), I, 272. For Duke Henry IV, see *Pol. Słow. Biog.*, IX, 405–8.

limitations of many of his contemporaries. The goal of his policy was nothing less than the crown of a reunited Poland. His plans received a serious setback, however, when the nobles of Little Poland refused to accept his rule. They turned instead to the ambitious Łokietek, who made himself master of the city of Cracow, though with some opposition.

The importance of this step should not be underestimated. The visitor to Cracow today is impressed by the magnificence of the many remaining monuments of late medieval times, some of them the work of Łokietek himself and, after him, Casimir. What may be overlooked is the fact that Cracow is a city of great military significance, since its acropolis, Wawel Hill, is an excellent strongpoint which in 1288 was already well fortified. Located in a curve of the Vistula River and commanding the countryside, Wawel provided an important base for Łokietek. The city of Cracow, however, possessed more than military significance. As Oswald Balzer, dean of an earlier generation of Polish scholars, has pointed out, by the end of the thirteenth century the city had become the focus of sentiment for Polish unity.[7] Not only was it the capital of Little Poland, it emerged in this period as a rival to the archiepiscopal city of Gniezno for ecclesiastical primacy in the whole of Poland.[8] By the time Łokietek seized control, Cracow was known in Poland as "the seat of the kingdom" and "the royal city and dwelling place," where "the Polish crown . . . had been since antiquity." In addition to this military and ideological basis for Cracow's ascendancy, there were also important material reasons involved. The city had long been on the major trade routes, and its commercial and economic significance by the end of the thirteenth century was spreading far beyond its own locale.[9] He who achieved control of Cracow, therefore, had taken a major step toward the restoration of the kingdom.

It is doubtful that Łokietek held any such sophisticated concept. He had not yet begun to look beyond the narrowly dynastic interests of his contemporaries. It was just as well, for only a few months later Henry IV sent an army from Silesia to lay siege to Cracow. The siege was unnecessary. The citizenry opened the gates to the troops and Łokietek fled hastily in disguise.[10] This was the first of many reverses he was to suffer.

After his victory in Little Poland, Henry undertook to consolidate his rule

7. Balzer, *Królestwo Polskie*, I, 172–97.

8. This was largely as the result of the growth of the cult of the martyred St. Stanisław in Poland, with its center in Cracow. See Baszkiewicz, *Powstanie zjednoczonego państwa*, pp. 440–46; and D. Borawska, *Z dziejów jednej legendy* (Warsaw, 1950), pp. 50 ff.

9. Stanisław Kutrzeba, "Handel Krakowa w wiekach średnich na tle stosunków handlowych Polski," *R.A.U.*, XLIV (1903), 1–196, but pp. 121 ff. especially. See also the more recent remarks by Krystyna Pieradzka in her contribution to the cooperative work, edited by Jan Dąbrowski, *Kraków, Studia nad rozwojem miasta* (Cracow, 1957), pp. 150–54.

10. For much of the foregoing narrative, see Edmund Długopolski, *Władysław Łokietek na tle swoich czasów* (Wrocław, 1951), pp. 1–4.

there. He did so in a manner which threatened to alienate many of the supporters who had brought about his success. He imprisoned the bishop of Cracow, Paweł of Przemanków, forcibly repressed opposition, and allowed his lieutenants extensive liberties which verged on abuse. Despite this, Henry was in a strong position to achieve his goal of the Polish crown: he was a prince of the Piast dynasty, which despite the vicissitudes of the twelfth and thirteenth centuries had never lost its standing as the ruling house of Poland; he had succeeded in uniting under his rule most of Silesia and little Poland, thus becoming master of two of the major regions of the former kingdom; he was the most powerful individual prince in Poland; and finally he was supported in his ambitions by the archbishop of Gniezno, Jakub Świnka. Before his plans could be fulfilled, however, Henry was treacherously poisoned, and he died on June 23, 1290. He was thirty-seven years old.

His death did not mean the end of the movement toward Polish unity, for by his will he provided for the ascendancy of Duke Przemysł II of Greater Poland. To him Henry gave Little Poland, while to Duke Henry of Głogów he gave the duchy of Wrocław. Behind this division of his territories lay Probus's recognition of the fact that Przemysł, who also was heir to Pomorze, was himself without heir, and, on the basis of an earlier agreement, his holdings were to go to Henry of Głogów. This would in effect have reunited all of the major divisions of the Polish kingdom.[11] Events quickly overwhelmed these statesmanlike plans, for both Henry of Głogów and Przemysł failed to seize the territories willed to them.

The citizens of Wrocław refused to grant Henry possession of the city and instead forced him to cede the principality to his older cousin, Henry of Legnica, one of Henry IV's generals. In Little Poland, Przemysł did indeed visit Cracow in July, 1290, remaining there until sometime after September 12. During his short stay he appropriated the traditional royal insignia, thus indicating his intention to seek the royal dignity for himself. When he left to go to Gniezno for a conference with Duke Mszczuj of Pomorze, his position appeared very strong for such a purpose, for, as he styled himself on September 23, 1290, he was "Duke of Greater Poland and Cracow" as well as, on the basis of an earlier agreement with the childless Mszczuj, "heir to Pomorze."[12]

His position in Little Poland was first disputed by Łokietek, who despite his earlier defeat still held Sandomir, Sieradz, and Brześć; but these territories were insufficient for his success, and a third claimant now appeared. King

11. For the will of Henry IV and the problems connected with it, see *Historia Śląska*, general editor Karol Maleczyński, vol. I, *do roku 1763*, in four parts (Wrocław, 1960–64), pt. i, pp. 526 ff. The topic is also treated by Balzer, *Królestwo Polskie*, I, 261 ff., and Baszkiewicz, *Powstanie zjednoczonego państwa*, pp. 207 ff.

12. This agreement is in *Pomm. U.B.*, # 333. For the political background of this arrangement, see Kazimierz Jasiński, "Zapis Pomorza gdańskiego przez Mszczuja w roku 1282," *Przegląd Zachodni*, VIII, pt. ii (1952), 176–89.

Václav II of Bohemia, who sought domination over Poland, represented the most formidable challenge yet to Łokietek's ambitions, Przemysł's pretentions, and the national unity of Poland.

This brilliant ruler, son of King Přemysl Otakar II, claimed suzerainty over the lands of Henry IV; and Emperor Rudolf of Habsburg recognized his claims in three separate documents in 1290.[13] Václav then turned his attentions to Little Poland. He invited Przemysł to Prague and late in 1290 or early 1291 (perhaps by threatening to urge on Bohemian allies in Brandenburg against Pomorze) obtained from him complete renunciation of all claims to the Duchy of Cracow.[14] At about the same time Václav gained the feudal allegiance of several Silesian princes, thus accelerating the process by which Silesia was permanently lost to the Polish kingdom.[15] Now the Přemyslid ruler was disputed in southern Poland only by Łokietek, who still clung tenaciously to Sandomir, harrying the Czech lieutenants.

Václav proceeded wisely to consolidate his rule in Cracow before turning to the problem of Łokietek. On September 1, 1291, in a successful attempt to gain the support of all elements of the population of Little Poland, he issued from Litomyšl in Bohemia two great charters confirming the traditional rights, privileges, and prerogatives of the knights, clergy, and towns of Little Poland. He further guaranteed the income of both the bishop and the cathedral chapter at Cracow. In return he was accepted as Duke of Cracow and Sandomir.[16] In order to make good upon the latter part of this title, however, he was forced to mount a military expedition against Łokietek. In early autumn, 1292, Václav led an army into Sieradz, and despite determined opposition Łokietek was captured. On October 9 Łokietek renounced all claim to Cracow and Sandomir and recognized Václav as his suzerain, retaining Sieradz and Brześć as compensation.[17]

---

13. July 22 and September 25 and 26. See Colmar Grünhagen and E. Markgraf, eds., *Lehns- und Besitzurkunden Schlesiens und seiner einzelnen Fürstentümer im Mittelalter*, 2 vols. (Leipzig, 1881–83), I, # 2–4.

14. Joseph Fiedler, "Böhmens Herrschaft in Polen. Ein urkundlicher Beitrag," *Archiv für Kunde österreichischer Geschichtsquellen*, XIV (1855), pp. 176 f., 182–85. See also Baszkiewicz, *Powstanie zjednoczonego państwa*, p. 266, n. 140, for Przemysł's motivation in the renunciation.

15. Two variant narrative accounts of the process are given by *Historia Śląska*, I, pt. i, 528 ff., and *Geschichte Schlesiens*, I: *Von der Urzeit bis zum Jahre 1526*, published by the Historische Kommission für Schlesien, ed. Hermann Aubin, et al. (3d ed., Stuttgart, 1961), pp. 175 ff. An older account, in some respects much superior in its narration of political and diplomatic affairs, is Jan Dąbrowski, "Dzieje polityczne Śląska w latach 1290–1402," in *Historja Śląska od najdawniejszych czasów do roku 1400*, ed. Stanisław Kutrzeba, et al., 3 vols. (Cracow, 1933–39), I, 334 ff.

16. *Kodeks dyplomatyczny katedry krakowskiej ś. Wacława*, ed. Franciszek Piekosiński, 2 vols. (Cracow, 1874–83), I, # 94, 95. See also Baszkiewicz, *Powstanie zjednoczonego państwa*, p. 208, n. 374.

17. Fiedler, "Böhmens Herrschaft," pp. 174–76, 177–79; for Fiedler's discussion of these documents and that mentioned in note 14 above, see pp. 163–72. The chronology adopted in the text is not that of Fiedler, but of Długopolski, *Władysław Łokietek*, pp. 11–16.

Łokietek seemed now almost wholly excluded from Polish affairs. With Václav master of Silesia and Little Poland, and Przemysł's fortunes in Greater Poland and Pomorze in rapid ascent, he was reduced to insignificance. It was, in fact, only his position as a member of the dynasty which enabled him to participate in a conference with Przemysł late in 1292 and early in 1293. Under the general sponsorship of Archbishop Jan Świnka, these two princes, together with the even more impotent Duke Casimir of Łęczyca, gathered ostensibly to discuss financial support for the archbishop. But the nature of the support, the titles adopted by these rulers, and the political agreements arrived at in Kalisz mark this meeting as the formation of nothing less than, in the words of Balzer, an "anti-Czech coalition."[18] This conclusion is based upon the fact that shortly after Epiphany, 1293, Przemysł promised to pay to Gniezno, to the extent that he was able or would be in the future, the sum of 300 silver marks yearly from the income of the salt mines of Wieliczka (south of Cracow) and to continue in the first two years after he had obtained possession of Cracow to make payments of 100 silver marks from the same source. At the same time, in a second document, the three rulers together, styling themselves all "heirs to Cracow," agreed to the same financial arrangements as in the first document. Polish historians have almost universally understood the significance of these documents to be not only the intention of regaining the territory previously lost to Václav, but also that the right to rule over Cracow would, if necessary, pass in turn from the strongest, Przemysł, then to Łokietek, and finally to the weakest, Casimir.[19] In the wake of this agreement the personal relationship between Przemysł and Łokietek was greatly strengthened when the latter married his first and only wife, Jadwiga, daughter of Bolesław the Chaste (Duke of Greater Poland, d. 1279) and cousin of Przemysł.[20] For the moment, however, Łokietek's position was still a secondary one.

Meanwhile, Przemysł was still flourishing. In 1294 he finally inherited Pomorze and, after incorporating it into his holdings, began preparations for his coronation as ruler of a resurrected Polish kingdom. In this his closest ally was the archbishop of Gniezno. It was indeed Jakub Świnka who technically brought an end, however temporary, to the territorial division of Poland; but

18. Balzer, *Królestwo*, I, 290 ff. The texts of the two documents issued at Kalisz are found respectively in *C.D.M.P.*, II, # 692, and Kazimierz Raczyński, ed., *Codex diplomaticus Maioris Poloniae* (Poznań, 1840), # 76.

19. Scholarly opinion on this point is summarized in D. S. Buczek, "Archbishop Jakub Świnka (1283–1314), An Assessment," in D. S. Wandycz, ed., *Studies in Polish Civilization* (New York, n.d. [1971?]), pp. 54–65.

20. Balzer, *Genealogia Piastów*, pp. 252 and 341, originally placed the date of this marriage sometime before 1279, but in his magisterial *Królestwo*, I, 295, n. 1, he adopted the period 1292/93. Recent researches have vindicated Balzer's final conclusions. See Kazimierz Jasiński, "Uzupełnienia do genealogii Piastów," *Studia Źródłoznawcze*, V (1960), 106–9.

as to the nature and significance of the policy which culminated in the coronation, there has been great dispute. Historians from Długosz onward pictured the
future king and the prelate as the chief representatives of the concept of the
regnum Poloniae, rising above the narrow limitations of their contemporaries to
erect, by force of their personalities and their ideals, the revivified Polish state.
More recently, however, historians have tended to diminish their reputations,
suggesting instead that there was little about either to differentiate them sharply
from their times. Jakub Świnka did indeed work untiringly for the restoration of
the kingdom (he also was active later in Łokietek's cause), but he did this within
a program of trying to preserve the church from lay encroachments. Przemysł's
reign is too short to evaluate his intentions definitively, but it is probable that a
moderate program of dynastic aggrandizement was crucial in his activity.[21]

On June 26, 1295, Przemysł was crowned in the cathedral of Gniezno by the
Polish metropolitan. All of the Polish bishops participated, either in person or
by proxy, and there were representatives of the towns and the knights of
Greater Poland and Pomorze. The nobles of these territories, however, absented
themselves, for they bitterly resented Przemysł's pretentions. Though originally
suspicious, eventually the papacy was persuaded to ratify the act.[22] This step
was nearly unnecessary, for, on February 8, 1296, seven months after his coronation, Przemysł was assassinated. Although some later sources cast suspicion
upon Václav of Bohemia, the first reactions to the death were probably correct:
it was the work of the margraves of Brandenburg in league with the nobles of
Greater Poland.[23] In the early spring of Poland's revival, the first bud of
political unity had been prematurely cut. Nevertheless, Poland did not return to
the status quo ante, for the situation was greatly changed.

Despite the inadequacies and shortcomings of Przemysł, despite the fact his
kingdom was only a partial restoration of the ancient *regnum*, his coronation was,
as Baszkiewicz admits,[24] neither unnecessary nor premature. Przemysł in his
strivings had provided an example for others who were to be more successful and
who would be judged by their own contemporaries as following the tradition
established in 1295.[25] Because his coronation was approved by the whole of the

21. The glorification of these individuals perhaps reached its height in the work of Oswald
Balzer. See particularly his *Królestwo*, I, 214–314. At the other extreme is Baszkiewicz, *Powstanie
zjednoczonego państwa*, pp. 262–65, 311 ff.

22. Such approval was particularly needed in the case of Poland, which was traditionally
considered, by the native clergy and nobility, as well as by the papacy, to be *immediata subiectio
sedi apostolicae*. Długosz, *Historia*, II, 511 f., attributes to the coronation an almost mystical
quality: automatically there was in Poland an end to anarchy and the blooming of order and
stability.

23. See Karol Górski, "Śmierć Przemysława II," *Roczniki Historyczne*, V (1929), 170–200.

24. Baszkiewicz, *Powstanie zjednoczonego państwa*, p. 263.

25. This is particularly true of the proceedings of 1320 and 1339, where the witnesses spoke
of Łokietek as the successor of Przemysł. See, for example, *Lites*, I, 23: "Wladislaus rex, tunc
dux, succedens domino Premislio regi in regno Polonie."

Polish church and touched the interests of the laity of all classes throughout the rest of the country, the ideal in which his career culminated does indeed mark the beginning of the end of the territorial fragmentation of the kingdom. It can not be denied, however, that his death retarded the process of unification, for two men stepped forward to claim the succession: Łokietek and Václav.

According to the original intentions of Przemysł II (based partly upon the will of Henry IV Probus), Greater Poland was to go to Duke Henry of Głogów. But the identification of Łokietek with the dead king complicated this arrangement. Thus it is not surprising that the magnates of Greater Poland turned to Łokietek and recognized him as their ruler. The fragile nature of Łokietek's position, however, was demonstrated by the far-reaching concession he was forced to make to Henry of Głogów on March 10, 1296, at Krzywiń. There, in return for recognition of Łokietek, the Silesian obtained both the cession of certain lands along the western border of Greater Poland as well as the right to the duchy for his sons.[26] Łokietek's position in Pomorze also was not safe, for his nephew Leszek claimed hereditary rule here styling himself "by God's mercy Duke of Pomorze."[27] Though the details of the process are unclear, Łokietek soon overcame Leszek's opposition, and by the beginning of September had succeeded in making himself master of this region.

That his ambitions were not limited to these two regions is shown by his actions the following year. There is good reason to believe he led a military expedition into Little Poland, and perhaps even into Silesia, in an unsuccessful attempt to wrest these regions from Václav.[28] This confirms the suggestion made by *Rocznik świętokrzyski* that "in the following year Wladislaus, Duke of Cuyavia, surnamed Loktek, wanted to obtain the Kingdom of Poland, already having several of its territories."[29]

Despite these ambitions, the immediate future was not promising for Łokietek. He was, for example, confronted by powerful enemies from beyond his borders. Henry of Głogów maintained a close interest in Greater Poland; Václav II in Little Poland also had wider pretensions; and the Mark of Brandenburg had long cast covetous glances toward Pomorze and the extreme western territories of Greater Poland. Yet another reason for his unsure position arose from his political weakness. Only in his patrimonium of Kujavia did he have the base of support which assured his continued control. In both Pomorze and Greater Poland he was far weaker than Przemysł had been, and he was unable to maintain order and stability there. From 1298 onwards the shortcomings of his administration and the consequences of his own abuses, as well as those of his

---

26. *C.D.M.P.*, II, # 745.

27. As reflected in *Pomm. U.B.*, # 540–41 (dated May, 1296). See also *SS. rer. Pr.*, I, 695.

28. See Długopolski, *Władysław Łokietek*, p. 36, for a narrative treatment; and Baszkiewicz, *Powstanie zjednoczonego państwa*, p. 268 n. 145, for a discussion of the sources.

29. *Sub anno* 1296. *M.P.H.*, III, 77.

knights, became more pronounced.[30] The result was that the higher clergy of Greater Poland agreed at Kościan in June, 1298, to support Henry of Głogów. This marked the beginning of the end for Łokietek. By August, 1299, his position was so weak that when Václav demanded he recognize Přemyslid feudal suzerainty over Greater Poland, Pomorze, and Kujavia he was unable to refuse.[31] By the beginning of the next year, Łokietek was forced into exile when Václav occupied these regions.[32] Poland was now again under the rule of one individual, but this was the result of conquest rather than reunification.

Václav moved quickly to consolidate his position. In order to prevent either Łokietek or even Henry of Głogów from raising claims as heir to the kingdom of Poland, Václav put himself forward on the basis of his de facto position as ruler of all or most of the Polish lands. Despite the efforts of a special embassy, it proved impossible to obtain the sanction of Pope Boniface VIII for such a step. Václav turned therefore to the only other power whose claims to universal control could justify jurisdiction over Polish affairs. From Emperor Albert I of Habsburg he received on June 29, 1300, the support which he sought.[33] His next step was to identify himself as closely as possible with the royal tradition in Poland. For this reason he became betrothed to Ryska, the daughter of Przemysł II, sometime before the end of July. Upon these foundations he persuaded Archbishop Świnka to crown him in the cathedral of Gniezno late in September.[34] The ceremony was attended by many ecclesiastics, but most came from abroad. There was a notable lack of support for Václav among the Polish clergy, and the archbishop performed his task unwillingly. His strong national feelings were most explicitly directed against the German element in central Europe; when asked what he thought of the sermon delivered by the bishop of Brixen at Václav's coronation, he replied, "It would have been all right if it hadn't been given by a dog and a German."

---

30. For Łokietek's position, see the discussion in Kazimierz Tymieniecki, "Odnowienie dawnego Królestwa Polskiego," *K.H.*, XXXIV (1920), 53 ff. Reflections of instability may be observed in *M.P.H.*, III, 41: "cum temporibus ducis Wladislai ecclesia multas iniurias pateretur, tam a predicto duce, quam a militibus eius, scilicet violaciones cimiteriorum, et oppressiones pauperum, viduarum ac orphanorum, omnium bonorum ecclesiarum; ecclesie annichilacionem, et alia que loqui horrendum est," as well as in *Lites*, I, 150: "tandem, tum propter guerras et quia prefatus dominus Wladislaus . . . non erat bonus iusticiarius et multa dampna, iniurie et spolia et oppressiones fiebant in dicta terra Pomoranie."

31. See the documents printed by Fiedler, "Böhmens Herrschaft," pp. 185–88.

32. *M.P.H.*, III, 41: "Anno domini 1300 Poloni videntes inconstanciam ducis Wladislai predicti, vocaverunt Wenceslaum . . . et in dominum sibi propriis." An important contribution to an understanding of the literary sources in Greater Poland for this period is Brygida Kürbisówna, *Dziejopisarstwo Wielkopolskie XIII i XIV wieku* (Warsaw, 1959), pp. 239–51 especially.

33. *C.D.M.P.*, II, #832. This document justifies Albert's action on the basis of his feudal suzerainty over Poland. See Josef Šusta, "Václav II a koruna polská," *Český Časopis Historický*, XXI (1915), 314–46; and Balzer, *Królestwo*, II, 121 ff.

34. See the *Chronicon aule regiae*, in *Font. rer. Boh.*, IV, 82, for the details of the coronation.

Some have inferred from this that Świnka could possibly view Václav's accession as the formation of a Slavic coalition against the Germans, but his support of the Piast dynasty in both Przemysł and Łokietek suggests rather that a conscious "Polishness" motivated him rather than any embryonic feelings of pan-Slavic brotherhood.[35]

Despite Václav's success, Poland's future lay not with the foreign ruler, but with the already thrice-defeated Łokietek. The Piast had proved thus far to be only a poor administrator and a mediocre politician. He had, however, a remarkable capacity to learn and never failed to profit from his mistakes. In his struggle to unify Poland he proved to be a sturdy fighter, persistent in action, undaunted in defeat. He had, in addition, a shrewd instinct for Polish interests which enabled him to oppose foreign elements wherever they appeared. Since these elements now held power in Poland, Łokietek became in exile the focus of these native forces tending toward national and dynastic unity. Nevertheless, it would be most incorrect to judge the rule of Václav II and his son as a brief, unfortunate interlude which preceded the ultimate victory of Łokietek. In order to suggest that it was more than this, it is necessary to trace both the activities of the Piast in exile and some details of Přemyslid rule from 1300–1306.

When Łokietek left Poland in 1300 he was forced to leave his wife at Radziejowo in Kujavia.[36] He spent the next years wandering throughout Europe in search of aid to regain his lost position.[37] He went first to Hungary and unsuccessfully requested aid from some of the magnates there, then turned to Rome for the support of Pope Boniface VIII. The reasons for his hope of assistance in both cases are clear. Less than a decade before, he had been allied with these magnates in the dispute over the succession in Hungary; while Poland's position as a papal dependency, the regular taxes gathered there, and the extraordinary levy of Peter's Pence provided the basis for an active papal interest in Poland.[38]

---

35. The former interpretation is best represented in Šusta's important article, "Václav II," pp. 314 ff. That this may have been the view of Czech observers is suggested by the *Chronicon aule regiae*, p. 81, which comments on the Polish-Czech union, "qui non multum dissonant in idiomate slavice lingwu. Nam qui idem lingwagium locuntur, plerumque amoris se arcioris nexibus complectuntur."

36. This at least is the inference which Długopolski, *Władysław Łokietek*, p. 47, draws from a later document issued to a certain Gerek, giving him a minor position in return for having sheltered Łokietek's wife during the period of exile.

37. There are two main literary sources for Łokietek's activity in this period: *Rocznik Traski*, in *M.P.H.*, II, 859; and Długosz, *Historia*, III, 5, 11. They are at some points contradictory. See Dąbrowski, "Z czasów Łokietka, Studya nad stosunkami polsko-węgierskimi w XIV w.," *R.A.U.*, series II, XXXIV (1916), 304–7.

38. After the death of Ladislaus III in 1290, Łokietek had supported those favoring the candidacy of the Angevin Charles Martel of Naples, the papal candidate. For Poland's position as a papal dependency and the significance of Peter's Pence, see in general *Historia Polski*, I, pt. i, 323–26. A somewhat less hostile view of this former tradition is found in the *Camb. Hist. of Pol.*, I, 21, 77.

Łokietek's efforts in Rome eventually bore fruit, for on June 10, 1302, Boniface VIII, as a part of his general anti-Přemyslid policy, lent the prestige of the Holy See to Łokietek's cause outside—and to that of the anti-Bohemian party inside—the kingdom. The letter which he sent that day denied Václav's right to the crown and ordered him to renounce the position, never to use the title, and to refrain in the future from all interference in Polish affairs.[39] This letter undoubtedly encouraged the anti-Přemyslid opposition within Poland, but the day when princes trembled as prelates spoke was as quickly passing in central Europe as in the west. What Łokietek really needed was military support. He turned again to Hungary, and in the political chaos there he this time found armed assistance.

The death of the last Árpád ruler of Hungary in 1301 had touched off a bitterly contested struggle for succession. The Magyar nobles were theoretically free to choose anyone they wished, but because of the almost mystical appreciation of royal blood, no matter how diluted, that much of medieval and early modern Europe seemed to possess, the choice of the magnates lay between Václav of Bohemia, son of King Václav II, or the Angevin Charles Robert, son of Charles Martel of Naples. Both were descended from the Árpád dynasty through the female line, and each was supported by a faction. Those favoring Václav actually succeeded in having him crowned in 1301, but his position was by no means secure. Those supporting Charles Robert were led by, among others, Amadeus of Kassa; and it was to him that Łokietek appealed in 1303. Seeing an opportunity to weaken the Přemyslid family, Amadeus agreed, and the following year Łokietek began his return from exile.[40]

With an unknown number of Hungarian troops, in September, 1304, Łokietek marched via the valleys of the Poprąd and Dunajec rivers into Poland. This brought him near Cracow itself, and his first victories were the towns of Pełczysk, Wiślica, and Lelów. They provided a military base for him, and early the next year[41] he marched successfully against the much more important center of Sandomir. At his side, in an army already swollen with

39. Theiner, *Mon. Hung.*, I, # 628. The political basis for Boniface's anti-Bohemian policy was the temporary Přemyslid victory in Hungary over the pope's Angevin candidate for the succession in the wake of the extinction of the Árpád dynasty in 1301.

40. The confused history of Hungary in the last years of the thirteenth and early years of the fourteenth centuries is most conveniently followed in English in C. A. Macartney, *Hungary, A Short History* (Edinburgh, 1962), pp. 35–40; Denis Sinor, *History of Hungary* (New York, 1959), pp. 82–88; and Bálint Hóman, "Hungary, 1301–1490," in *The Cambridge Medieval History*, VIII (Cambridge, 1936), 590–93. See also Dąbrowski, "Z czasów Łokietka," pp. 300–308; and Adam Kłodziński, "Problem węgierskiej pomocy dla Łokietka w r. 1304–6," *S.A.U.*, XLI (1936), 132–34.

41. *Rocznik Traski*, p. 853, simply indicates the year; Długosz, *Historia*, III, 22–23, specifically puts these events after Václav II's death, that is, in the second half of the year. A document cited by Dąbrowski, "Z czasów Łokietka," p. 308 n. 5, however, shows they may have taken place before February 1.

Polish allies, were nearly all the important civil officials of Sandomir. Shortly afterward he also recaptured his old territorial base of Sieradz. The city of Cracow had not yet fallen, but Łokietek had nearly succeeded in surrounding it. The unexpected death of Václav II in June, 1305, only aided the Piast, and despite the succession of Václav III, Łokietek's momentum remained unchecked. Finally in the spring of 1306, with an army composed more of peasants than of knights and nobility,[42] he laid siege to the Czech garrison in Cracow. The city fell, and with it the rest of Little Poland.

In the wake of Václav's death, Bohemian rule in Poland began to crumble. Not only was Little Poland lost, but in Greater Poland the nobles chose to recognize the rule of Duke Henry of Głogów. Václav III had not given up claim to Poland, however, and moved quickly to reestablish Czech control. He first gained the support of the emperor, then prepared an expedition to attack Łokietek. Before he could do so, he was murdered at Olomouc (Olmütz) on August 4, 1306. In its inspiration this act was unrelated to Polish affairs, but its effect was to aid Łokietek immeasurably. He began to consolidate his position in Little Poland, traveled to Pomorze to prevent the expansion of the Ascanians from Brandenburg, and received the allegiance of the nobles and cities of Pomorze, including the city of Gdańsk.[43]

The most immediate reason for the failure of Přemyslid rule in Poland was the extinction of the dynasty. Yet even before that, there were features of the reign of Václav II (with his young son, who in effect never had a chance to rule, we are not concerned) which suggested that an adequate legal and popular base for his rule was lacking. Despite the imperial approval and the archiepiscopal participation, the coronation of a foreigner while there still lived direct representatives of the Piast dynasty was never fully accepted. In recognition of this, Václav always remained a ruler in absentia, governing through appointed representatives who frequently were of Czech background. Nevertheless, he did have supporters. Those "new" people, recent settlers to whom he gave position and preferment could be counted on his side; and there were members of the clergy, particularly Bishop Jan Muskata of Cracow, who supported him. But to most of the inhabitants of the land, Václav was a foreigner; when there was a native alternative to him, he and his successor rapidly were abandoned. All this is not to deny that there were some positive contributions of Přemyslid rule. More specifically, two tangible results stand as the Czech heritage from this period.[44]

42. See Długosz, *Historia*, III, 21.

43. See ibid., pp. 24–27; and, for a modern narrative account, Długopolski, *Władysław Łokietek*, pp. 56–75.

44. The significance of the period of Czech rule in Poland has been variously treated by historians. In general, Polish scholars have been loath to admit any positive contribution from the Přemyslids. See Paul W. Knoll, "Władysław Łokietek and the Restoration of the *Regnum Poloniae*," *Medievalia et Humanistica*, XVI (1966), 57 n. 28.

The first came in the area of the economy. The multiplicity of coinages which circulated in central Europe in the late Middle Ages reflects the international character of commerce and the weakness of the rulers, who were unable to impose any uniformity in fiscal practices. It was not until much later that a state could limit the use of currency to that of its own issue. Nevertheless, some steps in this direction were taken by Václav (and after him—both chronologically and by way of imitation—by Casimir).

In July, 1300, the Czech king initiated an extensive fiscal reform in the lands of the Bohemian crown. The chief feature of this reform was the introduction of the Prague groschen (*grossus Pragensis*), a coin modeled upon the older *denarius grossus* of northern Italy and the *grossi Turonenses* minted by Louis IX of France.[45] This coin had an average weight of 3.86 grams and a silver assay of 93 percent. It quickly provided a stable coinage within the kingdom and soon spread beyond the borders. Though later in the century its quality declined greatly, it retained its value long enough to circulate widely through central Europe and as far west as Holland and Flanders.[46] It is therefore not surprising, particularly in view of the dynastic union of Poland and Bohemia, that the coin should appear in Poland. Early in Václav's reign in Poland there is evidence that "at the time of this same king, silver groschen were brought to Cracow."[47] It is somewhat surprising that the coin should have continued to circulate after the breakdown of Czech control. It is noted in Cracow and Little Poland in 1306, in Greater Poland in 1307, in Silesia in 1309, and in Kujavia in 1312; it may have been widely circulated until Łokietek's coronation in 1320.[48] The persistence of the Prague groschen is one measure of the continuing legacy of Přemyslid rule in Poland. Another is the fact that the later *grossi Cracovienses* of Casimir the Great were patterned upon the earlier coin.[49] Despite the existence of his own coin, Casimir continued to use the Prague money in later transactions.[50]

The second Přemyslid contribution is related to the machinery of government. The means by which Václav ruled Poland was by the development of a

45. See G. Skalský, "Mincovní reforma Václava II," *Český Časopis Historický*, XL (1934), 12 ff.; and K. Castelin, *Česká drobná mince doby předhusitské a husitské 1300–1411* (Prague, 1953), pp. 12 ff.

46. Castelin, "Pražske groše v cizině," *Numismatické Listy*, XI (1956), 69 ff.

47. Roman Grodecki, "Pojawienie się groszy czeskich w Polsce," *Wiadomości Numizmatyczno-Archeologiczne*, XVIII (1936), 77.

48. I have followed Jaroslav Pošvář, "Česká grošová reforma a Polsko," *Studia z dziejów Polskich i Czechoslowackich*, I (1960), 133 ff. See, however, the discussion of Grodecki, "Pojawienie się groszy czeskich," pp. 76–87.

49. See Ryszard Kiersnowski, *Wstęp do numizmatyki polskiej wieków średnich* (Warsaw, 1964), pp. 128–31.

50. The dowry for his daughter Kunegunde was paid in the Czech coin. See *Monumenta Wittelsbacensia: Urkundenbuch zur Geschichte des Hauses Wittelsbach*, ed. F. W. Wittmann, 2 vols. (Munich, 1857–61), II, 384.

territorial official, an office which was to have a long and distinguished future. Because Václav ruled in absentia he needed representatives in Poland to protect his interests. He chose to appoint men designated as *capitanei* (or in Polish, in the singular, *starosta*) whose responsibility was to exercise judicial powers, control the troops in both the countryside and in city garrisons, and levy and collect taxes. The *starosta* was, in effect, a territorial prince.[51] It is therefore not surprising that they were frequently mistrusted by their nominal superior Václav, who reassigned and reshuffled them from time to time in order to prevent them from growing too powerful. For example, four individuals represented the king in Little Poland from 1292 to 1300. These men, as well as most others appointed by Václav, were all Silesians or Bohemians, and were apparently despised by the native population. This type of official was not totally unknown to late thirteenth-century Poland, for in 1290 Łokietek had appointed a personal representative for Sandomir.[52] Václav, however, both made broader use of these representatives and endowed them with more extensive powers. Such an official was a virtual regent who acted in the absence of the ruler.

Later in the fourteenth century, during the reign of Casimir, the *starosta* was one of the most important royal officials. At that time, however, his power was more sharply circumscribed than under Václav, for he became a royal official, directly responsible to the monarch, interposed between the crown and the organs of local government. He merely represented royal interests (whether legal, military, or administrative) within a particular region of the kingdom. It is this distinction between the earlier Czech and later Polish *starosta* that has led some historians to deny that the latter was in any way modeled upon the former. Such a view is too extreme, for the later *starosta* was a modification of the Czech institution to suit the specific needs of the kingdom and the times.[53] Thus it is possible to see in this area also the extent of Přemyslid influence.

By the end of 1306 Władysław Łokietek was the single most powerful prince in Poland. Only in Greater Poland and Silesia had he failed to establish himself. He was thus at least as powerful as Przemysł had been in 1295, but he made no move to have himself crowned. He styled himself simply "Wladislaus by the Grace of God, Duke . . . ."[54] It was evident, however, that he was not

---

51. See the analysis of the *starosta* in Długopolski, *Władysław Łokietek*, p. 46.

52. *C.D.P.M.*, I, # 119.

53. See, for the former view, S. Kutrzeba, "Starostowie, ich początki i rozwój do końca XIV wieku," *R.A.U.*, XLV (1903), 90 ff. The latter is essentially the position taken by Długopolski, *Władysław Łokietek*, p. 17; and Baszkiewicz, *Powstanie zjednoczonego państwa*, p. 426. The view which argues that the Polish starosta is based upon not only the Czech official in Poland but also upon the Bohemian counterpart, is best represented by Šusta, *Dvě knihy českich dějin*, 2 vols. (Prague, 1917–19, 2d vol., 2d edition, 1935), I, 318. Shorter accounts of the early development of the starosta are found in Kutrzeba, *Historia ustroju Polski: Korona*, 8th ed. (Warsaw, 1949), pp. 107–11; and Juliusz Bardach, *Historia państwa i prawa Polski do połowy XV wieku*, 2d ed. (Warsaw, 1964), pp. 256–57.

54. See, for example, *C.D.M.P.*, II, # 906, # 919.

limiting his ambitions to these territories alone. By titling himself on occasion "heir to the Kingdom of Poland,"[55] he proclaimed that he considered himself heir to the crown and that he was only waiting to claim it until he had sufficiently strengthened himself. He could not do this, however, without defending himself against threats from abroad, overcoming resistance at home, and gaining control of Greater Poland. For the next decade, these three themes dominate the Polish scene.

It was from the west that the most immediate threat came. Under the Ascanian house, the Mark of Brandenburg had pursued a vigorous program of eastward territorial expansion in the late thirteenth and early fourteenth centuries. It had in the process seized minor Polish holdings in the Oder river valley. The most coveted goal of the margraves, however, was Pomorze. Because of the family ties with the Přemyslids and because the Bohemians ruled in Poland through representatives, it is not surprising that the margraves were asked to represent Bohemian rule in Pomorze. In July, 1306, when King Václav III granted margraves Hermann and Woldemar title to Pomorze as a fief of the Polish crown it appeared they had obtained this prize.[56] Shortly thereafter, Přemyslid rule in Poland deteriorated and collapsed. In the aftermath, neither Łokietek nor the cities of Pomorze recognized Václav's grant, and the Ascanians were forced to seek other means of making good their claims. They found their opportunity in the inveterate hostility toward Łokietek of the representatives of aristocratic interests in Pomorze, the Święca family and its head, Peter of Nowe.

Negotiations were opened between the two parties, and on July 17, 1307, a treaty was signed. Peter recognized the margraves as the lawful rulers of Pomorze and promised to support them against Łokietek. For their part, the Ascanians enfeoffed the Święcas with several local strongholds.[57] The Święcas immediately began agitating for the overthrow of Łokietek's rule and the acceptance of Ascanian domination. When news of this treachery reached Cracow several months later, Łokietek was outraged. He sent a deputy to Pomorze to arrest the whole family (the elderly Count Święca alone escaped) and bring them to Brześć in Kujavia; there they were imprisoned for two years. But it was too late to stop the revolt which they had fomented, and by spring of 1308 it reached Gdańsk. There the pro-German sentiment of many of the citizens forced Łokietek's local representative to travel to Cracow to seek aid in quelling the rebellion.

The uprising in Pomorze provided precisely the kind of situation the Ascan-

55. *C.D.P.M.*, II, # 544. See also Theiner, *Mon. Pol.*, I, 226: "dux, heres, et possessor," and "cum plenum ius predicto duci tanquam ipsius regni domino naturali et heredi legitimo, cui successio iure nature a suis progenitoribus debebatur, in regno competeret predicto."

56. Hermann Krabbo and Georg Winter, eds., *Regesten der Markgrafen von Brandenburg aus askanischem Hause*, 12 vols. (Berlin, 1910–55), II, # 1966, 1988, 1992. See also Johannes Schulz, *Die Mark Brandenburg* (Berlin, 1961–), I, 201.

57. Krabbo-Winter, *Regesten*, II, # 2024.

ians could exploit, and in August margraves Otto and Woldemar invaded Pomorze. They encountered few obstacles, and after a short siege of Gdańsk, the city was surrendered to them by its citizens. The fortress of the city remained, however, in the hands of troops loyal to Łokietek. Their situation soon became desperate, for without reinforcements the garrison could not hold out. Again a deputation was sent to Łokietek at Sandomir. There the fateful decision was made to request help from the Knights of the Teutonic Order. The offer was quickly accepted, for the Order looked with dismay upon Ascanian expansion. The terms of the agreement apparently called for the Knights to occupy one-half of the fortress and defend it at their own cost. The Polish garrison was to be limited to the other half. When the siege was ended, the Knights were to be reimbursed by Łokietek for their expenses and were then to leave the city. The aid of the Knights was instrumental in lifting the siege, and late in September the Ascanians withdrew.[58]

To this point, events are clear. What happened next is uncertain, due to lack of documentation and to six centuries of polemicism which has contributed greatly to the preservation of the Teuton-Slav antipathy. The description which follows must therefore be regarded as a reasonably probable one; total accuracy is impossible. So long as a common danger confronted the Knights and the Poles, they lived peacefully together in the crowded conditions of the fortress. After the lifting of the siege, however, the absence of a mutual enemy caused them to turn upon one another. During the night of November 14, 1308,[59] the Knights occupied and conquered the city.

Soon after the conquest, the rumor spread through Europe that the Knights had precipitated a bloodbath. Pope Clement V even went so far as to write Archbishop Frederick of Riga, on July 19, 1310, saying he had heard the Knights had killed ten thousand men in the conquest of Gdańsk. He asked the archbishop to investigate.[60] This accusation was denied by the Order when it learned of it, but there was an investigation. In 1312, in connection with another matter, papal legate Franciscus de Moliano charged the Order with this crime. The testimony of the witnesses in this action is contradictory, vague, and nearly worthless in determining the truth of the matter.[61] But without a doubt the charge that the Knights killed ten thousand people in Gdańsk is impossible. The city did not at that time have that large a population, even if Polish soldiers were included.[62]

58. The terms of the agreement and the details of the siege are reflected in *Lites*, I, 150–51, wit. 2; I, 373, wit. 102; and I, 389, wit. 116.

59. The date is established from the testimony in 1320 of Knight Shyra (*Lites*, I, 24, wit. 8).

60. Theiner, *Mon. Pol.*, I, #204.

61. See A. Seraphim, *Das Zeugenverhör des Franciscus de Moliano 1312* (Königsberg, 1912); and Walter Friedrich, *Der Deutsche Ritterorden und die Kurie in den Jahren 1300–1330* (Könisgberg, 1912), pp. 36–49, 83–86.

62. Erich Keyser, "Der bürgerliche Grundbesitz der Rechtstadt Danzig im 14. Jahrhun-

Less fantastic charges than these may have some validity. Our knowledge of these charges is based in large measure upon testimony given in 1320 and 1339 in two legal proceedings against the Knights. It was charged that, after the siege of Gdańsk had been lifted, the Knights went down into the city and killed all the soldiers and nobles in the service of Łokietek. As to how many were killed, most of the witnesses succumbed to that infuriating impreciseness which characterizes most medieval statistics. They speak only of "others," "many," or an "infinite number."[63] There was one Polish soldier who reported more precisely. Knight Shyra testified in 1320 that the Order in its conquest had killed sixteen of Łokietek's men.[64] This charge the Knights had already admitted, though they put a different light on the matter. In 1310 the grand master had explained to the pope that the citizenry of Gdańsk had given refuge to sixteen robbers whose clandestine activities were directed against the Order. Several times the Knights requested the citizens to give up these robbers, but in vain. Only after an ultimatum threatened retaliation against the citizenry were the sixteen delivered. The grand master said nothing of their fate, but it is probable they did not long survive.[65] There can be little doubt that the sixteen "robbers" are identical with the remnants of the Polish garrison described by Knight Shyra. Only differing points of view are responsible for the difference in description.

On the basis of these facts most historians have been hard pressed to be very specific about the actual number of deaths. German writers have tended to minimize casualties, while Polish historians have tried to maximize them.[66] The number of deaths is not, however, the prime issue (except as it affected popular sentiment and future relations between Germans and Poles). What is important is that Poland had lost its chief seaport and was soon to lose its Baltic coastline. Gdańsk had become Danzig.

---

dert," *Zeitschrift des westpreussischen Geschichtsvereins*, LVIII (1918), 45–46. According to Tadeusz Ładogórski, *Studia nad zaludnieniem Polski XIV wieku* (Wrocław, 1958), pp. 167 ff., Gdańsk did not approach a population of 10,000 until the beginning of the fifteenth century.

63. *Lites*, I, 304, wit. 51; I, 254, wit. 32; and I, 28, wit. 19.

64. *Lites*, I, 24, wit. 8.

65. See Seraphim, *Das Zeugenverhör*, pp. 62 ff.

66. From the German side, see Irene Ziekursch, *Der Prozess zwischen König Kasimir von Polen und dem Deutschen Orden im Jahre 1339* (Berlin, 1934), pp. 81–106, p. 94 especially: "Als Resultat aus der Untersuchung der Zeugenaussagen . . . ergibt sich daher, dass damals zunächst 16 polnische Ritter . . . hingerichtet wurden, und dass dann wahrscheinlich im Strassenkampf auch Danziger Bürger, jedoch ohne Ansehen der Nationalität, getötet wurden. Die genaue Zahl dieser Bürger lasst sich nicht mehr ermitteln, von mehrerer Tausend kann aber dabei keine Rede sein." From the Polish side, see K. Górski, *Państwo Krzyżackie w Prusach* (Gdańsk and Bydgoszcz, 1946), p. 78; Kazimierz Piwarski, *Dzieje Gdańska w zarysie* (Gdańsk, Bydgoszcz, and Szczecin, 1946), p. 27; Długopolski, *Władysław Łokietek*, pp. 118–19; *Historia Polski*, I, i, 430. The most recent edition of Stefan M. Kuczyński, *Wielka Wojna z Zakonem Krzyżackim w latach 1409–1411* (Warsaw, 1966), p. 75, returns, however, to the earlier tradition and speaks of the Knights in Gdańsk having murdered "all of its citizens."

Following the conquest of Gdańsk, the Knights of the Teutonic Order moved quickly to acquire the rest of Pomorze. Their actions were both military and diplomatic. They marched on Tczew and captured it, and then successfully laid siege to Świecie. By the end of 1311 most of the region was in their hands. In the meantime they had taken steps to legitimize their position by attempting to purchase the Ascanian claim to Pomorze. In a series of transactions between September, 1309, and June, 1311, the Order paid Woldemar 10,000 marks for final and absolute renunciation of Brandenburg's claims. Upon the death of the last of the Święca family, two years later, the Order obtained the territory of Nowe. Their conquest of Pomorze was complete, and Polish access to the Vistula north of Wyszogród was cut off.[67]

The reasons why the Order undertook to conquer Pomorze are more complex than they first appear. On the surface the conquest was, as Irene Ziekursch described it, simply the result of the Order taking advantage of a situation which existed: the lack of Polish control over the area, as seen in the pro-Brandenburg sympathies of the citizens of Gdańsk and in the threat of Ascanian expansion. Thus the Knights simply became practitioners of an early version of realpolitik.[68] Gotthold Rhode was closer to the truth when he wrote recently, "Undoubtedly the Order utilized the many difficulties of the Duke [Łokietek] for its own advantage and proceeded systematically. This corresponded to the general tendencies of the time which were predicated upon territorial expansion, the rounding-out of possessions, and utilization of all resources."[69] But it was two nineteenth-century historians, the one hostile to the Order, the other sympathetic, who succeeded in penetrating to the real reasons for these actions. For Jacob Caro, it was "difficult to believe that these events [in Gdańsk] were only the result of happenstance for the Knights of the Order. Rather, in these efforts it is possible to see a foundation of a consciously thought-out plan [of conquest], in the course of which the expulsion of the Poles from the fortress was only a prelude."[70] Such an analysis seems harsh, yet Caro was essentially correct, for after establishing themselves in Prussia in the half-century after 1230, the Knights faced the problem of their relationship to their homeland in the empire. To resolve this they initiated a process of expansion toward the west which emerged over the years as a consciously developed policy. Heinrich von Treitschke best expressed its nature and goal when he observed, "Not

---

67. The best narrative treatment of the conquest is Marjan Małuszyński, "Zabór Pomorza przez Krzyżaków (1308–1309)," *Rocznik Gdański*, VII–VIII (1933–34), 44–80; while the negotiations and stages of the Knights' payment may be followed in *Pomm. U.B.*, # 676, 682, 683, 685, 686, 697, and 698. The course of the border at this point is described in detail by Erich Sandow, *Die Polnisch-pommerellische Grenze 1309–1454 (Beihefte zum Jahrbuch der Albertus-Universität Königsberg Pr.*, VI) (Kitzingen/Main, 1954), pp. 4–9.

68. Ziekursch, *Der Prozess*, p. 105.

69. Rhode, *Geschichte Polens*, p. 65.

70. Caro, *Geschichte Polens*, II, 42–43.

merely the restless nature of a military state, but a serious political necessity drove the Order in this path [of conquest]. With the increasing development of the land, the Vistula ceased to be a natural boundary, and without direct connection with the strong root of its power, Germany, the young colony could not exist."[71]

The conquest of Pomorze was a blow from which Łokietek never recovered. To the end of his life he continued to style himself "heir to Pomorze," and the reconquest of the territory was the cardinal goal of his foreign policy after he became king. Before he could devote his attention to these matters, however, he had first to overcome opposition at home.

There were two sources of this opposition; the one ecclesiastical, the other municipal. The former existed in the person of Bishop Jan Muskata of Cracow. By birth a Silesian, Muskata had been one of the chief supporters of the Přemyslids in Poland. His role in this respect had been so extreme that even before the expulsion of the Czechs Archbishop Jan Świnka had instituted a canonical investigation of Muskata's policies.[72] This process came to nothing, but after Łokietek's victory in Little Poland in 1306 the issue was again taken up. In the course of the controversy serious charges were made that indicate, among other things, a sharpened anti-German sentiment in Poland. It was charged that Muskata "always promoted, not Polish clerics, but German ones," that "he appointed only Germans in the diocese of Cracow," that "he did not even promote worthy Poles, calling them unfit for a benefice."[73]

On another level the conflict between Łokietek and Muskata had to do with matters of finance and the relationship between ecclesiastical and princely power. Łokietek, in his victory in 1305–6, had been forced to depend upon financial support gathered by expropriation, frequently from church holdings. So bitter did the dispute become that in one instance Łokietek imprisoned the bishop, whereupon Muskata excommunicated the prince. Not until 1310, when the dispute was laid before the papal legate for arbitration, was the matter settled. Muskata went into exile which continued until after 1318. In the course of the conflict with Muskata, it is noteworthy that Łokietek's greatest ecclesiastical support came from Archbishop Jan Świnka, who henceforward becomes Łokietek's greatest supporter. Although Greater Poland was still in the hands of the Duke of Głogów, it was clear to contemporaries that Archbishop Świnka already intended for Łokietek a wider role in Poland.[74]

71. Heinrich von Treitschke, *Das Deutsche Ordensland Preussen* (reprinted, Göttingen, 1955), p. 29.

72. For Muskata and the conflict with Łokietek, see the following: Władysław Abraham, "Sprawa Muskaty," *R.A.U.*, XXX (1894), 122–80; Adam Kłodziński, "Polityka Muskaty (1304–6)," *S.A.U.*, XLI (1936), 334–38; and Długopolski, *Władysław Łokietek*, pp. 75–105.

73. The trial of Muskata before papal legate Gentilis is recorded in *M.P.V.*, III, # 121.

74. See especially the comments made by Muskata to the papal legate in 1309, *C.D.P.M.*, II, # 547.

The second source of opposition was unwilling, however, to grant the Duke even that which he already had. Especially among the German citizens of Cracow and other locations in Little Poland opposition soon coalesced into rebellion.[75] In 1311, under the leadership of Albert, *advocatus* of Cracow, and Henry, provost of the monastery of the Holy Sepulcher in Miechowo, revolt broke out and spread quickly. In addition the exiled Muskata played a role in this development. The political goal of this movement was the restoration of Bohemian rule in Poland (John Luxemburg had established himself as the successor of the Přemyslids and was already claiming the crown of Poland on that basis). Łokietek himself was personally threatened by this revolt. He was forced to take refuge, together with his wife and infant son Casimir, in the fortress on Wawel Hill, and it was some days before he was relieved.[76] The aid which Łokietek received in this uprising came from many sources, from Hungary as well as from towns in Little Poland which remained loyal, and was sufficient to slow the momentum of the revolt. Its leaders turned in desperation to Duke Bolesław of Opole and requested military assistance from him. He responded, but the combined forces which Łokietek had gathered carried the day. By the end of summer, 1312, the revolt had been crushed. The lands and property of those who had revolted were confiscated[77] and, following the method of Jephthah and the men of Gilead, those who were unable to demonstrate their Polishness by successfully repeating *Soczewica, koło, miele, młyn* were assumed to be German or Bohemian and were executed.[78]

The suppression of this revolt broke the back of all opposition to Łokietek. In doing this, the Piast was able to stigmatize his defeated opponents as traitors to Poland and identify himself as the representative of that which they had betrayed.[79] It was now obvious that he had moved far beyond the narrow limitations of his earlier policy. Before he could realize any new goals it was necessary to broaden his territorial base. Thus he turned his attention to Greater Poland.

In the months after the extinction of the Přemyslid dynasty, Henry III of Głogów obtained control of Greater Poland. His position was not wholly undisputed—Łokietek was supported by some of the noble families there. But

---

75. The revolt of 1311–12 is treated by Michał Bobrzyński, "Bunt wójta krakowskiego Alberta z roku 1311," *Biblioteka Warszawska*, XXXVII, iii (1877), 329–48; Długopolski, "Bunt wójta Alberta," *Rocznik Krakowski*, VII (1905), 135–86; and Kłodziński, "Jeden czy dwa bunty wójta Alberta," *S.A.U.*, XLIII (1938), 47–51, and "Z dziejów pierwszego krakowskiego buntu wójta Alberta," *Zapiski Towarzystwa Naukowego w Toruniu*, XIV (1948), 45–56.

76. See *Cod. Dipl. Pol.*, III, 174, where Łokietek recalls taking refuge in the fortress.

77. For traces of these confiscations, see *Libri antiquissimi civitatis Cracoviensis 1300–1400*, edited by Franciszek Piekosiński (Cracow, 1878), pp. 27, 28, 30, 35, 38, 39, 46, 47, 58, 63, 81.

78. *Rocznik Krasińskich*, in *M.P.H.*, III, 133.

79. This is quite explicit in a document issued April 17, 1312: "in nos, heredes nostros et gentem Polonicam prodicionaliter" *C.D.P.M.*, II, # 557.

on the whole he was able to establish his rule with a minimum of disruption, and the Greater Poland chronicle records that "in his time there was great peace in Greater Poland." It is also recorded, however, that he was "not a perfect friend of the Poles."[80] Henry ruled largely in absentia and those who acted as his representatives were resented by the populace. Even more resented were the strong German proclivities of Henry and his advisors. This situation was exacerbated in 1309 when Henry's five sons succeeded to his lands after his death. About them, the chronicle of Greater Poland bitterly says that they depended entirely upon German advisors and even sought advice on how best to remove all Poles from both ecclesiastical and secular positions.

It is not surprising therefore that the sons failed to maintain control. That power did not immediately slip from their hands was because the only possible alternative, Łokietek, was forced to devote himself to the affairs sketched above. Opposition to the Silesians thus devolved upon the local nobility, and in a spasmodic, though bitterly contested, conflict Henry's sons were driven out by 1314.[81] Łokietek took an active part in the last stages of this process and was soon recognized as the ruler of Greater Poland. In January, 1314, he styled himself "heir to Greater Poland," and by the following year the title "Duke of all Greater Poland" was commonly used.[82] This success in Greater Poland marks, in the words of Stanisław Zachorowski, "The end of the first period of Łokietek's reign, for in this moment he obtained the complex of territories which formed the central framework of the Polish state until the Jagiellonian union."[83]

Mere possession was not sufficient to gain for Łokietek the position to which he now aspired: king of Poland. It was necessary to obtain the support of those elements that might influence the elevation to the kingship: the clergy, the nobility, and above all the papacy. Unfortunately for Łokietek, it was at this time that Archbishop Świnka died, leaving him without the individual whom Oswald Balzer called the *primus movens* of the goal of a reunified *regnum*.[84] Nevertheless, the Duke was able to pursue a policy which brought him success.

The nobility were drawn to support Łokietek because he had achieved

---

80. *M.P.H.*, III, 41.

81. See Długosz, *Historia*, III, 50–51. The cathedral in Poznań was on one occasion transformed into a fortress, and besieged. The problem of Łokietek's seizure of Greater Poland has been thoroughly studied by Karol Potkański, "Walka o Poznań (1306–12)," *R.A.U.*, XXXVIII (1899), 275–94, and "Zajęcie Wielkopolski (rok 1313 i 1314)," *R.A.U.*, XLVII (1905), 158–71.

82. The former title in *C.D.M.P.*, II, #965; the latter, *C.D.M.P.*, II, #976. On January 11, 1314, Łokietek actually styled himself "Vladislaus, Dei gratia rex Polonie, dux" (*C.D.M.P.*, II, #964). Outside of the title—six years premature—there is nothing to indicate this is a false document. It may simply have happened that Łokietek felt the future would confirm his de facto position.

83. Stanisław Zachorowski, "Wiek XIII i panowanie Władysława Łokietka," *Encyklopedya Polska*, V, i (Warsaw, Lublin, Łódź, and Cracow, 1920), p. 264.

84. Balzer, *Królestwo*, I, 268–72.

military stature in his doggedly persistent struggle; the clergy, with the exception of a few adherents of Muskata, supported him because they recognized him to be the only possible candidate for the throne. In addition, he had succeeded in making himself in recent years the focus of Polish national consciousness, and he thus could draw upon sentiments which might be only indirectly connected with him. Only with Avignon was the matter more serious. It was eventually won over because of the de facto reunification of the state and its reappearance as a factor in the state system of central Europe. The financial support that Poland provided for the papacy was also a factor, especially after 1316 when the fiscally oriented Jacques Duese surveyed Europe from the papal throne. The most important factor in winning over the papacy, however, was the overwhelming support which Łokietek had within Poland.

Poland's reemergence as a state was symbolized by the treaty signed with King Eric VI Menved of Denmark.[85] This powerful monarch looked with suspicion upon his neighbors in Brandenburg. The margraves there, despite their setback in Pomorze, still pursued an aggressive policy which threatened surrounding princes. It was in response to this policy that King Eric attempted to weld together an anti-Ascanian coalition. On June 27, 1315, Łokietek formally adhered to this coalition by agreeing to attack the eastern border of the Mark. The next year he apparently did just that, though without apparent success. It was nevertheless evident that Poland was again a factor in international affairs.

The question of Polish financial support for the church in general and the papacy in particular is a difficult one to analyze, for records are fragmentary at best. It is possible to say that because of the nearly unique tax, Peter's Pence, Poland did occupy a special place in the financial considerations of Avignon.[86] During the decades of territorial division collection of all taxes, including ecclesiastical, had been sporadic. But with the gradual coalescence of the kingdom, this had been changed. Thus the papacy was better disposed to grant Polish requests than it might otherwise have been.

It was the Polish clergy which took the initiative in presenting the request for Łokietek's coronation. Despite the earlier strained relations with the clergy, Łokietek actively courted their favor after his success in Greater Poland.[87] As a result, time healed past injuries and the clergy gradually forgot previous

85. *C.D.M.P.*, II, # 976. See also Leon Koczy, "Przymierze polska-duńskie w roku 1315 na tle stosunków polsko-brandenburskich," *Roczniki Historyczne*, VIII (1931), 31–81.

86. On Peter's Pence in Poland, see Jan Ptaśnik, "Denar świętego Piotra obrońcą jedności politycznej i kościelnej w Polsce," *R.A.U.*, LI (1908), 133–218; and Erich Maschke, *Der Peterspfennig in Polen und dem deutschen Osten* (Leipzig, 1933). For Pope John XXII and Peter's Pence, see Emil Göller, *Die Einnahmen der apostolischen Kammer unter Johann XXII* (Paderborn, 1910), pt. i, pp. 122–34; and William E. Lunt, *Papal Revenues in the Middle Ages* (New York, 1934), I, 65–71.

87. See, for example, the generosity of his grants and endowments, *C.D.M.P.*, II, # 964 and 965.

complaints. It was events after the death of Jakub Świnka that provided the first opportunity for the Polish clergy to take their program of support for Łokietek to Avignon. Canon Borzysław of Gniezno, formerly archdeacon of Poznań, was elected on May 1, 1314, to succeed Świnka. He was admirably suited to his new task, for he had both an ecclesiastical and a political background. He had served as chancellor for Duke Bolesław of Płock and was known to be a lifelong partisan of Łokietek. Borzysław departed for Avignon, but the extended papal vacancy which followed the death of Clement V prevented his immediate confirmation as archbishop. In this period the archbishop-elect actively labored on behalf of Łokietek in the papal court.[88] Upon the eventual election in 1316 of John XXII, Borzysław was confirmed, but he failed to return to his homeland. Sometime in mid-1317 he sickened and died, and to replace him the new pope named Jan Janisław, an archdeacon of Gniezno and also a supporter of Łokietek.[89]

The new archbishop remained for a time in Avignon, involved in negotiation relating to financial and political matters in Poland. As late as May 20, 1318, he was there, and his efforts are reflected in two bulls issued by John XXII that day. The first provided for the regularization of the diocesan administration of Cracow during the continued exile of Bishop Muskata, and the second exhorted the Polish church to a more effective collection of Peter's Pence.[90] Following this, the new archbishop returned to Poland, perhaps arriving in time for a political and ecclesiastical convention which was crucial in the program of obtaining the crown for Łokietek.

The preparations for this gathering had been laid in March of 1318 at a meeting of Łokietek and the abbot of Sulejów at Chęciny. It was agreed then that the matter of Łokietek's coronation would be considered, as well as certain church affairs. To the village of Sulejów, located almost in the center of Łokietek's holdings, came churchmen and most of the important civil representatives of the four regions from which Łokietek drew his power: Cracow, Sandomir, Łęczyca, and Sieradz. No representatives from Greater Poland attended.[91] Three decisions of importance came from this meeting. First, it was agreed to prosecute more vigorously the inquisition against Beghards and Beguines in Poland. Next, a compromise was reached between Łokietek and Bishop Muskata, who was allowed to return to his see. Finally, the question of

---

88. See Władysław Abraham, "Stanowisko kurii papieskiej wobec koronacji Łokietka," *Księga pamiątkowa wydana przez Uniwersytet lwowski ku uczczeniu 500-letniego jubileuszu Uniwersytetu krakowskiego* (Lwów, 1900), p. 11.

89. His early identification with Łokietek is reflected in *Lites*, I, 367. On the new archbishop, see Zbigniew Szostkiewicz, "Katalog biskupów ob. łac. przedrozbiórowej Polski," *Sacrum Poloniae Millennium* (Rome, 1954–62), I, 479.

90. *M.P.V.*, III, # 144; I, # 53.

91. The presence, or absence, of specific individuals is reflected in the witnesses to documents issued by Łokietek at the meeting. See *C.D.P.M.*, II, # 573–74.

a revised system of payments for Peter's Pence was put forward. Bishop Gerward of Włocławek, acting as Archbishop Jan's representative, suggested that henceforth this tax be levied on the basis of one *denarius* per adult rather than three per household.[92]

Bishop Gerward appears in this convention not only as an important ecclesiastical figure, but as "defender and advocate of the Polish crown."[93] Such was not always the case, however, for as late as 1311 (three years after the seizure of Pomorze), Gerward still maintained good relations with the Teutonic Order, siding with them against his ecclesiastical superior, the archbishop of Gniezno.[94] In some matters, particularly in the case of the church of Świecie, the Knights gradually alienated Gerward by infringing upon what he conceived as his interests. When an appeal to the papacy over a vacancy at Świecie was decided in the Order's favor on June 7, 1317,[95] Gerward firmly attached himself to the cause of Łokietek, seeing in him a protector for his own interests and Poland's best hope for unity. Thus it was Gerward at Sulejów who took the initiative in drafting a formal petition to the papacy for the coronation of Łokietek. He played the same role some weeks later, in late June, at a convention at Pyzdry of the nobility and clergy of Greater Poland. At that time, those earlier decisions of Sulejów which affected Greater Poland were confirmed and Gerward's proposal approved.[96] Not surprisingly, the bishop was chosen by both conventions to carry the request to Pope John.

Sometime in the second half of 1318 Gerward travelled to Avignon, bearing a remarkable document from the whole kingdom, clergy, nobility, and city-dwellers.[97] All directed their heartfelt request to the pope to restore the kingdom and save its traditions by granting to Władysław Łokietek the crown of a united Polish kingdom. Two of the arguments put forward in this document are particularly noteworthy: first, that such a dignity would greatly facilitate Łokietek's struggle against the pagan Lithuanians and schismatics as well as

92. *Rocznik miechowski*, in *M.P.H.*, II, 883. For the problem of heresy, see Abraham, "Stanowisko Kurii," pp. 11–14. A document issued in Sulejów in June but dated October 8 (*Kod. dypl. kat. krak.*, I, # 119) suggests Łokietek and Muskata had been reconciled. For Peter's Pence in this context, see Ptaśnik, "Denar świętego Piotra," pp. 174 f., 181–97. The importance of this change for the demographic history of Poland is discussed by Ladogórski, *Studia nad zaludnieniem Polski*, pp. 67–123.

93. *M.P.H.*, II, 944; II, 859.

94. See Kazimierz Tymieniecki, "Studya nad XIV wiekiem: Proces polsko-krzyżacki z lat 1320–1321," *P.H.*, XXI, (1917–18), pp. 131–48, Appendix: "Gerward, biskup Kujawski."

95. *C.D.Pr.*, II, # 80.

96. Długosz, *Historia*, III, 86.

97. The date of Gerward's departure is difficult to determine. Długosz, *Historia*, III, 80, sets the trip in 1316, but his chronology in this whole section is badly confused. Caro, *Geschichte Polens*, II, 80, suggests early 1318, but Ptaśnik, "Denar świętego Piotra," p. 153, shows him to have been present in Poland at Sulejów. Abraham, "Stanowisko Kurii," p. 15, sets the date at the end of the year. The request Gerward carried has not survived and its contents must be reconstructed from the papal response of August 20, 1319. See Theiner, *Mon. Pol.*, I, # 224.

enabling him to be more active in promoting missionary activity to the east; second, that Poland's immediate dependency upon the Holy See and the payment of Peter's Pence provided justification for papal approval.

Łokietek's cause was given further impetus this same year by the appointment of Gabriel da Fabriano as apostolic nuncio to Poland. His task was to oversee the collection of papal funds and also to report on ecclesiastical affairs in general in Poland. This he did, and his information substantiated and strengthened Bishop Gerward's position when he presented his own request. Gabriel was also lavish in his praise of Łokietek as a true son of the church.[98]

When Gerward stood before Pope John to deliver his petition, there seemed to be no reason why it should not be approved. But the presence at Avignon of representatives of the Teutonic Order and of John of Bohemia indicates that such was not to be the case. The former, as allies of the Luxemburgs, and the latter, in the interests of their king, protested Łokietek's ambitions and demanded that John reject the petition. The basis for such action lay in John of Bohemia's claim to the Kingdom of Poland as heir of the last Přemyslid.[99]

This challenge was enough to cause the pope to temporize. Already deeply involved in the disputed succession within the empire which would eventually lead to the conflict with Lewis of Bavaria, he could ill-afford to alienate the important Luxemburg family. His response to Gerward's petition, in a letter dated August 20, 1319, was to suggest that the matter needed more study, even though he sympathized with the desires of the clergy and nobility. He did not absolutely deny the request; he simply did not approve it.

Gerward left Avignon and, less than six months later, attended the coronation of Władysław Łokietek, *dei gracia rex Polonie*. This event did not take place in contravention of papal wishes. As with so much else in the practice of international diplomacy, there were factors which were not made public. Gerward returned to Poland bearing copies of two secret letters, one directed to Łokietek, the other to the archbishop of Gniezno and the Polish bishops.[100] The first outlined the papal understanding of the significance of the traditional immediate subjection of Poland to the papacy and delineated Łokietek's responsibilities toward the church. It concluded by giving papal blessing to the

---

98. Theiner, *Mon. Pol.*, I, # 223.

99. Balzer attempted in his *Królestwo* to minimize the extent of King John's claims, suggesting they were at this time limited only to Greater Poland (II, 249–320, pp. 281 f. especially). He has been followed by some Polish scholars. See Długopolski, *Władysław Łokietek*, pp. 193–94. The Czech historian Šusta has demonstrated, however, that John did indeed intend the whole of the kingdom; see his *Král cizinec* (Prague, 1939), pp. 426–68. He has been followed by most other students of the question. See also Baszkiewicz's criticism of Balzer (*Powstanie zjednoczonego państwa*, p. 218); and *Historia Polski*, I, i, 434–35.

100. Władysław Abraham discovered regests of these letters in Cambrai and printed them in his "Stanowisko Kurii." The question of whether Łokietek had papal permission for the coronation is now therefore academic, but it intrigued many scholars in the nineteenth century. See Knoll, "Władysław Łokietek," p. 66, n. 89.

proposed coronation. The second letter explicitly granted permission for the coronation.

Before he left Avignon, Gerward also arranged for the institution of a papally sponsored legal proceeding against the Teutonic Knights over the question of Pomorze. He persuaded Pope John to issue, on September 11, 1319, a letter appointing three judges to undertake the investigation.[101] Finally, the bishop succeeded in gaining for himself and members of his family substantial benefits and preferments.[102] He then departed and returned to Poland, where he conferred with Łokietek and with his fellow prelates. Out of that conference arose the decision to proceed with the coronation, to be held in the cathedral at Cracow.

This decision confirmed earlier developments of the twelfth and thirteenth centuries and signalized one of the most important characteristics of the newly restored Kingdom of Poland, the dominance of Little Poland. Whereas in the older Piast state Greater Poland had dominated, under Łokietek and, after him, Casimir the regions of Cracow and Sandomir stood in the forefront. Later observers, such as Długosz,[103] might explain (with some justice) that the choice of Cracow as capital reflected military advantages: the more easily defended fortress and the further distance from two chief external threats to the state, Brandenburg and the Teutonic Order. But Łokietek probably also remembered the hostility of Greater Poland in the years before 1300 and after the end of the Přemyslids, and he preferred to make his royal residence in an area where he had a stronger political base. These reasons, plus the earlier rise of this city to predominance in the state, help to account for the choice of Cracow and the gentle but definite shift in the political center of gravity in the *regnum*.

On Sunday January 20, 1320, Archbishop Jan Janisław placed the crown of a reunited kingdom upon Łokietek's head. The cathedral of Wawel, where the ceremony was performed, was not the splendid gothic structure that it became under future kings. The setting of the scene was appropriate, however, for the coronation of the simple, direct warrior; and to the assembled multitude, including the higher clergy and nobility of Poland as well as Łokietek's family, it was enough that the ceremony took place. More definitely than the coronations of either Przemysł or Václav, this act marked the end of the divided kingdom.

The actual crowns which Łokietek and his wife, Jadwiga, wore were newly fashioned for the purpose, since earlier ones had been taken by Václav to Bohemia. The coronation sword, *Szczerbiec*—The Jagged Sword—was regarded as the weapon of Bolesław Chrobry, notched when he struck the Golden Gate of

101. Theiner, *Mon. Pol.*, I, # 231.

102. See Długopolski, *Władysław Łokietek*, pp. 196–97.

103. Długosz, *Historia*, III, 88.

Kiev in 1018. In reality it was of thirteenth-century manufacture, probably in Silesia. One member of the assembled multitude undoubtedly found little to enjoy that day. Bishop Muskata attended, but he can hardly have approved of the ceremony.[104]

Already sixty years old, Łokietek had still more than a decade remaining to him in which to defend the kingdom in the vigorously direct manner to which he was so accustomed; thirteen years in which to govern and strengthen the state with those administrative talents which had been so slow to ripen. To him, this was the climax of his life, for he had achieved that goal for which he had striven, the unification of the kingdom. But his coronation was more than a personal triumph. It was even more than simply the end of the process of reunion begun in the preceding century and guided in turn by Henry IV Probus, Przemysł, Václav, and Łokietek, for this process was more than the sum total of their individual efforts. What was celebrated that Sunday was the triumph of an idea. The concept of the *regnum Poloniae* is central to this period; and although it is hardly possible to deal here with the various, and sometimes varying, interpretations of that concept by generations of Polish scholars, it is nevertheless appropriate to delineate briefly those factors which seem to be constant. In this way we may see a significance to Łokietek's coronation which lies beneath the surface of events.[105]

The earlier Polish state was in large measure regarded as having a dynastic character. When the dynasty was unable to rule over a particular region or when it was personally divided, the very existence of the state was in doubt. In the course of the extended territorial division of the twelfth and thirteenth centuries, however, there was a gradually dawning awareness that the *regnum* continued to exist, even though it was not united. For example, the *Vita Major S. Stanislai* of the thirteenth century speaks of the "kingdom divided within itself."[106] That there was this independent entity of the *regnum* is shown even more clearly in the *Rocznik świętokrzyski* about 1300: "Wladislaus . . . wanted to obtain the Kingdom of Poland, already having several of its terri-

---

104. This description of the coronation could be considerably amplified by drawing upon fuller accounts of later coronations, since patterns and traditions in a formal event such as this changed little in the Middle Ages. I have chosen, however, to hold fairly closely to Długosz's briefer account in *Historia*, III, 93. See also Marian Gumowski, "Szczerbiec polski, miecz koronacyjny," *Małopolskie Studia Historyczne*, II, pts. ii/iii (1959), 5–18.

105. It is necessary to distinguish here between *corona regni Poloniae*, that is, the symbol, and *regnum Poloniae*, the real entity independent of any individual. The former concept is clear by the end of Casimir's reign; the latter has clearly evolved by the time of Łokietek's coronation. On the concept of the *regnum*, see Stanisław Krzyżanowski, "Regnum Poloniae," *S.A.U.*, XIV (1909), pt. v, 14–16, and XVIII (1913), pt. ix, 20–26; Marian Łodyński, "Regnum Poloniae w opinii publicznej XIV wieku," *K.H.*, XXVIII (1914), 38–54; Zygmunt Wojciechowski, *W sprawie Regnum Poloniae za Władysława Łokietka* (Lwów, 1924); Balzer, *Królestwo*, II, 321–536, and III, 143–266; Baszkiewicz, *Powstanie zjednoczonego państwa*, pp. 401–11.

106. *M.P.H.*, IV, 392.

tories."[107] Considered in this context the *regnum* appears to have chiefly a constitutional significance, and this is the sense in which Oswald Balzer later brilliantly described it.[108] This is certainly true, and the efforts of early "reuniters" were largely directed towards giving political expression to this concept within a constitutional framework.

But by the second decade of the fourteenth century, a broader concept may be observed, one containing ethnic, territorial, and historical elements. Of these, the historical and territorial are perhaps the most easily understandable, for that which had been part of the state before would easily be assumed to be still part of it. This is the reason why a citizen of Wrocław, writing to the pope in 1312, could remark, ". . . the Polish kingdom, in which Wrocław is located, as is well known."[109] These same precedents are utilized by the witnesses against the Teutonic Knights in 1320 and 1339, where the phrases "part of the Kingdom of Poland" and "land which has belonged to the Kingdom of Poland from antiquity" appear frequently.[110] But the most striking use is in reference to Chełmno, which had not been ruled by any Polish prince since the early thirteenth century. This region is also regarded as part of the *regnum*, "and . . . this is public knowledge and well known."[111] The ethnic element is closely related to the development of a Polish national consciousness in this period. On this basis, the *regnum* includes those regions whose inhabitants bear the badge of Polishness by the fact that they speak Polish. This would of course encompass those regions politically under the control of the *regnum*, such as Little Poland and Greater Poland but it also was extended to those areas now ruled by others—Silesia and Pomorze.[112]

This ideological formulation of the *regnum Poloniae* is partially necessary as a framework for the understanding of certain aspects of Łokietek and Casimir's foreign policy. Their persistent attempts to regain Silesia and Pomorze were more than simple dynastic or personal aggrandizement. They were more than the expression of economic concerns, though they had these aspects also. They were in fact a kind of crusade in which the *regnum* was the motivating consideration.[113]

107. *M.P.H.*, III, 77.

108. Balzer distinguished here between a pre-1320 ethnographic concept (see his "Polonia, Poloni, gens Polonica," in *Księga pamiątkowa ku czci Bolesława Orzechowicza* [Lwów, 1916], I, 71–93, especially pp. 75 ff.), and the post-1320 constitutional understanding (see *Królestwo*, III, 144 ff. especially).

109. *Breslauer Urkundenbuch*, ed. Georg Korn (Wrocław, 1870), # 95.

110. *Lites*, I, pp. 149, 365, 397, 398, 402.

111. Ibid., pp. 148, 182, 187, 210, 226, 230, 237, 241, 249, 253, 281, 294, 347, 391.

112. Ibid., 144, 163, 201, 256, 262, 271.

113. The ideal of the whole *regnum* is reflected in the late thirteenth century in the chronicle of Mierzwa, in *M.P.H.*, II, 300: "ut idem regnum Deus in statum pristinum restauret."

2
FATHER AND SON

Following his coronation, Łokietek took up immediately his already pressing problems of foreign policy. He began by diplomatic efforts, securing for himself and Poland a powerful ally against the ambitions of his Luxemburg, Wittelsbach,[1] and military-religious neighbors. In central Europe it was only to Hungary that he could look for such an ally. The Angevin supporters there had granted him aid in 1304; now it was with the Angevin ruler himself that he dealt. As early as 1315 formal relations had been developed between him and Charles Robert.[2] The most important factors in this relationship were a common anti-Luxemburg policy and the increased prestige of the Piast dynasty as a result of Łokietek's coronation. The death of the Angevin's second wife made a marriage pact between the two houses natural. Late in June, 1320, Łokietek's daughter Elizabeth, then some fourteen years old, travelled to Hungary to meet her bridegroom. On July 6 she and Charles Robert were married at Székesfehérvár (Stuhlweissenburg). Though apparently there was

1. When the Ascanian line died out in Brandenburg the year before Łokietek's coronation, a period of anarchy ensued. Gradually the Wittelsbach family of Lewis of Bavaria gained control; and although Margrave Lewis (der Ältere) was not formally enfeoffed with Brandenburg until 1323, his effective control came much earlier. The establishment of this dynasty there posed a grave threat to Polish interests. The Wittelsbachs were as aggressively expansionistic as the Ascanians, as reflected in *Pommersches Urkundenbuch*, 7 vols. (Szczecin, 1868–1958), VI, # 3775. They had good relations with the Knights, which caused Łokietek to fear the two would work in concert against Poland (see *C.D.Pr.*, III, # 8). For the history of the Mark in this period, see Johannes Schulz, *Die Mark Brandenburg* (Berlin, 1961–), I, 273 ff., II, 9–24.

2. See Jan Dąbrowski, "Z czasów Łokietka, Studya nad stosunkami polsko-węgierskimi w XIV w.," *R.A.U.*, series 2, XXXIV (1916), pp. 315 ff.

no formal alliance connected with this,[3] both countries were to benefit greatly in the future. For Poland, Łokietek and Casimir could count upon tangible assistance to complement the moral support of the papacy; for Hungary, it meant the eventual union of the two kingdoms under Louis the Great, the son of Charles Robert and Elizabeth.

In the meantime, Łokietek was involved in a legal action against the Teutonic Knights. Polish complaints against the Order had since 1308 unceasingly been directed to Avignon, and on September 11, 1319, Pope John appointed Archbishop Jan Janisław, Bishop Domarat of Poznań, and Abbot Mikołaj of Mogiłno to determine the validity of the Polish charges.[4] If they concluded the Poles were correct, the Order was to be commanded to return Pomorze to Łokietek and pay an indemnification equal to the damages it had caused and the income it had in the meantime received. The partisan nature of the forth-coming proceeding was foreshadowed by the tenor of John's commission and the composition of the court: all were Poles sympathetic to Łokietek.[5]

The proceeding began when the judges, on February 19, 1320, ordered the grand master and certain of his subordinates to appear before them in Inowrocław on April 14 to answer charges.[6] The grand master, who had no intention of appearing, appointed a deputy to represent the interests of the Order. His first act was to lodge an appeal with the papacy against the whole proceeding,[7] but this was in vain. The Polish prosecutors—Philip, chancellor of Greater Poland, Zbigniew, canon of Cracow and vice-chancellor of that city, and Jan, canon of Rudda—leveled seven formal articles of complaint which in sum charged the Order with having unjustly and forcibly seized Pomorze from Łokietek and from Poland. The prosecutors demanded that the Order be expelled from Pomorze and fined 30,000 Polish marks plus the cost of the process. Then they called a series of witnesses to testify to the validity of the charges. These included two bishops, three dukes, as well as lesser ecclesiastics and a variety of lay people. All agreed that the charges brought against the

---

3. Edmund Długopolski, *Władysław Łokietek na tle swoich czasów* (Wrocław, 1951), p. 222, implies that there was, though Dąbrowski, "Z czasów Łokietka," p. 317, and "Elżbieta Łokiet-kówna," *R.A.U.*, LVII (1914), 306, mentions none. Cooperation between the two states and dynasties, which were not in a permanent alliance, was usually on an ad hoc basis.

4. Theiner, *Mon. Pol.*, I, #281.

5. There has never really been any attempt by modern Polish scholars to portray the court as objective. As early as Adam Naruszewicz, *Historya narodu polskiego od początku chrześciaństwa*, V (Warsaw, 1784), 376 f., the lack of objectivity was noted. Despite this, some German historians have tended to use this partisanship as the justification for deprecating the eventual verdict.

6. The documents relating to this proceeding are printed in *Lites*, I, 7–51. The best secondary accounts are given by Kazimierz Tymieniecki, "Studya nad XIV wiekiem: Proces polsko-krzy-żacki z lat 1320–21," *P.H.* XXI (1917–18), 77–130; Długopolski, *Władysław Łokietek*, pp. 201–14; and Stanisław Zajączkowski, *Polska a Zakon Krzyżacki w ostatnich latach Władysława Łokietka* (Lwów, 1929), pp. 20–31.

7. *C.D.Pr.*, II, #94.

Order were correct, and some, as eyewitnesses to many of the events in Pomorze, were in an excellent position to make such a judgment.[8]

By October 1 the testimony was complete. The Order had made no defense at all, preferring to limit its activity to protesting the legality of the proceeding. These protests and other maneuvers prolonged events, and it was not until February 9, 1321, that the decision was published in Inowrocław. When the sentence was first read representatives of the Order proceeded to raise innumerable questions on points of legal procedure. These tactics again delayed the end of the process. But on the next day the definitive sentence was read. The judges sentenced the Order to return Pomorze to Łokietek, pay him an indemnification of 30,000 marks, and pay 150 marks for the costs of the proceeding. Again the Order appealed, but the work of the judges was done and the process came to an end. Łokietek had succeeded in obtaining a judgment against the Order but in following months it became apparent that he had failed to obtain the return of Pomorze.

Both the judgment and the appeal to the papacy were buried in the morass of a renewed struggle between pope and emperor. The Knights were able to ignore the decision and go their own way; and because law without enforcement is no law at all, the matter seemed to have been dropped by all parties. But this was not true, for whatever the shortcomings of the court, it had been legally constituted by the papacy and had ruled in Poland's favor; and Łokietek was later to use this as justification when he abandoned diplomacy and took up the sword.

Though Łokietek was to concentrate as king upon affairs in the west, he was not unaware of the significance of the east. At about this time the *regnum Galiciae et Lodomeriae* and the nascent Lithuanian state under Gedymin began to play roles in his policy. This former kingdom had emerged in the territorial dissolution of the Kievan state in the twelfth century. Under the leadership of Prince Roman (ruled 1199–1205) the regions of Halicz and Vladimir were united, and Roman ruled as an independent prince. The house of Roman had prospered after its founder's death, and in 1253 Pope Innocent IV had sent a crown to Roman's son Daniel, hoping that he and his subjects would recognize the supremacy of Rome and henceforth follow the Latin rite rather than the Orthodox. The papacy also hoped that Daniel would make his kingdom into Christendom's eastern bulwark against the Tatars, who only the decade before had swept into central Europe before being turned back, first by the Poles, then the Hungarians. The Asiatic threat was still a very real concern to Europe, but the papacy and the Western powers failed to mount the crusade which Daniel demanded, and Innocent's hopes were not realized. After the death of Daniel his two sons had divided the kingdom between them. The elder, Leo I, founded a new capital which later became one of the major cities

---

8. See particularly *Lites*, I, 23–24, wit. 8.

of eastern Europe: Lwów, or Leopolis. (For other forms of place names, see Appendix A.)

When Leo II and Andrew, the last direct descendants of the house of Roman, died in 1323,[9] Łokietek was forced to consider the safety of his eastern border. Because the descendants of Roman had at one time recognized Tatar overlordship, Łokietek feared the Horde might claim this territory for itself. He wrote to Pope John on May 21, 1321, outlining the threat to Poland and western Christendom. He suggested a crusade and requested other subsidies against the Tatars.[10] John was apparently not alarmed, for two years elapsed before he thought it necessary to respond. In a series of four letters, written between June 20 and August 1, 1325, he granted to Łokietek, the clergy, and all the faithful in Poland full indulgences for the fight "against schismatics, Tatars, pagans and other confused nations of unbelievers."[11] Such a response was too little, too late, for Łokietek had already undertaken a campaign into Ruthenia.

The paucity of our sources makes it nearly impossible to establish the precise nature and results of this campaign, and the description which follows is highly inferential and tentative. Sometime between midyear 1323 and early fall 1325, with the aid of his son-in-law Charles Robert, Łokietek travelled to Ruthenia. Although he was related by marriage to the last of the Romanoviči, he did not attempt to seize the rule himself. He recognized the weakness of Poland's position and that he would be overextending himself by such an act. Instead he was content to support the candidacy of a distant cousin, Bolesław Trojdenowicz. This youth, born between 1310 and 1314, was the son of Duke Trojden of Sochaczew and Czersk in Mazovia, and Maria, the sister of the deceased Romanoviči, Leo II and Andrew. He was therefore the nearest blood relative in the line of succession, and sometime prior to mid-1325 he was, with Łokietek's backing, recognized as *dux Russiae* by the boyars of Ruthenia. Bolesław converted to Orthodox Christianity and ruled under the name George II until 1340.[12]

9. The circumstances and dates of their deaths were difficult for historians to determine. See Gotthold Rhode, *Die Ostgrenze Polens, Politische Entwicklung, Kulturelle Bedeutung und geistige Auswirkung*, vol. I: *Im Mittelalter bis zum Jahre 1401* (Cologne and Graz, 1955), p. 122 n. 105. The most reliable sources are Johannes Vitoduranus, *Chronicon a Frederico imperatore ad annum 1348*, in *M.G.H. SS.*, *n.s.*, III, 184: "imperator Tartarorum duos paganos [that is, "Scismatici," see Antoni Prochaska, "W sprawie zajęcie Rusi przez Kazimierza Wielkiego," *K.H.*, VI (1892), 5] reges satis idoneos Ruthenis praefecerat"; and Łokietek's letter to the pope (see note 10 below) from which the date 1323 may be inferred.

10. *M.P.V.*, I, # 83.

11. See Theiner, *Mon. Pol.*, I, # 316, 334, 335, 338.

12. Charles Robert's claims to this region were based upon earlier Árpád claims. See Bálint Hóman, *Geschichte des Ungarischen Mittelalters*, 2 vols. (Berlin, 1940–43), II, 12–14, 22–24, 30–32. The complicated genealogical considerations involved in Polish claims are reflected in Oswald Balzer, *Genealogia Piastów* (Cracow, 1895), pp. 347 ff., 438. The persons of Bolesław and

Against this reconstruction of events in 1323–25 might be cited certain documents issued by Bolesław-George indicating his friendship toward, and support of, the Teutonic Order;[13] some historians have suggested that Łokietek would hardly have aided anyone who was sympathetic toward his most bitter enemy.[14] This argument is not wholly convincing, for these documents were all issued after Bolesław-George had been established in Ruthenia. In addition, as Gotthold Rhode has recently pointed out, none of the agreements with the Teutonic Order indicate hostility toward Łokietek. They suggest rather that "Bolesław-George II, and the Boyars ruling with him, sought to occupy as neutral a position as possible between the great powers of the day."[15]

Łokietek himself sought to improve his position against one of these great powers, the Teutonic Knights. He did so by seeking a rapprochement with Prince Gedymin of Lithuania. Despite previous hostility between Poland and Lithuania,[16] there was an overriding reason why the two were likely allies: each saw the Order as its chief enemy. It was probably this attitude which had governed Gedymin's earlier dealings with the west.

As early as 1317 Gedymin had made some attempt to obtain the good will of the newly elected Pope John. As a result, John had written him on February 3, 1317, exhorting him to become a Christian and give up his pagan ways.[17] This letter seemed to bear no fruit, but six years later western Europe was astounded to hear that six letters, purportedly from Gedymin, had been sent to the pope, Christendom in general, two religious orders, and certain commercial cities. They hinted that Gedymin might consent to be baptized.[18] The effect was sensational, but by the time any concrete decisions were made in the West, it was evident that Gedymin had no real wish to become a Christian. The only specific result had been that the Order was, by the course of events, maneuvered

---

George for many years created confusion among scholars, and the first to establish the identity between them was the Czech scholar Jan Řežabek, whose "Jiří II, poslední kníže veškere Malé Rusi," first appeared in *Časopis Musea království Českého*, LVII (1883), 120–218.

13. *C.D.Pr.*, II, # 116; and *Pr. U.B.*, II, # 537. This friendship was three times repeated; in 1327, 1334, and 1335. See *Pr. U.B.*, II, # 582, 826, and III, # 28.

14. So Mykhailo Hruschevsky, *Istoria Ukrainy-Rusy*, 10 vols. (New York, 1955), III, 123; Stanisław Zachorowski, "Wiek XIII i panowanie Władysława Łokietka," *Encyklopedya Polska*, V, pt. i (Warsaw, Lublin, Łódź, and Cracow, 1920), p. 390; Abraham, *Powstanie*, I, 192.

15. Rhode, *Die Ostgrenze Polens*, I, 126, who also points out that Bolesław-George's marriage in 1331 to Gedymin's daughter Eufemja (see Balzer, *Genealogia*, pp. 451 ff.) is part of the same picture. This element of "cautious neutrality" was previously pointed out by Długopolski, *Władysław Łokietek*, pp. 224 f.

16. In the three-quarters of a century before the alliance of 1325, the Lithuanians invaded Polish territory sixteen times. See Rhode, *Die Ostgrenze Polens*, I, 134 n. 13 for documentation.

17. The text of this letter is printed in Abraham, *Powstanie*, I, 365–67.

18. The texts of these letters, taken from later copies, are printed in *Liv-, Est-, und Kurländisches Urkundenbuch nebst Regesten*, ed. F. G. Bunge et al., 10 vols. (Reval, Riga, and Moscow, 1853–1910), II, # 687–690, V, # 3069.

into an extended truce with Gedymin. This may well have been the Lithuanian's intention all along.[19]

Such an ephemeral victory was not sufficient for Gedymin, however, and he was open to the alliance with Poland suggested in negotiations in 1324 and 1325. The result was the signing in the fall of 1325 of a formal Polish-Lithuanian treaty. Its details are not fully known, but there is no doubt that it was directed against the mutual enemies of the two states.[20] To seal the arrangement, Gedymin's daughter Aldona was engaged to Łokietek's son Casimir. After the bride had converted to Christianity, adopting the name Anna, the two were married on October 16, 1325. Part of Anna's dowry was the return of all Poles held prisoner by the Lithuanians, though the figure of 24,000 given by some sources is hardly credible.

The bride in this marriage pact proved to be a great source of joy for her husband. To the somewhat restrained Polish court she brought a gaiety and joie de vivre which gladdened the hearts of those around her. She delighted in worldly pleasures, games, and dances; and whenever she went in public or rode with her handmaidens, she was accompanied by drummers, flutists, and other musicians. She was not highly regarded by her contemporaries, but she was beloved by her husband, who deeply mourned her passing in 1339.[21]

That he should have done so was not wholly surprising, for Casimir was a sensitive, emotional individual in personal matters. This future king of Poland was born on April 30, 1310, the third son and the sixth and youngest child of Łokietek and Jadwiga.[22] His older brother, Stefan, had died in 1306, while a second brother, Władysław, died in 1312. Casimir was thus heir to the throne almost from birth and received a training commensurate with his future. From his tutors, Spicymir of Melsztyn and Archdeacon (later Archbishop) Jarosław Bogoria, he received a formal, though limited, education and an awareness of the importance of two factors which were to dominate his reign: the art of diplomacy and the value of the written law. From his father he learned more

---

19. I have here accepted the view that Gedymin's letters were genuine, or at least sent with his knowledge. This does not imply religious motivation, for their language and subsequent political events indicate quite another motivation. The letters have been accepted as genuine by Prochaska, "Stosunki Krzyżaków z Gedyminem i Łokietkiem," *K.H.*, X (1896), 20–21; Abraham, *Powstanie*, I, 183–85; Chodynicki, "Próby," pp. 260 ff.; Friedrich, *Der Deutsche Ritterorden*, pp. 114–18. Their authenticity has been denied by Theodore Schiemann, *Russland, Polen und Livland bis ins 17. Jahrhundert*, 2 vols. (Berlin, 1886–87), I, 224–29; Johannes Voigt, *Geschichte Preussens von den ältesten Zeiten bis zum Untergange der Herrschaft des Deutschen Ordens*, 9 vols. (Königsberg, 1827–39), IV, 626–37; and, with qualifications, by Forstreuter, "Die Bekehrung Gedimins," pp. 255–61.

20. See Stanisław Zajączkowski, "Przymierze polsko-litewskie 1325 r.," *K.H.*, XL (1926), 608–10.

21. *Rocznik małopolski*, in *M.P.H.*, III, 199.

22. Biographical data on Casimir, together with citations, are given by Balzer, *Genealogia*, pp. 10, 380. The date given in *Pol. Słow. Biog.*, XII, 264 (April 3) is a misprint.

practical arts: the military elements of statecraft and the need for laying long-range plans. As he matured he accompanied his father on military campaigns.

The young heir entered the world of international politics for the first time in 1322, when Łokietek betrothed him to Jutta, the daughter of John of Bohemia. Had this match been successful, it would perhaps have reconciled the Piast and Luxemburg dynasties and might even have provided a powerful ally for Poland against the Teutonic Knights. It failed however, and Łokietek was forced to look elsewhere for dynastic combinations. As we have seen, he was successful. It perhaps was high time that Casimir be sobered by the responsibilities of a wife and family, for he had already demonstrated those high, passionate spirits which remained vital till his death. In this respect he, as well as his wife, contrasted sharply with the sober austerity of the Polish court. Łokietek found his time so filled with maintaining Poland's position and defending its borders that he was unable to emulate, for example, the Angevin splendor of his daughter and son-in-law's court in Hungary. The nature of the Polish court was also shaped by the piety of Casimir's mother. Among her other religious austerities, she counted it a blessing to be able to eat and sleep once a year in the nunnery of St. Clare in Stary Sącz.[23]

In the same year that Casimir married Anna, Łokietek gained another ally who could be helpful against both the Teutonic Knights and the Wittelsbachs in Brandenburg. It was a community of interests which brought the Polish king and Dukes Warcisław, Otto, and Barnim of Western Pomorze together. In an alliance signed on June 18, 1325, the two sides bound themselves in a defensive treaty. From the standpoint of the dukes this provided aid against Brandenburg in their struggle to regain independence, while for Łokietek the treaty allowed him to strengthen his border against both the Knights and the Wittelsbachs.[24] It was in connection with this treaty that next year the Polish-Lithuanian alliance was first applied.

Early in 1326, between February 10 and March 11, a joint Polish-Lithuanian force invaded Brandenburg. The 1,200 troops wreaked great devastation upon the land, but the campaign failed when the army was stopped at Frankfurt on the Oder.[25] This invasion of Brandenburg marked a turning point in Łokietek's career. With this act, he abandoned the arts of diplomacy which he had followed so successfully in the preceding decade. Henceforth until his death he was involved in almost yearly military campaigns against

23. For this characterization of her, see Theiner, *Mon. Pol.*, I, # 423.

24. The text of the treaty is printed in *Lites*, I, 431 f., and Otto Heinemann, "Das Bundniss zwischen Polen und Pommern vom Jahre 1325," *Zeitschrift der historischen Gesellschaft für die Provinz Posen*, XIII (1898), 342–44. See also Zajączkowski, *Polska a Zakon*, pp. 85–86; Prochaska, "Stosunki Krzyżaków," pp. 50 f., Stanisław Nowogrodzki, "Pomorze Zachodnie a Polska 1323–1370," *Rocznik Gdański*, IX-X (1935–36), 6–28.

25. The sources for this campaign are found in *M.P.H.*, III, 229; Johannes Vitoduranus, *Chronicon*, p. 102; Henricus de Rebdorf, *Annales imperatorum et paparum, 1294–1362*, in *M.G.H. SS., n.S.*, I, 39; Peter of Dusburg, *Chronica terre Prussie*, in *SS. rer. Pr.*, I, 287.

one or another of his mighty enemies. The significance of these years will be considered below, but it is sufficient here to note that the young Casimir, who accompanied his father on many of these campaigns, could hardly fail to be impressed by the nearly unrelieved series of reverses his father suffered. The first of these came in the struggle with Brandenburg, where the campaign of 1326 had initiated a three-year conflict. It was desultory in nature, however, largely because neither side concentrated upon its prosecution. The Wittels-bachs were too involved in their struggle against Pope John XXII, while Łokietek was forced to direct his attention to the attempted recovery of Pomorze and the aggressive aspirations of John of Bohemia. Thus negotiations for a truce progressed rapidly when they were initiated in 1328. Finally on August 18 of the following year a three-year truce was signed at Landsberg.[26] Each party was now free to concentrate upon its other interests. While Edmund Długopolski has seen this as a major diplomatic triumph for Łokietek,[27] it was more in the nature of a pragmatic recognition of the realities of Poland's position and the nature of its true interests.

Łokietek conceived this interest to be the recovery of Pomorze. Toward this end he had first tried peaceful means, but the last attempt of this kind probably came in 1324. In that year the new grand master of the Teutonic Order sent a representative to Brześć in Kujavia to meet with the king. Johannes Grot, later Bishop of Cracow, was present at the meeting and reported in 1339 that its purpose was "to obtain an agreement of peace and concord with ... Wladislaus about the aforementioned regions of Chełmno and Pomorze."[28] When Łokietek presented his claims, Sieghard denied their validity but offered to pay the king 10,000 marks for renunciation of Polish claims; this was refused, and the meeting accomplished nothing. Recognizing that recourse to arms was all that remained to him, Łokietek set about obtaining allies for that end. It is against this background of heightened tension between Poland and the Order that we must see the aforementioned treaties with Western Pomorze and Lithuania of the next year.

In the meantime, the Order was not idle, for it set about the task of diplomatically isolating Łokietek. It persuaded Duke Warcisław of Western Pomorze to renew an earlier treaty in September, 1325.[29] This was strictly a defensive arrangement in which the Order promised to support the Duke against his

---

26. *C.D.M.P.*, II, # 1103 and 1117. For the problems of dating this truce, see A. Kłodziński, "Rokowanie polsko-brandenburskie w r. 1329," *R.A.U.*, XLVII (1905), 57–124, pp. 63–67, 110 ff. especially. See also Zajączkowski, "Polska a Wittelsbachowie w pierwszej połowie XIV wieku," in *Prace Historyczne w 30-lecie działalności profesorskiej Stanisława Zakrzewskiego* (Lwów, 1934), pp. 69–75.

27. Długopolski, *Władysław Łokietek*, p. 285.

28. *Lites*, I, 287. Caro, *Geschichte Polens*, II, 110, concludes incorrectly that a truce was signed in this meeting to last until Christmas, 1326. See Zajączkowski, *Polska a Zakon*, pp. 52–55.

29. *C.D.Pr.*, II, # 115.

enemies, that is, the Wittelsbachs. For his part, Warcisław agreed to withhold aid from any enemy of the Order. Since this included Łokietek, the Polish king was thus deprived of support which only a few months before he had gained. Several months later the Order scored another victory. In January, 1326, Dukes Ziemowit and Wacław of Mazovia signed a treaty of friendship with the Order.[30] This was by no means an offensive alliance, neither was it a defensive arrangement. It merely asserted strong ties of friendship and regulated contacts between the two. It did, however, remove a possible ally for Łokietek.

The uncertain peace between Poland and the Order gave Łokietek pause as he prepared for the Brandenburg expedition. In order to protect his rear, he met with representatives of the Order in Łęczyca in February, 1326. At that time agreement was reached which provided that "there should be ordained a treaty [*treugas*] valid from this day [February 7] until the nearest future day of Christ's birth."[31] Though we have no evidence to indicate that fighting had broken out, the use here of the technical word *treugas* suggests that both sides recognized a state of war.[32] In the next year there is evidence of formal hostilities.

In July 1327, while there were still Hungarian troops in Cracow to defend against John of Bohemia (see below), Łokietek invaded Mazovia. Marching north from Cracow through Kujavia and Dobrzyń, the Polish troops struck directly at the capital of Duke Wacław, the ancient city of Płock. Attacking at night, Łokietek sacked and burned the city, then marched toward Sochaczew. At the same time Lithuanian troops may also have attacked from the east, but their contribution was negligible. In response the Knights marched to the aid of their Mazovian allies. Under the leadership of provincial commander Otto von Luterberg the Knights drove the Polish army out of Mazovia, back toward Brześć in Kujavia. Łokietek successfully prevented the capture of this town, and when the Knights offered a truce he accepted. A month's campaigning had settled nothing.[33]

The field remained empty during 1328, the battle continuing, for the time being, in the papal court. To Avignon both sides constantly addressed complaints against the other. The better lobby was Łokietek's and the Polish prelates', for most papal decisions in this period went against the Knights. None of the decisions succeeded in returning Pomorze to Poland, however, and Łokietek simply waited for a new opportunity to take up arms for that purpose.

---

30. *Pr. U.B.*, II, # 540–42; *Lites*, I, 432–33.

31. *Lites*, I, 433.

32. See Zajączkowski, *Polska a Zakon*, p. 87, and "Przymierze polsko-litewskie," p. 610.

33. The chief sources for this campaign are the testimony of the witnesses in 1339 (*Lites*, I, *passim*); *Chronica Olivensis*, in *M.P.H.*, VI, 327; and Długosz, *Historia*, III, 115, who incorrectly sets these events in 1325. See, however, Zajączkowski, *Polska a Zakon*, pp. 108–9. Tadeusz Żebrowski, in *Dziesięć wieków Płocka* (Płock, 1966), p. 45, abides by Długosz's dating.

Ironically it was his bitter foe, John Luxemburg, who provided him with the opening he needed.

Late in 1328, King John, in emulation of his predecessor, Otakar II, announced he would lead a crusading campaign into Lithuania and Samogitia.[34] He left Prague on December 6 and spent Christmas in Wrocław, where several Silesian princes joined his retinue. His party also included, as unofficial historian, the great French poet-musician, Guillaume de Machaut. By January 1, 1329, John had reached Toruń; there he joined forces with the Order, and the combined army marched to Königsberg where arrangements were made with Łokietek's representatives to prolong the truce between Poland and the Order.[35] After that the armies departed for Samogitia, where the crusade resulted in a remarkable number of conversions. In one instance their swords reportedly brought baptism to six thousand inhabitants of the region. These gains for Christendom proved, however, to be ephemeral, for when the Knights and King John precipitously broke off the campaign, the natives relapsed immediately into paganism.

That the allies returned so soon was the result of the news that Łokietek had invaded Chełmno. The unprotected rear of the Knights proved to be too tempting for the Polish king, and on February 1 he led an army of some six thousand into the heart of the Order's territory. For five days and nights, apparently with Casimir at his side, he devastated the countryside; but his success came to an abrupt end upon the return of the Knights and King John. On March 12 they signed a solemn pact of alliance against Łokietek in Toruń,[36] then counterattacked, crossing the Drwęca River into Dobrzyń. For a month they ranged at will there, and by early April John could claim to have conquered the region, for on April 3 he granted one-half the territory to the Knights as a reward for their help. A year later he sold them his claim to the other half.[37] This was not the only territory which fell into John's hands, for Duke Wacław of Płock in Mazovia was forced to surrender his land to the Bohemian king. On March 29, he accepted John as his feudal overlord and

---

34. There are a great many sources for this campaign and the year's events. In addition to those from the Polish and Order sides, there are Czech chronicles, particularly the *Chronicon aule regiae*, in *Font. rer. Boh.*, IV, 281, and the record left by the French poet Guillaume de Machaut. See T. Puymaigre, "Une campagne de Jean de Luxembourg, roi de Bohème," *Revue des questions historiques*, XLII (1887), 168–80.

35. The sources are unclear on this point, and many historians have doubted that such a truce was signed. See Zachorowski, "Wiek XIII," p. 393; Prochaska, "Stosunki Krzyżaków," pp. 57–58. On the other hand, Zajączkowski, "Przymierze polsko-litewskie," p. 613 (and after him Długopolski, *Władysław Łokietek*, pp. 267–68), have suggested that Łokietek sent representatives to Königsberg to protest the campaign against his ally and was offered instead the extension described above. See also Wigand of Marburg, *Chronica nova Prutenica*, in *SS. rer. Pr.*, II, 463.

36. *C.D.M.P.*, II, #1097. On the same day, John, as *rex Bohemie et Polonie*, confirmed the Knights in their possession of Pomorze. See *Pr. U.B.*, II, #638 and 639.

37. *C.D.Pr.*, II, #126; *Pr. U.B.*, II, #643, for the first. *Pr. U.B.*, II, #682, for the second.

1

Poland in East Central Europe
— 1320 —

——————— Boundaries of The Polish Kingdom in 1320
.... Other political boundaries

0   50   100   200   300   400   Miles

Pskov

LIVONIA

Kalmar

Copenhagen

Baltic Sea

Memel

SAMOGITIA

Polotsk

Königsberg

Vilno

LITHUANIA

POMORZE

BRANDENBURG

MEISSEN

← See Map 2

KIEV

Prague

Elbe

Vistula

VLADIMIR

BOHEMIA

Moldau

LWOW

PODOLIA

MORAVIA

HALICZ

Bug

SLOVAKIA

MOLDAVIA

Dniester

AUSTRIA

Esztergom

Buda Pest

HUNGARY

Danube

Adriatic
Sea

Black
Sea

Baltic Sea

WESTERN POMORZE

GDAŃSK-POMORZE

Gdańsk

Königsberg

Malbork

TEUTONIC ORDER

Vistula

Drwęca

Noteć

Chełmno

Toruń

Santok

Inowrocław

Płowce

Dobrzyń

Wkra

Narew

Gniezno

Brześć

Płock

Bug

Miedzyrzecz

Poznań

Warta

Zakroczym

Warsaw

Oder

GREATER POLAND

M A Z O V I A

Kalisz

Łęczyca

Głogów

Sieradz

Legnica

S

I

L

E

S

I

A

Wrocław

Lublin

Świdnica

Chęciny

L I T T L E   P O L A N D

Opole

Sandomierz

Elbe

Bytom

Wiślica

Raciborz

Cracow

Vistula

San

Opava

Oder

Olomouc

Cieszyn

Dunajec

B O H E M I A

Nowy Sącz

Przemyśl

Sanok

Vah

H U N G A R Y

Danube

received Płock as a fief of the Bohemian crown.[38] In the weeks after Easter the Knights continued to take their revenge, this time on the left bank of the Vistula, where they razed the city of Raciąż and sacked Włocławek, burning its cathedral to the ground.[39]

Forced to withdraw from Chełmno in order to defend himself elsewhere, Łokietek had been unable to stem the tide of conquest. He had watched helplessly as superior forces held the field time after time. His foolhardy invasion had ended in disaster with the loss of important land and widespread devastation. He willingly accepted a truce, recognizing the weakness of his position. As soon as possible, however, he set about altering this. He turned to Charles Robert for aid, and late in 1329 dispatched Casimir to Hungary as his representative.

The Latin splendor of the court at Wyszegrad contrasted strikingly with Casimir's home in Cracow, and it is not surprising that the nineteen-year-old prince did not spend all his time in negotiations with Charles Robert. The purpose of Casimir's visit was in fact soon accomplished, with the Angevin ruler agreeing to send troops to Poland for next year's campaigns. Casimir did not, however, immediately return home. He found the atmosphere of the court congenial to his lively nature, and spent some time in a dalliance with one of the young attendants to his sister, the Hungarian queen.[40] Only after some weeks did more martial concerns draw him back to Poland.

The Hungarian troops which Casimir had obtained were needed in 1330, for the conflict between Poland and the Order again broke out. The issue which precipitated this was the Knights' position in Dobrzyń, where attempts to consolidate their position were hampered by the commanding position of the Polish fortress of Wyszogród on the Vistula. They felt this to be a threat to their position, and in May they invaded Kujavia and besieged the fortress. Their eventual success came at the cost of heavy casualties on both sides. Further campaigning by the Knights resulted in the destruction of the fortified towns of Radziejów, Nakeł, and probably Bydgoszcz.[41]

By early autumn, Łokietek had prepared his revenge. Strengthened by the Hungarian troops sent by Charles Robert,[42] he attacked the garrisons of the

38. *Kodeks dyplomatyczny księstwa mazowieckiego*, edited by T. Lubomirski (Warsaw, 1863), #59.

39. The witnesses of 1339 are explicit in their descriptions of this activity. See *Lites*, I, 179, wit. 7; I, 213, wit. 17, particularly.

40. Casimir's Hungarian visit, together with certain problems connected with it, are best treated by Zdzisław Kaczmarczyk, *Polska czasów Kazimierza wielkiego* (Cracow, 1964), pp. 13 ff.

41. The sources for this campaign and those of 1331 and 1332 are rather more full than for previous years. See Peter of Dusburg, *Chronica*, p. 216; Wigand of Marburg, *Chronica*, pp. 465–66; Franciscus Thorunensis, *Annales Prussici, 941–1410*, in *SS. rer. Pr.*, III, 67; *Chronica terrae Prussiae*, in *M.P.H.*, IV, 39; *Rocznik Traski*, p. 854; *Rocznik małopolski*, p. 190; and the various witnesses in *Lites*, I.

42. The figures for the extent of this aid, as well as figures for sizes of armies in general in

Order in Kujavia, retaking several of the towns. Then he crossed the Vistula and Drwęca rivers into Chełmno. For a month his army ravaged the countryside, but it was unable to capture and hold any territory. Nevertheless the season's campaigning had been sufficiently demanding upon the resources of both sides that a truce was easily arranged. Sometime in early October representatives of the Order approached Łokietek, and on October 18, 1330, a truce until May 26 of the following year was signed.

The nature of this truce must be noted briefly here, because one of its conditions was repeated in succeeding truces and eventually was utilized by Casimir to undertake preliminary settlement with the Knights in 1335. This condition called for Łokietek and the Order to submit its dispute to kings John of Bohemia and Charles Robert of Hungary for arbitration. Whether this condition was binding in any way was not further specified, but it was a promising first step in the process which eventually removed the conflict from the battlefield. According to Wigand of Marburg, this provision for arbitration was the work of one of Łokietek's Hungarian lieutenants.[43] This suggests the agency of Charles Robert, who may have hoped thereby to establish more firmly his influence in central Europe. The truce of 1330 also provided for the return of Bydgoszcz and Wyszogród to Poland, but the significance of this gesture was minimal, since the razing of these fortresses had greatly reduced their immediate military importance. In balance, then, Łokietek had gained nothing from the campaign of 1330, and had in fact lost ground. He was not, however, willing to give up the struggle, and the campaigns of 1331 and 1332 were fought on an even greater scale than those before. These years saw the culmination of Poland's military conflict with the Order.

The eve of this culmination was marked by two important events which bear directly upon the relationship between Poland and the Knights. The first was the murder of Grand Master Werner von Orseln, who was succeeded on February 17, 1331, by Luter von Braunschweig. At the beginning of von Braunschweig's reign, he adopted a much more hostile policy toward Poland; with the numerous troops he brought with him from the empire he began preparations to invade Poland. In the meantime, Łokietek was providing for his son a baptism of fire as future king. According to the *Rocznik małopolski*, at a convention of representatives from throughout the kingdom in Chęciny, Łokietek "handed over control of Greater Poland, Sieradz, Kujavia to his son Casimir . . . so that he [the king] as well as his son might attempt to improve

---

this period, are grossly exaggerated. A common factor of reduction is to divide by ten. This at least brings the numbers within the realm of possibility. *M.P.H.*, III, 190 f., puts Hungarian troops at 10,000 and the total size of Łokietek's army at 50,000: 2,000 heavy cavalry, 20,000 light cavalry; and nearly 30,000 archers and foot soldiers. Peter of Dusburg, *Chronica*, p. 216, sets Łokietek's Hungarian help at 8,000.

43. Wigand of Marburg, *Chronica*, p. 466.

the borders of the kingdom."[44] The exact significance of this act has been disputed by Polish scholars,[45] but it appears that, first, from a constitutional standpoint Casimir occupied a position identical, or very similar, to the *starosta* (*capitaneus*); that is, he represented the interests of the king in this area. Second, from the standpoint of Łokietek's motives, it is probable that he intended to provide his heir with administrative experience. At the same time this would preserve Poland's strength in the north while Łokietek was able to devote his attention to the southwest where John of Bohemia was laying plans for an invasion of Poland.

It was not from John, however, but from the Knights that invasion first came. The initial wave of a double assault[46] began in late July when Grand Marshal Dietrich von Altenburg and Commander Otto von Luterberg of Chełmno entered Kujavia, raiding and devastating the countryside as they moved swiftly toward Inowrocław. A short, unsuccessful siege there was followed by the sacking of Słupsk and the attempt to take Pyzdry, where Casimir was at the time. After this other villages were attacked, Gniezno suffered some damage, and two small towns were destroyed before the Knights returned to Toruń. This whole campaign probably took less than three weeks.

Its speed was due to the absence of any machines of war, for the Knights in this instance depended wholly upon cavalry and infantry. This somewhat unusual approach, combined with the Knights' attempt to take the otherwise unimportant city of Pyzdry, raises the question of why they undertook the campaign. Most Polish scholars have followed the tradition of the *Rocznik małopolski*[47] and suggested the campaign was connected with the treachery of Vincent of Szamotuły, who had been the starosta of Greater Poland before he was replaced by Casimir. He had decided to revenge himself upon the prince and informed the Knights of his whereabouts. Thus one of the reasons for their invasion may have been to capture Casimir and perhaps obtain from him renunciation of Polish claims to Pomorze.[48]

During the July invasion of the Knights, Łokietek had remained in Cracow. The need for his watchfulness from the capital was shown not long after when

44. *M.P.H.*, III, 192–93.

45. Compare the following: Adam Kłodziński, "W obozie cesarskim, 1331–1332," *Przegląd Polski*, CLIII (1904), 300; Stanisław Kętrzyński, "Zapis Kazimierza Wielkiego dla Kazimierza Bogusławowice," *P.H.*, XIV (1912), 58; Oswald Balzer, *Królestwo Polskie, 1295–1370*, 3 vols. (Lwów, 1919–20), II, 441–52.

46. Kłodziński, "Ze studjów krytycznych nad rokiem 1331," *K.H.*, XIX (1905), 35–38, first suggested the possibility of two separate waves of invasion. This was more clearly demonstrated by Stanisław Kaniowski, "Przyczynki do dziejów wojny polsko-krzyżackiej z r. 1331," *P.H.*, XII (1911), 128–48.

47. *M.P.H.*, III, 193: "Predictus igitur Vincencius regni pessimus defraudater et gentis, et inpaciens huius alienacionis circa festum beate Marie Magdalene callide et occulte cruciferos eduxit, qui fere Cuyaviam et Wladislaw civitatem ceperant."

48. See Kłodziński, "W obronie zdrajcy," *S.A.U.*, VI, pt. vii (1901), 18–19.

King John invaded Poland in an attempt to link forces with the Knights. But the more immediate threat from the Order caused him to forsake his southern strategy of defense and gather an army for an invasion of the lands of the Knights. Before he could do so, they attacked again. Early in September Dietrich von Altenburg and Otto von Luterburg left Toruń at the head of a cavalry contingent of some 2,000, plus many support troops. This army followed a route which took them to Płock, Łęczyca, and Uniejów.[49] At Uniejów they divided forces, with one group marching into Sieradz and devastating this region, while the other went directly to Kalisz to await the arrival of John of Bohemia. Eventually the two contingents rejoined, but John did not appear. Finally, on September 23 they began their return to Toruń via Radziejów, plundering and raiding along the way as they had done all month.

In the meantime, Łokietek, with Casimir at his side, had dogged the route of the Knights. His forces were too small to meet them in an open battle or to relieve any of the beleaguered cities of the kingdom, but he was able to harry the Order in semiguerrilla fashion. When the return from Kalisz began, however, he was forced to pull back. Then came a stroke of fortune of which Łokietek was quick to take advantage. Early Friday, September 27, the Knights separated their forces into three groups. One of them, led by Dietrich with about one-third of the total strength but with the preponderance of the officers, left Radziejów and began the march toward Brześć via the village of Płowce. Just east of this place, about mid-morning Łokietek attacked. In the ensuing three-hour battle, the Polish troops, with the cry of "Cracow, Cracow" on their lips, succeeded in badly defeating the Knights, even taking the wounded Dietrich von Altenburg captive.

Despite this victory the army of the Knights had not been destroyed. News of the attack had been relayed to Otto von Luterberg and Heinrich Reuss von Plauen, who were in command of the other two divisions of the army. They hurried to relieve their brothers and by mid-afternoon had made contact with the Polish army. The fighting which followed, the second phase of the battle of Płowce, was no less vigorous than before, but apparently it was less bloody. Both sides took many prisoners, however (Heinrich Reuss was one who fell into Polish hands), and at dusk both sides broke off contact. A clear victory had been Łokietek's in the first phase, with nothing decisive emerging from the second. Losses had been high on both sides; the bishop of Włocławek later reported he had counted 4,187 bodies after the battle. In balance it had been a Polish victory; and even though fighting was not resumed the next day, Łokietek could take pride in his destruction of the myth of the Knights' military invincibility. A source of embarrassment, however, lay in the fact that his son and heir, Casimir, had fled in panic from the field of battle.[50] Shortly there-

---

49. For the route the Knights took, see Kaniowski, "Przyczynki," pp. 134–46.

50. *SS. rer. Pr.*, II, 6: "Der junge Kunic gegen Crakau vlôh/Daz er wênic den zogil zôch."

after the Knights returned to Toruń, to lick their wounds and prepare for another day.

That day came the following year about Easter, when the Order demonstrated that despite the defeat at Płowce, it was still the dominant military power in the region. After negotiations earlier in the year had failed to effect an exchange of prisoners and the signing of a peace between Poland and the Knights,[51] the Order invaded Kujavia in April and began a two-week siege of Brześć. In this instance they came not to raid and plunder, but to conquer, for "with siege machines and other instruments of war," they took the city and moved on to Inowrocław, which fell to them on April 26. As the two most important defenses for the region, the fall of Brześć and Inowrocław meant that the whole of Kujavia now lay open to the Knights. It is ironic that in the futile defense in following months, Wincenty of Szamotuły perished in the service of King Łokietek. Despite his earlier traitorous activity, the former starosta, now reinstated as Wojewoda of Kujavia, had made his peace with his ruler and served faithfully in the events of 1331 and 1332.[52]

Łokietek was unable to respond immediately to this new aggression. Not until August 15 did he invade Chełmno through Mazovia; but despite Hungarian assistance,[53] he was unable to accomplish anything. Soon thereafter he entered into negotiations with the Knights, and shortly a truce was signed which was to last until Pentecost, 1333. The provisions of this agreement, however, mark it as more than a simple cessation of hostilities. Following the precedent of 1330, it became in effect the preliminaries of peace, since both sides agreed to submit the conflict to kings John of Bohemia and Charles Robert of Hungary for arbitration.[54] Łokietek did not live to implement this arrangement but Casimir, building upon this foundation, eventually erected a stable peace with the Order, first in 1335 in Wyszegrad, and finally in 1343 at Kalisz.

The young prince probably had accompanied his father upon this last campaign. After the signing of the truce, Łokietek returned to Cracow, but Casimir proceeded into Greater Poland. There, at the head of a combined Polish-Hungarian army, he stormed some fifty fortified places and captured the city of Kościan. His activities should be seen, not as the chronicler of *Małopolska*

I have found extremely valuable the recent study by Marian Biskup, "Analiza bitwy pod Płowcami i jej dziejowego znaczenia," *Ziemia Kujawska*, I (1963), 73–104.

51. See Długopolski, *Władysław Łokietek*, p. 319.

52. See Karol Potkański, "Zdrada Wincentego z Szamotuł. Studya nad XIV wiekiem," *R.A.U.*, XXXVIII (1899), 374–95.

53. According to Długosz, *Historia*, III, *sub anno* 1332, Hungarian troops participated in the whole campaign. See Dąbrowski, "Z czasów Łokietka," p. 325, n. 3.

54. *M.P.H.*, II, 857; III, 196: "treugas usque ad pentecostes interim consiliandi et de negocio colloquendi cum ipsis accipiens." See also Zajączkowski, *Polska a Zakon*, pp. 264–77.

suggested, as an attack upon "fugitive commanders attacking the kingdom of Poland,"[55] but as a successful attempt to recover for the *regnum* territory from Greater Poland which Łokietek had failed to obtain from the heirs of Duke Henry of Głogów in the years 1312–14.[56]

The preceding two years had been important ones for the heir to the Polish throne. Casimir had taken an increasingly important role in the administration of the kingdom, he had accompanied his father on military campaigns, meeting Poland's enemies personally, and he had redeemed his failure of 1331 by his success of 1332. It is not surprising that it was reported "he returned to Cracow in triumph." This glory was overshadowed by the losses to the Knights, by the slow but sure inroads of Luxemburg influence in Silesia, and by John of Bohemia's claims upon the Polish crown. With these last two threats Łokietek and Casimir had also to deal.

As early as 1319 John had put forward claims to the crown of Poland.[57] These he had maintained after Łokietek was crowned, continuing to style himself "John, King of Bohemia and Poland" and referring scornfully to "Wladislaus, called Loktek, King of Cracow."[58] John was less interested in the crown itself than in using his claim as a lever upon Łokietek (and after him, Casimir) in quite another regard. What the Luxemburger really wanted was domination over Silesia and Polish recognition of the Bohemian position there.[59]

Originally part of the Kingdom of Poland, Silesia had followed an independent path of political and, even, cultural development during the decades of territorial fragmentation of the kingdom. One of the most striking features of that development had been the gradual but steady penetration into the region of German and Bohemian influences.[60] These influences had been cultural, legal, and economic rather than ethnic in nature, but they had nevertheless brought significant changes in the region. Among the nobility and urban aristocracy especially, it had become more natural by the beginning of the

55. *M.P.H.*, II, 857; III, 196.

56. See Długopolski, *Władysław Łokietek*, pp. 323–25.

57. Theiner, *Mon. Pol.*, I, # 224.

58. See, for example, *C.D.M.P.*, II, # 1097; *Pr. U.B.*, II, # 638 and 682.

59. For this motivation, see Bronisław Włodarski, "Polityka Jana Luksemburczyka wobec Polski za czasów Władysława Łokietka," *Archiwum Towarzystwa Naukowego we Lwowie*, XI, iii (1933), 17–60. See also *Historia Śląska*, general editor Karol Maleczyński, vol. I: *do roku 1763*, in four parts (Wrocław, 1960–64), I, pt. i, 544–59.

60. Zachorowski, "Wiek XIII," pp. 265–76, 335–38, 403 f.; Jan Dąbrowski, "Dzieje polityczne Śląska w latach 1290–1402," in *Historja Śląska od najdawniejszych czasów do roku 1400*, ed. Stanisław Kutrzeba, et al., 3 vols. (Cracow, 1933–39), I, 327 ff.; *Historia Śląska*, I, pt. i, 251–55, 291–94, 443–46, 447–54; and M. Z. Jedlicki, "German Settlement in Poland and the Rise of the Teutonic Order," in *The Cambridge History of Poland*, W. F. Reddaway et al., 2 vols. (Cambridge, 1941–50), I, 124 ff.

fourteenth century to look toward Prague and Magdeburg, rather than Cracow.[61]

Not surprisingly, this process of change was greatly accelerated during the years of Přemyslid domination in Poland. Moreover, it had taken on political overtones, for in 1291 Václav II had gained the allegiance of several Silesian princes. In the years after the extinction of the Přemyslid dynasty, Łokietek had been unable to establish his rule in Silesia; and with the accession of the Luxemburgers in Bohemia, John had tried to extend his control there. He was at first unsuccessful, and for two decades Silesia was for all intents and purposes politically independent. This situation changed sharply in 1327.

For some years, both before and after Łokietek's coronation, the several princes of this region, while not recognizing the new king as their overlord, had nevertheless continued to consider themselves part of the *regnum Poloniae*.[62] But from 1323 onward, this attitude began to disappear. Among the Silesian princes, there was increasingly a feeling that Silesia was threatened by three great dynasties which bordered the region: the Piasts, the Luxemburgs, and the Wittelsbachs. Why it was the second of these which established its control there remains partially inexplicable to some Polish scholars,[63] but the combination of traditional Bohemian influence with the aggressive boldness of King John was undoubtedly the crucial factor.

Early in 1327, John led an army out of Bohemia toward Cracow, intending to invest it and perhaps extract from Łokietek some advantage either for himself or his informal allies, the Teutonic Order. He marched through Silesia and before mid-February had conquered the fortress Sławków, lying between Bytom and Cracow. Very soon afterward, however, he broke off his campaign because Charles Robert of Hungary had threatened war against him if

61. The question of the nature and extent of what might be called "Polish characteristics" in Silesia at this time is one of the most difficult problems of Polish historiography. Evidence of both "native" and "foreign" influences may easily be found, but they are not numerous enough to enable us to make meaningful generalizations. Even the tendency toward "quantification" in postwar scholarship has not wholly succeeded in this regard. Anna Lipska, "Der polnische Hochadel im 14. und in der ersten Hälfte des 15. Jh. und das Problem der Vereinigung Schlesiens mit Polen," in Ewa Maleczyńska, ed., *Beiträge zur Geschichte Schlesiens* (Berlin, 1958), p. 190, argues for the essentially Polish nature of Wrocław and Silesia as late as the mid-fourteenth century, because the nobility still bore Polish names, the language of the city was Polish, and preaching in the churches was in Polish. She is, however, overoptimistic. Nevertheless, she does represent the general orientation of Polish scholarship in this matter. See the cooperative work *Dzieje Wrocławia do roku 1807*, ed. Wacław Długoborski, Józef Gierowski, and Karol Maleczyński (Warsaw, 1958), pp. 194–96. An interesting comparison may be made by reference to *Geschichte Schlesiens*, vol. I, *von der Urzeit bis zum Jahre 1526*, published by the Historische Kommission für Schlesien, ed. Hermann Aubin, et al. 3d ed. (Stuttgart, 1961), pp. 333 ff.

62. See for example, *Regesten zur schlesischen Geschichte*, ed. Colmar Grünhagen, et al., 8 vols. (Wrocław, 1875–1925), V, # 3885, 3899, 3916, 3990, 4051, 4138, 4149, 4271.

63. "Even today it is difficult to understand why the Silesian princes, who as late as 1323/24 had stood solidly in Łokietek's corner . . . should seven years later enter unexpectedly into feudal agreement with the Czech King." *Historia Śląska*, I, pt. i, 544.

he persisted against Łokietek.[64] John then turned his attention to Silesia proper. On February 18 and 19 he received the feudal allegiance of Dukes Bolko of Niemodlin, Casimir of Cieszyń, Władysław of Kożel, and Leszek of Racibórz. He accepted control of their duchies and returned them as fiefs of the Bohemian crown. Five days later, on February 24, the process was repeated with John of Oświęcim. Before the coming of summer, John had gained further successes. In March, Duke Henry VI of Wrocław sought out the king in Prague and transferred his duchy, the traditional capital of Silesia, into Bohemian hands. Henry was to retain possession during his lifetime, along with the territory of Kłodzko, plus receiving a pension of 1,000 groschen yearly. The last act in the events of 1327 came in early April, when Duke Bolko of Opole became a Bohemian vassal. Thus in the space of less than three months many of the most important Silesian principalities were formally lost to Łokietek and to Poland.[65]

Further successes were John's in 1329 after the campaign in Lithuania and the seizure of Płock and Dobrzyń. In Wrocław, between April 20 and May 10, he received the feudal allegiances of the Dukes of Ścinawa, Oleśnica, Żagań, and Legnica. Having gained physical possession of much of Silesia, John now wanted to force Łokietek into a renunciation of Polish claims to the region. He saw an opportunity to do this during the height of the Polish-Teutonic Order conflict. In 1331 he agreed to join forces with the Knights at Kalisz in Greater Poland in order to bring Łokietek to his knees. But John was delayed in leaving Prague, and the battle of Płowce was two days past when he arrived in Wrocław. A further delay came when he marched to Głogów, where he forced the new duke to accept his overlordship. Only then did he invade Poland, but his brief siege of Poznań accomplished little. Łokietek was able to open negotiations for a truce, which, partially through the influence of Charles Robert, was granted.[66] Łokietek was spared a reopening of hostilities, for John, seldom able to devote himself long to a single task, decided that the forthcoming coronation

64. There is confusion as to whether John led this campaign personally or whether he was present in Nagyszombat with Charles Robert. Compare Dąbrowski, "Z czasów Łokietka," pp. 321–22, and Długopolski, Władysław Łokietek, pp. 252–53. See also Historia Śląska, I, pt. i, 552–53. Charles Robert also held out to John a marriage pact between his son Ladislaus and John's daughter Anna.

65. M.P.H., IV, 14 f. See also III, 45 and 228. The few remaining documents from this process are in Colmar Grünhagen and E. Markgraf, eds., Lehns- und Besitzurkunden Schlesiens und seiner einzelnen Fürstentümer im Mittelalter, 2 vols. (Leipzig, 1881–83), I, 66 f., II, 379, 417, 560, 677. The text has described briefly the results of a complicated process in which the Silesian dukes did not always willingly acquiesce. One side of this story, which emphasizes the political aspects, is found in Włodarski, "Polityka Jana Luksemburczyka," pp. 34–40. Another viewpoint, which gives more attention to economic factors, reasons of dynastic policy, and cultural ties, is found in Josef Šusta, Král cizinec (Prague, 1939), pp. 433–41; Historia Śląska, I, pt. i, 535–58; and (more briefly), Długopolski, Władysław Łokietek, pp. 248–57. Dąbrowski, "Dzieje polityczne Śląska," pp. 371–80, occupies a middle ground, as does the excellent study by Roman Grodecki, Rozstanie się Śląska z Polską (Katowice, 1938).

66. M.P.H., II, 857; III, 195. See also Kłodziński, "Ze studjów krytycznych," pp. 31–35; Włodarski, "Polityka Jana Luksemburczyka," pp. 60–70; and Šusta, Král cizinec, pp. 535 ff.

of Philip VI of France required his presence more than affairs in Poland and Silesia. Even though John spent most of 1332 in western Europe, the Silesian situation was hardly bright for Łokietek. Only Świdnica, Jawór, and some other minor areas, including some ecclesiastical territories, remained independent. Nevertheless, it was not to be his role to bring about a resolution of Polish-Bohemian conflict over Silesia, just as the question of Pomorze and the Knights remained unanswered in his lifetime.

The last vestiges of the south Polish winter had not yet disappeared when the final illness of the king began. Łokietek realized he would not see his seventy-third birthday, so early in March, 1333, he called his Dominican confessor to him in Wawel castle, made his peace with the church, and received the sacraments. After this ceremony, various nobles and friends were admitted to the king's presence. Two of them, Castellan Spicymir of Melsztyn and Archdeacon Jarosław Bogoria of Cracow, apparently representing the nobility and clergy, approached Łokietek. They praised him for his fair and just rule and urged him to indicate clearly to all that his son Casimir was his rightful successor. Although he was already speaking and breathing with difficulty, Łokietek, recognizing that their intentions were to spare the kingdom from contention over the succession, did what they requested. He pointed out Casimir and commanded all to follow and love him as they had his dying father. Then in the presence of his nobles, his churchmen, and his son, Łokietek died.[67] His burial some days later in the cathedral of Cracow on the left of the choir near the altar of St. Stanisław was the occasion for an outpouring of sorrow and mourning from the whole kingdom. Some years later Casimir commissioned a fitting monument for his father. Constructed of white granite with a life-size relief of Łokietek upon it, this memorial now contrasts sharply with the later and more refined late-Gothic, Renaissance, and Baroque features of the cathedral. Its simplicity is stark and direct. It may in fact more truly reflect the character of the king it honors by these very features.

The ceaseless rovings to and fro of foreign armies across Poland, the devastation which the land suffered, and the important territorial losses to Bohemia and the Teutonic Order became in the last years of Łokietek's rule details which obscure the full significance of his achievements. There is no doubt that the losses of Silesia, Pomorze, Kujavia, Dobrzyń, and other minor lands cast a shadow across his reign. Internally also, the condition of the kingdom was far from happy. Though details are obscure, the chronicler of Little Poland informs us that Łokietek "left behind a great chaos of error and license." This probably was due to the necessity in his last years for Łokietek to focus his attention upon the borders and beyond. As a result the effectiveness of internal administration had broken down.

---

67. *M.P.H.*, II, 858, and III, 197, are identical. Długopolski *Władysław Łokietek*, p. 326, suggests that Łokietek had suffered a paralytic attack.

But we must not let these negative considerations prevent us from recognizing the fact that Poland's existence as a state was a far more important phenomenon. A generation before, Poland had seemingly been hopelessly divided into petty principalities. Now it had been reconstituted, had maintained itself against its foes, and carried on the several functions of a state. It is worth examining briefly Łokietek's role in some areas that have not been touched upon to this point.

Although Łokietek was not the famous builder that his son was, he did initiate several projects which are indicative of the more general Polish revival. The kind of building he did is also important, for his activity gave great impetus to the development of stone and brick construction. Not surprisingly, his greatest contribution came in his capital. The beginning of a major renovation of Wawel Cathedral, the initiation of a rebuilt Draper's Hall in the central market square, the building of new fortifications for the city and the castle, and continuing improvements upon St. Mary's Church were Łokietek's most important achievements there. Elsewhere in the kingdom, Łokietek also was active. The erection of a great new parish house in Olkusz, the building of a chapter house in Wiślica, and the completion of several Dominican and Franciscan monasteries were all carried out under his aegis.[68] Although he was again overshadowed in this respect by Casimir, Łokietek was moderately active in the foundation of markets and villages.[69] In other areas the work of Łokietek and his times seems to merge with that of his son, and the separate responsibilities of the two become indistinguishable.

Compared with the brilliant reigns of Casimir the Great and the Jagiellonians, Łokietek's contribution seems modest indeed. But we must not minimize it and judge him too severely.[70] Seen against the background of the late thirteenth and early fourteenth centuries, he emerges as an important figure in his own right; just as Henry VII of England prepared the way for his nation's

---

68. See Andrzej Wyrobisz, *Budownictwo murowane w Małopolsce w XIV i XV wieku* (Wrocław, Warsaw, Cracow, 1963), pp. 57, 64, 72 f. and Józef Lepiarczyk, "Fazy budowy kościoła mariackiego w Krakowie wieki XIII–XV," *Rocznik Krakowski*, XXXIV, pt. iii (1959), 193–95.

69. Some suggestive comments in this regard are made by Karol Buczek, *Targi i Miasta na prawie polskim (okres wczesnośredniowieczny)* (Wrocław, Warsaw, and Cracow, 1964), pp. 51, 62, 101, and 119 n. 30.

70. The severely negative judgment of Zachorowski, "Wiek XIII," p. 301, has been, correctly I think, disputed by Długopolski, *Władysław Łokietek*, pp. 327 ff. The former saw the king as a weak politician and administrator, who was little more than a hard-bitten knight pursuing narrow, particularist policies. That he may have been this early in his career is perhaps true; but his successful Hungarian policy was a farsighted one; he laid the foundation for Poland's expansion—both by conquest and diplomacy—into Ruthenia; and he firmly supported the church, partially as a means of opposing German influence and policies. Had he not been forced to devote so much attention to the borders, he might well have left a more significant record on the matter of internal administration. See, for example, the judgment of Jan Baszkiewicz, *Polska czasów Łokietka* (Warsaw, 1968), pp. 192–96.

future greatness, and Henry IV is regarded as the founder of modern France, so must Łokietek be regarded as the indispensable factor which made later reigns so impressive. But he is rightfully regarded as only a beginning. To see the fulfillment of this beginning in the area of foreign policy, we turn to great Łokietek's greater son.

3
A TIME
TO MAKE PEACE
FROM THE CORONATION
TO THE CONGRESS OF WYSZEGRAD

While Łokietek lay yet unburied, plans were made for the coronation of his son. Under normal circumstances such haste would not have been necessary, but it was too soon after the reunification of Poland to say just what was normal. John of Bohemia claimed to be heir to the Polish throne and might even march on Cracow. The Knights of the Teutonic Order might at any time renew their struggle with Poland, in which case internal uncertainty or an interregnal period might be disastrous. Even the nobles of Poland, perhaps not yet completely reconciled to revivified royal power, might attempt self-aggrandizement. There were, in short, too many uncertainties to delay the coronation of Łokietek's successor. For these reasons the late king's son-in-law and closest ally chose to act to ensure Casimir's accession. The chronicler of Little Poland reports that "Casimir entered upon his rule with the advice and initiative of his relative, King Charles [Robert] of Hungary, for an early coronation."[1]

Casimir became King of Poland, therefore, by right of hereditary succession, a fact clearly recognized by Janko of Czarnków, writing some years after Casimir's death: "Łokietek left his single son as heir to the kingdom and as his successor."[2] By the end of the century, however, due to changed constitutional conditions within Poland, the principle of elective kingship had been established. As a result there grew up a tradition of Casimir's election, which finds expression in the *Rocznik Kujawski*: "In that same year all of the inhabitants of the kingdom with a single will accepted Łokietek's son, Duke

1. Elements of internal instability and traces of Charles Robert's initiative are reflected in *M.P.H.*, II, 859 f.; III, 198. See also Zdisław Kaczmarczyk, *Polska czasów Kazimierza Wielkiego* (Cracow, 1964), p. 17.

2. *M.P.H.*, II, 619.

Casimir, as King of Poland." [3] In Długosz's history a century later the tradition is repeated.[4] Such an interpretation of the events of 1333 is wholly without foundation, however, as later scholarship has amply demonstrated.[5] Whatever the Polish monarchy later became, it was at this point hereditary and endowed with the potential for strong, centralized rule in the hands of a vigorous, intelligent ruler. Casimir was that man.

No one raised a voice to dispute the succession of Casimir, who in addition to his hereditary position was already well known to the kingdom because of his military and administrative participation in the reign of his father. On April 25, 1333, in the cathedral half transformed by Łokietek into a Gothic edifice, Archbishop Jan Janisław of Gniezno consecrated and crowned Casimir and his Lithuanian wife, Anna. In addition to the archbishop, other members of the ecclesiastical hierarchy were present, including Bishop Jan Grot of Cracow, with whom Casimir was to have much difficulty, and the papal nuncio, Peter of Alvernia. From the secular world came the knights and nobles of Poland, the Duke of Braunschweig, a personal representative of Charles Robert of Hungary, and the grand master of the Teutonic Knights, Luther of Braunschweig.[6] There was some unpleasantness connected with the coronation, but it quickly passed. The queen mother Jadwiga refused at first to allow Anna to be crowned queen of Poland. She was dismayed at the thought of sharing the royal glory with her daughter-in-law. Casimir himself intervened, however, and Jadwiga agreed to the double coronation. She was present for the festivities of Casimir's elevation, but shortly thereafter betook herself to her beloved nunnery of St. Clare at Stary Sącz, where she spent the rest of her life in peace and good works.

Even before his coronation, Casimir had turned to the important problems of foreign policy which were the heritage of his father. The most pressing of them, the conflict with the Teutonic Order, was in temporary abeyance following Łokietek's truce of the previous summer. This truce would shortly expire, however, and there was danger the strife would break out anew. Casimir recognized that this might be disastrous for Poland, for the kingdom

3. *M.P.H.*, III, 211.

4. Długosz, *Historia*, III, 162.

5. See Jacob Caro, *Geschichte Polens*, 4 vols. in 5 (Gotha, 1863–86), II, 174; Stanisław Kętrzyński, "Zapis Kazimierza Wielkiego dla Kazimierza Bogusławowica," *P.H.*, XIV (1912), 17–18; and, above all, Oswald Balzer, *Królestwo Polskie, 1295–1370*, 3 vols. (Lwów, 1919–20), III, 83–87.

6. The date is variously given as April 24 or 25. Janko of Czarnków, *Chronicon Polonorum*, in *M.P.H.*, II, 619, gives the former in his description of the coronation; Długosz, *Historia*, III, 163, gives the latter. Most modern scholars have followed Długosz; see, however, Caro, *Geschichte Polens*, II, 175 n. 1, who argues that since there were apparently negotiations between Casimir and the Knights on April 25, the coronation must have been the day before: "es ist wohl nicht anzunehmen, dass man am Krönungstage zu solchem Geschäft Zeit gehabt habe." For the presence of Peter of Alvernia, see Theiner, *Mon. Pol.*, I, # 456.

did not have the resources with which to prolong the struggle.[7] Despite Poland's victory at Płowce in 1331, the Knights were still militarily superior, and further conflict might result in greater territorial losses to the kingdom. Thus Casimir resolved for the moment to follow a more pacific policy than his father. He sent representatives to Toruń early in April to negotiate an extension of Łokietek's truce.

These negotiations, of which we are not further informed, were successful, and on April 18 Grand Master Luther of Braunschweig agreed to a prolongation of the truce until the day of Pentecost, 1334.[8] Seven days later, in the midst of the festivities and ceremonies which accompanied his coronation and probably in the presence of the grand master, Casimir announced Poland's adherence to the extension.[9] As had been true a year earlier, this prolongation was no mere cessation of hostilities, for it again provided for the mediation of the conflict by the kings of Bohemia and Hungary. Though it may not have been readily apparent at the time, this prolongation represented confirmation of the end of the Polish-Teutonic Order conflict that had been achieved the year before. Those negotiations which remained before the treaties of Kalisz in 1343 were the diplomatic maneuverings for a settlement. The fighting had ended, and, despite the presence of bitter enmity, it was not resumed for three-quarters of a century.

The details of interim terms, until the proposed mediation could be accomplished, were further elaborated in the course of the year as the result of continued negotiations. One of the factors instrumental in bringing about a compromise between Poland and the Order was the interest which King Charles Robert, Casimir's closest ally, took in the matter. He sent his personal representative to Cracow and Toruń to urge that some agreement be reached.[10]

7. The question of Polish strength can be partially approached through demography, which for this period of Polish history has the potential of preciseness. See, however, the varying estimates of J. Mitkowski, "Uwagi o zaludnieniu Polski na początku panowania Kazimierza Wielkiego," *Roczniki Dziejów Społecznych i Gospodarczych*, X (1948), 121–31; T. Ladenberger *Zaludnienie Polski na początku panowania Kazimierza Wielkiego* (Lwów, 1930); and E. Vielrose, Ludność Polski od X do XVIII wieku," *Kwartalnik Historii Kultury Materialnej*, V, pt. i (1957), 42–48. I have generally found the estimates of Tadeusz Ładogórski, *Studia nad zaludnieniem Polski XIV wieku* (Wrocław, 1958), pp. 139 ff., more reliable. Caro, *Geschichte Polens*, II, 173–74, gives a moving description of the "thränenerfulltes Land" which Casimir inherited. See also Oskar Halecki, "Kazimierz Wielki, 1333–1370," *Encyklopedya Polska*, V, pt. i (Warsaw, Lublin, Łódź, and Cracow, 1920), pp. 312 ff.; Jan Dąbrowski, *Dzieje Polski od r. 1333 do r. 1506*, vol. II of Roman Grodecki, Stanisław Zachorowski, and Jan Dąbrowski, *Dzieje Polski średniowiecznej* (Cracow, 1926), pp. 7–8.

8. *Lites*, I, 441–42.

9. Ibid., 443. The documents cited in this note and the preceding one are actually dated 1334. The records of negotiations and agreements from 1333 have not survived, but it is possible to reconstruct the broad outlines on the basis of a second prolongation the following year. See Henryk Paszkiewicz, "Ze studjów nad polityką krzyżacką Kazimierza Wielkiego," *P.H.*, XXV (1925), 189 and n. 5.

10. See Dąbrowski, "Elżbieta Łokietkówna," *R.A.U.*, LVII (1914), 361, and *Dzieje Polski*, II, 10; Halecki, "Kazimierza Wielki," p. 316.

As a result of these negotiations, a compromise was reached whereby the disputed fortress and territory of Brześć in Kujavia were to be given into the hands of a neutral third party until a permanent solution was accepted. Duke Ziemowit was appointed to receive Brześć; if he refused, the responsibility was to fall to Bishop Matthias of Włocławek. Whoever accepted the role of receiver was to hold the fortress until the expiration of the truce. If by that time the dispute had not been settled, Brześć was to be returned to the Knights within a month.[11]

Little was accomplished in the remaining months of 1333 or early 1334 toward settling the dispute, and, as the day of Pentecost approached, negotiations were opened between Poland and the Order to prolong the truce once more. The Knights' attitude was such that an agreement was easily reached, and on April 30 Luther granted a formal extension until June 24, 1335. Casimir accepted this on May 15.[12] In this second extension, the grand master promised obedience to the truce, not only for the Knights, but also for King John of Bohemia (who had shown no inclination to renew his attack on Poland) and Dukes Ziemowit and Trojden of Mazovia. Casimir spoke for himself and Dukes Przemysław of Kujavia and Władysław of Łęczyca and Dobrzyń.

These negotiations had not really solved or in any substantial way ameliorated the controversy between Poland and the Teutonic Order. The two parties were still far from reaching any accord. The Knights steadfastly protected their holdings; Casimir, though for now resolved upon a more pacific policy, had not given up any of the goals of Łokietek. Nevertheless the fighting had stopped, and a kind of peace had been established during which Poland rested and recuperated. In addition, a foundation had been laid upon which a more durable agreement might be reached: both parties had agreed to submit to outside arbitration, though the meaning of this word was very imprecisely understood. Casimir had supported these developments, because he saw that the strategy, if not the policy, of Łokietek toward the Order had been fruitless and was not in the best interests of Poland.

While he had been dealing with the Knights, Casimir had also been carrying on negotiations with Poland's Wittelsbach neighbors in Brandenburg. Although Łokietek had manifested little but hostility toward them, such an attitude did not suit the purposes of the young king. Thus he broke sharply with the policy of his father and issued to Margrave Lewis of Brandenburg an invitation to confer in Poznań. In the weeks after his coronation, Casimir traveled about his kingdom and in midsummer came to the traditional capital of Greater Poland. There, after preliminary negotiations, he signed a two-year friendship pact on

---

11. The details of this compromise are reflected in a document of the following year. See *C.D.Pol.*, II, # 665; *C.D.Pr.*, II, # 146 and 149; and *C.D.M.P.*, II, # 1129.

12. *Lites*, I, 441–42; *C.D.Pr.*, II, # 146 and 149, for the former. For the latter, *Lites*, I, 443; *C.D.Pol.*, II, # 665; and *C.D.M.P.*, II, # 1129.

July 31 with Lewis.[13] Casimir promised to withhold aid from all enemies of the Mark and guaranteed that his subjects would do likewise. Margrave Lewis made similar promises for his part in the agreement, thus assuring Poland of Wittelsbach neutrality in the struggle with the Order. In addition, Casimir promised to accept the decisions of the advocates of the Mark in all disputes arising over the contested city of Drezdenko, so long as the decisions were made according to local law, not the *ius theutonicum* of Magdeburg.

This treaty was the beginning of an important rapprochement between Poland and the Mark, and in succeeding months their relationship became even closer. Finally, in early December, 1334, Casimir proposed a meeting for February 9, 1335, and issued a safe-conduct for the margrave and his party to come to Poznań.[14] Lewis decided against a personal visit to Poland, however, and suggested instead a meeting at Frankfurt on the Oder to be held in mid-May. Casimir declined to go in person, but sent two of his highest officials as representatives.

After a short period of negotiation, a formal alliance was proposed on May 16 in which Casimir, through his representatives, and Lewis promised to prevent their subjects from any act which might damage the position of the other party. It was proposed to seal the alliance by the marriage of Casimir's oldest daughter, Elizabeth, to Lewis the Roman, youngest son of the emperor and younger brother of the margrave. In addition, four arbiters were appointed, two from each side, to adjudicate all disputes over boundaries and property. Finally, June 24 was fixed as the date for a meeting between Casimir and Lewis at some point between Wieleń and Dobiegniew to work out final details for the alliance and the marriage.[15]

Once again the two rulers did not attend in person, but Casimir empowered his representatives to travel to Königsberg in the Mark, where on June 20 agreement was reached. Each side was to support the other with three hundred mounted knights against all enemies for a period of three years, and the marriage pact was agreed upon. Casimir was to give Elizabeth a dowry of two hundred thousand Prague groschen, and Lewis the Roman promised to endow Elizabeth with land on the east bank of the Oder worth two thousand silver

---

13. *C.D.M.P.*, II, # 1126. See also Stanisław Zajączkowski, "Polska a Wittelsbachowie w pierwszej połowie XIV wieku," in *Prace Historyczne w 30-lecie działalności profesorskiej Stanisława Zakrzewskiego* (Lwów, 1934), p. 82, who suggests the initiative for this treaty came from Casimir, as do Halecki, "Kazimierz Wielki," p. 317; Dąbrowski, *Dzieje Polski*, II, 10; and Kaczmarczyk, *Polska czasów Kazimierza*, p. 22. On the other hand, F. W. Taube, *Ludwig der Aeltere als Markgraf von Brandenburg 1323–1351* (Berlin, 1900), pp. 58, 62, and Emil Werunsky, *Geschichte Kaiser Karls IV. und seine Zeit*, 3 vols. in 4 (Innsbruck, 1880–96), I, 131, both hold strongly for Wittelsbach initiative.

14. *C.D.M.P.*, II, # 1141.

15. *C.D.M.P.*, II, # 1147. See the document issued by the emperor empowering his oldest son to undertake these additional negotiations, dated June 6, 1335, in Ludewig, *Reliquiae*, II, 291.

marks for her lifetime. September 8, 1335, was decided upon for a conference between Casimir and the margrave to ratify the treaty and marriage pact.[16]

The appointed day came and went, and although an official party of Polish dignitaries had left Cracow in August, it had travelled south to Trenčin in Hungary, rather than northwest to Brandenburg.[17] Not until September 17 did Casimir send a letter of apology to Lewis, explaining that other affairs of state had been of such great concern that he had been unable to meet the margrave on the appointed day. Moreover it did not appear that he would be able at this time to ratify the marriage pact and alliance.[18] This action resulted in an immediate cooling of Polish-Brandenburg relations, although in later years the marriage pact and alliance were again taken up in different circumstances.

On the surface it appears that Casimir had foolishly sought an alliance with the Wittelsbachs without taking his own actions seriously enough to pursue the matter to a successful conclusion. This appearance is most misleading, however, for an examination of other facets of Casimir's diplomacy in these first two years of his reign makes it clear that in addition to any benefit he might receive against the Order, Casimir's dealings with the Wittelsbachs were only part of a larger plan which aimed at nothing less than breaking the Luxemburg half of the Bohemian-Order pincer which threatened Poland. In order to understand these dealings with King John and Margrave Charles of Moravia, it is necessary to examine briefly certain aspects of the King's relationship with the church at this time.

Although the papacy had been the bitter opponent of both the Wittelsbachs and the Teutonic Order, Casimir's dealings with Brandenburg and his peaceful policy toward the Knights did not cause any straining of Polish-papal relations. The chief reason for this was that the inveterately hostile John XXII died in 1334 and was succeeded by Benedict XII, who pursued a much more conciliatory policy.[19] It was also due to the fact that Casimir throughout his reign attempted, in the main successfully, to adopt a friendly attitude toward the papacy and the church in Poland. This posture was strained, however, by events within the kingdom soon after his coronation.

These events centered upon the person of Jan Grot, bishop of Cracow since 1326 and a previous adversary of King Władysław Łokietek.[20] This

16. *C.D.M.P.*, II, #1148. See also Taube, *Ludwig der Aeltere*, pp. 62 ff.; Zajączkowski, "Polska a Wittelsbachowie," pp. 85 ff.

17. See Kaczmarczyk, *Kazimierz Wielki (1333–1370)* (Warsaw, 1948), p. 41, and *Polska czasów Kazimierza*, p. 24.

18. *Codex diplomaticus Brandenburgensis*, ed. Adolph Friedrich Riedel, 41 vols. (Berlin, 1838–69), II, #718.

19. For the differences between John's and Benedict's policies, particularly toward the empire, see G. Mollat, *The Popes at Avignon, 1305–1378* (London, 1963), pp. 219–24.

20. The earlier dispute had concerned the collection of church monies and certain ecclesiastical prerogatives with which Łokietek had interfered. On Jan Grot, see *Pol. Słow. Biog.*, IX,

imperious churchman had attempted in the months following Łokietek's death to become a kind of *eminence grise* for the young king. When this failed, he turned instead to opposing the pacific orientation of Casimir's policy. Thus, in the spring of 1334, at a secret gathering of dignitaries of the kingdom in Cracow, Jan Grot had stood at the head of those who advocated renewed war against the Knights.[21] In 1333 and 1334 these elements of political opposition were combined with earlier jurisdictional conflicts over church funds in the diocese of Cracow. Bishop Jan accused the papal nuncio in Poland, Peter of Alvernia, of mismanagement and corrupt practices in the gathering of Peter's Pence and the papal tenth. He also published an anathema on Casimir and laid the diocese of Cracow under interdict. A papal investigation into the charges discovered some truth to the allegations against Peter of Alvernia, who was recalled and replaced by the great Polonophile, Galhard de Carceribus.[22] But in the matter of the bishop's charges against the king, the pope did little more than urge a compromise. The bitter controversy was to continue for many years.[23]

Nuncio Galhard's first task in Poland, beyond the matter of church income, was to effect a peace between Poland and the Teutonic Order.[24] His urgings in this regard undoubtedly reinforced the already peacefully oriented desires of both sides;[25] and although the aforementioned compromise over Brześć proved unworkable in practice, there was no resumption of conflict by either side in 1335 after the expiration of the twice-prolonged truce. This respite enabled Casimir to reap from Bohemia the fruits of the pressure he had applied by his dealings with Brandenburg.

In the great struggle between empire and papacy in the first decades of the fourteenth century, the House of Luxemburg in Bohemia supported the papacy

---

15–18; and Mieczysław Niwiński, "Biskup krakowski Jan Grotowic i zatargi jego z Włodzisławem Łokietkiem i Kazimierzem Wielkim. Ustęp z dziejów stosunku Kościoła do Państwa w Polsce w w. XIV," *Nova Polonia Sacra*, III (1939), 57–99.

21. See Kaczmarczyk, *Polska czasów Kazimierza*, pp. 22 f.

22. Caro, *Geschichte Polens*, II, *passim*, and Kaczmarczyk, *Kazimierz Wielki*, *passim*, as well as many other authors, incorrectly use the name Galhard of Chartres. This is a misreading of the Latin "de Carceribus," which in my judgment refers to the Benedictine priory of Carcés in the French diocese of Fréjus. See L. H. Cottineau, *Répertoire topo-bibliographique des Abbayes et Prieurés* (Macon, 1939), I, 601. Helena Chłopocka has promised a thorough study of Galhard's career, including an analysis of the geographical location connected with his name. See her *Procesy Polski z Zakonem krzyżackim w XIV wieku* (Poznań, 1967), p. 32, n. 13.

23. Details of the controversy are reflected in papal letters in Theiner, *Mon. Pol.*, I, # 445, 456, 480, 481, and 495.

24. See the papal letters in Theiner, *Mon. Pol.*, I, # 473 and # 474.

25. Representatives of the Order in Avignon had made clear to the papacy that the grand master was well disposed toward a peaceful settlement with Poland. See the letter to Galhard in Theiner, *Mon. Pol.*, I, # 470. The death of Grand Master Luther on April 18, 1335, also threw the Order into confusion so that it had no desire to pursue an aggressive foreign policy. See Marjan Tumler, *Der Deutsche Orden im Werden, Wachsen und Wirken bis 1400* (Vienna, 1955), p. 345.

and was the bitter foe of the Wittelsbachs. Thus the Luxemburgers were alarmed at any activity which might possibly strengthen Lewis IV and his family. Casimir was fully cognizant of this and realized that by his dealings with the Wittelsbachs he could bring pressure upon King John and his son Charles. This pressure could be used to resolve certain aspects of the Polish-Bohemian conflict. By mid-1335 the policy had born fruit.

Margrave Charles of Moravia, later Emperor Charles IV, had seen with dismay the rapprochement between Casimir and the Wittelsbachs. With his customary clear insight into the affairs of his day, he recognized the Polish-Wittelsbach treaty of July, 1333, as dangerous for Bohemia. Not only would the treaty strengthen a mortal enemy, it might well include at some future date Poland's firmest ally, Hungary. The threat of this partial encirclement of the Luxemburgers' eastern holdings caused Charles to resolve to break the Polish-Wittelsbach alliance by offering Casimir an advantage superior to that which the Wittelsbachs could offer. He was in excellent position to do this since his father still claimed the crown of Poland, while Bohemian influence in Silesia was so strong as to render Polish claims there ineffectual. Charles recognized that Casimir could be wooed from Brandenburg by an offer to trade, in effect, renunciation of John's claim to Poland in return for the abandonment of Polish claims to Silesia.[26]

Negotiations were suggested to Casimir by Czech representatives late in 1334, and the suggestion was eagerly welcomed. It was to his advantage (and was in fact what he had striven for) to achieve normal relations with Bohemia and to be reconciled with King John before the latter began his work as one of the arbiters of the Polish-Teutonic Order struggle. Thus the negotiations were assured of a successful outcome, and on May 28, 1335, representatives of Casimir and Charles signed a truce in Sandomir which was to last until the feast of St. John the Baptist (June 24), 1336.[27] Both rulers promised that their nobles and other subjects would maintain the truce. In addition, the complaints of Polish subjects against Bohemian rule and Bohemian subjects against Polish rule were to be adjudicated by specially appointed arbiters in respectively, Wrocław and Kalisz. Free passage was also guaranteed subjects of both rulers between Barcz (near Kalisz) and Wrocław. In the treaty, Casimir spoke also for King Charles Robert of Hungary and Dukes Przemysław of Kujavia and Władysław of Łęczyca and Dobrzyń.[28]

It is impossible to overestimate the importance of this treaty as a first step

26. This motive is analyzed by Werunsky, *Karl IV*, I, 131 f.; Šusta, *Karel IV, Otec a Syn, 1333–1346* (Prague, 1946), pp. 130 f.; Halecki, "Kazimierz Wielki," p. 317; Dąbrowski, *Dzieje Polski*, II, 11; Kaczmarczyk, *Kazimierz Wielki*, pp. 39–41.

27. Ludewig, *Reliquiae*, V, 596; *C.D.Mor.*, VII, # 60. See also Caro, *Geschichte Polens*, II, 185 n. 1.

28. See Dąbrowski, "Dzieje polityczne Śląska w latach 1290–1402," in *Historja Śląska od najdawniejszych czasów do roku 1400*, ed. Stanisław Kutrzeba et al., 3 vols. (Cracow, 1933–39), I, 414; Dąbrowski, *Ostatnie lata Ludwika Wielkiego 1370–1382* (Cracow, 1918), p. 82.

in the resolution of the Polish-Czech conflict. Moreover it also had a bearing upon Polish-Teutonic Order relations, since for the first time in recent years the Luxemburgers had been detached from the Knights. Casimir was also fortunate that in these early negotiations with Bohemia his dealings were with Margrave Charles. The two had much in common, not the least their youth; both were far less impetuous and more farsighted in their personal lives and public policies than their fathers. In addition they faced similar problems in countries where internal administration had suffered from the neglect of their fathers: both Łokietek and John had been more the knight than the careful governor. Later meetings between Casimir and Charles gave rise to a friendship which endured despite dynastic disputes and misunderstandings of state.

In the summer of 1335, Casimir empowered several of his most important civil officials to undertake further negotiations with the Bohemians concerning a peace treaty for all the princes and lands of the kingdom and the whole kingdom itself.[29] On August 9, these representatives left the Polish capital to begin two weeks of negotiations with the Bohemian representatives in the Slovak-Hungarian town of Trenčin, chosen because of its neutral location. Shortly thereafter the negotiators were joined by John and Charles in person, and on August 24 an agreement was reached.[30] The Luxemburgers formally agreed to renounce all claims for themselves and their heirs to the Kingdom of Poland and swore never again to use the title *rex Poloniae* under pain of excommunication. Casimir for his part agreed to renounce, again on pain of excommunication, all claims to suzerainty over those Silesian princes who had sworn allegiance to King John; and over Wacław of Płock in Mazovia, who had become a vassal of John in 1329. Through his plenipotentiaries, Casimir promised to ratify this agreement by October 16, the feast of St. Gallus.

Although Casimir had informed his representatives that he would be willing to pay John an indemnification of up to six hundred thousand Prague groschen for Bohemian renunciation of the Polish crown, there is no mention of such an indemnity in the documents from Trenčin.[31] Nevertheless, this provision may well have been discussed, for it was incorporated into the agreements of Wyszegrad in November. It was also agreed at Trenčin that the kings of Poland, Bohemia, and Hungary would meet personally to arrange further details and to arbitrate the conflict between Poland and the Teutonic Order in accord with the truces between Casimir and Luther of Braunschweig.[32]

29. Ludewig, *Reliquiae*, V, 585, with the incorrect date of 1345.

30. *C.D.Mor.*, VII, # 76. See also Otakar Bauer, "Poznámky k mírovým smlouvám česko-polským z roku 1335," in *Sborník prací věnovanych prof. dru. Gustavu Friedrichovi k šedesátým narozeninám 1871–1931* (Prague, 1931), pp. 9–22.

31. See Bauer, "Poznámky k mírovým smlouvám," pp. 13–15; Šusta, *Karel IV*, pp. 198–200.

32. Werunsky, *Karl IV*, I, 143. Caro, *Geschichte Polens*, II, 186, confuses the ratification of the Trenčin agreements with the conference at Wyszegrad. See Halecki, "Kazimierz Wielki," pp. 317 f.

Later events show that John was anxious to gain from Casimir an offensive-defensive alliance against the Wittelsbachs, but he was unable to achieve this at Trenčin. Casimir's relationship to Brandenburg was still too close to allow this, though as we have seen the relationship was already beginning to cool. The Polish king, despite his youth, had a shrewd sense of future possibilities which might be advantageous to Poland. Although now embarked upon a program of peace, Casimir recognized that at some future time Wittelsbach assistance might be welcome and so hesitated to close off his options completely. Casimir's evolving peaceful policy is well shown at Trenčin, but its fulfillment in the early years of his reign came in November at Wyszegrad.

The fact that the negotiations between Poland and Bohemia had been carried out in Hungary at Trenčin, that Charles Robert had seen fit to send observers to the negotiations,[33] and that the forthcoming royal congress was also to be held on Hungarian soil is not without significance for the nature of Casimir's policy. It is obvious that Charles Robert, as Casimir's strongest ally, would have taken an interest in the course of Polish-Bohemian relations. In addition, a more profound reason of state lay behind this action. Casimir's union with Anna of Lithuania had not been blessed with male issue, despite ten years of marriage. Even though the young king was only twenty-five, there was a growing possibility that no legitimate heir would be forthcoming. Thus Charles Robert had resolved upon a policy which aimed at nothing less than the acquisition of the crown of Poland for his own house in the event the Piast line should fail. To accomplish this, he had first to ensure that no one else had any legitimate claim to the crown. For this reason he followed closely the negotiations at Trenčin to assure a final Bohemian renunciation of claims to Poland.[34]

At the same time Charles Robert felt it necessary to achieve closer relations with the house of Luxemburg. King John for his part also wished to strengthen the ties between the two dynasties, for in the past Charles Robert had often allied himself with the increasingly powerful Habsburg family in Austria, whose policy conflicted sharply with that of the Luxemburgers. Thus Bohemian negotiators remained in Hungary after the meeting at Trenčin to discuss with Angevin representatives an alliance between the two houses. Their efforts bore fruit on September 3 in Wyszegrad, where a defensive-offensive alliance was signed.[35] Charles Robert and his oldest son, Louis, swore to protect King John and his sons against all enemies, with the exception of the Angevin King Robert of Jerusalem and Sicily, Casimir of Poland, and all other members of the Neapolitan branch of the house of Anjou. In case any of the Luxemburgers undertook a campaign outside their kingdom, the Angevin swore to lend them

33. Dąbrowski, "Elżbieta Łokietkówna," p. 361.

34. Dąbrowski, *Ostatnie lata*, p. 83.

35. *C.D.Mor.*, VII, #81; Ludewig, *Reliquiae*, V, 483.

military aid. In the case of invasion however, Charles Robert would personally lead an army to aid the Luxemburgers. For their part the Bohemians promised the same support, even if one of them should attain a more important position than King of Bohemia (thus indicating John had higher goals in mind for his house). Finally both sides promised not to close a separate peace in the event of conflict with the Habsburg Dukes of Austria.

In accord with the Trenčin agreements of August, the three kings came to Wyszegrad in late fall, 1335. Fortunately we are not dependent for our knowledge of this congress entirely upon the official acts decided there. We have in addition the detailed narrative of Johannes of Thurócz, a protonotary of King Matthias Corvinus of Hungary (1458–90).[36] It is he who describes the glittering congress of kings and princes in the second Hungarian capital and tells us that the first royal arrival was King John, who came late in October with a large and impressive retinue which included Bishops John of Olomouc and Witago of Meissen, as well as many nobles and knights of the Bohemian crown. John and his party were received most hospitably by Charles Robert and given suitable quarters. Shortly thereafter came Casimir with a no less impressive following. He was accompanied by papal nuncio Galhard, many civil officials, and several nobles of the kingdom including Duke Władysław of Łęczyca and Dobrzyń.[37] He and his party were also well received by the host. The most numerous and distinguished body of representatives came, naturally enough, from Hungary. Somewhat belatedly, but still in time for the final negotiations, Margrave Charles hurried from Silesia to meet his father in Wyszegrad.[38]

The physical surroundings of the congress were appropriate to the distinguished character of its participants. The guests were housed in the sumptuous royal palace, which reportedly had 350 separate rooms. From the windows it was possible to look down upon the majestic sweep of the Danube. The food matched the setting. The Czechs consumed daily 2,500 loaves of bread, while the Polish retinue contented itself with a mere 1,500. To insure sufficiently relaxed camaraderie between all concerned, 180 barrels of good Magyar wine were distributed daily. Nor did Charles Robert's munificence end with this. To John he gave fifty silver vessels, two quivers and jeweled swordbelts, a

---

36. Johannes de Thurócz, *Chronica Hungarorum*, in *Scriptores rerum Hungaricarum veteres ac genuini* . . . , ed. J. G. Schwandtner, 3 vols. (Vienna, 1746–48), I, 165 ff.

37. See the lists in *C.D.Mor.*, VII, # 89; Theiner, *Mon. Pol.*, I, # 519; Ludewig, *Reliquiae*, V, 604. It has been correctly pointed out by Kaczmarczyk, *Polska czasów Kazimierza*, p. 25, that Casimir was accompanied only by officials from Little Poland. This is surprising when it is remembered that the congress was to deal with the question of Pomorze and the Knights, thus affecting closely the interests of Greater Poland. What we see here is a manifestation of that Little Poland political base upon which Casimir built his reign. This problem has recently been studied in detail by Stanisław Gawęda, *Możnowładztwo Małopolskie w XIV i w pierwszej połowie XV wieku* (Cracow, 1966), pp. 17–50 especially.

38. *Vita Caroli IIII*, in *Rerum Bohemicarum antiqui scriptores* . . . , ed. C. V. Marquard Freher (Hanover, 1602), p. 96. See also Werunsky, *Karl IV*, I, 150 n. 8.

beautifully wrought tureen of mother-of-pearl, a decorated chessboard, two costly saddles, and a mace. To Casimir he presented a handsome gift of 500 gold marks.[39]

This congress, with its glittering array of kings, ecclesiastics, nobles, and knights meeting amid the splendor of the Angevin court of Hungary, marked Casimir's coming of age. He was the son of a simple warrior who had risen from obscurity to become king, a warrior who had once fled to this same country seeking refuge and aid. In the councils of central Europe, Casimir was a mere youth—only twenty-five years old—and ruler of a state that had been reconstituted as a kingdom only within the last fifteen years. Yet at this congress he was a peer of the two powerful and famous kings with whom he negotiated. The congress was the point at which he was accepted as one worthy of the dignity which he bore. Nevertheless, one must not forget that the problems of Poland were being arbitrated by foreign rulers. Casimir was not yet completely master of Poland's destinies.

Although the ostensible purpose of the congress was to provide an opportunity for John and Charles Robert to decide between the conflicting Polish and Teutonic Order claims to Chełmno, Pomorze, Kujavia, Dobrzyń, and other minor districts, this was the last subject be discussed by those present. Each had individual interests of his own which were given by mutual consent precedence over the Polish-Order conflict. Thus King John desired to make the Luxemburg rapprochement with Poland more permanent by signing with Casimir an alliance to be directed against the Wittelsbachs. This would at the same time accomplish the purpose which Margrave Charles had pursued in May at Sandomir: the sundering of Polish-Brandenburg ties. To achieve his purpose John had already shown himself willing to renounce his claims to the Polish crown. Casimir was willing in principle to follow the Luxemburger lead, but showed more hesitancy in matters of detail. He wanted to break the Bohemian-Teutonic Order pincer which had endangered the kingdom since 1329, and was therefore willing to ratify the Trenčin agreement (he had failed to do this before the feast of St. Gallus), even though such an act would formally cost Poland an important province. King Charles Robert, in addition to his role as arbiter, wished to protect his own dynastic interests by avoiding, if possible, any Piast-Luxemburg marriage alliance, as well as to insure that his brother-in-law was fairly represented in his dispute with the Order.[40] This was the context within which the month-long negotiations of the congress took place.

Less than two weeks after the congress began, the question of the status of

39. For these details see Johannes de Thurócz, *Chronica*, pp. 165–66. On the nature and significance of Casimir's gift from his brother-in-law, see Palacky, *Geschichte von Böhmen*, II, pt. ii, 207; Caro, *Geschichte Polens*, II, 189 n. 1; Šusta, *Karel IV*, p. 208 n. 1.

40. An analysis of the aims of each of the parties to the congress is given by Jan Leniek, "Kongres Wyszegradzki w roku 1335," *Przewodnik Naukowy i Literacki*, XII (1884), 264–71, 356–60.

the Trenčin agreements was decided, for on November 12 John formally renounced all claims for himself and his heirs to the Kingdom of Poland and promised never again to use the title *rex Poloniae*. To obtain this renunciation Casimir agreed to pay an indemnification of four hundred thousand Prague groschen. Some two hundred thousand were paid immediately to John, while another eighty thousand went to the noble Henry of Lippa, who may have been a creditor of King John's.[41] Casimir, whose word was guaranteed by a dozen of his civil administrators, promised to pay the remaining one hundred twenty thousand before Easter, 1336, at either Opawa or Racibórz. If he were late in this payment, the guarantors were to deposit the money in Opawa in a manner to be designated by John. In addition Casimir was to pay twenty thousand groschen in penalty. Should the guarantors fail to do this, then Charles Robert, with whom the document of John's renunciation had been deposited, was to return John's deposition. In such an instance, Casimir was still obligated to pay the penalty.[42] Apparently feeling this arrangement to be somewhat cumbersome, Charles Robert promised one week later to pay the remaining one hundred twenty thousand groschen if Casimir defaulted. The document of renunciation was then to remain in his hands.[43]

Although this stage of the congress was concerned with the agreements of Trenčin, there was no mention made in any of the extant documents about the question of Silesia. Margrave Charles states clearly in his autobiography that the matter was indeed discussed and that Casimir formally renounced Silesia in favor of the Bohemian crown.[44] There is no other evidence to support this contention and in fact the definitive Polish renunciation to Silesia did not come for another four years. At that time, Casimir made no mention or reference to any such renunciation from Wyszegrad. Charles may be correct that the topic was discussed (it would be surprising if it had not been), but for the rest he undoubtedly reads back into the events of 1335 that which actually took place in 1339. It is not surprising that Casimir was unwilling for the moment to recognize de jure the de facto loss of Polish influence in Silesia. It is more difficult to understand why John apparently did nothing to press the issue. It must, however, be remembered that he wanted to win Casimir to an alliance against the Wittelsbachs and dared not push the young king too hard. For the moment, therefore, the matter of Silesia remained unresolved, though as may be seen below, certain implications about the status of Silesia arose in the further negotiations between John and Casimir.

Next the rulers turned to the question of the treaty between Poland and

41. This suggestion is made by Werunsky, *Karl IV*, I, 151, n. 1.

42. *C.D.Mor.*, VII, # 89; Ludewig, *Reliquiae*, V, 593.

43. *C.D.Mor.*, VII, # 90; Ludewig, *Reliquiae*, V, 603.

44. *Vita Caroli*, p. 96: "Rex vero Cracoviae [Casimir] renunciavit patri nostro et regno Bohemiae, pro se et successoribus suis regibus inferioris Poloniae, in perpetuum de omni actione omnium Ducatuum Silesiae, et Opoliae et civitatis Wratislaviae."

Bohemia which John so desired. On November 19 a simple treaty of friendship and border-regulation accord was signed between the two. By its terms, disputes which might arise over boundaries were to be settled by a panel of arbiters appointed by both sides, with appropriate penalties for those who might break the peace by rapacious forays into neighboring territories. Further, if such acts of robbing or pillaging did take place, the superiors of those responsible were to destroy their castles and confiscate their possessions. A transgressor from one country was to be regarded as a criminal in the other, as well as in Hungary, a provision to which Charles Robert readily agreed. One of the most important points of discussion in these negotiations had been the fortress of Bolesławiec, which lay in Polish territory athwart the great commercial route from Kalisz to Wrocław. It had been held by individuals sympathetic to John who had, moreover, used it as a refuge from which they preyed upon merchants going from Poland to Silesia and Bohemia. It was further decided in this agreement that this fortress was to be razed by John before January 5, 1336, and that the territory would remain in Polish hands but Casimir would never rebuild the fortress there.[45]

The details of this agreement were to be sealed by a marriage pact agreed upon the same day. Casimir's oldest daughter, Elizabeth, previously promised to the Wittelsbach Lewis the Roman, was engaged to King John's grandson. The marriage was to take place as soon as the two children had reached maturity. Casimir promised Elizabeth a dowry of one hundred thousand Prague groschen, and John bound himself to endow his grandson with an amount half-again as great.[46] Charles Robert may well have been displeased with this marriage alliance, though there was little he could do about it. If the marriage were consummated with male issue, the house of Luxemburg would have a claim to the same throne which Charles Robert coveted for his own family. Fortunately for him, the marriage never took place.

Despite John's efforts, Bohemia did not gain at Wyszegrad the defensive-offensive alliance for which he had hoped. Casimir had been unwilling to go that far, and had been able to hold open other options in the field of foreign policy which he later utilized. He did this, however, at the cost of failing to woo John completely away from the Knights. As a result, although Polish-Bohemian relations had been put on a more friendly basis—a condition which lasted eight years—Casimir still faced Luxemburg hostility in the matter of the Teutonic Order.

Though the pacific attitudes of 1333 and 1334 appeared to guarantee that a settlement between Poland and the Knights could be easily reached, when the details of each side's position were explored in negotiations it became obvious that reconciliation would be more difficult than had been anticipated. The

---

45. *C.D.Mor.*, VII, # 91; Ludewig, *Reliquiae*, V, 507, 588.

46. *C.D.Mor.*, VII, # 90; Ludewig, *Reliquiae*, V, 592, though with the incorrect date of 1305.

delegation from the Teutonic Order had arrived in Wyszegrad early in November to present to arbiters the demands of the Order as formulated by the recently elected Grand Master Dietrich of Altenburg.[47] Perhaps because he remembered the indignity of defeat and capture at Płowce, perhaps because he desired to begin his mastership with a striking program, Dietrich adopted a much less compromising tone than his predecessor.

The Order demanded the legal recognition by Casimir of their possession of Chełmno, Pomorze, Michałowo (mortgaged to the Order by Łokietek in 1317),[48] Xenithen, the castle of Nieszawa, one hundred hides (*Hufen*) of land on the right bank of the Drwęca River (about 4,090 square acres),[49] and certain enclaves in the regions of Słupsk and Sieradz. They further demanded that Casimir guarantee seven Polish cities as security against any future boundary disputes between Poland and the Order, and also grant free passage through Polish lands for the Order and its allies in their battles against the heathens. To show their good faith, they were willing to return to Poland the conquered territories of Kujavia and Dobrzyń.[50]

These demands were far more than Casimir was willing to grant, even though he was inclined toward a peaceful solution. In the three weeks of negotiations which followed, Charles Robert tried to defend the position and rights of his brother-in-law, while John, as a friend and ally of the Knights, attempted to uphold the claims of the Order. By no means were the two kings neutral arbiters. Rather they acted as counterweights to balance each other's partisanship. Charles Robert was perhaps less successful in his efforts than John, for the decision handed down on November 26 fulfilled most of the demands of the Order.

According to the terms of the judgment, the territories of Kujavia and Dobrzyń, including the disputed fortress of Brześć, were to be returned to the Kingdom of Poland, with the exception of the district of Gniewkowo, which belonged to Duke Casimir of Kujavia. This part of the decision was modified slightly by reserving to the Order all property and possessions in these territories which it had claimed before the outbreak of the war with Poland. The territory of Chełmno, including Toruń, was to remain in the hands of the Order. There was no mention of the district of Michałowo by the arbiters, who apparently accepted the Order's claim that the district had passed permanently into its hands as a result of Łokietek's deed of mortgage.

47. Werunsky, *Karl IV*, I, 153; Leniek, "Kongres Wyszegradzki," pp. 359 ff.

48. *C.D.Pr.*, II, # 112. See Caro, *Geschichte Polens*, II, 74–75; Stanisław Zajączkowski, *Polska a Zakon Krzyżacki w ostatnich latach Władysława Łokietka* (Lwów, 1929), p. 61 n. 1; and Irene Ziekursch, *Der Prozess zwischen König Kasimir von Polen und dem Deutschen Orden im Jahre 1339* (Berlin, 1934), pp. 127–37.

49. The *Hufe*, usually a variable measure in western Europe, was far more regular in the lands of the Teutonic Knights. See F. L. Carsten, *The Origins of Prussia* (Oxford, 1954), p. 28 n. 2, p. 53 n. 9.

50. *C.D.Pr.*, II, # 199; *Lites*, I, 445–47.

The most important part of the decision concerned Pomorze, the province for which Łokietek has risked, and lost, so much. Pomorze, according to its ancient boundaries (this itself was a highly imprecise phrase), was to be given to the grand master and the knights of the Teutonic Order by Casimir for the salvation and health of his soul and the souls of his predecessors and heirs as a perpetual alm of the Polish crown. Further, Casimir was to renounce in the Order's favor all claims, rights, and privileges which he claimed in Pomorze. The arbiters also refused to consider any question of indemnification for either side. Finally they declared that all who fled from Kujavia and Dobrzyń to Chełmno or Pomorze during the war were to be allowed to return to their homes. If, however, they chose to settle elsewhere, they were to be allowed to sell the property they had left.[51]

The arbitration of Kings John and Charles Robert in effect proposed the restoration of the *status quo ante bellum*, except for the district of Płock, which now recognized the suzerainty of John of Bohemia. The return of the important territories of Kujavia and Dobrzyń would be a significant aid to Casimir in his strengthening and rebuilding of the kingdom. Nevertheless, the fundamental problem of Poland's foreign policy in the north had not been solved: the Teutonic Order still cut Poland off from the Baltic, and the Order's presence across the kingdom's northern border presented a constant threat of the possibility of renewed conflict. For Poland, however, the wording of the decision had injected a new factor into the problem. This was the tacit recognition that Pomorze belonged technically to the Polish crown and was held by the Order only on the sufferance of the king. This certainly was the interpretation made by some of the Polish nobility and clergy, and in succeeding years they attempted to prevent the implementation of the decrees of Wyszegrad.

John immediately recognized such a possibility. Since the arbitration was by no means binding, it was expected that all parties concerned would have to ratify the decision. From the Knights no difficulty was expected in this regard, but it was not an impossibility that Casimir would be loath to renounce Pomorze in perpetuity. Thus John wrote the grand master on December 3, promising to do all in his power to obtain from the Piast formal confirmation of the decrees and to gain a similar renunciation from all the heirs and relatives of the king, including the royal couple of Hungary.[52]

The problem of implementing the decisions of Wyszegrad and bringing about a stable peace with the Teutonic Order began shortly after the judgment was handed down. Had Kujavia and Dobrzyń been returned to the kingdom as immediate possessions of the crown and as integral parts of the *regnum*, at least

---

51. The document of arbitration has been frequently printed. See J. Dumont, ed., *Corps universel diplomatique du droit des gens* . . ., 8 vols. (Amsterdam and The Hague, 1726–31), I, pt. ii, # 216; Dogiel, *Codex*, IV, # 57; Długosz, *Historia*, III, 167–70; *Lites*, I, 447–49.

52. *C.D.Pr.*, II, # 154.

one of the problems would not have arisen. On December 3, however, Casimir returned the territory of Dobrzyń to his cousin Duke Władysław, from whom it had been taken by the Knights in 1329 and to whom Łokietek had then given Łęczyca to replace the loss. Instead of accepting the decision of the arbiters, however, Władysław demanded indemnification from the Knights for the losses which he had suffered at their hands.[53] Casimir was for the moment unable to persuade the duke to abide by the Wyszegrad decree, and in the future Władysław was in the forefront of opposition by the nobles to the king's policy of accepting and implementing the decision of the congress.

Once the final negotiations at Wyszegrad (our sources tell us nothing of them) were disposed of, those in attendance began the return trip home, although Casimir did not immediately return to Cracow since he had accepted an invitation from King John to visit him in Prague.[54] It is difficult to avoid the impression that the young king felt himself honored and flattered to be in the company of one whose knightly reputation was famous throughout Europe.[55] Such an attitude was hardly displeasing to John, for whom any kind of adulation was simply his due. This attitude and the visit suited well his policy of attempting to persuade Casimir to ratify the acts of Wyszegrad. The trip also suited Casimir's purposes. He wished to continue the good relations with Bohemia which had been begun at Sandomir, developed at Trenčin, and brought to fruition at Wyszegrad, for peace with the Luxemburgers would allow him to devote his attention to Poland's other problems. Early in December, John and Casimir arrived in the Bohemian capital where the latter stayed nine days during which he was received and entertained by the Bohemian court in a manner befitting his position. During this time he had no contact with Margrave Charles, who had gone from Wyszegrad to Wrocław in order to re-establish Bohemian control following the death of Duke Henry VI.[56] By mid-December Casimir had returned to Cracow.[57]

A reign that had begun overshadowed by national mourning for the death of a beloved king and by threats to the kingdom from beyond its border had in thirty-two months emerged into the bright dawning of peace. The congress of Wyszegrad marked the accomplishment of the minimum goals of Casimir's early policy. He had firmly established himself as king of Poland, strengthened relations with Hungary, broken the Bohemian-Teutonic Order pincer by allying himself with John of Luxemburg, obtained clear title to the crown of

---

53. Ludewig, *Reliquiae*, II, 604. See also Leniek, "Kongres Wyszegradzki," p. 360.

54. *Chronicon aulae regiae*, in *Mon. Hist. Boem.*, V, 488.

55. This assumption is made by several other authors. See, for example, Caro, *Geschichte Polens*, II, 192; Werunsky, *Karl IV*, I, 155; Kaczmarczyk, *Polska czasów Kazimierza*, p. 29.

56. See Dąbrowski, "Dzieje polityczne," pp. 419–20; Šusta, *Karel IV*, pp. 210–12.

57. The assertion of Długosz, *Historia*, III, 171, that Casimir stayed in Hungary, celebrating Christmas with his sister and brother-in-law, is incorrect.

Poland as a result of John's renunciation, neutralized the hostility of Brandenburg and even turned it to Poland's advantage, and laid the foundation for
peace with the Teutonic Order. These were important successes to have gained
in such a short time. They demonstrated clearly the pacific orientation of his
early policy and show him to be that which every successful statesman must be:
master of the art of the possible.

A common judgment upon this policy of Casimir is that it was essentially a
continuation of Łokietek's, and that it is a mistake to oppose the two.[58] In many
respects this is true, but although the policy of Casimir may not have been
very different from his father's, there were important differences in strategy.
Casimir made far more use of diplomacy than his predecessor, especially in
dealing with Bohemia and the Teutonic Order. Łokietek had felt it necessary to
prove the power of Polish arms to gain respect for the newly reconstituted
kingdom. Casimir recognized that, although Poland could defend itself, it was
still unable to wage offensive war. He was willing to accept what he viewed as
the temporary loss of Silesia to Bohemia, for he could do nothing to alter that
situation for the moment. He was also inclined to accept the arbitration of
John and Charles Robert at Wyszegrad, again because he was not in a position
to dispute the Order's possession of Pomorze. That he did not immediately
ratify the decisions of the congress was due to factors which will be considered
below.

One must not be misled by the splendor of the gathering at the Hungarian
capital into thinking that the external problems of Poland and Casimir were
solved by the negotiations there. Only a first step, a cautious, peacefully
oriented beginning had been made. The first years of Casimir's reign were
indeed a time to make peace, but the fulfillment of that time had yet to come.

---

58. See Halecki, "Kazimierz Wielki," p. 407, and "Casimir the Great," in *The Cambridge
History of Poland*, ed. W. F. Reddaway et al., 2 vols. (Cambridge, 1941–50), I, 167; and *Pol.
Słow. Biog.*, XII, 268 (article by Kaczmarczyk).

4
THE ROAD TO STABILITY
FROM WYSZEGRAD TO KALISZ

From the spectacular Angevin capital on the Danube to the ancient commercial city of Greater Poland, Kalisz, it is not, under ordinary circumstances, a difficult journey. For Casimir, however, in the eight years after 1335, this route proved to be twisting and uncertain. Although in the first years of his reign Casimir had displayed remarkable consistency in the policy he pursued, after that he tried unsuccessfully to reap the fruits of two mutually contradictory programs. As a result, the liquidation of the problems left by his father and the achievement of a stable peace in the west was delayed. The culmination of the beginning made at Wyszegrad did not come until 1343. Though there is less internal consistency to the events covered in this chapter, this is not a new period in the king's policy. Casimir dealt with the same problems and issues in many of the same ways as before. In the end, he achieved his goals.

At the end of 1335, despite an understandable reluctance to confirm Poland's losses, Casimir was disposed to accept the decisions of the arbiters at Wyszegrad, for he recognized this would end the conflict with the Teutonic Order and give Poland the much needed opportunity to consolidate the gains made during Łokietek's reign. There were, however, certain elements within the kingdom which were not convinced of the wisdom of this policy. One faction which opposed the king came from the nobility. Another was composed of certain members of the clergy in Poland. In general, opposition from the former was disorganized and largely inarticulate. The most prominent figure in this camp was Duke Władysław of Łęczyca and Dobrzyń, whose motivation was his desire for indemnification from the Teutonic Order for damage to his territory and loss of income during and after the war.[1] A more subtle, yet nevertheless potent,

---

1. Suggested by the document in Ludewig, *Reliquiae*, II, 604.

reason also motivated the opposition of the nobility of the kingdom. For the most part they were contemporaries of Władysław Łokietek and had played important roles in the successes which he had achieved. The roots of their allegiance to Łokietek and to the aggressive policies which he had pursued against John of Bohemia and the Teutonic Order went deep into the past. They were loath to see policies for which they had risked life and property so easily abandoned, as Casimir seemed to be doing. They looked with suspicion, and even hostility, upon the programs of Casimir's early years.[2]

The opposition from the clergy was focused around Bishop Jan Grot of Cracow and papal nuncio Galhard de Carceribus. Though these two prelates differed widely on many other matters, in their opposition to Casimir's policy they were united. Of the two, the bishop was the more dangerous, since he harbored ambitions of personal and priestly power which had hitherto been frustrated. To gain his ends, Jan Grot used every pretext possible to embarrass the king. For example, not long after the Congress of Wyszegrad, on an occasion when Casimir was absent from the capital, the bishop besieged Queen Anna in Wawel castle claiming gratuitously that several ecclesiastics were imprisoned there. On another occasion he abruptly broke off the celebration of mass and refused to continue because Casimir had entered the church. The pope later admitted there was no excuse for such action.[3] The full force of the bishop's opposition to the king, and its chief goal, is summed up by the following epigram, circulated by Jan Grot throughout the kingdom:

O, King Casimir, you shall never have peace with Prussia
Until you recover Gdańsk, that is, the land of Pomorze.[4]

The activities of nuncio Galhard, a noted Polonophile, were of a different sort but were equally opposed to Casimir's policy. He strove zealously to protect the rights and prerogatives of the church in Poland and in the process worked against the best interests of the kingdom and its people. In the first place Galhard clung to an interpretation of the relationship between prelate and prince which in the second third of the fourteenth century was already a hundred years outdated. It was his idea to bend Polish policy to conform to what he conceived the papal position to be. A further element in his opposition was a financial consideration. Poland's loss of Pomorze and Silesia and the

2. See Jacob Caro, *Geschichte Polens*, 4 vols. in 5 (Gotha, 1863–86), II, 193. This factor is not treated by Kaczmarczyk, *Kazimierz Wielki (1333–1370)* (Warsaw, 1948), and *Polska czasów Kazimierza Wielkiego* (Cracow, 1964). He sees instead a more coherent, direct policy followed in these years than the process described in the text.

3. Both these events are reflected in a papal letter to the bishop in early 1338. See Theiner, *Mon. Pol.*, I, # 533. It is difficult to determine when they took place or how Pope Benedict learned of them. Kaczmarczyk, *Kazimierz Wielki*, pp. 62–63, suggests some time late in 1337. This may be a little late.

4. Cited by Zygmunt Wojciechowski, "Z dziejów pośmiertnych Bolesława Chrobrego," in his *Studia Historyczne* (Warsaw, 1955), p. 221.

resignation of claims to these areas would reduce papal income from these areas, an eventuality which Galhard devoutly hoped to avoid, for the unique tax of Peter's Pence, which the kingdom paid directly to Avignon could not be collected in the lands of the Bohemian crown or the territories of the Teutonic Order.

A final consideration also played a role in the opposition to Casimir, and although it found clearest expression with Jan Grot and Galhard, this position may well reflect the views of members of the nobility. According to their understanding, Casimir was not sympathetic enough to the native Polish element. The fact that he had become so friendly with the German Wittelsbachs and Luxemburgers and was desirous of making peace with the Teutonic Order, compounded with his many grants of foundation *de jure theutonico*, made it appear that the king was "pro-German." What these individuals did not adequately realize was that Casimir needed the friendship of Brandenburg and Bohemia, and peace with the Order, to safeguard Poland's national interests, and that Polish law was not yet a satisfactory instrument for administration.[5] Thus despite the fact that complaints of favoritism to Germans were unfounded, Jan Grot and Galhard brought their fears to the attention of Pope Benedict. In 1337 they wrote that Casimir was bringing many Germans into Poland, and that wherever Germans were in control the rights of the church were disregarded.[6]

By early 1336 opposition to Casimir's policies was pronounced enough to cause the Teutonic Order concern. The great days of conquest had temporarily come to an end for the Order, and under Grand Masters Luther of Braunschweig and Dietrich of Altenburg, the Knights had turned to the task of consolidating their gains and developing their internal administration.[7] They were anxious to maintain peaceful relations with Poland, and the aggressive attitudes of some there disturbed them. When Casimir demanded the return of Kujavia and Dobrzyń in accord with the arbitration of Wyszegrad, Dietrich in turn requested that the king first obtain from his nobles formal ratification of the Wyszegrad decrees. This he was unable to do.[8]

Neither was he able completely to preserve the de facto peace which existed between Poland and the Order. Urged by Pope Benedict to continue their mission against the heathens and supported by troops led by Margrave Lewis

5. The shortcomings of Polish law were to be remedied by one of Casimir's greatest achievements: the codification of native law. For brief treatment, see Kaczmarczyk, *Monarchia Kazimierza Wielkiego*, 2 vols. (Poznań, 1939–46), I, 45–96, and *Polska czasów Kazimierza*, pp. 77–93.

6. Theiner, *Mon. Pol.*, I, # 519.

7. See Marjan Tumler, *Der Deutsche Orden im Werden, Wachsen und Wirken bis 1400* (Vienna, 1955), pp. 344–46; and Johannes Voigt, *Geschichte Preussens von den ältesten Zeiten bis zum Untergange der Herrschaft des Deutschen Ordens*, 9 vols. (Königsberg, 1827–39), IV, 532.

8. Długosz, *Historia*, III, 171–72, makes it clear the grand master recognized that in this matter, no action of the king would be permanent without the approval of his nobles and prelates. See Voigt, *Geschichte Preussens*, IV, 534 n. 1.

of Brandenburg, the Knights sallied forth in early 1336 into Samogitia where they besieged the fortress of Pillenen and also built a fortification of their own which they christened Baiersburg, in honor of Lewis.[9] In the meantime, certain of the knights in Poland carried out a brief foray into the lands of the Order, but withdrew when the troops of the Order threatened to retaliate. The Knights contented themselves, however, with greatly strengthening the fortifications of Gdańsk and Świecie.[10] This situation threatened to undo all the achievements of Casimir's first years and might indeed have done just this had not the grand master recognized the foray by the Polish knights to be due to the intrigues of those who opposed Casimir and not the king himself. Thus Dietrich contented himself with issuing formal protests to the pope, Emperor Lewis IV, and the arbiters at Wyszegrad. In response to inquiries, especially from John and Charles Robert, Casimir issued on May 26 an assurance to the Order that he intended to remain true to the decisions at Wyszegrad and bound himself to maintain the peace for another year, until June 24, 1337. In case conflict did break out between the two states, he promised that the Order would receive indemnification.[11] Thus the fragile peace was maintained.

The course of Polish-Teutonic Order relations was closely followed by King John of Bohemia. He considered himself a friend and ally of the Knights and wished to ensure that their rights and prerogatives were defended; but also, in his role as an arbiter at Wyszegrad, he still felt a responsibility to see that those efforts were not in vain. Thus he had written to Casimir urging him to remain true to those decisions. In this same letter John raised the question of Luxemburg interests in Carinthia and the Tyrol and invited Casimir to meet with him to discuss common action against other claimants for the succession there—the Wittelsbachs and the Habsburgs. Casimir agreed, and on June 21 he arrived in the border town of Marchegg, some ten miles northwest of Pozsony. Shortly thereafter King Charles Robert joined his fellow monarchs. John was resolved upon war in Austria and Bavaria and persuaded the others to join him. Casimir agreed to contribute 200 heavy and 300 light cavalry, while his brother-in-law sent 600 helmeted troops and several thousand light archers.[12] Though the campaigns which followed consisted largely of devastation and pillage, they were not so indecisive as some have suggested;[13] for when peace negotiations were opened in late September in the Austrian city of Enns, the

9. Długosz, *Historia*, III, 174; and *Chronica Olivensis*, in *M.P.H.*, VI, 333. See also F. W. Taube, *Ludwig der Aeltere als Markgraf von Brandenburg, 1323–1351* (Berlin, 1900), p. 66.

10. *Chronica Cracoviae*, in *Silesiacarum rerum Scriptores aliquot adhuc inediti*, ed. Wilhelm Sommersberg, 3 vols. (Leipzig, 1729–32), II, 98; *Chronica Olivensis*, p. 333.

11. Dogiel, *Codex*, IV, #58; *Lites*, I, 451.

12. The details of these negotiations and of the following campaign are reflected in *Chronicon aulae regiae*, in *Font. rer. Aust.*, VIII, pt. i, 526 f.; and Albertus Argentinus, *Chronicon integrum . . .*, in Christian Urstisius, ed., *Germaniae Historicorum illustrium . . .*, 2 vols. (Frankfurt, 1585), II, 125.

13. For example, Caro, *Geschichte Polens*, II, 196.

Luxemburgers were able in the peace treaty of October 9 to obtain possession of the Tyrol.[14] Although Casimir had given military support to the Bohemians, he had not taken part in the campaign and was not present at Enns. Nevertheless, he had shown his friendship to the Luxemburgers and in effect assured them that recent Polish hostilities with the Teutonic Order had not altered the tenor of Polish-Bohemian relations.[15]

While Polish troops were fighting in Austria and Bavaria, Casimir had been fighting his own battle at home. He was still a young man, subject to the indecision and enthusiasm of youth. The intrigues of nuncio Galhard brought considerable pressure to bear upon Casimir to abrogate his promise to abide by the decisions of Wyszegrad. The king was not entirely unreceptive to such an idea, for although reason and statesmanship demanded a pacific, conciliatory policy, national ambition desired the recovery of Pomorze. Because Casimir's youthful idealism convinced him that this might be done without recourse to arms, he became more sympathetic to the policy of Galhard. This policy was clearly expressed by the nuncio in mid-1336, when he suggested to Avignon that the basis for negotiation with the Knights should be, not the arbitration of Wyszegrad, but the decision of the papal judges of Inowrocław in 1321. This judgment had sentenced the Teutonic Order to return Pomorze to Poland, pay an indemnification of 30,000 marks, and reimburse the court for the expenses of the trial. Galhard boldly bid for papal support in this policy by arguing that the papacy would prosper if these negotiations were successful, since Peter's Pence could again be collected in Pomorze. In addition he promised that the king would pay half his indemnification into papal coffers.[16]

Had Casimir agreed to such a policy, his reversal would have been complete. Yet by the end of 1336 he was wavering, fully aware of the consequences of an about-face and at the same time seduced by the possibility of success. He knew he risked more than failure. His reputation would also be at stake, for such a tergiversation would surely cast doubt upon his good faith and the validity of his word.[17] Before he finally cast his lot with his nuncio, who soon gained the

14. See the documents in *C.D.Mor.*, VII, # 132–40.

15. There is some reason to believe that these relations may have been somewhat strained at this time, for the year 1336 saw another great increase in Bohemian influence in Silesia. The unexpected death without heir of Duke Henry VI of Wrocław on November 24, 1335, was followed—on the basis of an earlier agreement with John—by the incorporation of the duchy into the Bohemian crown. Then in August, Duke Bolko of Ząbkowice accepted the feudal suzerainty of King John. See *Historia Śląska*, general editor Karol Maleczyński, vol. I, *do roku 1763* in four parts (Wrocław, 1960–64), pt. i, p. 562. On the question of the summer's campaigning in Bavaria and Austria, see Emil Werunsky, *Geschichte Kaiser Karls IV. und seine Zeit*, 3 vols. in 4 (Innsbruck, 1880–96), I, 159–68; Josef Šusta, *Karel IV, Otec a Syn, 1333–1346* (Prague, 1946), pp. 215–21, 231–34; Jan Dąbrowski, *Dzieje Polski od r. 1333 do r. 1506*, vol. II of Roman Grodecki, Stanisław Zachorowski, and Jan Dąbrowski, *Dzieje Polski średniowiecznej* (Cracow, 1926), p. 18.

16. See Galhard's letter in Theiner, *Mon. Pol.*, I, # 506.

17. There is a Polish historiographical tradition which takes the point of view that Casimir was justified in eventually adopting Galhard's policy because it offered an opportunity of

support of Avignon, he waited to see what the outcome of his policy up to that point would be.

The position of the papacy in these affairs and its reaction to the Congress of Wyszegrad was highly ambivalent. It had been Pope John XXII, and Benedict XII after him, who had urged the Poles and the Teutonic Order to conclude peace.[18] Slowly, however, the papacy changed its policy, largely through the persuadings of Galhard, but influenced also by a rapprochement of the Order with the Wittelsbachs, with whom Benedict's relations were slowly worsening after an auspicious beginning. Within a year of Wyszegrad, the papacy also was wavering and was not well disposed toward the original policy of Casimir.

Early in 1336, while the spirit of Wyszegrad still prevailed, Casimir had sent a message to Avignon asking for papal confirmation of the settlement suggested the previous November. He also requested a revision of the method established in 1318 for paying Peter's Pence, so that this tax would not weigh so heavily upon the Polish people, and demanded the removal of two Polish bishops because of their opposition to the king. The first of these was Jan Grot of Cracow,[19] and the second was probably Nanker of Wrocław.[20] Casimir also complained to the pope that the Knights had violated Polish possessions in a breach of the truce between the two states, and asked that Benedict take appropriate action to punish the Order.

The papal reply, issued late in 1336, was most discouraging to all of Casimir's requests. Benedict refused to approve the decision of Wyszegrad, saying that these agreements outraged good reason and were compatible neither with the honor nor the best interests of the king. Further, the pope felt that in Polish diplomacy of the recent past there had been too little regard for the position of

---

regaining Pomorze. It may be discovered in Jan Kochanowski, *Kazimierz Wielki* (Warsaw, 1900), p. 44, and Kaczmarczyk, *Kazimierz Wielki*, pp. 56–57, but it is clearest in Oscar Halecki, "Kazimierz Wielki, 1333–1370," *Encyklopedya Polska*, V, pt. i (Warsaw, Lublin, Łódź, and Cracow, 1920), p. 320, and "Casimir the Great," in *The Camb. Hist. of Pol.*, I, 169–70. I find it difficult to agree with the assumption of success, and sense more than a trace of nationalist pride in evaluating this aspect of Casimir's policy. I would rather suggest that however interesting the events which culminated in the Warsaw process of 1339, they nevertheless mark a deviation from the wiser policy which found expression in the treaties of Kalisz in 1343. The aberration of 1337–39/40 did much to delay Poland's return to an important international position. It was only from such a position that Poland might hope to recover Pomorze, as in fact it did in the fifteenth century.

18. See especially on this question, Kazimierz Gorzycki, "Wpływ stolicy apostolskiej na rokowania pokojowe Kazimierza Wielkiego z Czechami i Zakonem niemieckim," *Przewodnik Naukowy i Literacki*, XXI (1893), 78–87, 170–77, 266–74, 366–70, 448–55.

19. See Mieczysław Niwiński, "Biskup krakowski Jan Grotowic i zatargi jego z Włodzisławem Łokietkiem i Kazimierzem Wielkim. Ustęp z dziejów stosunku Kościoła do Państwa w Polsce w w. XIV," *Nova Polonia Sacra*, III (1939), 71–72.

20. Raynaldus, *Annales Eccl.*, XXV, *a.d.* 1336, par. 62: "Rogaret etiam pontificem Casimirus, ut Wratislaviensem et Cracoviensem episcopos sibi minus gratos ad alias sedes traduceret." See also Caro, *Geschichte Polens*, II, 197 n. 2; and Kaczmarczyk, *Kazimierz Wielki*, p. 57.

the papacy. He went on to deny Casimir's request concerning Peter's Pence, saying that after consulting the record books of the papacy he had found no legitimate reason to consider a change in the present system. In reference to the request for the transfer of the two bishops, Benedict loftily replied that it was not the custom of the apostolic see to translate ecclesiastics without sufficient cause, and he could find none in this instance. Finally the pope wrote that he was surprised Casimir should make charges against the Teutonic Order, since the Order had lodged similar complaints against him and his nobles. Therefore there was nothing he could do until the situation had become a bit clearer.[21]

It was a grim Advent season which Casimir celebrated in 1336. Only a year before, he had recently returned from Wyszegrad and Prague where the cautious maneuverings of the previous two and a half years had enabled him to achieve modest success in international affairs. Now the picture was far less bright. Casimir had been thoroughly rebuffed by the pope, openly opposed by some of his nobles, and secretly undermined by various of the clergy. He was bound by formal promises to Bohemia and the Teutonic Order to honor the judgments of Wyszegrad, yet at the same time he was inclining toward a totally contradictory policy. Casimir and his policy were adrift in the sea of international affairs. It was perhaps sometime in this Christmas season that the king went cautiously over to the program of Galhard, for the nuncio was able to write Benedict in 1337 of the king's qualified support for his policy.[22] A new element had thus been added which was to complicate and confuse the events of the next years.

Though a certain aimlessness of policy is evident in the affairs of 1337, as the contradictory implications of Casimir's program became evident, it is possible in retrospect to see events in this year which brought the problems the king faced into perspective and ultimately enabled him to resolve them. The element which precipitated this development was the restless wandering of John of Bohemia.

Early in January, 1337, John and his son Charles arrived in Wrocław for conferences with several Silesian princes.[23] With Duke Henry of Jawór John signed a treaty of friendship on January 4 in which Henry agreed to cede his duchy to the Bohemian crown if he died without heir. In return he was to receive the usufruct of the duchy for his lifetime. Two days later the duke signed a defensive-offensive alliance with the Luxemburgers.[24] In the meantime John had also undertaken negotiations concerning the important duchy of Racibórz, whose ruler had died without heir in 1336. On the basis of the pact of 1327, on January 14 an agreement was reached in which Racibórz was annexed to the

---

21. Theiner, *Mon. Hung.*, I, # 910.
22. See Theiner, *Mon. Pol.*, I, # 519.
23. See the list in Werunsky, *Karl IV*, I, 177.
24. *C.D.Mor.*, VII, # 150–51; Ludewig, *Reliquiae*, VI, 2, 9.

Bohemian crown under the administration of Duke Nicholas of Opawa. Thus, as a result of John's stay in Wrocław, Bohemian authority and influence were further extended in Silesia, bringing even closer the king's goal of complete control there.[25]

Following this Silesian sojourn, John and Charles, accompanied by many princes and nobles from Silesia and the empire, led an army across Polish lands to the *Ordensstaat*, where they joined the Knights for a campaign into Lithuania. After leaving Königsberg late in January, the united army travelled across the Kur gulf to the lower reaches of the Memel River, where they completed the building of a fortified outpost named Marienburg (not to be confused with the greater fortress of the same name on the lower Vistula). Then the question of actual campaigning against the Lithuanians was considered. Since the Lithuanians refused to meet the Knights in open conflict and since the winter was so mild that sure interior passage could not be guaranteed, the campaign was finally given up. By mid-February the two armies had returned to Toruń.[26]

While John had campaigned with the Knights, other matters of mutual interest had been discussed, including the state of Polish-Teutonic Order relations. This was of great concern to the Bohemian, and acting as mediator and arbiter, he wrote Casimir from Toruń to suggest a meeting of the two kings with Grand Master Dietrich. Casimir agreed and promised to meet them as soon as possible in Inowrocław.[27] John and Dietrich went immediately to the appointed city for preliminary negotiations.[28] By this time the Order was increasingly aware of Casimir's acquiescence in Galhard's policy, and the grand master took considerable pains to provide for John a clear exposition of the

25. For the details of these negotiations, see Werunsky, *Karl IV*, I, 177–78; Šusta, *Karel IV*, pp. 240–45; Dąbrowski, "Dzieje polityczne Śląska w latach 1290–1402," in *Historja Śląska od najdawniejszych czasów do roku 1400*, ed. Stanisław Kutrzeba, et al., 3 vols. (Cracow, 1933–39), I, 421–29; *Historia Śląska*, I, pt. 1, 562–63.

26. For the details of this campaign, see *Vita Caroli IIII*, in *Rerum Bohemicarum antiqui scriptores . . .*, ed. C. V. Marquard Freher (Hanover, 1602), p. 97; *Chronica Olivensis*, p. 333; Wigand of Marburg, *Chronica nova Prutenica*, in *SS. rer. Pr.*, II, 493–94. The modern accounts of this campaign given by Voigt, *Geschichte Preussens*, IV, 542–46, and Caro, *Geschichte Polens*, II, 199–200, should be supplemented by the shorter, but more critical, treatments in Werunsky, *Karl IV*, I, 179–81; Šusta, *Karel IV*, pp. 245–46; and Kaczmarczyk, *Kazimierz Wielki*, p. 58.

27. Henryk Paszkiewicz, "Ze studjów nad polityką krzyżacką Kazimierza Wielkiego," *P.H.*, XXV (1925), 187–221, particularly p. 216, where he shows that this meeting took place in Inowrocław, not Włocławek, as earlier writers had stated. See for example, Caro, *Geschichte Polens*, II, 200.

28. The chronicle of Wigand of Marburg, who wrote about the end of the fourteenth century, is particularly full on this point, but must be used with caution. In addition to an obvious error, such as saying that Poland was represented by "Locut [Łokietek] rex Cracoviensis," he also states that there were two meetings between Casimir, John, and Dietrich: one in January, before the Lithuanian campaign; the other in March, the subject of our present consideration. This first meeting is not confirmed by any other source, and since the first critical edition of Wigand by Hirsch in 1863, scholars have tended to disregard his testimony about two meetings. See *SS. rer. Pr.*, II, 268–70, 493 f.

basis for the Order's possession of Pomorze. As a result, John confirmed the Order's position on March 2 and renounced again all claims to the province in their favor. Margrave Charles also signed this document. Three days later the Bohemians took the Order under their special protection, promising to respect all its rights and privileges in the lands it now held and might in the future conquer, and to represent it in the best possible light at Avignon.[29]

The next day Casimir arrived, accompanied by Archbishop Jan Janisław of Gniezno, the dukes of Łęczyca-Dobrzyń and Mazovia, and the palatines of Poznań, Kujavia, and Kalisz. Bishop Matthias of Włocławek was already present, and Bishops Otto of Chełm and Berthold of Marienwerder had accompanied the grand master and John.[30] From the number and rank of the dignitaries gathered in Inowrocław, the meeting took on the appearance of a minor congress. Unfortunately, the results of the negotiations did not correspond to the importance of those in attendance.

The day of Casimir's arrival in Inowrocław, Duke Władysław of Łęczyca and Dobrzyń formally renounced all claim to the latter territory in favor of Casimir, in return for confirmation of his position in Łęczyca.[31] This puzzling decision can only be explained by assuming (there is no direct evidence) that Casimir had urged him to do this in order to obtain a free hand in dealings with the Knights. By such an act, the problem of Władysław's demands for indemnification from the Teutonic Order was solved. That Casimir should urge the duke to do this indicates that he was still interested in pursuing a conciliatory policy toward the Order and further suggests the indecision which the king exhibited in this period. The impression of a certain schizophrenia in his thinking is strengthened by an examination of the treaty which he signed with the Order after two days of negotiations.

In the treaty he agreed to recognize the rights of the Order to Pomorze, Michałowo, Chełmno, and other border districts, and never again to use the title or seal, *heres Pomoraniae*.[32] He further promised to obtain from the Hungarian royal couple a formal renunciation of their possible claims to these territories as relatives of the Polish crown. In this treaty, Casimir promised in the names of the archbishop of Gniezno, the bishops of Włocławek and Poznań, the dukes of Kujavia and Dobrzyń, and the nobles of the kingdom that all would abide by the terms of this treaty and none would claim indemnification from the Teutonic Order for losses and damages suffered during the war.

The names of those who witnessed this document and those in whose names Casimir made his promises are of significance, for they show that some of the ecclesiastics and nobles of Poland were in support of Casimir's original policy.

29. The first document is in *Lites*, I, 452; the second in *C.D.Mor.*, VII, # 155.
30. These are all mentioned as witnesses in *C.D.Pr.*, II, # 163.
31. Dogiel, *Codex*, IV, # 59.
32. *C.D.Pr.*, II, # 163; *Lites*, I, 453–58.

Moreover, the inclusiveness of the king's promise "for the barons, counts, knights, and the other nobles of our kingdom," though it surely was not meant to imply that all in the kingdom supported him, does allow the inference that Casimir had support enough to feel confident that his promise would be respected. The most significant name in the list was that of Duke Władysław, who had originally opposed the similar Wyszegrad agreements.[33]

Before this august meeting of rulers came to an end, it was agreed that Casimir was formally to ratify these agreements by July 15, 1337. When he had done this, the Teutonic Order would renounce all claim to Kujavia and Dobrzyń in accord with the Wyszegrad decision and return these territories to Casimir and Poland. In the meantime the lands were to be held in the name of the king of Bohemia by a Czech representative, who was to make his residence in Brześć in Kujavia.[34]

Despite Casimir's apparent desire to achieve a final settlement with the Order, the agreements of Inowrocław never went into effect. One reason was that Charles Robert and Elizabeth of Hungary failed to ratify the renunciation of claims to Pomorze, Michałowo, and Chełmno made for them by Casimir.[35] More important, Casimir himself decided not to ratify these agreements. Increasingly, he was under the influence of nuncio Galhard's urgings to follow a more aggressive policy toward the Order.[36] July 15 came and went, and the dispute between Poland and the Order remained in the same state as before.

Following the meeting in Inowrocław, King John returned to Bohemia, accompanied as far as Poznań by Casimir. Before parting, the two discussed the problem of Silesia, and on March 12 they signed an agreement. Taking as their point of departure the peace treaty of Sandomir in 1335,[37] they appointed a panel of arbiters, two from each kingdom, to settle all disputes which might arise over the boundaries between Silesia and Poland. This treaty went much

33. Caro, *Geschichte Polens*, II, 200–201, 201 nn. 1, 2, attempts to argue that there was never any thought on Casimir's part of the ratification of this treaty and that these negotiations were only a sham. This I think is too strong a judgment, for the king was of pacific orientation in the matter of the Order. That this treaty was in fact never ratified is due more to the indecisiveness of the king than to any conscious duplicity.

34. *C.D.Pol.*, II, # 448.

35. See Dąbrowski, *Ostatnie lata*, pp. 88, 95, 100. There is no evidence to indicate that Casimir actually attempted to obtain such a ratification.

36. Długosz, *Historia*, III, 175, says that Bishop Jan Grot of Cracow went to Avignon to petition Benedict to oppose this settlement with the Order. Caro, *Geschichte Polens*, II, 203 n. 1, has correctly pointed out, however, that the emissary was only the nephew of the bishop and that he was the personal representative of Galhard. See the report of the nuncio in Theiner, *Mon. Pol.*, I, # 519. This fact points up again where the initiative lay.

37. This is clearly demonstrated by Otakar Bauer, "Poznámky k mírovým smlouvám českopolským z roku 1335," in *Sborník prací věnovaných prof. dru. Gustavu Friedrichovi k šedesátým narozeninám 1871–1931* (Prague, 1931), pp. 16–17. His further argument, however, that there is also a direct relationship to the agreements of Wyszegrad is less tenable, since the question of Silesia did not really figure in those decisions.

further than the one of 1335, and it was far more specific. It was to last for ten years; Czech infractions of the treaty were to be judged by the *capitanei* of Wrocław and Głogów in either Syców or Wschowa, while Polish breaches were under the jurisdiction of the *capitanei* of Poznań and Kalisz, who were to hear cases in Ostrzeszów and Kościan; finally, appropriate penalties were also suggested.[38] Though it has been concluded that both kings felt this treaty settled all differences between them,[39] this could hardly have been the case. The treaty did not directly touch the real point of conflict, that is, the question of who legally controlled Silesia. In a sense Casimir had tacitly recognized Bohemian suzerainty by allowing Bohemian interests to be represented by Silesian officials, but even this did not go as far as the Trenčin agreements of 1335. It was not for another two years that this problem was finally resolved.

It is appropriate at this point to analyze briefly one of the most revealing documents relating to Casimir's early reign. Either explicitly or by its assumptions, the document touches upon most of the major problems of Poland's policy at this point. It is the report of nuncio Galhard to Pope Benedict XII on July 10, 1337.[40]

After appropriate opening phrases, Galhard reviews the financial aspects of his commission. He emphasizes the large sums which Poland has raised for papal coffers by various taxes and tributes.[41] In this discussion of money, Galhard had a twofold purpose. He first wished to indicate how well he was fulfilling this aspect of his responsibilities; but he also wanted to create a favorable impression on Benedict in order to assure himself a sympathetic hearing when he stated his complaints against the Teutonic Order and the Bohemians. His tactics were completely successful.

The nuncio had never shown himself friendly to foreign interference in Poland, and this attitude was clearly reflected in the next part of his report. According to him, wherever Poles were in the majority or exercised positions of leadership, the interests of the church and the papacy were well protected and encouraged; however, where there were Germans or Bohemians, there was a noticeable lack of regard for these same interests. This was especially true in the bishoprics of Kamień and Lubusz ("which, as is well known, have belonged to Poland from antiquity")[42] and of Chełm, where the bishop all but refused to

---

38. *C.D.M.P.*, II, #1166; Dogiel, *Codex*, I, 3; Ludewig, *Reliquiae*, V, 589. There is no specific mention of the Silesian-Polish boundary in this treaty. It speaks only of the boundary between the two kingdoms. The fact, however, that the Bohemian judges came from Wrocław and Głogów, both in Silesia, would seem to justify the more specific boundary definition given in the text. See Werunsky, *Karl IV*, I, 185; Dąbrowski, "Dzieje polityczne," p. 427; Kaczmarczyk, *Kazimierz Wielki*, pp. 60 f.

39. By Caro, *Geschichte Polens*, II, 202.

40. Theiner, *Mon. Pol.*, I, #519, pp. 391–97.

41. On the question of papal taxes in Poland, see Kaczmarczyk, *Monarchia*, II, 29–38.

42. Neither of them at this point belonged politically to Poland. On the bishopric of Lubusz, see Kaczmarczyk, *Monarchia*, II, 146 ff.

pay the papal taxes. The most glaring example of opposition to the church was in Wrocław, where one of the canons refused to recognize the authority of the nuncio. Galhard went on to request that the pope take special care when filling any vacancies which might occur in these places, suggesting that they be filled by Poles appointed by the pope, lest an election result in the elevation of another German or Czech. Finally he raised one of the most sensitive issues between King John of Bohemia and the church: the fortress of Milicz. Galhard exhorted the pope to admonish Bishop Nanker of Wrocław not to alienate this episcopal property to John, for Milicz was the key to Poland. If it were in Luxemburg control, the whole of the surrounding territory might be swallowed up by the crown of Bohemia.[43]

The combination of Galhard's supplications and the eloquence of the nuncio's personal representative, who had been given a special commission to present the report orally to Benedict, evoked an almost immediate response, for on September 12, two months after the report had been sent, the pope issued four letters. The first two went to the nuncio, instructing him about the contents of the others and urging him to utilize all necessary ecclesiastical tools to obtain the payment of church monies. A third letter was sent to Casimir. How different in tone it was from that which the king had received from Benedict nine months before! After the conventional politeness of the opening formulas, Benedict alluded to the praiseworthy things that had been said about the king by Galhard. He further complimented him on the steadfastness of his faith and closed by urging him to continue firm in his devotion to the church. The fourth letter was directed to Bishop Nanker and ordered him not to divest himself of Milicz.[44]

This heavily fortified castle stood thirty miles northeast of Wrocław astride the heavily travelled trade routes leading into the heart of Greater Poland. Like the fortress of Bolesławiec, it often served as a refuge for those who preyed upon merchants travelling between Poland and Bohemia. Its strategic position made it a place which could easily be garrisoned by Polish troops and used as a forward position for an attack upon Silesia. Thus King John wished to gain control of it and have it razed. The problem was complicated by the fact that the fortress was not under the jurisdiction of the temporal ruler of Wrocław, who owed allegiance to John, but was instead the personal property of the Bishop of Wrocław, who was still subject to Gniezno.[45] When John was in Wrocław, in March, 1337 (after returning from Poznań), he had begun negotiations with Bishop Nanker which he hoped would result in a cession of Milicz

43. See below for Milicz. The nuncio's report is discussed by Caro, *Geschichte Polens*, II, 202–4; Kaczmarczyk, *Kazimierz Wielki*, pp. 61 ff.

44. Theiner, *Mon. Pol.*, I, # 520, 521, 523, and 522 respectively.

45. See Karol Maleczyński, *Dzieje Wrocławia do roku 1526* (Katowice and Wrocław, 1948), pp. 180–81; Dąbrowski, "Dzieje polityczne," pp. 429–33; *Historia Śląska*, I, pt. i, 566–67.

to the crown of Bohemia. In addition to the ecclesiastical implications of such an act, this eventuality would have left Poland partially unprotected from the southwest in case of renewed Polish-Bohemian conflict. Galhard strove in every way to bring pressure upon Nanker to refuse to cede Milicz.[46] Now the pope had added his authority to that of his nuncio, and for the moment the fortress remained in the hands of the bishop, preventing John from achieving his goal.

Late in 1337 or early in 1338, Pope Benedict took steps which greatly strengthened the policy which Galhard, and now, increasingly, Casimir, was pursuing. To ease the load of his nuncio in the collection of Peter's Pence, he sent an assistant to Poland—Peter Gervais, a canon of Viviers in Spain.[47] In addition, as the result of various charges and allegations against the Teutonic Order and its continuing conflict with Poland, the pope decided to initiate an investigation into the whole matter. Thus two years after the Congress of Wyszegrad, it was clear that the papacy was becoming increasingly well disposed toward Poland and more and more hostile to the Order.[48]

The policy of King John of Bohemia toward Poland during this period was based upon his desire to establish his legal claims to Silesia. He was the de facto suzerain of much of this region, for most of the dukes and princes had recognized his overlordship; but despite the agreements of Trenčin, Casimir had not formally renounced his claims to this area. There was thus some question as to the legitimacy of John's claims. In 1338 John turned to Casimir's closest ally and brother-in-law, Charles Robert of Hungary, for help in obtaining his goal.[49] The Angevin also had plans which concerned Casimir and Poland. He wished to provide a throne for each of his three sons: Sicily's for Andrew, Hungary's for Stephen, and Poland's for Louis.[50] To obtain his goal for Louis, he needed to determine that the Luxemburgers would in no way oppose him. Thus the two dynasties had mutual interests which made them allies.

In February, 1338, Margrave Charles travelled to Wyszegrad to meet with Charles Robert, and on March 1 a treaty was signed. Charles promised for

46. According to a document in *Sil. rer. SS.*, I, 132 n. 4, Nanker tentatively agreed in March to give up the fortress if John would take over the protection of the bishopric. This decision was never ratified, however; see Werunsky, *Karl IV*, I, 187, and Dąbrowski, "Dzieje polityczne," pp. 430–31.

47. Already papal nuncio in Hungary, Peter of Gervais is first mentioned as having responsibility also in Poland on February 28, 1338. See Theiner, *Mon. Pol.*, I, # 529.

48. See Halecki, "Kazimierz Wielki," pp. 321–22; Dąbrowski, *Dzieje Polski*, II, 21; Gorzycki, "Wpływ," pp. 74–77.

49. Werunsky, *Karl IV*, I, 219–20; Šusta, *Karel IV*, p. 278.

50. Janko of Czarnków, *Chronicon Polonorum*, in *M.P.H.*, II, 636: "Habebat enim Karolus rex memoratus protunc tres filios, Lodvicum, Andream et Stephanum, conceperatque in animo, quod Lodvicum in Polonia, Andream in Sicilia et Stephanum in Ungaria praeficeret in reges." See also Halecki, "O genezie i znaczeniu rządów andegaweńskich w Polsce," *K.H.*, XXXV (1921), 36.

himself and his heirs to help the Angevins gain the throne of Poland for Louis should Casimir die without a male descendant. Charles Robert for his part promised that neither he nor his heirs would lend Casimir any help if the Polish king attempted to seize any of the Silesian principalities. He also promised to do all in his power to dissuade Casimir from any such act and to persuade him to renounce finally and forever his claims to Silesia. Should the Angevins actually gain the throne of Poland, Charles Robert also promised not to attempt to regain Silesia for Poland and even to return it to Bohemia should Casimir have succeeded in retaking it before his death.[51] This alliance was supplemented and sealed by a marriage pact. Charles Robert's twelve-year-old son was engaged to the Margrave's three-year-old daughter, Margaratha. By the end of September, 1339, she was to move to the Hungarian court to be brought up and educated there. Each promised substantial dowries for the prospective couple. The alliance was to remain in force even if Casimir died before the proposed marriage.[52]

Although this alliance worked to the benefit of both Bohemia and Hungary, it presented the possibility of a serious threat for Poland, for it momentarily strained Polish-Hungarian relations. By his promise to withhold aid from Casimir, Charles Robert removed the support of Poland's only real ally in central Europe. The kingdom was not ready to stand alone among its powerful neighbors, and it was fortunate that this alliance was only a momentary enfeeblement of the Cracow-Wyszegrad bond.[53] For Bohemia, the alliance meant Hungarian support in its attempt to obtain Casimir's renunciation of his Silesian claims. It further secured the Luxemburg eastern border, since Hungary promised to withhold aid in the event of a Polish attack upon Silesia. The Angevins by this treaty had removed a possible stumbling block in their program of gaining the crown of Poland, since Bohemia had promised to assist them in this policy. Previously Charles Robert had feared that the Luxemburgers might oppose his program if they wished to revive their claims to the Polish throne.

The Luxemburgers were the first to obtain their goals. During 1338, Charles Robert made it clear to his brother-in-law that he would be well advised to seek a resolution of the problem of Silesia with Bohemia. Casimir was willing to do this, for in the face of his increasingly hostile policy toward the Teutonic Order, he desired, at the very least, Bohemian neutrality. In addition he recognized that he had no effective control over Silesia. Negotiations were opened between

51. Ludewig, *Reliquiae*, V, 492; *C.D.Mor.*, VII, # 187.

52. Ludewig, *Reliquiae*, V, 487; *C.D.Mor.*, VII, # 188. See also *Vita Caroli*, p. 99. Compare Caro, *Geschichte Polens*, II, 206 n. 1; and Werunsky, *Karl IV*, I, 221.

53. One of the factors which brought about a rapprochement between the two dynasties was Casimir's visit to Wyszegrad later in 1338, at which time important decisions were made concerning Polish-Hungarian plans in Ruthenia. See Paszkiewicz, *Polityka Ruska Kazimierza Wielkiego* (Warsaw, 1925), p. 40; and below, chap. 5.

Casimir and Charles, and on February 9, 1339, the Piast issued in Cracow a renunciation in favor of King John of his rights, privileges, and claims to all duchies in Silesia which had accepted Bohemian overlordship, as well as to the cities and territories of Wrocław and Głogów. He also renounced all claim to the principality of Płock in Mazovia, whose prince had recognized Bohemian suzerainty since 1329.[54]

Casimir's renunciation was complete, although it did not take into account any of the developments in Silesia since 1335 and failed to mention any Polish claims to territories which had not yet come under Bohemian control.[55] Nevertheless, John had achieved his goal, since, unlike the Trenčin agreement of 1335, this pact was speedily ratified. There is no hint of opposition by the clergy or nobility to this act. In character, the renunciation was not a simple act of ratifying the Trenčin agreement on Silesia; neither was it merely an extension of the Wyszegrad agreement, for the subject of Silesia was not formally treated in it.[56] This renunciation of February 9 was an independent act, preceded, to be sure, by previous unsuccessful attempts to achieve the same goal. It brought to an end for the time being the Bohemian-Polish conflict over Silesia.

The unexpected death on May 26, 1339, of Casimir's Lithuanian wife, Anna, led to a rapprochement between Casimir and Charles Robert, for it raised in a very immediate manner the question of the succession in Poland. There had been no male heir from the marriage, and since there were strong reasons to avoid turning to a collateral line of the Piasts Casimir was receptive to the efforts which Charles Robert was making on behalf of his dynasty.[57] The Angevin received further support from the Luxemburgers in March, 1339, when Charles visited Wyszegrad and reassured the king of Bohemian support for his plans.[58] Charles Robert's cause had other advocates. Two of Casimir's most important civil officials, Zbigniew, chancellor of Cracow, and Spycimir, castellan of Cracow, had long been in favor of Angevin succession in Poland if

54. *C.D.Mor.*, VII, # 224; Colmar Grünhagen and E. Markgraf, eds., *Lehns- und Besitz-urkunden Schlesiens und seiner einzelnen Fürstentümer im Mittelalter*, 2 vols. (Leipzig, 1881–83), I, 4.

55. See especially on this point *Historia Śląska*, I, pt. i, 564–65.

56. See Dąbrowski, "Dzieje polityczne," p. 435, n. 1. Otakar Bauer, "Poznámky k mírovým smlouvám," pp. 17–19, attempts to show that this agreement was a simple ratification of the earlier agreement. Despite impressive evidence based on similarity of language in the two documents, his argument is not wholly convincing. The language is indeed similar, but there is much of a formula nature to it, and it does not necessarily indicate that the later agreement is based upon the earlier one or that the later one is a simple ratification. Caro, *Geschichte Polens*, II, 214, incorrectly implies this was an extension of both Trenčin and Wyszegrad. Such an assumption can only be based upon the later testimony of Charles IV.

57. Halecki, "Kazimierz Wielki," p. 326, and "Casimir the Great," p. 186, suggests that Casimir felt his Piast relatives to be unworthy of the crown.

58. See Werunsky, *Karl IV*, I, 235; Šusta, *Karel IV*, pp. 300 ff.

Casimir had no male heir.[59] They recognized, as did Casimir also,[60] that such an arrangement would tie Hungary even more closely to Poland and would provide additional resources for Poland against its enemies, particularly the Teutonic Order. Casimir found that his nobles and magnates were generally in favor of the Angevin succession, and early in July he travelled to Wyszegrad to meet with Charles Robert.[61]

There negotiations resulted in the designation of Casimir's sister Elizabeth as heir to the throne of Poland and, through her, Charles Robert or one of his sons.[62] This agreement achieved the goal of the Hungarian king and made provision for a successor to Casimir. Charles Robert promised, for himself and his heirs, to spare no effort, once the Angevins had gained the crown, in attempting to regain those territories and provinces which had been torn from the Polish crown, especially Pomorze. This they were to do at their own cost and not with Polish monies. He also promised to appoint no foreigners to government positions in Poland, but to rely only upon native Poles. Finally he swore not to

59. They had been open advocates of this since at least the Congress of Wyszegrad; see Janko of Czarnków, *Chronicon*, p. 638. And perhaps before that; see Balzer, *Królestwo Polskie, 1295–1370*, 3 vols. (Lwów, 1919–20), III, 89 f.

60. Dąbrowski, *Ostatnie lata*, p. 93, n. 3, correctly attacks the treatment of Casimir's position on this question by Caro, *Geschichte Polens*, II, 184 ff., who saw the Piast as the victim of intrigues by John and Charles Robert. Nothing could be farther from the truth, for Casimir was well aware of Angevin intentions and approved of them. See also Antoni Prochaska, "W sprawie zajęcia Rusi przez Kazimierza Wielkiego," *K.H.*, VI (1892), 17, who makes a similar error.

61. Długosz, *Historia*, III, 192 f., writing at a time when there were more limitations upon the Polish crown, described a gathering of ecclesiastical and secular hierarchy under the name *conventus generalis*. According to him, this body deliberated for some days, then approved by acclamation Louis as Casimir's successor. No contemporary sources mention this event, though Długosz may have utilized a source not now available. He was followed by later Polish historians, such as Marcin Kromer, *Kronika Polska* (Warsaw, 1767), p. 345; and Naruszewicz, *Historya narodu polskiego*, VI, 77. There are, however, certain errors in Długosz's account. He was certainly mistaken in calling this a *conventus generalis*, or *Sejm* (the Polish equivalent of parliament or estates general), for such an institution did not develop until the fifteenth century. (Naruszewicz is careful to distinguish between this and what he calls a *sąd powszechny królewski*, or general royal council.) In addition, Długosz was probably incorrect in setting this meeting in 1339 and in attributing to it such extensive rights. The question is thoroughly discussed by Balzer, *Królestwo*, III, 87–99, who is challenging not only the fifteenth-century historian, but also his contemporary Stanisław Kętrzyński, who had discussed this same matter in his long article "Zapis Kazimierza Wielkiego dla Kazimierza Bogusławowica," *P.H.*, XIV (1912). Finally, though Długosz speaks of the designation of Louis and Casimir's meeting with him, in actuality the events of 1339 simply established the principle of Angevin succession, that is, of Charles Robert or one of his three sons.

62. The complex question of succession in general is fully discussed by Balzer, "O następstwie tronu w Polsce. Studya historyczno-prawne," *R.A.U.*, XXXVI (1897), 289–431. More specifically focused upon this period is Balzer, *Królestwo*, III, 1–142, pp. 86 ff. especially. See also Dąbrowski, "Elżbieta Łokietkówna," *R.A.U.*, LVII (1914), 362–63. The position of Casimir's sister is clearly shown in a papal letter of 1369: "utpote soror eius et sibi proximior immediate seu primo loco et Ludovicus rex . . . secundo loco." Theiner, *Mon. Hung.*, II, #171. Casimir's choice fell upon his sister rather than one of his daughters because she already had a husband and sons.

levy any new taxes upon either the nobility or the land without the permission of those concerned; and to respect all rights, privileges, and immunities of the clergy and the nobility. When these limitations had been accepted, Casimir and the nobles of Little Poland who had accompanied him formally recognized the Angevin dynasty as the source of Casimir's successor should the Piast die without heir.[63] As soon as these negotiations were finished, Casimir returned quickly to Poland to follow the progress of the legal suit being brought against the Teutonic Order.

Two important trends may be observed in Poland's dealings with its neighbors in the years 1337–39. The first, which resulted in the legal process in Warsaw, was a noticeable hardening of the Polish attitude toward the Knights. The second was the increasingly friendly ties binding Poland, Hungary, and Bohemia. This second trend was viewed with dismay by Emperor Lewis IV. He recognized the growing power and influence of the Luxemburgs in central Europe and saw that Polish and Hungarian support for them might be dangerous to his cause in the empire and elsewhere. His first move to counteract Polish influence was to strengthen the Teutonic Order. In mid-December, 1337, he granted to the Knights the whole of Lithuania, together with all other heathen lands bordering thereon.[64] Despite the fact that this territory remained yet to be conquered, such a grant was of considerable importance to the Order both for the prestige it brought and for the military opportunities it provided.

More important imperial support for the Knights came the following year when the hostility of the papacy toward the Teutonic Order had become more apparent. To reassure the Knights of imperial support and to warn them not to flag in opposition to Polish attempts to regain Pomorze, Lewis wrote to Grand Master Dietrich on July 22, 1338, that the Order was an imperial institution and that the basis of its position rested upon imperial, not papal, authority; it need obey only those decisions and commands which came from the emperor. Further, the efforts of "Casimir, who calls himself King of Poland," to regain Pomorze should not cause the Order to lose heart in its struggle with him, for the cause of the Order would be protected by the Emperor.[65] Strange advice indeed to be given to a military-religious Order, whose raison d'être was the crusade against heathens and schismatics and *propaganda fidei*!

While Lewis was giving with the right hand to the Order, his left hand was not unoccupied, for in the fall of 1338 he made an attempt to woo Casimir away from Bohemia. He tried to revive the alliance and marriage pact which the

63. The documents issued at this time appear to have perished. The negotiations are described and the agreements are detailed from the Hungarian side by Johannes de Thurócz, *Chronica Hungarorum*, in *Scriptores rerum Hungaricarum veteres ac genuini . . .*, ed. J. G. Schwandtner, 3 vols. (Vienna, 1746–48), I, 166 f.; and from the Polish side by Janko of Czarnków, *Chronicon*, pp. 638–39. See Dąbrowski, *Ostatnie lata*, pp. 96–106.

64. Ludewig, *Reliquiae*, I, 336. See also Voigt, *Geschichte Preussens*, IV, 559 n. 1.

65. *C.D.Pr.*, III, # 8.

Polish king had so unceremoniously dropped with Margrave Lewis three years before. The marriage proposed at that time was to have taken place in the fall of 1338, though in the meantime the intended bride had been promised to a member of the Luxemburg house. Pretending to have taken no note of events in the preceding three years, Lewis wrote Casimir on September 15, 1338, saying that upon the request of his son Margrave Lewis, he had empowered him and Duke Rodolf of Saxony to negotiate all details concerning the marriage, including the dowry. He requested Casimir to meet his son someplace in Brandenburg.[66]

Lewis could hardly have been more undiplomatic in this letter, for he addressed Casimir as "King of Cracow." It is not surprising that the emperor failed to achieve what he proposed. Casimir apparently never replied to the letter. Another reason for the emperor's failure is that Casimir was increasingly occupied with Polish policy toward the Teutonic Order and with exploiting the growing hostility of the papacy toward the Knights.

Pope Benedict XII had kept well informed on the status of Polish-Teutonic Order relations. He regularly received news from nuncio Galhard, and from time to time special pleaders from the kingdom and the *Ordensstaat* made their appearance in Avignon. It appears, however, that the conflict between the two after 1336 was purely verbal. Nevertheless, from Galhard's point of view, the original points at issue had not been settled, and he was resolved to pursue his policy to a conclusion successful for Poland and the papacy. By 1338 he had convinced the king to follow the same policy, and together they urged the pope to investigate the whole dispute. Before Benedict could do so with any effectiveness, he had to restore peace within Poland by ending the strife between Casimir and the bishop of Cracow. In April, 1338, he sent letters to Casimir urging him to forgive Jan Grot; to the bishop, castigating him sharply for his despicable actions against the king and queen; and to Galhard, telling him to do all in his power to reconcile the two parties.[67] Eventually an uneasy peace was established between the various parties in Poland.[68]

The reports which the pope had received induced him to undertake a further investigation of the Polish-Teutonic Order controversy. Early in 1338, he appointed a commission to investigate the situation and recommend to him what course to follow.[69] News of this act and of the investigations of the commission soon reached the Order, which was quick to deny the validity of the allegations made against it. For example, the abbot of the monastery in Oliva wrote to Benedict in May, 1338, to complain of the unjust treatment given the Order, implying that only ill-will lay behind the actions of those who leveled

66. Ludewig, *Reliquiae*, II, 293.

67. Theiner, *Mon. Pol.*, I, # 532, 533, 534.

68. See Gorzycki, "Wpływ," p. 267; Niwiński, "Biskup krakowski Jan Grotowic," pp. 72–75.

69. Theiner, *Mon. Pol.*, I, # 541.

charges against the Knights.[70] Despite this, it was the report of the papal commission which finally decided Benedict. The report substantiated in many details the complaints lodged against the Order by Galhard. As a result, Benedict resolved to follow the example of his predecessor, John XXII, and bring formal suit against the Order. On May 4, 1338, he appointed two representatives in Poland, Galhard and Peter Gervais, to act as judges.[71]

Benedict's commission to the judges rested upon three points. First, he regarded the judgment of 1321 to be still in force; second, he stated that the judges should determine whether the territories conquered by the Order had been illegally taken from Poland; third, the tribunal should consider whether the damage the Order had caused in Poland called for indemnification and, if so, in what amount. Finally, he called upon the court to inform the Knights that they had six months in which to prepare a defense and to present representatives before the tribunal with those documents and privileges which they believed to support the Order's position.

In accord with Benedict's order, Galhard and Peter formally notified the Order on October 27 that the papacy had established a tribunal to hear arguments in a legal process concerning Chełmno, Pomorze, Kujavia, Dobrzyń, and Michałowo. This process was to be held in the Mazovian city of Warsaw (chosen undoubtedly to give the appearance of neutrality, since its duke was technically independent of both Casimir and the Order[72]). The judges informed the Order of the charges to be brought against it, and commanded it to appear before them on February 4, 1339, prepared to defend itself.[73] Then on November 15 Galhard published a general letter to all the churches in Poland and Pomorze which set forth the charges to be leveled against the Order and which called upon all who might have evidence to give to come forward.[74] This was followed by three other letters of similar nature directed to the general public.[75]

In the meantime the Poles had not been idle. Soon after news first arrived from Avignon of the process, Polish prosecutors were appointed to present the Polish case against the Order in Warsaw. Those who were chosen, Barthold of Racibórz, Albert of Bochnia, and Archdeacon Jarosław Bogoria of Cracow,[76]

70. Partially printed by Voigt, *Geschichte Preussens*, IV, 561 n. 2.

71. Theiner, *Mon. Pol.*, I, # 542.

72. Halecki, "Casimir the Great," p. 170, and Kaczmarczyk, *Kazimierz Wielki*, p. 69 (repeated in *Polska czasów Kazimierza*, p. 35), have both remarked that Warsaw makes its first historical appearance in this process. This is not strictly true, however, for Warsaw is mentioned in a document from 1321. See *Kodeks dyplomatyczny księstwa mazowieckiego*, ed. T. Lubomirski (Warsaw, 1863), p. 43.

73. *Lites*, I, 71–73.

74. Ibid., 73–77.

75. Ibid., 77–82, dated November 28, 29, and December 20.

76. Barthold of Racibórz is probably identical with the Barthold who some years earlier had

were appointed by Casimir. The Order had also begun preparations for the process. In early December Grand Master Dietrich went to Toruń and empowered representatives to guard the interests of the Order in Warsaw.[77] They were instructed not to defend the Order in any way against the Polish charges. Rather, following the example of his predecessor nineteen years before, Dietrich had resolved merely to present passive resistance by lodging objections and appeals through his representatives.

When the deadline set by Galhard arrived, everyone concerned gathered in the house of *wójt* Bartholomew of Warsaw. The surroundings were modest, for Warsaw was not yet the elegantly sumptuous baroque city of the seventeenth and eighteenth centuries. Now it was merely a village without municipal rights, though the settlement there did have a defensive wall.[78] It was here that the Polish prosecutors formally presented their demands to the tribunal. They gave a short recapitulation of the events which had brought about the conflict between Poland and the Teutonic Order, then declared that the Knights were illegally holding the territories of Pomorze, Chełmno, Kujavia, Dobrzyń, and Michałowo. They reaffirmed the validity of the Inowrocław decision of 1321 and demanded that the members of the Order be excommunicated, be forced to return the aforementioned territories to Poland, and be sentenced to pay Casimir an indemnification of 149,000 Polish marks.[79] The immediate reaction of the Order was to protest the proceeding and lodge a formal appeal with the two judges. The Knights' representative stated that in doing so he was in no way recognizing the legality of Galhard and Peter as judges over the Order. He regarded them rather as reasonable men before whom he protested the erection of the tribunal and the convocation of the proceeding itself. In the first place, Casimir had no right to be represented before such a body because he had been excommunicated for imprisoning a cleric.[80] Second, despite a solemn oath to keep the peace, he had invaded Chełmno with his father in 1329 while the Order was fulfilling its mission by crusading in Lithuania with King John of Bohemia. Thus he was guilty of breaking an oath and should be regarded as untrustworthy. Third, he and his father had allied themselves with heathens

been involved in certain Silesian affairs; see Maleczyński, *Dzieje Wrocławia do roku 1526*, p. 114, and *Historia Śląska*, I, pt. i, 543. Albert of Bochnia had received some higher education, earning the degree *magister in artibus*; see S. Fischer, *Kazimierz Wielki i jego stosunek do Bochni i Bochen-szczyzny* (Bochnia, 1934). Archdeacon Jarosław later became archbishop of Gniezno and was one of Casimir's closest advisors; see *Pol. Słow. Biog.*, XI, 1–3.

77. *Lites*, I, 85–87; Dogiel, *Codex*, IV, 60–61. See also Voigt, *Geschichte Preussens*, IV, 566, n. 2.

78. Some interesting comments about Warsaw's regional significance and status of development are made in Stanisław Pazyra, *Geneza i rozwój miast mazowieckich* (Warsaw, 1959), pp. 60–65.

79. *Lites*, I, 82–85.

80. This was a reference to Casimir's recent bitter conflict with Bishop Jan Grot. See Niwiński, "Biskup krakowski Jan Grotowic," pp. 72–75.

(that is, Lithuanians) against Christians (that is, the Teutonic Order), and should further be regarded as enemies of civilization. Fourth, despite his oaths to abide by the arbitration of Kings John and Charles Robert at Wyszegrad, Casimir had refused to do so and continued to be hostile toward the Order. Finally, if the facts had been presented to the Holy Father in Avignon in this light, the present proceeding would never have been initiated. Thus the Order must refuse to recognize the jurisdiction of the court and whatever decision it might hand down.[81]

In reply the Polish prosecutors stated that if Casimir were indeed excommunicated, the judges as papal representatives had the power to revoke that sentence, which they had in fact done in summoning the representatives of the king before them. As to the second charge, it was commonly known that Casimir and his father had had great provocation for their invasion. Thus, there was no reason to impugn the integrity of the court. The judges agreed with the Polish prosecutors, for they rejected the appeal of the Order, saying it was frivolous and thoughtless.[82] Such a reproach induced the Order's representative to direct a formal appeal to the pope the next day (February 6), whereupon he and his colleagues left Warsaw and returned to Toruń.[83] For the remainder of the process, they seldom returned to Warsaw, preferring to ignore the events there.

The decision of the Order not to attend the process did not bring it to a close. Instead it simply allowed the Polish prosecutors a free hand in the presentation of their case. Their first step was to present thirty articles charging the Order with a variety of misdeeds.[84] Taken together they show the comprehensive nature of the Polish case and the pains which the prosecutors had taken in its preparation. The first three articles concerned the territory of Chełmno. There it was asserted that Chełmno, together with all its districts and cities, including Toruń, had since antiquity belonged to the kingdom of Poland and that its princes held the territory in the name of the king of Poland. Further, the prosecutors intended to prove that the unique tax, Peter's Pence, was collected only in Poland for payment to the Holy See; that Peter's Pence had been collected in Chełmno before the Order had prevented this; and that therefore Chełmno in this sense also was a part of the kingdom. The next five articles were devoted to the question of Pomorze. First it was asserted that Pomorze and all of its territories and districts were located within the *regnum Poloniae* and had been a part of this *regnum* from antiquity. Next the prosecutors claimed that the whole duchy was ecclesiastically subject to the episcopal dioceses of Gniezno and Kujavia, which were both within the kingdom and part of the archiepiscopal

81. *Lites*, I, 89-92; *C.D.Pr.*, III, # 15.
82. *Lites*, I, 92-93.
83. Ibid., 99-101.
84. Ibid., 94-98.

province of Gniezno. In article six the claim was made that former King Władysław ruled Pomorze as a part of the kingdom (that is, Pomorze had a constitutional relationship to the kingdom, not simply an incidental one because both were ruled by the same person). It was next asserted that the order, "by violence and with a strong army divided into companies which massacred many soldiers and men," had conquered Pomorze from Łokietek, causing more than 45,000 Polish marks damage. The last article concerning Pomorze referred to the legal processes of 1320–21, and asserted that its sentence was still valid. Articles nine through eleven concerned Kujavia. In the first of these the prosecutors claimed that Kujavia, together with its cities, castles, and villages was a part of the kingdom of Poland and that Łokietek ruled it as a part of that kingdom. Next they charged that the Knights in the year 1332 had conquered Kujavia and were continuing to occupy it; and that this conquest and occupation had caused more than 15,000 marks damage. The next four articles of complaint referred to the region of Dobrzyń. Here Barthold and his associates indicated that Dobrzyń had been a part of the kingdom of Poland, that Łokietek had ruled it as a part of this kingdom, that the Knights in 1329 had conquered and occupied Dobrzyń illegally, in the process causing more than 7,500 marks damage. The last area dealt with in these articles was the little region of Michałowo, lying on the Drwęca river. Number sixteen claimed Michałowo was a part of the kingdom, number seventeen that it had been mortgaged to the Knights thirty years before, and number eighteen that the income in these thirty years had been 1,200 Polish marks—an amount which far exceeded the amount of the mortgage—and that therefore the region should be returned to Poland. The next eleven articles, nineteen through twenty-nine, detailed the devastation wrought in Poland by the Order, chiefly in the disastrous campaigns of 1331. In general these charges focused upon three areas: the burning and destruction of churches, monasteries, and residences; casualties caused by the Knights; and the "appropriation" of animals and other moveable goods. For all these things the prosecutors demanded in article thirty an indemnification of 115,000 Polish marks. Together with other claims presented, the total damages and losses for which restitution was demanded reached the sum of 194,500 silver Polish marks. (This was an amount about double the income of the Polish crown in most years.)

The deliberations of the process were carried out in the following manner. The Polish prosecutors, to prove the validity of the charges outlined above, called a total of 126 witnesses to testify. This was done on twenty-three different occasions between February 4 and April 30 in a variety of places. Depositions were taken in Warsaw, Łęczyca, Uniejów, Kalisz, Pyzdry, Gniezno, Sieradz, and Cracow.[85] Each of the witnesses was first asked his name and his station in life, then whether he needed the articles of complaint read to him. When this

85. Ibid., 98–122.

had been done, each individual gave testimony on those points about which he was qualified to speak. Thus in addition to the historical evidence presented, the record of this testimony provides an invaluable insight into the social makeup of Casimir's Poland.[86] The witnesses came from all walks of life. Some were relatives of the king; others, higher or lower clergy. Some were citizens of Polish towns and villages; others, merchants from Cracow. Many were former members of the Polish army. Not all were Poles. Some of the Cracow merchants may have been German, and some of the witnesses had been members of the army of the Order.[87]

The mechanics of taking testimony proved to require much more time for the process than had previously been envisioned. This was partially the result of the great number of witnesses, but was due also to the difficulty of obtaining testimony.[88] The process was further delayed in March when the tribunal recessed, and Galhard and Peter traveled to Toruń at Casimir's request.[89] There they met with Grand Master Dietrich and suggested to him that Casimir would be willing to conclude peace with the Order for a payment of 14,000 florins indemnification. Since he considered this proposal too vague, and because he still hoped for some result from the Order's appeal to Avignon, Dietrich declared that such an arrangement was unacceptable. He would, nevertheless, continue to maintain the peace. He also repeated his objection to the process in Warsaw, saying that if a tribunal composed of men of scrupulous fairness and honesty were to hand down a decision calling for the Order to pay an indemnification, then he would abide by that decision. At the present time, however, he could see no benefit to further discussions. Rebuffed, the judges returned to Warsaw to continue the process.

As a result of all these factors, the proposed day of judgment was postponed until March 2, then rescheduled for March 30, then again postponed until May 11.[90] Further delays prevented the publishing of the decision until late

---

86. See the use made of this data by Marian Łodyński, "Regnum Poloniae w opinii publicznej XIV wieku," *K.H.*, XXVIII (1914), 41–43.

87. The merchants are recorded in *Lites*, I, 384 ff.; former members of the Order's army in *Lites*, I, 253, wit. 32; 274, wit. 41; 304, wit. 51. It is a common feature of German historiography to state that all the witnesses were Poles and therefore their testimony was one-sided and unreliable. See, for example, Tumler, *Der Deutsche Orden*, p. 255 n. 24. A slightly different position is taken by Ziekursch, *Der Prozess*, p. 153, who argues only that all the witnesses were partial to the Polish point of view. This is closer to the truth. But she also reaches essentially the same conclusions as outlined above. From another point of view, it is hardly necessary to condemn the Polish prosecutors for summoning only those witnesses who could give testimony to support their claims. Any good lawyer would do the same. The Order had the opportunity to balance the record, but chose not to do so.

88. For example, Galhard was forced to issue several citations to the merchants of Cracow before they would appear before the tribunal. See *Lites*, I, 112–13.

89. *C.D.Pr.*, II, #16: "nuncios speciales sanctissimi principis domini Kazimiri Regis Polonie."

90. *Lites*, I, 99, 114.

September. In the meantime the evidence given by the witnesses was collected. In general this tended to confirm the charges which the prosecutors had levied against the Order.[91] Supplementary contemporary evidence which has been assembled by Irene Ziekursch, who has analyzed both the testimony and the witnesses more thoroughly than any other non-Polish scholar, modifies some of the conclusions which might be reached on the basis of the transcript of the testimony alone.[92] This supplementary evidence was not, however, the basis upon which the judges made their decisions. Considered in this light, the judgment given appears reasonable and well founded (if wholly unrelated to the political realities of the day), and those historians who have criticized the conclusions reached by Galhard and Peter[93] fail to realize that the fact that supplementary evidence was not presented was the responsibility of the Order, not the Polish prosecutors or the judges.

The most difficult point to establish on the basis of the testimony was whether or not the damage which the Order had done did in fact amount to the sum demanded by the Polish prosecutors. Thus, although testimony was completed by late spring, the judges were unable to reach a conclusion which they felt was justified, and the process was prolonged several times until a decision was reached. Finally, in order to resolve the problem, Casimir himself issued a sworn affidavit on September 9 to the effect that the sum demanded indeed corresponded to the actual damage suffered.[94] Following this, the judges prepared their decision.

The church of St. John the Baptist in Warsaw was the site of the publication of the sentence by the judges on September 15.[95] Galhard and Peter, after one final attempt to summon the Order to Warsaw,[96] judged the Knights guilty of all the charges leveled against them, and laid the Order under papal ban, to be removed only if the Order made restitution for the ecclesiastical property which it had destroyed. The Order was also sentenced to return Pomorze, Chełmno, Kujavia, Dobrzyń, and Michałowo to Poland, to pay an indemnification of 194,500 silver marks to the Polish crown, and to reimburse the judges for

91. See Łodyński, "Regnum Poloniae," pp. 43–48.

92. See Ziekursch, *Der Prozess*, pp. 153–54. Her evidence does not modify these conclusions as much as she believes, however; see below, note 97.

93. See, for a sampling, Voigt, *Geschichte Preussens*, IV, 570–71; Heinrich von Treitschke, *Das Deutsche Ordensland Preussen* (reprinted, Göttingen, 1955), p. 34; Erich Sandow, *Die Polnisch-pommerellische Grenze, 1309–1454 (Beihefte zum Jahrbuch der Albertus-Universität, Königsberg, Pr., VI)* (Kitzingen/Main, 1954), pp. 23–24; Theodore Schiemann, *Russland, Polen und Livland bis ins 17. Jahrhundert*, 2 vols. (Berlin, 1886–87), I, 490; Tumler, *Der Deutsche Orden*, p. 255 n. 24; Bruno Schumacher, *Geschichte Ost- und Westpreussen* (Königsberg, 1937), p. 49.

94. *Lites*, I, 132.

95. Caro, *Geschichte Polens*, II, 213, incorrectly gives the date as September 25. The date of September 16 given by Naruszewicz, *Historya narodu polskiego*, VI, 88, apparently rests upon an older manuscript tradition.

96. *Lites*, I, 130.

the costs of the process in the amount of 1,600 marks.[97] The process had lasted 224 days, during which the judges had been maintained by Casimir.[98] The results of the process appeared to mark the total success of the policy which Galhard had advocated and in which Casimir had acquiesced. Such was not to be the case, however; for just as in the 1321 case there was no power to enforce the judgment.

Immediately following the pronouncement of the sentence, the Order issued another appeal to Benedict, claiming again that the tribunal had no jurisdiction in this matter and refusing to recognize the decision.[99] This appeal and the one lodged by the Order on February 5 apparently had some effect upon the pope, for he refused to ratify the Warsaw sentence immediately. He slowly realized the significance of what had been demanded of the Order, for the loss of Pomorze and Chełmno would virtually destroy the power and prestige of the Knights. This consideration became increasingly important in the months following the process, for the eastern gates of Christendom were again attacked by the Tatars. As early as 1337 they had attacked Lublin in eastern Poland, and under their vigorous khan they were enough of a threat to arouse the attention of western Europe.[100]

97. The text of this judgment has been printed several times. See *Lites*, I, 137 ff.; Dogiel, *Codex*, IV, 63; Długosz, *Historia*, III, 181–92. There is no adequate extended secondary treatment of the proceeding. Ziekursch, *Der Prozess*, fails to fill this gap on at least three counts. She limits herself to the modest, though important, task of analysis of the witnesses and their testimony, and draws only a few general conclusions about the significance of her findings. In addition, however, her study is based upon an edition of the manuscripts which is now outdated. The manuscript material upon which our knowledge of the processes of the fourteenth and fifteenth centuries against the Knights was gathered by Jan Długosz late in the fifteenth century. See Kaczmarczyk, *Polska czasów Kazimierza*, p. 36: "With his own hand he copied out the acts from Warsaw." But the printed version of the nineteenth century must now be supplemented by new finds. See, on this question, Helena Chłopocka, "Dotychczasowe edycje Lites ac res gestae w świetle krytyki," *Studia Źródłoznawcze*, X (1965), 109–15, and her important study *Procesy Polski z Zakonem krzyżackim w XIV wieku* (Poznań, 1967). The most fundamental weakness of Ziekursch's study is both her lack of scholarly balance ("Der Deutsche Orden, und damit das Deutschtum überhaupt, hatten und haben rechtmässige Ansprüche auf das Kulmerland, Pommerellen und auf das Michelauerland," p. 154) and her misunderstanding of Polish constitutional history and development. This latter is particularly true in her treatment of the question of whether Pomorze was part of the *regnum Poloniae*. Because Łokietek had not been king when he ruled there, she concludes (pp. 76–77) that it was neither true Polish territory nor part of the *regnum*. To correct this view, see Balzer, *Królestwo*, III, 150–58.

98. This is the number of days from February 4 to September 15. In a document in Theiner, *Mon. Hung.*, I, # 957, however, Peter says the process lasted 266 days, during which he was the guest of Casimir.

99. *Lites*, I, 141.

100. The earlier attack is recorded by *Rocznik świętokrzyski*, in *M.P.H.*, III, 78. Because the chronology of this chronicle is so frequently incorrect, some historians have suggested that this date also is incorrect. Most, however, have accepted it as valid. See Halecki, "Kazimierz Wielki," p. 325; Berthold Spuler, *Die Goldene Horde. Die Mongolen in Russland, 1223–1502* (Leipzig, 1943), pp. 97 f. Compare, however, Paszkiewicz, "Sprawa najazdu tatarskiego na Lublin w roku 1337," *Teka Zamojskiego* (1920), pp. 158 ff. Western European echoes of Tatar expansion

The threat from the Tatars was not the only reason why Benedict hesitated to confirm the Warsaw sentence. The Order kept permanent representatives at Avignon to protect its interests. This lobby continually protested the actions of the process, and this influenced Benedict in 1340 to reexamine the whole question of Polish-Teutonic Order conflict. He appointed a new commission of cardinals for this purpose, and when news of this decision reached Prussia the bishops of Chełmno, Marienwerder, and Sambien wrote to Benedict to strengthen the cause of the Knights. They first apologized because the grand master had not come personally to Avignon to represent the Order, but he was busy defending Christendom from the heathen Tatars; thus it was all the more to be regretted that certain people still were trying to create division between Poland, also threatened by the Tatars, and the Order by insisting on confirmation of the Warsaw process and nullification of the reasonable decisions made at Wyszegrad in 1335. Therefore, the newly appointed commission should disregard the sentence of the Warsaw tribunal, for the arbitration of Kings John and Charles Robert was the proper basis upon which a lasting peace between Poland and the Order might be built.[101]

This remarkable petition arrived while the cardinals were deliberating the merits of both sides of the question. By summer, 1341, Benedict had recognized that it would be impossible for the papacy to support fully the sentence handed down by its own judges in Warsaw, so on June 22, 1341, he wrote to the bishops of Meissen, Chełmno, and Cracow requesting them to exhort the Order to return Kujavia and Dobrzyń to Poland and to pay Casimir an indemnification. As far as Chełmno, Pomorze, and Michałowo were concerned, a more careful examination was being made to determine what their status should be.[102] Within a month this decision had been made, for on July 18 Benedict wrote to Casimir saying that there were important grounds upon which to doubt the validity of the Warsaw decision. There appeared to have been too much partisan spirit shown in the process, and therefore he must refuse to grant papal ratification. Instead he urged Casimir to be content with some kind of compromise agreement with the Order and exhorted him to reach a final settlement as soon as possible.[103]

Once he had been persuaded to follow the policy of Galhard, Casimir had held hopes of actually accomplishing by diplomatic means what his father's wars had been unable to do. The process of 1339 had encouraged him in this, but in the following two years his hopes had waned. By mid-1341, the realities

are reflected in Johannes Vitoduranus, *Chronicon a Friderico II Imperatore ad annum 1348 procedens*, in J. G. Eccardus, ed., *Corpus Historicum Medii Aevi . . .*, 2 vols. (Leipzig, 1723), I, 1860–62.

101. *C.D.Pr.*, III, # 21. See also Voigt, *Geschichte Preussens*, IV, 574–76.

102. *Urkundenbuch des Bistums Culm*, edited by K. P. Wölky, 2 vols. (Gdańsk, 1884–87), I, # 214.

103. Theiner, *Mon. Pol*, I, # 568.

of papal policy had become apparent, and the king was forced to reexamine his goals and tactics. He soon recognized that his original pacific policy had been correct, and he became more amenable to a compromise with the Order. The first attempt to mediate such a compromise was made by Margrave Charles of Moravia.

Casimir had spent part of the summer of 1341 in Prague as a guest of the Luxemburgers. When Casimir returned to Poland in the fall, Charles accompanied him, having suggested himself as a mediator between Poland and the Order. This was gladly accepted by Casimir, so in early October Charles travelled on to Toruń. He was accompanied there by several of Casimir's civil officials and by Archbishop Jan Janisław of Gniezno. The party was greeted in Toruń by Grand Master Dietrich, who despite old age and ill-health, had travelled from Małbork. He was accompanied by a personal representative of King Charles Robert of Hungary.[104] Negotiations were immediately begun upon the basis suggested by Benedict in his July letter to Casimir, and so much progress was made that an agreement seemed imminent.

Suddenly the picture changed. After retiring on October 5, Charles was unexpectedly awakened by comture Ludolf König, who informed him that Grand Master Dietrich had taken ill and was near death. He wished, however, to speak to Charles. The young margrave hurried to his host's bedside and the two talked briefly about the Order's relations with Poland. Completely exhausted, Dietrich soon fell asleep and died shortly thereafter.[105] The death of Dietrich made impossible for the moment any renewal of negotiations over Polish-Teutonic Order relations, for the election of a successor was delayed for several months. In the meantime another stumbling block to peace between the Order and Poland had been discovered.

In 1339, when the Angevins had been granted the expectancy to the Polish crown, they had also agreed to recover Pomorze from the Knights. This stipulation had in succeeding months become common knowledge, and the Order demanded, before agreeing to any peace with Poland, that Casimir obtain a renunciation of this claim from Charles Robert and his heirs. Casimir was unable to do this, however, and negotiations were not resumed by the Order.[106] Thus at the end of 1341, despite the Congress of Wyszegrad, the process at Warsaw, and numerous other negotiations, there still existed between Poland and the Order, in effect, the *status quo post coronationem.* The only hopeful sign which pointed to a possible settlement was that both sides now seemed more conciliatory and willing to work out a compromise. Before discussing this final

104. *SS. rer. Pr.,* II, 498. See also Voigt, *Geschichte Preussens,* IV, 583 n. 2; and Dąbrowski, *Ostatnie lata,* p. 114.

105. This narrative is based upon Wigand of Marburg, *Chronica,* p. 498, and *Chronica Olivensis,* p. 337. For the date of death, see Voigt, *Geschichte Preussens,* IV, 584, n. 2.

106. Dąbrowski, *Ostatnie lata,* pp. 102–3; and Caro, *Geschichte Polens,* II, 239, and note 2.

settlement, it is necessary to examine the fluctuations in Casimir's relations with his other western neighbors in the years 1339–43.

Two personal losses in 1339–40 played an important role in these relations. In May, 1339, Casimir's wife of fourteen years died after a lingering illness. Though Casimir was hardly a model of conjugal fidelity, he had been very close to Anna and apparently loved her deeply. Without her, the king's life was far less pleasant. Casimir was equally shaken the following year when his mother died peacefully in the nunnery of St. Clare in Stary Sącz. Despite the sharp contrast between the personalities of his gay, lively wife and his pious, ascetic mother, the loss of the latter was painful. To fill his time and distract his attention from personal matters, the king busied himself in the details of a visit to Cracow by Charles of Moravia in May, 1340. Casimir was flattered by the presence of his contemporary, and the friendship between the two young rulers was strengthened.

The margrave's visit to Cracow was not wholly of a social nature; there were also important dynastic considerations involved. The possibility, now greatly increased since the death of Anna, that Poland and Hungary would be united under one ruler dismayed Charles, for such an eventuality would create a central European power able to threaten the Luxemburgers' attempts to consolidate and expand their holdings; this would be especially true in regard to Silesia. Charles wished to persuade Casimir to remarry in the hope that a new union would produce an heir. Such a possibility was certainly not displeasing to Casimir, but Charles had further plans. He wished Casimir to marry his sister, Margaretha, who had also been recently widowed. This might prevent an Angevin ascendancy, and would at the least assure the continuance of Polish-Bohemian friendship.[107] In pursuing his plan, Charles utilized all the considerable cleverness he possessed to win Casimir to a marriage agreement. His success was so complete that the Piast reportedly fell in love with Margaretha before he saw her.[108] (Unfortunately her feeling was not mutual, and John and Charles had to overcome her active opposition before she agreed to marry Casimir.) Fully convinced of the propriety of remarriage and the advisability of a union with the Luxemburgers, Casimir agreed to come to Prague in July of the following year for the ceremony.

The preparations for the forthcoming wedding in the Bohemian capital foreshadowed those improvements which Charles later undertook as emperor

107. Suggested by Franz Palacky, *Geschichte von Böhmen*, 5 vols. in 10 (Prague, 1836–67), II, pt. ii, 321; clearly stated by Werunsky, *Karl IV*, I, 263, and Šusta, *Karel IV*, p. 332. See also Kaczmarczyk, *Kazimierz Wielki*, pp. 85–86, who suggests Charles's interests were related more closely to the rise of Wittelsbach influence and that Casimir was interested in gaining further support against the Order.

108. These and following details from Matthias Nuewenburgensis, *Chronica 1272–1350*, in *Font. rer. Ger.*, IV, 213. See also the sources cited in Caro, *Geschichte Polens*, II, 233 n. 1. Werunsky, *Karl IV*, I, 264, describes Casimir at this point as "der liebesbedürftige," perhaps an exaggeration.

to make Prague the most beautiful city of central Europe. Buildings were cleaned, rebuilt, and gaily decorated, and the populace was given the responsibility of cleaning the streets. By June, 1341, everything was in readiness. Casimir arrived in Prague accompanied by a large retinue, only to find his intended bride seriously ill. Despite all the efforts of the doctors, she grew rapidly worse; on July 11 she died.[109]

With Margaretha's death there was the possibility that all Charles's maneuverings would have been in vain. To prevent this, the margrave took advantage of Casimir's unsettled state to make new arrangements. On the day that the intended bride was buried, Casimir was persuaded to sign an alliance with Kings John and Charles in the presence of the Bishop of Olomouc and Dukes Bolesław of Legnica, Bolko of Świdnica, and Nicholas of Opawa-Racibórz. He promised to honor and love John as a father and Charles as a brother and to support them against all enemies, except Duke Bolko and King Charles Robert.[110] In his grief he was persuaded to go even further, for he promised Charles that he would always seek advice from him and not remarry without his consent.[111] After these events Casimir did not immediately return to Poland. He remained in Prague consulting with Charles about an acceptable bride for himself. Finally a decision was reached to request the hand of Adelheid of Hesse, and a deputation was sent to her father to ask his consent. Henry of Hesse was a minor princeling of the empire and such a request was unexpected. He agreed to the marriage and announced he would accompany his daughter to Poznań for the wedding.[112] This marriage was in no way to the political advantage or disadvantage of Casimir, and it is easy to see Charles as the driving force in it, since he hoped to be able to retain, because of the weakness of Duke Henry, considerable influence in Polish affairs.

Late in September the two rulers travelled from Prague to Poznań, where in the first days of October Casimir was married to Adelheid by Archbishop Jan Janisław, and the bride was crowned queen of Poland. Duke Henry promised his daughter a modest dowry which he was to pay within the year, while Casimir presented his wife with sumptuous gold and silver gifts and assigned her the income from several royal properties in Sandomir. At the same time the duke and the king signed a defensive alliance in which Casimir promised to protect his new father-in-law against all enemies, except the king of Hungary and Duke Bolko of Świdnica.[113] Following the marriage, Margrave

109. The sources for Casimir's stay in Prague are particularly full. See Franciscus Pragensis, *Chronica Pragensis 1125–1353,* in *Font. rer. Aust.,* VIII, 566; Beneš Krabice z Weitmil, *Chronicon Ecclesiae Pragensis, 1283–1374,* in *SS. rer. Boh.,* II, 278; Matthias Nuewenburgensis, *Chronica,* p. 213.

110. Dogiel, *Codex,* I, 4; Ludewig, *Reliquiae,* V, 504; *C.D.Mor.,* VII, # 333, 334.

111. *C.D.Mor.,* VII, # 374.

112. See Johannes Victoriensis, *Chronicon Carinthiue 1211–1343,* in *SS. rer. Aust.,* I, 960.

113. *C.D.Pol.,* I, 190, for the dowry; and the sources cited in Caro, *Geschichte Polens,* II, 234 n. 3, for Casimir's agreement.

Charles left Poznań immediately for his unsuccessful negotiations with the Teutonic Order in Toruń.

Casimir's second wife is a shadowy figure. Still in her teens when she married the king, she more closely resembled the late queen mother than she did her predecessor. She was withdrawn and aloof and did not well suit the more lively nature of her husband. Shortly after her marriage, Casimir dispatched her to a distant castle and never thereafter visited her. She spent her married life alone and unloved, though she bore her exile with patience and fortitude.[114] The heir for which Casimir hoped, therefore, did not issue from this marriage.

The events of 1341 marked the zenith of Polish-Bohemian relations in this period. Following Casimir's marriage and Charles's return to Prague, the friendship between the two states and dynasties began to cool, and eventually points of contention arose which made enemies of the two. One of the most important points of controversy was the position of Duke Bolko of Świdnica. On two occasions (noted above) Casimir had exempted him from the list of those against whom he would defend first King John and later Duke Henry. The political reality which lay behind these actions was that Bolko was one of the last independent Piast princes of Silesia. He was generally hostile to John, who was still attempting to consolidate and centralize his control over Silesia, and frequently sympathetic to Casimir, who was his cousin.[115] Thus through Bolko, Poland still retained a toehold in Silesia. It soon became evident that Casimir hoped he might expand this.

Another problem between the two states was the matter of borrowed money. When Charles was designated by his father as sole administrator in February, 1342, he had promised to pay John a rent from the kingdom amounting to 5,000 silver marks for two years. This sum exceeded his resources, and Charles was forced to seek additional sources of income. He ultimately resorted to borrowing money from Casimir. Such an arrangement frequently provides grounds for misunderstanding and bad feeling, and this proved to be the case in this instance, for Charles frequently was delinquent in his repayments.[116]

Casimir's interference in Silesian affairs also created resentment between the two countries. While Casimir was in Prague in 1341, he had become involved in the financial dealings of Duke Bolesław of Brześć. Bolesław had mortgaged some of his holdings to Duke Casimir of Cieszyń, but found himself unable to

114. These and other details are reflected in a papal letter to Casimir in 1353. See Theiner, *Mon. Pol.*, I, # 723. Adelheid was finally moved to protest when her own situation worsened and when Casimir's behavior overstepped the bounds of good taste and legality. See below, chap. 8.

115. See the comments of Dąbrowski, "Dzieje polityczne," p. 446. An older and a more recent treatment of the career of Bolko may be compared in Erich Gospos, *Die Politik Bolkos II von Schweidnitz-Jauer 1326–1368* (Halle, 1910); Krystyna Pieradzka, "Bolko II Świdnicki na Łużycach," *Sobótka*, II (1947), 93–109.

116. See Werunsky, *Karl IV*, I, 297; Šusta, *Karel IV*, pp. 387–88; Caro, *Geschichte Polens*, II, 240.

repay the money which he had received. In a series of negotiations in Prague, Poznań, and Cracow, King Casimir agreed to buy up the mortgage. Then in Cracow, Casimir finally purchased proprietary rights to the cities of Namysłów, Kluczborek, Byczyna, and Wołczyń from Bolesław for 3,000 groschen. Since Bolesław owed allegiance to the Bohemian crown, these lands technically could not be alienated to Casimir. When the Bohemians objected to these dealings, Casimir agreed to return the lands if his money was returned.[117] The extremely confused nature of these dealings enabled Casimir in later years to push his claims to these cities. As it was, the king's involvement in Silesian affairs exacerbated his steadily deteriorating relations with the Luxemburgers.

Of all the points at issue between Bohemia and Poland, none was more troublesome than the question of Wrocław. There, in the years before 1341, increasingly dramatic confrontations took place between Bishop Nanker and nuncio Galhard on the one hand and the substantial German element of the city and King John on the other.[118] The specific issues were the matter of Peter's Pence and the ecclesiastical fortress of Milicz, but these were fought out against the background of Wrocław's divided allegiance: political subjection to Bohemia and ecclesiastical subordination to Gniezno. The payment of the special tax was deeply resented by many but, by dint of zealous prosecution of papal prerogatives, Nanker and Galhard maintained its collection.[119] The battle was clearly joined in 1339 when John occupied the fortress of Milicz. Nanker's response was to excommunicate him and his adherents in Wrocław and lay the diocese under interdict.[120]

Thus affairs stood on April 10, 1341, when Bishop Nanker died. In his place the cathedral chapter in Wrocław elected Canon Přeslav of Pohořelce, a young Czech nobleman who had studied in Bologna. He was, not surprisingly, sympathetic and even friendly to King John and Margrave Charles, and they were pleased with his election. When he petitioned his immediate ecclesiastical superior, the archbishop of Gniezno, for confirmation, however, he was refused, because Casimir opposed the election of a non-Polish bishop for Wrocław.[121] With this Přeslav turned to Avignon for support, and despite the protests of

117. Grünhagen and Markgraf, *Lehns- und Besitzurkunden*, I, 314–16, 316–18; II, 643. See also the detailed treatment in Dąbrowski, "Dzieje polityczne," pp. 446–47.

118. The treatment of this issue in the *Geschichte Schlesiens*, vol. I: *von der Urzeit bis zum Jahre 1526*, published by the Historische Kommission für Schlesien, ed. Hermann Aubin et al., 3d ed. (Stuttgart, 1961), p. 213, portrays Galhard as an external interference in what had been an essential harmony between King John and Bishop Nanker. In reality, Nanker had long been an opponent of the king. See Grünhagen, "König Johann von Böhmen und Bischof Nanker von Breslau," *Sitzungsberichte der Philosophische-Hist. Classe der Kaiserliche Akademie der Wissenschaften* (Vienna), XLVII, pt. vii (1864), 35 ff. An extended treatment of the whole of Nanker's career may be found in Tadeusz Silnicki, *Biskup Nanker* (Warsaw, 1953).

119. See *Historia Śląska*, I, pt. i, 566–67.

120. See *Chronica principum Poloniae*, in *M.P.H.*, III, 522.

121. "Sed impeditus est per regem Polonie Kazimirum." *M.P.H.*, III, 523.

nuncio Galhard, Benedict XII confirmed him as bishop of Wrocław on January 28, 1342.[122]

Immediately following this, Charles took steps to bring about an understanding with the new bishop. He arranged a meeting in the Silesian town of Nysa late in April, 1342, where preliminary agreements were made. The two then returned to Wrocław, and on May 6 Přeslav informed the cathedral chapter that the bishop had been reconciled with the Bohemian crown through the efforts of Charles. He then lifted the excommunication and interdict which Nanker had imposed.[123] Later negotiations resulted in the signing of a formal treaty on July 1 in which Přeslav recognized the king of Bohemia as the legal successor to Duke Henry VI of Wrocław as the patron and protector of the bishopric. He further promised to give no aid or assistance to any enemy of either John or Charles, agreeing finally to use all ecclesiastical means at his disposal to insure that those Silesian princes who had recognized the suzerainty of the Bohemian crown would remain true to their oaths. In return, the same day Charles confirmed all the rights, privileges, and immunities granted by the several Silesian princes to the secular and regular clergy of the diocese and chapter of Wrocław. He promised further to protect them against all who had recognized Bohemian suzerainty in Silesia, and finally bound himself not to levy any new taxes upon the clergy.[124]

The real point of controversy between John and Nanker had been Milicz, and this problem had not been touched by any of the formal agreements between Charles and Přeslav. It is obvious that it had been discussed, however, for on November 13, Charles removed the Bohemian garrison and confirmed the diocese of Wrocław in its possession of the fortress, promising not to interfere in any way with the administration of it.[125] He felt justified in doing this because so long as Milicz was in the possession of a bishop friendly to the Luxemburgers, there was little danger it would be alienated to the king of Poland or be utilized in any way which might prove harmful to Bohemian power in Silesia. This was an important setback for Casimir, for even though he had formally renounced all claim to Silesia, he still had an interest there. Charles's dealings with the new bishop had now greatly decreased Polish influence in Wrocław and in all of Silesia. Casimir soon sought to reverse this trend by more direct means.

With the cooling of Polish-Bohemian relations, Casimir recognized that his policy of attempting to break the southern half of the Luxemburg-Teutonic Order pincer had, despite some temporary success, ultimately proved unfruitful.

122. Theiner, *Mon. Pol.*, I, # 571.

123. *Chronica principum Poloniae*, pp. 526–27.

124. *C.D.Mor.*, VII, # 424; and 423 and 425 respectively. One of the privileges which was confirmed was the right of collecting Peter's Pence.

125. *C.D.Mor.*, VII, # 306, p. 879.

Thus he turned elsewhere to find defensive strength against the Knights. He directed his attention to Pomorze-Zachodnie, and revived an interest which had first been aroused in 1337 while negotiating with King John in Poznań.[126] In Pomorze-Zachodnie a relatively strong principality had arisen under the leadership of Bogusław V of Pomorze-Wołogoszcz.[127] Casimir recognized that the strategic position of this principality, lying athwart the Oder to the west of the *Ordensstaat*, enabled Bogusław to control one of the major access routes from the empire to Prussia. Moreover, Bogusław was sympathetic toward Casimir's overtures because he also sought allies against the Wittelsbachs.[128] After preliminary negotiations early in 1343, a defensive alliance was signed between the two rulers and sealed with a marriage pact. Bogusław promised to let no one pass through his territory from the empire to Prussia without Casimir's permission and to send at least 400 heavy cavalry to Casimir's aid should Poland become involved in a war with the Teutonic Order. The engagement of Casimir's oldest daughter, Elizabeth, to Bogusław and the king's bequest of a handsome dowry was followed on February 28, 1343, by the marriage of the two.[129] Thus Casimir had formed strong defensive ties against the Order in the north. They were never tested, however, for the same year the Piast came to terms with the Knights.

That he did so was the result of several factors. One was that, three years before, Casimir had entered the lists to contend for the succession in the ancient *regnum Galiciae et Lodomeriae*, thus committing Poland to an extended struggle there. It had quickly become apparent that success in Ruthenia, as this area is frequently called, would come only if the resources of the kingdom were concentrated upon this task. This meant that Casimir must for the moment come to terms with the Order. Another factor which influenced the king's decision was his awareness that the pressing internal problems of Poland needed his attention. The first decade of Casimir's reign had been largely devoted to the liquidation of problems of foreign policy which he had inherited from Łokietek. Now it was necessary to undertake reforms in the currency, in the military, and in legal matters.[130] To do this required peace. A third consideration was also

126. While John had been in Poznań negotiating with Casimir, he had also signed a defensive alliance against the Wittelsbachs with several princes of Pomorze Zachodnie. See Karol Maleczyński, *Polska a Pomorze Zachodnie w walce z Niemcami w wieku XIV i XV* (Gdańsk, Bydgoszcz, and Szczecin, 1947), pp. 26–27. It has been suggested by Wiktor Fenrych, *Nowa Marchia w dziejach politycznych Polski w XIII i XIV wieku* (Poznań, 1959), p. 57, and Kaczmarczyk, *Kazimierz Wielki*, p. 61, that Casimir may also have signed a treaty with these same princes. This is certainly not an impossibility, though it is not supported by any contemporary evidence.

127. See Stanisław Nowogrodzki, "Pomorze zachodnie a Polska w latach 1323–1370," *Rocznik Gdański*, IX–X (1935–36), 23–27.

128. For the background to this see *Dzieje Szczecina wiek X-1805* (Warsaw, 1963), pp. 109–13; Fenrych, *Nowa Marchia*, pp. 52–56.

129. Dogiel, *Codex*, I, 568.

130. These important subjects have not yet received adequate attention in the west European languages.

involved, that of the attitude of the church. For some months the papacy had waged a campaign to establish peace between Poland and the Teutonic Knights; and although the papal letter of June 8, 1343, exhorting both parties to conclude a peace treaty would have arrived in Poland too late to have had any influence upon the peace proceedings,[131] Avignon's attitude was well known. Casimir had no desire to oppose the wishes of the church, especially when they were congruent with his own.

It was Poland's diplomatic isolation, complete by early 1343, which finally confirmed Casimir in his intent to make peace with the Knights. Casimir's closest ally, Hungary, had recently suffered the loss of its first Angevin king, Charles Robert, who had died on July 16, 1342, at the age of fifty-five. The succession of his sixteen-year-old son Louis was peacefully accomplished, but immediately thereafter Hungarian attention was drawn to Italy, where the Angevins sought to acquire the kingdom of Naples.[132] This concern effectively prevented them from lending any aid to Casimir to support his claim to Pomorze. Neither could the Piast place any reliance upon help from the Bohemians. The Luxemburgers were reluctant to see Poland strengthened by regaining Pomorze and securing access to the sea, while as allies of the Knights both John and Charles favored maintaining the status quo between Poland and the Order. In addition, as we have seen, Polish-Luxemburg relations had steadily deteriorated. They were further strained by the margrave's visit to Cracow in April, 1343. His purpose was again to borrow money. Casimir lent him 4,000 score Prague groschen and two wealthy citizens of Cracow added 3,333 score more. Concerned because Charles had not yet fully discharged his previous debts, the king demanded assurance that full repayment would be made. Charles promised to repay all debts within three weeks and, if he did not, granted Casimir the right to call upon Louis of Hungary to help force the margrave to repay the money.[133] Charles defaulted on this debt also, and a further chill set in between Poland and Bohemia which augered against Luxemburg support of Casimir. Neither from the east nor the west could Poland expect aid. The Wittelsbachs were friendly, but were unwilling to proffer assistance unless the marriage pact of previous years was fulfilled. Another reason for their reluctance lay in the fact that some of their recently acquired lands on the Baltic were threatened by the Order, and they feared support for Poland might bring retaliation by the Knights.[134] The Lithuanians no longer had with Poland the good relations of 1325, or even of the whole lifetime of Casimir's wife, Anna.

131. Theiner, *Mon. Pol.*, I, # 590; see also Raynaldus, *Annales Eccl.*, XXV, a.d. 1343, pars. 38–40.

132. See Denis Sinor, *History of Hungary* (New York, 1959), p. 91; Eugen Csuday, *Die Geschichte der Ungarn*, 2 vols. (Vienna, 1900), I, 344–51; Mollat, *The Popes at Avignon*, pp. 173–77.

133. Ludewig, *Reliquiae*, V, 510; *C.D.Mor.*, VII, # 471. See also Werunsky, *Karl IV*, I, 334 nn. 1, 2.

134. See Voigt, *Geschichte Preussens*, V, 3–4.

By now the two had become bitter enemies over the succession in Ruthenia, and Lithuania had little desire to help Poland against the Order.

From the papacy, also, came little support for the aggressive policy of 1339. In his last years Benedict XII had become convinced that compromise was necessary over the question of Pomorze. His death in April, 1342, had only reinforced this trend in papal policy, for his successor, Pierre Roger (Clement VI) was as peacefully oriented as he was extravagant. One of his first acts had been to reaffirm the position taken in an earlier letter by Benedict by continuing the policy outlined there. He wrote the bishops of Cracow, Chełmno, and Meissen, urging them to establish peace between Poland and the Order.[135] In this letter he indicated that the papacy felt the judgment of 1339 to be too severe and unfair and that a more appropriate solution would be for the Order to return Kujavia and Dobrzyń and pay an indemnification of 10,000 florins to Casimir. The Polish king, for his part, should recognize the Order's possession of Chełmno, Pomorze, and Michałowo. This was essentially the agreement reached in 1343 between Poland and the Order, and the papal exhortations undoubtedly played a role.

Two fundamental problems remained to be solved before peace could be achieved between Poland and the Order. The first was the papal insistence upon an indemnification of 10,000 florins and the return of Kujavia and Dobrzyń. Though the Knights had been ready to do the latter since Wyszegrad, they refused to pay an indemnification; and in the face of such obstinance, the matter of indemnification was apparently dropped. Nothing more is heard of it in later negotiations. The second problem was more difficult to solve. As Casimir's heir-presumptive, King Louis of Hungary had promised to regain Pomorze for Poland. The Order thus demanded of Casimir that he obtain a renunciation of this promise from the Angevin. The Piast was unable to do this, for Louis feared such a renunciation might be construed by the nobility as a failure to fulfill the promises he had made to gain the Polish throne, thus costing him the succession.[136] On this point of contention, negotiations with the Knights might have foundered.

Casimir did succeed in working out, however, with the assistance and advice of the new archbishop of Gniezno, Jarosław Bogoria, an ingenious compromise which was accepted by the Order and became the preliminaries upon which the peace was ultimately based. As a substitute for the Hungarian renunciation and as a means of assuring peace, Casimir suggested that he obtain the following agreements: (1) the three dukes of Mazovia and the two dukes of Kujavia and Łęczyca-Dobrzyń, who as relatives of the king had some claim to succeed him should he die without an heir, were to promise to renounce all claims they might ever have to Pomorze, Chełmno, and Michałowo; (2) Casimir was to obtain from his son-in-law, Duke Bogusław V, the promise to be responsible for

135. Theiner, *Mon. Pol.*, I, # 580–81.
136. *C.D.Pr.*, III, # 37. See also Dąbrowski, *Ostatnie lata*, p. 115.

maintaining whatever peace might be signed; (3) Casimir was to obtain from the nobles of Greater and Little Poland and from the citizenry of seven of the chief Polish cities[137] the promise that they would never grant aid to any person, even if it were the king himself, who sought to alter the peace in any way.[138]

Early in July, Casimir, accompanied by an extensive retinue of churchmen, nobles, and civil officials from Poland and by Duke Bogusław, arrived in Kalisz, the site chosen for the peace negotiations. Shortly thereafter came the plenipotentiaries of the Order. Several days of intense negotiation followed, and on July 8 the two sides came to terms. Casimir formally renounced all his claims to Chełmno, the castles of Nieszawa, Orłów, and Murzyń in favor of the Order, and renounced for himself, his wife, and his heirs all claims to Pomorze and Michałowo, promising never again to use the title Duke of Pomorze.[139] For its part, the Order agreed to return Kujavia and Dobrzyń to Poland, together with all their cities, castles, and fortresses.[140] Casimir also bound himself to represent the interest of the Order at the Hungarian court and to restrain the Angevins from hostile acts against the Knights;[141] he promised further not to give aid or advice to any of the heathen enemies of the Order, to grant an amnesty to all members of the Order who had been involved in the conflict, and to grant the same to all Poles who had fled to the territory of the Order during the war. Finally, he promised to obtain from the civil officials of the kingdom a renunciation of all claims to indemnification from the Order.[142] While these negotiations were being conducted, separate dealings between the Order and the clergy of Poland resulted in a statement by several Polish ecclesiastics on July 8 that they had received satisfactory indemnification from the Order for their losses. Then in the name of all the clergy of the kingdom they abjured the judgment issued by the papal tribunal in Warsaw and promised to do nothing to harm the peace which had been fashioned between Casimir and the Knights.[143]

After the events of July 8, arrangements were made for a meeting between

---

137. Poznań, Kalisz, Inowrocław, Brześć, Cracow, Sandomir, and Sącz.

138. *C.D.Pr.*, III, # 37.

139. *Lites*, II, 372; Dogiel, *Codex*, IV, 62.

140. The documents issued by the Order in these negotiations have perished, purposely destroyed by the Knights according to Józef Szujski, "Warunki traktatu kaliskiego r. 1343," in his *Opowiadania i roztrząsania historyczne* (Warsaw, 1882), p. 65. The documents issued by the Poles, however, do allow us to make inferences about what the Knights agreed to. The document in *C.D.Pol.*, II, 269, and *Lites*, II, 375, has been shown by Caro, *Geschichte Polens*, II, 252 n. 1, to be a fabrication.

141. Dogiel, *Codex*, IV, 63; *Preussische Sammlung*, III, 297. See, however, *Preussische Sammlung*, III, 301, and Caro, *Geschichte Polens*, II, 253 n. 1.

142. *Preussische Sammlung*, III, 304, 303, 302, 299 respectively.

143. *C.D.Pr.*, III, # 32. Długosz, *Historia*, III, 207–8, suggests that Archbishop Jarosław and other Polish bishops advised Casimir against signing peace with the Order. Though this may have been true in the case of Jan Grot of Cracow, who was conspicuously absent from the dealings in Kalisz, it most certainly was not true in the case of Jarosław, who had been one of the moving spirits behind the treaty from the Polish side.

Casimir and Grand Master Ludolf König to ratify the peace. Then the king turned to the task of obtaining the guarantees he had promised as the substitute for the Hungarian renunciation. On July 9 he obtained from the higher officials of Greater Poland and Kujavia and the civil representatives of Poznań, Kalisz, Brześć, and Inowrocław the promise they would never lend support to anyone who attempted to renew the war between Poland and the Order.[144] The same promise was obtained on July 15 from the officials, nobles, and chief cities of Little Poland.[145] On July 11 Duke Bogusław of Pomorze-Wołogoszcz formally renounced any claim he might have to the territory under discussion and swore not to alter the terms of the peace treaty.[146] Six days later the Dukes of Kujavia, Łęczyca-Dobrzyń, and Mazovia signed an eternal peace with the Order and made promises similar to those of Duke Bogusław.[147] Finally on July 20 the bishop of Chełmno renounced all claims to indemnification from Casimir due to losses suffered during the war, and promised to protect and honor the peace.[148]

On July 23 the treaties negotiated at Kalisz some two weeks before were ratified by Casimir and Ludolf König at Wierzbiczan, between Inowrocław and Murzyń. Two pavilions were erected for the rulers, and in the presence of the archbishop of Gniezno, who read the agreements to the assembled multitude, the king and the grand master exchanged the documents of peace. They swore a solemn oath, Casimir upon his crown and Ludolf upon his pectoral cross, to fulfill all the provisions of the treaties, then kissed each other to seal the agreement.[149] The ratification of these agreements was confirmed by the archbishop of Gniezno and the bishops of Kujavia, Poznań, and Płock, all of whom were present and who testified that both sides had sworn to keep the peace and that Casimir had truly renounced for himself and his heirs all rights and privileges to Chełmno, Michałowo, and Pomorze.[150] On the same day certain prelates from the lands of the Order wrote Pope Clement describing the events and requesting speedy papal confirmation of the peace.[151] With the ratification of the treaties of Kalisz, the first phase of Casimir's reign came to an end. In his first decade of rule, he had been largely concerned with the problems left as the

144. Dogiel, *Codex*, IV, # 65; *C.D.M.P.*, II, # 1221–22.

145. *Lites*, II, 379; *C.D.Pr.*, III, # 36; *C.D.Pol.*, I, 191; *Preussische Sammlung*, III, 742.

146. *C.D.Pr.*, III, # 33; *Lites*, II, 375. Voigt, *Geschichte Preussens*, V, 9, calls this document the "erste der Friedensurkunden," despite the clear "actum et datum . . . feria sexta ante diem S. Margarete virginis," thus July 11 at the earliest, three days after the original peace documents.

147. *C.D.Pr.*, III, # 34–35; *Lites*, II, 376, 378; *Preussische Sammlung*, III, 737. These treaties and promises were made by the dukes as independent and sovereign princes, not as members of the Polish crown. See Balzer, *Królestwo*, III, 171, 200 f.

148. Dogiel, *Codex*, IV, # 66; *Lites*, II, 380.

149. The notarial record of this ceremony is printed in *Lites*, II, 381 ff., and *C.D.Pr.*, III, # 37.

150. Dogiel, *Codex*, IV, # 64; *Lites*, II, 383.

151. *C.D.Pr.*, III, # 38.

heritage of Władysław Łokietek. These had by 1343 been liquidated: Casimir had brought peace to Poland and assured it a safe place on the eastern frontiers of the *res publica Christiana*. This peace had been bought at a high price, however, for both Silesia and Pomorze had been lost to the kingdom. This much is obvious. But it still remains to assess the significance of Kalisz and to answer the question as to why Casimir made peace with the Order.

One answer, which has proved particularly durable, was given in the fifteenth century by Johannes Długosz. He wrote: "King Casimir of Poland, seeing himself involved in war with the Ruthenians and Lithuanians and not wishing to fight with three enemies at one and the same time, requested peace terms from the Grand Master and the Order."[152] In other words, the Cracow canon suggested that Casimir made peace because his attention had become focused upon the east. There is undoubtedly an element of truth to this, for only the most foolhardy ruler willingly fights a two-front war. Despite the fact that the years from 1332 to 1343 had seen no formal hostilities, it could hardly be said that relations were normal between Poland and the Knights. It appears, therefore, that it was Ruthenia which drew him away from Pomorze. Conversely, it is possible to see in this question a wholly different dimension, for it has been recently suggested[153] that it might be more appropriate to say that it was Pomorze which drew Casimir to Ruthenia, that is, the king saw in the kingdom of Halicz and Vladimir an opportunity to strengthen the state and provide himself with a power base from which he could later return to the recovery of Pomorze. Such a view would suggest that whatever Casimir intended the Order to think when he signed an eternal peace with them, he reserved to himself the right to recover Pomorze whenever he felt himself and Poland equal to the task.[154]

It is neither appropriate nor possible at this point to determine the validity of this latter argument. Such a judgment can only be made after the question of Ruthenia and the remaining twenty-seven years of the king's reign have been carefully examined. Let us provisionally suggest that the argument has much to recommend it; we shall in succeeding pages, both implicitly and explicitly, return to it.

152. Długosz, *Historia*, III, 207.

153. Stanisław Zakrzewski, *Zagadnienie Historyczne*, 2 vols. (Lwów, 1936), II, 147: "Casimir the Great turned toward Ruthenia . . . in order that he might strengthen himself from this side to return to Pomorze." See also Sieradzki, *Polska wieku XIV*, pp. 175 ff., and most explicitly Sieradzki and Rafał Łąkowski, "Traktat kaliski z roku 1343," in *Osiemnaście wieków Kalisza*, 2 vols. (Kalisz, 1960–61), II, 41–53, pp. 47–48 especially.

154. On the significance of the treaties of Kalisz as viewed by various authors, see the works cited in the preceding note, and Caro, *Geschichte Polens*, II, 258–59; Kaczmarczyk, *Kazimierz Wielki*, pp. 96 f.; Dąbrowski, *Dzieje Polski*, II, 40–43; Halecki, "Kazimierz Wielki," pp. 334–35; Karol Górski, *Państwo Krzyżackie w Prusach* (Gdańsk and Bydgoszcz, 1946), pp. 103 ff.; Gorzycki, "Wpływ," pp. 366–70; *Historia Polski*, general editor Tadeusz Manteuffel, vol. I: *do roku 1764*, in three parts, ed. Henryk Łowmiański (Warsaw, 1958–61), pt. i, 406–8; and Szujski, "Warunki traktatu kaliskiego," pp. 52–66.

5
THE TURN TO THE EAST
1340–1349

To the east of Cracow, rising out of the Vistula valley and the historic lands of Piast Poland, the landscape gradually begins to take on a different character. Though cut by many rivers, the region is really one great plateau stretching out into the vast reaches of the Ukraine. The climate is harsh, and although there were several important cities in the region in the fourteenth century, the land was more sparsely populated than the relatively crowded area around Cracow. This was the region of the *regnum Galiciae et Lodomeriae*. Lying chiefly in the basin of the Dniester River, this ancient kingdom was composed of several separate territories. Przemyśl, Lwów, and Halicz to the south were commonly considered to belong to the general area of Galicia (or Halicz); while to the north, Chołm, Bełz, Włodzimierz (Vladimir), and Łuck traditionally formed the area of Lodomeria (or Vladimir). The whole region is known either as Halicz-Vladimir, or Ruthenia, despite the impreciseness and slightly anachronistic nature of this latter term.[1]

Ruthenia was hardly a terra incognita to fourteenth-century Poland. The kingdom of Bolesław Chrobry had included a part of it, King Casimir II had had dealings with both Ruthenia and Kiev, and Duke Leszek the White had

---

1. Medieval sources speak of the whole region of the east Slavic peoples as "Rus," from which comes the territorial name "Russia" and the ethnographic appellation "Rutheni." By the end of the fourteenth century, however, "Rus" applied to the territory of Muscovy as well as to what we today call the Ukraine and Byelorussia. Increasingly, the former was called Russia and the latter Ruthenia in order to distinguish between them. Such terminology was hotly debated in the nineteenth century, but at least in Polish historiography it had become accepted by the end of the First World War. See particularly Stanisław Smolka, *Die reussische Welt. Historisch-politische Studien, Vergangenheit und Gegenwart* (Vienna, 1916).

also intervened there.[2] In each case, however, Polish interest in this area had been incidental and sporadic. Despite Łokietek's support for Bolesław-George in 1324–25, this tradition remained unaltered by the early years of Casimir's reign. Thus when the last Piast marched into Ruthenia in 1340, there was no hint whatsoever of an attempt to recover a *Polonia irredenta*. His motivation was far different. But this campaign makes little sense without an understanding of his early attitude to the area and of the position and policy of Bolesław-George II, the last independent prince of Ruthenia.

This ruler, son of Duke Trojden of Sochaczew and Czersk in Mazovia, became master of Halicz and Vladimir in 1324 or 1325, entitling himself *dux Russiae*.[3] Although he was a collateral member of the Piast dynasty which ruled Poland, he carried out a totally independent policy. It was his goal to remain on friendly terms with the great powers which surrounded him by maintaining a careful neutrality. He had dealings with all his neighbors, but was bound to none of them by formal alliance. His closest ties were with the Teutonic Order, whom he four times assured of his good will and desire for peace.[4] At least one scholar has attempted to show that these assurances eventually assumed the form of an alliance with the Order against its enemies,[5] but such a conclusion is unsupported by the facts. Never at any time did Bolesław-George sign a formal alliance with the Order. The farthest he went was to promise free passage through Ruthenia for German merchants and to assure the Order he would not ally with anyone against it. To the north of Ruthenia lay the nascent Lithuanian state whose expansionist tendencies were a constant threat to Bolesław-George. To prevent encroachments upon his territory, he attempted to

2. For previous Polish interest in Ruthenia, see in general Roman Grodecki, "Dzieje Polski do r. 1194," in Roman Grodecki, Stanisław Zachorowski, and Jan Dąbrowski, *Dzieje Polski średniowiecznej*, 2 vols. (Cracow, 1926), I, 75–78, 120–21, 168–74; Zachorowski, "Wiek XIII i panowanie Łokietka," in *Dzieje Polski*, I, 224–27, 311–13, 328–29; Stanisław Kętrzyński, "The Introduction of Christianity and the Early Kings of Poland," in *The Cambridge History of Poland*, ed. W. F. Reddaway, et al., 2 vols. (Cambridge, 1941–50), I, 28–30, 40–41; A. Bruce Boswell, "The Twelfth Century: From Growth to Division, 1079–1202," in *Camb. Hist. of Pol.*, I, 54; Gotthold Rhode, *Die Ostgrenze Polens, Politische Entwicklung, kulturelle Bedeutung und geistige Auswirkung*, vol. I: *Im Mittelalter bis zum Jahre 1401* (Cologne and Graz, 1955), pp. 57–118; *Historia Polski*, general editor Tadeusz Manteuffel, vol. I: *do roku 1764*, in three parts, ed. Henryk Łowmiański (Warsaw, 1958–61), pt. i, pp. 167 f., 198 f., 212, 219, 227 f., 315–17. More specialized are M. Buxbaum, "Stosunki polsko-ruskie w latach 1288–1323," *Sprawozdanie Dyrekcji Państw. Gimnazjum w Końskich za r. 1931–1932* (Końskie, 1932); Ludwik Droba, "Stosunki Leszka Białego z Rusią i Węgrami," *R.A.U.*, XIII (1881), 361–426; Kazimierz Górski, "Stosunki Kazimierza Sprawiedliwego z Rusią," *Przewodnik Naukowy i Literacki*, III (1875), 572–84, 649–56, 750–57.

3. *C.D.Pr.*, II, # 116; *Pr. U.B.*, II, # 537.

4. In 1325 (*C.D.Pr.*, II, # 116, and *Pr. U.B.*, II, # 537); in 1327 (*Pr. U.B.*, II, # 582); in 1334 (*Pr. U.B.*, II, # 826); and in 1335 (*Pr. U.B.*, III, # 28). See also Henryk Paszkiewicz, "Ze studjów nad polityką Polską, Litewską i Krzyżaczką Bolesława Jerzego, ostatniego księcia Rusi halicko-włodzimierskiej," *Ateneum Wileńskie*, II (1924), 50–62.

5. Kurt Forstreuter, *Preussen und Russland von den Anfangen des Deutschen Ordens bis zu Peter dem Grossen* (Göttingen, Berlin, and Frankfurt, 1955), pp. 31–33.

win the friendship of Grand Prince Gedymin. His efforts were successful, and in 1331, at the court of his uncle, Wacław of Płock, he married Gedymin's daughter Eufemja.[6] The question of Bolesław-George's relation to the Tatars also bears upon this general problem, for at various times in the past Halicz and Vladimir had fallen under the suzerainty of the Tatars. Because of the decline in the power of the Horde before their rise to greatness in the last years of the rule of Khan Uzbek,[7] Bolesław-George had been able to rule with a minimum of interference; he was still responsible for the payment of tribute, which he apparently did without complaining.[8] The increasing threat of the Tatars to this region, however, is nowhere better shown than in the fact that the Horde was able to force the Ruthenians to aid them in a twelve-day siege of Lublin in 1337.[9] This incident was an exception to the normal neutrality maintained by the prince of Halicz-Vladimir, and in general he paid little attention to Tatar overlordship.

Polish-Ruthenian relations before 1340 are imperfectly reflected in those documents which have survived the vicissitudes of east central Europe's history. It is probable that Łokietek paid little attention to his eastern neighbor because of his involvement in the west. He may nevertheless have found occasion to broach to Bolesław-George the possibility of a reconversion to Roman Catholic Christianity, for in 1327 Pope John XXII wrote the king urging him to do all in his power to bring about such a return. At the same time John wrote the prince, addressing him by his Christian name, exhorting him to remain

6. Oswald Balzer, *Genealogia Piastów* (Cracow, 1895), pp. 451–57. Despite Bolesław-George's conversion to Orthodoxy, the religion of the majority of his subjects, the marriage was performed by a Roman Catholic priest.

7. See Berthold Spuler, *Die Goldene Horde. Die Mongolen in Russland, 1223–1502* (Leipzig, 1943), pp. 77–85; and George Vernadsky, *The Mongols and Russia* (New Haven, Conn., 1953), pp. 174–78.

8. Direct evidence to demonstrate that he paid tribute to the Horde is lacking. After Bolesław-George's death, however, the ruling Boyar Diet'ko complained to the Khan that Casimir had forbidden the Ruthenians to pay tribute. See Janko of Czarnków, *Chronicon Polonorum*, in *M.P.H.*, II, 622. From this it is possible to infer that payment may have been a normal act under Bolesław-George.

9. The question of a Tatar siege of Lublin in 1337 is one of the many disputed ones touching this period. According to *Rocznik świętokrzyski*, in *M.P.H.*, III, 78, "In 1337 the Tatars and Ruthenians besieged the fortress of Lublin for twelve days and nights, though strongly opposed, and devastated the whole region." Because no other source confirms this and because the chronology of this chronicle is not always correct (it sets Casimir's first marriage in 1335 and the peace of Kalisz in 1338, for example; see Paszkiewicz, *Polityka Ruska Kazimierza Wielkiego* [Warsaw, 1925], p. 36 and n. 5 for other mistakes), some scholars have rejected this source, setting the invasion instead in 1341. See Alexander Czuczyński's note in *K.H.*, V (1891), 173–78; Paszkiewicz, "Sprawa najazdu tatarskiego na Lublin w roku 1337," *Teka Zamojskiego* (1920), pp. 158 ff.; and, in less detail but more accessibly, *Polityka Ruska*, p. 37 n. 1. Most scholars, however, accept the 1337 date. See Oskar Halecki, "Kazimierz Wielki, 1333–1370," *Encyklopedya Polska*, V, i (Warsaw, Lublin, Łódź, and Cracow, 1920), p. 325; Spuler, *Die Goldene Horde*, pp. 97–98; Rhode, *Die Ostgrenze Polens*, I, 173.

steadfast in his desire to return to the church of Rome.[10] The question of whether these efforts bore fruit will be considered below.

Casimir displayed more interest in Halicz and Vladimir in the early years of his reign than had his father. In 1336 he wrote Pope Benedict XII to request that Catholic interests in Ruthenia be placed under the direct jurisdiction of the archbishop of Gniezno. Previously the bishop of Lubusz had been responsible for the ecclesiastical concerns of the church there, and such an arrangement had limited the effectiveness of the archbishop.[11] On December 12, 1336, Benedict replied to Casimir that he would do as the king requested after the death of the incumbent bishop of Lubusz, Stephan—all this so that the king and his kingdom might be strengthened.[12]

At least one Polish historian has seen in this action Casimir's first attempt to prepare for the eventual organization of Ruthenia under Polish rule.[13] In this he is undoubtedly correct and we may assume that the king was already laying plans for the acquisition of the territory. Another motive may also be detected beneath the king's action, however, for he was ever alert to future possibilities which would be beneficial to the kingdom. The diocese of Lubusz, while technically still subject to Gniezno, in practice followed its own program. Since the early part of the century, the territory of Lubusz had belonged, not to Poland, but to Brandenburg, and the bishop there was highly sympathetic to the Wittelsbachs and the Teutonic Order.[14] Casimir hoped to diminish the importance of the bishopric by weakening its jurisdictional powers, thus making it easier at some future time to regain the territory within which the bishopric lay. It is possible, then, to see a twofold purpose in the king's actions. His intentions toward Ruthenia, however, became even clearer in 1338.

Any Polish plans or ideas concerning Ruthenia had to take into account Hungarian attitudes. This was true in the first place because Charles Robert was Casimir's strongest ally and Hungarian help might well be needed for intervention in Halicz and Vladimir. In the second place, Angevin wishes had to be considered since Charles Robert had taken over Hungarian claims to the *regnum Galiciae et Lodomeriae* which dated back to the early thirteenth century. There is no doubt that Casimir and Charles Robert did come to some kind of agreement, for in 1340 there were Hungarian auxiliary troops sent into Ruthenia and in 1350 the then king, Louis, recalled such an arrangement.[15] The question is when this agreement was made.

10. Theiner, *Mon. Pol.*, I, # 384, 383.

11. See Władysław Abraham, *Powstanie organizacyi kościoła łacińskiego na Rusi*, vol. I (Lwów, 1904), 200–211.

12. Theiner, *Mon. Hung.*, I, # 910. This promise was not fulfilled.

13. Paszkiewicz, *Polityka Ruska*, p. 40.

14. On Lubusz and its pretensions, see Zdzisław Kaczmarczyk, *Monarchia Kazimierza Wielkiego*, 2 vols. (Poznań, 1939–46), II, 146–48; Abraham, *Powstanie*, pp. 262–73.

15. ". . . Support and help . . . in the same way and manner previously agreed upon between

More than four decades ago, in a brilliant youthful work, Jan Dąbrowski argued that at the Congress of Wyszegrad in 1335 the two kings had entered into discussions about the succession to Bolesław-George.[16] While it is not impossible that a pact was made at that time, the force of Dąbrowski's argument is greatly diminished because he used as an essential part of his proof a document which, although supposedly issued by Casimir in 1337, has since been proven to be a falsification.[17] Later scholars, most notably Henryk Paszkiewicz, have suggested that events of 1338 more probably gave rise to the Polish-Hungarian alliance.[18] In June of that year, according to nuncio Galhard, Casimir visited Charles Robert in Wyszegrad. At the same time either Bolesław-George or his representative also came to the Hungarian capital. There the Ruthenian requested assurances of aid and assistance from the two kings. They granted this while agreeing among themselves that Poland would undertake no action, either with or without Angevin aid, which would be prejudicial to Hungarian claims; and Charles Robert agreed to support Polish action there should Casimir intervene.[19]

Within two years, events in Halicz and Vladimir involved Casimir in the question of succession. Two factors were responsible for this: the revival of Tatar power and the policies of Bolesław-George. The Tatars invaded Hungary in 1332, 1334, and 1338,[20] and, as we have seen, laid siege to Lublin in 1337. In the winter of 1339–40 central Europe was again faced with the threat of a great Tatar invasion. So serious was the danger that Peter Gervasius, the collector of Peter's Pence, transferred all monies in his care to Zagreb for

---

our father Charles . . . and this same King of Poland." This document was first discovered and printed by Antoni Prochaska, "W sprawie zajęcia Rusi przez Kazimierza Wielkiego," *K.H.*, VI (1892), 31.

16. Dąbrowski, *Ostatnie lata Ludwika Wielkiego, 1370–1382* (Cracow, 1918), pp. 109–10.

17. *C.D.P.M.*, III, # 651, dated June 24, 1337. See Stanisław Kętrzyński, "Zapis Kazimierza Wielkiego dla Kazimierza Bogusławowica," *P.H.*, XIV (1912), 303 n. 2.

18. Paszkiewicz, *Polityka Ruska*, p. 40. See also Rhode, *Die Ostgrenze Polens*, I, 173 n. 6.

19. Galhard wrote to Benedict on June 11, 1338: "There is nothing else new to report, except the fact that the king of Hungary is gravely ill and the king of Poland has gone to visit him at his request." *M.P.V.*, I, 181. According to the *Chronicon Dubnicense*, in *Historiae Hungaricae fontes domestici*, ed. M. Florianus, 4 vols. (Fünfkirchen and Leipzig, 1881–85), III, 128: "In 1338, about the time of the feast of Saints Peter and Paul, Lothka Duke of the Ruthenians came to Wyszegrad with members of his army, promising King Charles of Hungary increased friendship." Abraham, *Powstanie*, p. 206, was the first to investigate the discrepancy between names. He concluded, correctly I believe, that "Lothka dux" is identical with Bolesław-George. At the very least, he was a plenipotentiary of the prince. The character of the *Chronicon Dubnicense*, the circumstances of its creation, and its historical value are analyzed in detail by C. A. Macartney, *The Medieval Hungarian Historians, A Critical and Analytical Guide* (Cambridge, 1953), pp. 111–33. On Charles Robert's attitude, see Prochaska, "W sprawie," pp. 17 ff.

20. György Pray, ed., *Annales regum Hungariae ab anno Christi CMXCVII ad annum MDLXIV . . .*, 5 vols. (Vienna, 1764–70), II, a.d. 1332, 1334, 1338. See also Prochaska, "W sprawie," p. 15.

safekeeping.[21] The Tatars were also a threat to Bolesław-George, and he appealed for help to Casimir and Charles Robert. In addition, he requested support from them against his boyars. Both kings gathered armies and by spring, 1340, were prepared to march into Ruthenia.

The prince's position had become increasingly more difficult in recent years. At least two things cost him the support of his boyars: Roman Catholic resurgence and the influx of Western influences into Ruthenia under his rule. Some scholars have concluded that he actually returned to Roman Catholicism.[22] If he did not, he certainly considered it and furthered this form of Christianity. The pope had urged him to persevere in his plans to reconvert, and Bolesław-George had chosen a Catholic priest for his marriage to Eufemja in 1331. He had also, in all probability, supported the erection of a Catholic bishopric in Przemyśl.[23] The culmination of this process came in early 1340, when rumors spread through Ruthenia that Catholicism was to be introduced by the prince.[24] The boyars of the region were equally disturbed by Bolesław-George's dependence upon the West. He had gone, for example, to the Angevins in 1338; and in the last public act of his rule he had bestowed German law upon the newly founded city of Sanok on January 10, 1339, and named someone from Little Poland instead of Ruthenia to administer it.[25] Other sources mention this aspect of the prince's policy.[26] These two tendencies were too much for the boyars, who took matters into their own hands. On April 7, 1340, they poisoned Bolesław-George.[27] Ten days later, Casimir invaded Ruthenia.

If one were to believe the testimony of medieval and renaissance historians, Casimir's invasion of Ruthenia in 1340 was an immediate success which resulted in the conquest of most of the kingdom of Halicz and Vladimir and its annexation to the kingdom of Poland on a par with Kujavia, Sandomir, or Łęczyca. This traditional interpretation was the work of Casimir's later vice-chancellor, Janko of Czarnków. According to him, Casimir entered the land, subjected its population, received an oath of allegiance from its citizens, and carried back to

21. See the report of Peter Gervais of February 20, 1340, in *M.P.V.*, I, 419. See also *Monumenta Vaticana historiam regni Hungariae illustrantia, Series prima*, 6 vols. (Budapest, 1887–91), I, 433; and below, n. 60.

22. Chiefly Jan Řežabek, "Jiří II, poslední kníže veškeré Malé Rusi," *Časopis musea království Českého*, LVII (1883), 205–6.

23. According to Abraham, *Powstanie*, pp. 239–41.

24. As reported by Johannes Vitoduranus, *Chronicon a Friderico imperatore ad annum 1348*, in *M.G.H. SS., n.S.*, III, 180. See also Vernadsky, *The Mongols and Russia*, p. 203.

25. *C.D.Pol.*, III, 88.

26. *Rocznik Traski*, in *M.P.H.*, II, 860: "introducing foreigners, namely Bohemians and Germans, over them."

27. For the sources concerning Bolesław's death, see Mykhailo Hrushevsky, *Istoria Ukrainy Rusy*, 10 vols. (reprinted, New York, 1955), III, 534–35. The date of April 7 is based on *Annales Posnanienses*, in *M.P.H.*, V, 880, although *Rocznik Traski*, p. 860, says "circa festum annunciancionis beate Marie," that is, March 25.

Cracow the princely treasury of Bolesław-George. A century later, Johannes Długosz, relying heavily upon Janko, presented essentially the same picture of the events of 1340. This description was not greatly modified by the earliest modern Polish historians, Marcin Kromer, bishop of Warmia (1570–89), and Maciej Stryjkowski, poet and historian (ca. 1547–ca. 1582).[28] With the more critical study of this problem which began in the eighteenth century, it soon became apparent that Casimir's conquest of Ruthenia was more complex than Janko and his historiographical successors had portrayed it. The historian is fortunately not without supplementary sources, both literary and diplomatic, upon which to base his researches; during the height of the Polish enlightenment Adam Naruszewicz was able to present a reasonably correct picture of the events of 1340.[29] In the nearly two centuries since then, many scholars have contributed to the refinement and correction of the story.

The sudden death of Bolesław-George without direct heir created a power vacuum in Ruthenia which could have been filled in any one of several ways. The most obvious alternative was for the Tatars to reestablish their overlordship in the territory and set up a puppet ruler. The threat of this possibility was an important factor in the plans which Casimir had made, for he could ill-afford to allow the hostile Horde to become his neighbor. The dukes of Mazovia also had grounds to claim the inheritance, for Bolesław-George had been the son of Duke Trojden (d. 1341) and the brother of Ziemowit III (d. 1381) and Casimir I (d. 1355). In addition, these three had other hereditary ties to Ruthenia, since the duke was the son-in-law, and the other two the grandchildren, of the former Ruthenian prince, George I (d. 1308).[30] That there was apparently no attempt on their part to claim the succession has suggested to most scholars that they deferred to Casimir as the senior representative of the Piast family.[31] In fact, Mazovian troops supported the king in the campaign of 1340, even though the dukes were independent of Casimir's control. A third possibility for the succession was Charles Robert of Hungary. In practice, however, such a claim would not have been a realistic alternative; for despite the justifiability of the Angevin assumption of Árpád claims, Hungary was less interested in the succession in Ruthenia than in Poland. Thus Charles Robert, and after him Louis, was willing to follow Casimir's lead lest they offend the Polish king and thereby spoil future possibilities.

28. Janko of Czarnków, *Chronicon*, pp. 620–22; Długosz, *Historia*, III, 196–97; Marcin Kromer, *Kronika Polska* (Warsaw, 1767), p. 346; Maciej Stryjkowski, *Kronika Polska, Litewska, Żmodzka* . . . (Warsaw, 1766), pp. 388–89.

29. Adam Naruszewicz, *Historya narodu polskiego od początku chrześciaństwa*, 8 vols. (Warsaw, 1780–1806), VI, 91–104.

30. George I's daughter Maria had married Trojden sometime before 1310. Maria's two older brothers, Andrew and Leo II, had jointly succeeded their father and ruled until 1323.

31. Zakrzewski, "Wpływ," pp. 104–5; Oswald Balzer, *Królestwo Polskie 1295–1370*, 3 vols. (Lwów, 1919–20), III, 173; Paszkiewicz, *Polityka*, p. 49; Rhode, *Die Ostgrenze Polens*, I, 176.

The two other claimants were more serious. The Lithuanians already had close ties through Bolesław-George's marriage to Eufemja. In addition, Lubart, one of the Gedyminowicze (sons of Grand Prince Gedymin), had married Buča, daughter of former Prince Andrew of Vladimir, sometime after 1325.[32] There was thus a twofold hereditary basis for the Lithuanian claim. This position was strengthened by two factors: the Lithuanian proximity to Ruthenia and the frankly expansionist attitude of Gedymin's sons.[33] The Polish candidacy of Casimir was based on an hereditary claim and upon practices of succession in the Piast family. Both Casimir and Bolesław-George were descendants of Conrad I of Mazovia (d. 1247) and were in addition brothers-in-law by marriage, for both had married daughters of Gedymin: Casimir in 1325, Bolesław-George in 1331. Casimir was thus as closely related to Bolesław-George as Lubart. Beyond this, Oswald Balzer has suggested that because Ruthenia was ruled by a member of the Piast family, the succession went to the senior member of that dynasty (that is, Casimir) in lieu of a direct descendant.[34] His argument is not related to the principles of feudal tenure; that is, Ruthenia did not escheat to the Polish crown. The basis of the argument is the complex system of familial and dynastic precedence which characterized relations among the Piasts.[35] It was upon this that the succession system of Bolesław Krzywousty had been established; that the Mazovian princes had deferred to Casimir; and, as other historians have agreed,[36] that Casimir understood his position in relation to Ruthenia. It is quite unnecessary to attempt to suggest that Bolesław-George had recognized the feudal suzerainty of Poland in 1338 at Wyszegrad, or even to argue that Bolesław-George had formally recognized Casimir as his successor in 1338.[37] The hereditary and familial ties were sufficient for the king.

Whatever the legal and hereditary basis, Casimir did not hestitate in claiming the succession and leading his troops into Ruthenia. Bolesław-George died on April 7, and on April 16 Casimir invaded Halicz and marched toward Lwów, where he was soon joined by Hungarian troops.[38] The speed with which

32. Many Russian sources note this marriage, but without precise reference to the date. Rhode, *Die Ostgrenze Polens*, I, 175 n. 17, has argued, with others, that the union must be dated after 1325, since before that date Lubart would have stepped forward to challenge Bolesław-George.

33. There is some evidence to indicate that even before 1340, the Lithuanians, perhaps Kiejstut, may already have taken part of Podlachia from Bolesław-George II. See Paszkiewicz, "Z dziejów Podlasia w XIV wieku," *K.H.*, XLII (1928), 139–43.

34. Balzer, *Królestwo*, II, 492.

35. Balzer, "O następstwie tronu w Polsce. Studya historycznoprawne," *R.A.U.*, XXXVI (1897), 430 n. 1, and, in much greater detail, *Królestwo*, III, 143–266.

36. Paszkiewicz, *Polityka Ruska*, pp. 48–49; Dąbrowski, *Dzieje Polski od r. 1333 do r. 1506*, vol. II of Grodecki, Zachorowski, and Dąbrowski, *Dzieje Polski średniowiecznej*, pp. 30–31; and Halecki, "Kazimierz Wielki," p. 327.

37. Zakrzewski, "Wpływ," p. 103, for the former approach. The latter in Abraham, *Powstanie*, pp. 215 ff.

38. Hruszevsky, *Istoria*, IV, 435–36, cites a document which demonstrates Hungarian

he responded to news of the duke's death suggests that previous preparations for an expedition into Ruthenia had been made, in all probability in accord with the agreements of 1338 to provide support for Bolesław-George against his boyars and against the Tatars. This would account for the small number of troops [39] utilized in the expedition and its relatively abbreviated nature, all of which suggests that Casimir did not at this time intend to undertake a campaign of conquest.

Casimir's decision to march upon Lwów is understandable. The easiest route of march (though not one which can be documented for this campaign of 1340) would take the Polish troops down the Vistula valley to the region of Sandomir, and from there either up the San River valley, or along the high ground between the San and the Tanew. The former route leads to Przemyśl, the latter to Lwów itself.[40] The route to Lwów is more probable, since Przemyśl was neither a military nor a political objective, whereas Lwów was both. Since its founding in the thirteenth century, Lwów had become the chief city of Halicz and Vladimir. It was the seat of the ruler, and at the same time an important commercial center where major trade routes between the Baltic and the Black Seas came together. Moreover, the city was well located for fortification with a splendid acropolis for military purposes.[41] It was the key to Ruthenia and had to be taken if Casimir desired to control the whole region.

The best source for this first campaign, and the only one which speaks of two

---

military activity in Ruthenia under William Druget before May 7, 1340. Abraham, *Powstanie*, p. 217, has concluded therefore that Casimir had returned to Poland in this time to prepare a new expedition. It is more probable that Polish and Hungarian military activity in Ruthenia was of a joint nature. See Paszkiewicz, *Polityka Ruska*, p. 54, and n. 11. The date of the invasion is based on *Rocznik Traski*, p. 860: "circa festum pasche."

39. *Rocznik Traski*, p. 860, says "in limited numbers," but Długosz, *Historia*, III, 196, describes the composition of the army as drawn "from his lancers and other barons, who had been assembled in great numbers." To my knowledge there is no documentary evidence for 1340 to validate the implication in Karl Bartels, *Deutsche Krieger in polnischen Diensten von Misika I. bis Kasimir dem Grossen ca. 963–1370* (Berlin, 1922), pp. 94 f.: "andererseits boten die Feldzüge Kasimirs gegen die russischen Teilfürstentümer Halicz und Wladimir den deutschen Rittern ein reiches Betätigungsfeld." K. Luck, *Deutsche Aufbaukräfte in der Entwicklung Polens* (Plauen, 1934), p. 47, more specifically says that German soldiers were on this 1340 campaign, but this statement rests only upon a very late (seventeenth-century) source. See Jacob Caro, *Geschichte Polens*, 4 vols. in 5 (Gotha, 1863–86), III, 58.

40. This is the reconstructed route shown by Kaczmarczyk and Stefan Weyman, *Reformy wojskowe i organizacja siły zbrojnej za Kazimierza Wielkiego* (Warsaw, 1958), p. 123, though it should be emphasized again that it is a route based on probability, not one which can be documented.

41. On the question of Lwów as a commercial center, see in general Stanisław Kutrzeba, "Handel Polski ze Wschodem w wiekach średnich," *Przegląd Polski*, XXXVIII (1903), cxlviii, 189–219, 462–96, cxlix, 512–37; cl, 115–45; and "Handel Krakowa w wiekach średnich," *R.A.U.*, XLIV (1903), 1–196; L. Charewiczowa, *Handel średniowiecznego Lwowa* (Lwów, 1925); Weyman, *Cła i drogi handlowe w Polsce piastowskiej* (Poznań, 1938). The city's military advantages are reflected in Długosz, *Historia*, III, 239–40.

separate expeditions in 1340, is the *Rocznik Traski*, whose author was an eye-witness to the events he described.[42] According to him, when Casimir arrived in Lwów, he found a general antiwestern reaction had set in following the death of Bolesław-George, and several Catholics had been killed.[43] In his role as Catholic prince Casimir took the responsibility of protecting other Catholics and taking them back to Poland. Because of his small army he made no attempt to conquer Ruthenia; but to prevent anyone else from seizing control, he besieged the fortress and razed it after its capture. After sacking the royal treasury, which included "two golden crosses, two jeweled crowns, the prince's mantle, and a gold-encrusted throne," he returned by mid-May to Cracow. It is probable that before he left Lwów Casimir had opened negotiations with the Ruthenian boyars, led by Dmitrij Diet'ko, palatine of Przemyśl and an important advisor of Bolesław-George.[44] Though nothing came of these contacts, they did provide a basis upon which agreement was quickly reached with Diet'ko during Casimir's second campaign.

During Casimir's return to Poland in late May and June, preparations were made for a new campaign. Fewer than forty days were required for the raising of a new, expanded army. On this occasion he utilized the recently developed *pospolite ruszenie* for the mobilization of troops.[45] On June 24 Casimir again entered Ruthenia, with an army of 20,000 men, according to Traska.[46] We may rightly regard this as a highly imaginative exaggeration, perhaps by a factor of five or ten.[47] This judgment is all the more necessary when the duration of the

42. *Rocznik Traski*, pp. 860–61: "Thraska eciam fuit ibidem." There are in addition three other valuable contemporary or near contemporary sources: (1) Janko of Czarnków, *Chronicon*, pp. 620–29; (2) Johannes Vitoduranus, *Chronica*, pp. 180–84; and (3) a letter from Pope Benedict to the bishop of Cracow on June 29, 1341, in Theiner, *Mon. Pol.*, I, # 566. Other sources which are useful are noted below. Despite Traska's explicit description of two campaigns, most early studies of this topic persisted in following Janko of Czarnków and compressing events into one campaign. See the historiographical comments in Paszkiewicz, *Polityka Ruska*, pp. 53–54.

43. See also Theiner, *Mon. Pol.*, I, # 566: "the schismatic Ruthenians treasonously poisoned Bolesław, Duke of Ruthenia, and savagely killed several other Christians who had followed this Duke while he lived," and Franciscus Pragensis, *Chronica Pragensis 1125–1353*, in *Font. rer. Aust.*, VIII, 564: "many Christians were killed by the sword and in other ways." Similarly, Diet'ko (see below for this individual) admitted not long after in a letter to the merchants of Toruń "indeed after the death of . . . the Duke of Ruthenia, several citizens of Lwów were injured" *C.D.Pr.*, III, # 61.

44. Janko of Czarnków, *Chronicon*, pp. 621 f.: "the Baron called Datko, who held the fortress of Przemyśl." Hrushevsky, *Istoria*, IV, 430–33, has assembled the available information about Diet'ko. There is some question as to whether "Diet'ko" is a name or a title, but most scholars prefer the former.

45. On the question of Casimir's military reforms, see particularly Kaczmarczyk and Weyman, *Reformy wojskowe*. According to Długosz, *Historia*, III, 198: "he led an army into Ruthenia gathered from all his lands."

46. *Rocznik Traski*, p. 860: "the same year about the feast of John the Baptist, Casimir again invaded Russia, having gathered a strong army of 20,000 men." See also Tadeusz Korzon, *Dzieje wojen i wojskowości w Polsce*, 3 vols. (Cracow, 1912–14), I, 84–85.

47. Since the days of Sir Charles Oman's *A History of the Art of War in the Middle Ages*, and

campaign is noted. Within a month, Casimir had returned to Cracow, having besieged and conquered, according to Długosz, Przemyśl, Halicz, Łuck, Vladimir, Sanok, Lugaczów, Trębowla, and Tustan, and having covered therefore more than 600 kilometers. In actuality, the achievements of the king, whatever his movements, were more modest. The greatest success of the campaign came in forcing the boyars of Halicz and Vladimir to make an agreement concerning the administration of Ruthenia and its relation to the *regnum Poloniae*.

No document of this agreement survives, and its nature, which must be inferred from independent documents, is difficult to ascertain. Scholarly opinion as to its significance has been sharply divided. M. Hrushevsky, the great Ukrainian historian, and I. L. Filevič, the Russian scholar, vigorously maintain that the agreement left Ruthenia completely independent of Poland and that Diet'ko was an autonomous ruler.[48] Polish scholars, chiefly Paszkiewicz, Prochaska, and Balzer, assert with no less vigor that Diet'ko was actually acting as Casimir's *starosta* (*capitaneus*) in Ruthenia.[49] In a sense both sides are correct, for each views the problem differently. The conflict is over the interpretation of de facto status versus de jure. To be sure both Traska and Janko of Czarnków report that Casimir was able to subject Ruthenia and obtain an oath of fealty from the boyars.[50] But such an arrangement was meaningless so long as Casimir had not fully conquered the territory and consolidated his control. In effect, Diet'ko, who was clearly the leader of the Ruthenian nobles and may even have been the local candidate for succession to Bolesław-George,[51] was an independent ruler subject only to the eventuality of Casimir's return, even though Diet'ko's legal status corresponded most closely to the Polish *starosta*. The nature of this arrangement becomes much clearer after Casimir's winter campaign against the Tatars, and there are several documents which bear on the problem.

Before tracing further Polish involvement in Ruthenia in 1340–41, it is instructive to note that in the same period the Lithuanians had not been totally

---

Hans Delbrück's *Geschichte der Kriegskunst im Rahmen der politischen Geschichte*, scholars have been generally aware of the unreliability of medieval statistics regarding the size of armies. Thus it is all the more surprising to find a consistently uncritical acceptance of these figures by even the most recent Polish scholarship. See, in the present instance, Kaczmarczyk and Weyman, *Reformy wojskowe*, p. 124, and Karol Olejnik, *Działalność militarna Polski w czasach Kazimierza Wielkiego* (Poznań, 1966), p. 80.

48. See Hrushevsky, *Istoria*, IV, 434 ff. I have been unable to utilize directly I. L. Filevič, *Borba Pol'ši i Litvy-Ruši za Galicko-Vladimirskoe nasledie* (St. Petersburg, 1890).

49. Paszkiewicz, *Polityka Ruska*, pp. 71–78; Prochaska, "W sprawie," pp. 21–22; Balzer, *Królestwo*, II, 501–3. Curiously, Józef Sieradzki, *Polska wieku XIV. Studium z czasów Kazimierza Wielkiego* (Warsaw, 1959), devotes only passing mention to the problem of Diet'ko.

50. *Rocznik Traski*, p. 860; Janko of Czarnków, *Chronicon*, p. 621.

51. This evaluation is strongly suggested by Kaczmarczyk and Weyman, *Reforma wojskowe*, p. 122.

inactive. In the summer of 1340 Gedymin's son Lubart had occupied the *ziemie* of Wołyń and Łuck, while another son, Kiejstut, had conquered Podlachia, perhaps even before the death of Bolesław-George.[52] It was obvious that the Lithuanians also would contend for the succession in Ruthenia. With these advances the scene was set for bitter and prolonged conflict between Casimir and the Gedyminowicze. This contention dominated Ruthenia and Casimir's eastern policy for the next quarter-century.

As soon as Casimir left Ruthenia in July and returned to Poland, there arose in Halicz and Vladimir a national party opposed to Polish rule.[53] To rid themselves of Polish influence, they turned to the Tatars, requesting aid and saying that Casimir had forbidden them to pay tribute to the Horde. Uzbek responded by gathering his army (an impossible 40,000, according to Traska) and by preparing to invade Poland in the fall.[54] Casimir had recognized the possibility of a Tatar invasion (one of the reasons for his Ruthenian campaign of April had been to prevent an expansion of Tatar power), and either before or immediately after the June expedition had requested aid from Avignon. On August 1, 1340, Benedict sent letters to the bishops of Poland, Hungary, and Bohemia announcing a crusade against the Horde.[55] In the meantime, Casimir had sought material support from his neighboring Catholic princes. He sent emissaries to Charles Robert of Hungary, Emperor Lewis IV, and the dukes of Mazovia.[56] Only the last responded to his appeal.[57]

Late in 1340 the Tatars began their invasion. Not only were they granted safe passage through Halicz and Vladimir, the Ruthenians actually lent the Horde aid and took part in the invasion.[58] Their campaign was at first highly

52. See Paszkiewicz, *Polityka Ruska*, pp. 85–87, and "Z dziejów Podlasia," pp. 229–45. See also Rhode, *Die Ostgrenze Polens*, I, 129 f., 178.

53. Janko of Czarnków, *Chronicon*, pp. 621–22, specifically mentions Diet'ko as a leader. Further reflections of these events are found in Diet'ko's letter to the merchants of Toruń in *C.D.Pr.*, III, # 61, where he speaks of "conflict . . . between King Casimir of Poland and us."

54. These preparations may be placed in the fall of this year on the basis of the letter of Pope Benedict to Uzbek, dated September 17, 1340. In it the pope exhorts the khan to keep the peace and give up his military plans. See *Codex diplomaticus Hungariae ecclesiasticus et civilis*, ed. György Fejer (Buda, 1829–44), VIII, pt. iv, 450–52. See also Theiner, *Mon. Hung.*, I, # 958 (papal letter of August 1, 1340).

55. Theiner, *Mon. Hung.*, I, # 959.

56. Johannes Vitoduranus, *Chronicon*, p. 181; Johannes Victoriensis, *Chronicon*, p. 438.

57. *Rocznik Traski*, p. 861: "there were many plain [simplices] Mazovians murdered and killed." Johannes Vitoduranus, *Chronicon*, p. 181, remarks, "In this conflict the Polish dukes participated vigorously." This also may refer to the Mazovians. The view in the text is supported by Paszkiewicz, *Polityka Ruska*, p. 64, but challenged by Ewa Maleczyńska, *Książęce lenno mazowieckie 1351–1526* (Lwów, 1929), p. 35. She argues that the Mazovians were undoubtedly members of the entourage of Bolesław-George II who had returned with Casimir from Lwów after the first campaign. This is, of course, not impossible, but Traska's use of the word "simplices" would hardly apply to the groups Professor Maleczyńska suggests. For that reason, I have preferred Paszkiewicz's interpretation. See also Rhode, *Die Ostgrenze Polens*, I, 207 n. 181.

58. The weaker description is given by Rhode, *Die Ostgrenze Polens*, I, 180. The stronger, by

successful. The Tatars probably followed the route of the river San into Little Poland, devastating the region around Sandomir. Casimir was able to prevent them from crossing the Vistula, and the invaders turned north toward Lublin, which they unsuccessfully invested.[59] It was the approach of the Polish army which forced them to withdraw, but they did so too late. Casimir overtook them and administered a crushing defeat, apparently in late January, 1341.[60]

Despite his successes in Ruthenia in the summer and his defeat of the Tatars that winter, Casimir recognized that he had by no means conquered Halicz and Vladimir. He was not yet strong enough to hold and defend the whole territory against the Tatars, the Lithuanians, and the native boyar party. Nevertheless he wished to maintain as much Polish influence there as he could until he was able to bring Ruthenia firmly under his control. Thus he chose to ally himself with the boyars, led by Diet'ko. Sometime early in 1341 he signed a treaty with Diet'ko, the nature of which may be reconstructed from three important sources: [61] a papal bull of June 29, 1341; a letter from King Louis of Hungary to Diet'ko in 1344; and Diet'ko's own letter to the merchants of Toruń, which may be most reasonably dated sometime in 1341.

According to the papal letter, which refers to a lost request of Casimir (see below), Diet'ko was named *capitaneus seu provisor terre Russie*, and he and the other boyars swore an oath of allegiance to Casimir, in return for which the king promised to respect their rights, privileges, and customs. The same oath

---

C.D.Pr., III, 21: "The Emperor of the Tatars with Ruthenian princes"; Janko of Czarnków, *Chronicon*, p. 622: "The Tatar Emperor . . . with the Ruthenians hostilely invaded Poland"; *Poczet królów polskich*, in *M.P.H.*, III, 295 (undated): "The Ruthenians and Tatars invested the fortress of Lublin"; Beneš Krabice z Weitmil, *Chronicon Ecclesiae Pragensis, 1283–1374*, in *Font. rer. Boh.*, IV, 490: "King Casimir of Poland had war with the Ruthenians and Lithuanians [sic]."

59. *Rocznik małopolski*, in *M.P.H.*, III, 199; *Annales Posnaniensis*, in *M.P.H.*, V, 881; Janko of Czarnków, *Chronicon*, p. 622; Johannes Victoriensis, *Chronicon*, p. 438, are the best sources for the military aspects of this campaign, plus the lesser sources discussed in Paszkiewicz, *Polityka Ruska*, pp. 66–70. These military aspects are treated also by Kaczmarczyk and Weyman, *Reformy wojskowe*, pp. 123, 125; and Olejnik, *Działalność militarna*, p. 80.

60. It is possible to be fairly precise about the date. Franciscus Pragensis, *Chronica*, p. 564, reports snow and frost (that is, wintertime) during the campaign; while two Italian sources indicate the turn of the year. Galvaneus Flamma, *Opusculum de rebus gestis ab Azone Luchino et Johanne vicecomitatibus ab anno 1328–1342*, in *Rerum Italicarum Scriptores . . .*, ed. by L. A. Muratori, 25 vols. plus indices (Milan, 1723–51), XII, 1037, says at the end of 1340; Johannes de Cornazanis, *Chronica abbreviata (Parmensis) ab a. 1085 ad a. 1355*, in *Rer. Ital. SS.*, XII, 742, says "Del mese di decembre 1340 e di gennaro 1341." The *Rocznik Poznański*, in *M.P.H.*, V, 881, sets the invasion after the death of Duke Trojden's wife Maria, that is, after January 11. Since Casimir was still in Cracow on January 15 (*C.D.P.M.*, I, # 213), it is possible to agree with Paszkiewicz, *Polityka Ruska*, p. 67, upon late January. In contradistinction to him, however, I set Peter Gervasius's statement in 1340: "Also, in the year 1340, on February 20, when the Tatars invaded the Kingdom of Poland and the whole of the Kingdom of Hungary was in tumult because of this, I quietly transferred the money to the city of Zagreb" *M.P.V.*, I, 419.

61. Theiner, *Mon. Pol.*, I, # 566; *Cod. Dipl. Hung.*, IX, i, 209; and *C.D.Pr.*, III, # 61, respectively.

seems to have been given to the Hungarian ruler also, for in his letter Louis refers to Diet'ko as "his servant, the highly esteemed Count Diet'ko, the *capitaneus* of the Ruthenians." The nature and use of these titles have led scholars to conclude that a kind of Polish-Hungarian condominium existed in Ruthenia with Diet'ko responsible equally to both rulers.[62] This was Diet'ko's legal position. In actual fact he was an independent ruler and considered himself to be such.[63] In his letter to Toruń he speaks of Casimir simply as *Dominus Kazimirus rex Polonie*, and omits the word *noster*, which should have been included had Diet'ko felt himself to be the king's subordinate. Even more significant in this connection is the way Diet'ko refers to previous rulers of Halicz and Vladimir as *predecessores nostri*.[64]

As Casimir reviewed the events of the preceding year early in 1341 and contemplated future plans for Ruthenia, he realized that he had promised too much to Diet'ko and the other boyars, for he could not extend Polish power and influence into Ruthenia without breaking his oath to them. He sent a long letter to Benedict XII in which he outlined the course of the preceding year and requested the pope to absolve him from his oath and give him a free hand in future dealings. This was not an unreasonable request; and since it did not involve other Catholic princes, the pope granted the request in the aforementioned letter of June 29, 1341.

The events of 1340–41 are quite correctly regarded as a turning point in Polish history.[65] Although Casimir had not yet made any lasting conquests in the east and did not actively return to the Ruthenian problem until 1349, in retrospect it is possible to see that he had firmly turned Poland's face to the east. This fact was important not only for the history of the king's own reign, but also for the next six centuries of Polish history. But whatever Casimir's motives in intervening in Ruthenia, he certainly did not intend that affairs in the west should thereby be excluded from Polish interests. His approach to this region was far more complex and, at the same time, better balanced. Unfortunately such an approach was not as true of succeeding generations; particularly after

62. This is accepted by Abraham, *Powstanie*, pp. 218–19, who discusses instances of this arrangement in central Europe; by Paszkiewicz, *Polityka Ruska*, pp. 78–79; by Balzer, *Królestwo*, II, 502; by Rhode, *Die Ostgrenze Polens*, I, 181.

63. There is no real evidence to suggest that Ruthenia was under Lithuanian control at this point, as argued by Hrushevsky, *Istoria*, IV, 29–30, especially. His view is also accepted by Korzon, *Dzieje wojen*, I, 85–86.

64. The whole question of Diet'ko as *starosta* is reviewed in detail by Paszkiewicz, *Polityka Ruska*, pp. 79–85. He takes some pains to minimize the significance of the two factors suggested above, but his efforts are not wholly convincing, chiefly because he attempts to judge Diet'ko by standards of the *regnum Poloniae*, when in reality the boyar stood outside this tradition.

65. This is the view of nearly every writer who has dealt with the subject. See, among others, Paszkiewicz, *Polityka Ruska*, pp. 46 ff.; Halecki, "Kazimierz Wielki," p. 328; Kaczmarczyk, *Polska czasów Kazimierza*, p. 41; Paweł Jasienica, *Polska Piastów* (Warsaw, 1966), pp. 322 ff.; *Historia Polski*, I, pt. i, 451.

the successful wars of the fifteenth century, noneastern affairs tended to play an increasingly minor role on the Polish scene. The lesson and example of Casimir had been forgotten.[66]

Despite the interest and involvement which Casimir had already shown in the east, he was unable to devote himself fully to this area in the period from 1341 to 1349. Dealings with the Luxemburgers, Wittelsbachs, and Teutonic Knights, as well as important domestic reforms, occupied much of his time and energy. This was particularly true before 1343, and for that reason there is practically no mention of Ruthenia until after the treaties of Kalisz. Then again the east made demands upon the king's interests.

In that year Casimir requested the new pope, Clement VI, for renewed help against the Tatars, Ruthenians, and Lithuanians. Clement responded in two bulls, dated December 1, 1343,[67] that granted Casimir a tenth of all ecclesiastical income from the archdiocese of Gniezno, with the exception of Wrocław,[68] plus the papal tenth in Poland for two years. In all probability this latter grant approximated 2,500 silver marks for the two years.[69] Despite this substantial financial support from the papacy, there is no evidence to suggest that Casimir actually undertook a campaign to the east in 1344. On the contrary, since Louis of Hungary stated in his letter to Diet'ko in May, 1344, that there were extensive commercial relations between Poland and Ruthenia, one may infer that Casimir was at peace with the area.

Soon thereafter there were changes. By 1345 Casimir was in possession of the city and territory of Sanok on the river San and had signed an agreement with Olgierd, Kiejstut, and Lubart (all sons of Gedymin) which granted them effective control over Ruthenia. The former fact is drawn from Casimir's privilege of May 9, 1345, granting certain rights to the merchants and citizens of Nowy Sącz;[70] and also from two royal documents issued in Sanok in 1352, which refer to Polish possession of the region at some time before 1349.[71] The

66. I have touched upon this problem in a slightly different context. See Knoll, "The Stabilization of the Polish Western Frontier under Casimir the Great, 1333–1370," *The Polish Review*, XII, pt. iv (1967), 28–29. In a much expanded manner, this problem of the significance of the eastern frontier in Polish history is central to the important study by Gotthold Rhode, *Die Ostgrenze Polens*.

67. Theiner, *Mon. Pol.*, I, # 604–5.

68. The income from Wrocław had been granted to John of Bohemia in July, 1343, even though the church there was under the ecclesiastical jurisdiction of Gniezno. See Theiner, *Mon. Pol.*, I, # 593.

69. According to Jan Rutkowski, *Historia Gospodarcza Polski*, 2 vols. (Poznań, 1946–50), I, 104. According to a 1333 index printed by Max Kirmis, *Handbuch der polnischen Münzkunde* (Poznań, 1892), p. 28, the total sum is the equivalent of 5,000 oxen or 7,500 cattle.

70. *C.D.P.M.*, I, # 218: "We grant free passage from Sącz to Ruthenia via Byecz, Smigrod, and Sanok."

71. *A.G.Z.*, VIII, 1; *C.D.Pol.*, I, 117. There is mention in these documents of "capitaneus de Sanok" which implies incorporation into the Polish administrative system.

latter fact is reflected in a papal letter to Casimir on October 18, 1345, which had been written in response to an *apologia* from the king about certain aspects of his foreign policy.[72] Casimir had defended in this statement his reconciliation with the Wittelsbachs, who were vigorously antipapal and anti-Luxemburg, and his seeming friendship for the heathen Lithuanians. The king contended that the vicious hostility of the Luxemburgers toward Poland was the real cause of his action, that he had merely sought others to defend Poland's interests and had not the slightest desire thereby to embarrass or restrict the church. This bland and somewhat self-serving letter obscures the more significant, and certainly more complex, problem of when Casimir gained Sanok and the reason why he had made an agreement with the Gedyminowicze which markedly minimized the Polish position in Ruthenia. In order to solve this problem it is necessary to read between the lines of the four relevant documents which are extant.

The most careful investigator of Casimir's Ruthenian policy, Henryk Paszkiewicz, was the first to document the itinerary of the king in the period under discussion, accounting for his presence from early 1343 until late June, 1344, and from January, 1345, until the end of the year. On this basis he concludes that the territory of Sanok was captured by Casimir on a campaign into Ruthenia during this interval.[73] In this conclusion he is probably correct, but his analysis of the circumstances of the campaign is less sound. He takes Casimir's statements to the pope (discussed above) at face value and concludes that, in order to gain the alliance of the Lithuanians, Casimir had in effect established spheres of influence in Ruthenia. Paszkiewicz sees the campaign into Sanok as part of a common effort with the Gedyminowicze, who at the same time took control of much of the rest of the territory.[74] It is difficult to understand, however, why Casimir should have had to withdraw so completely from Ruthenia in order to gain the alliance of the Lithuanians. It is this consideration which suggests that events in the east were somewhat more complex than

---

72. Theiner, *Mon. Pol.*, I, # 628.

73. Paszkiewicz, *Polityka Ruska*, pp. 92–95. This is also the conclusion reached by Halecki, "Geografja polityczna ziem ruskich Polski i Litwy 1340–1569," *Sprawozdania z posiedzeń towarzystwa naukowego Warszawskiego, wydział I i II*, X (March 16, 1917), 5 ff. Hrushevsky, *Istoria*, IV, 31, suggested sometime in 1344 or 1345; Abraham, *Powstanie*, p. 219 n. 2, says 1345; and Dąbrowski, *Ostatnie lata*, p. 126 n. 5, concludes sometime in 1344. The conclusions of Halecki and Paszkiewicz have generally been followed.

74. Paszkiewicz, *Polityka Ruska*, pp. 102–8. He would leave Lwów under nominal Polish control by this argument, for he further suggests that Janko of Czarnków's statement ("Lubart the son of Gedymin, Duke of the Lithuanians possessed the Duchy of Ruthenia," *Chronicon*, p. 629) should be understood to include only Vladimir. In this instance, Hrushevsky, *Istoria*, IV, 32, is more probably correct when he says Lubart ruled the whole of Ruthenia. Paszkiewicz's suggestion leaves open the question of who was ruling in Przemyśl and Halicz, for as we shall mention below, it is probable that Diet'ko was by this time dead.

Paszkiewicz has shown.[75] The following reconstruction by Gotthold Rhode is more acceptable.[76]

Sometime after May, 1344, Diet'ko died. When Lubart learned of this in Łuck, he immediately marched into Ruthenia and was able to occupy the region before Casimir, who was involved with the Bohemians in the west, could do anything to hinder him. Belatedly, Casimir turned to the east and was able to conquer the territory of Sanok. He was able to gain nothing else because Lithuanian power was too strong. The king was then forced to agree to a compromise with Lubart, which in effect recognized the latter as the legal overlord of Ruthenia. It was this arrangement which prompted Janko of Czarnków to comment, after describing events of 1340: "Lubart the son of Gedymin, Duke of the Lithuanians, possessed the Duchy of Ruthenia."[77] This reconstruction of the events of 1344 conforms to the king's itinerary for the period, accounts for the manner in which Poland gained Sanok, and explains why Casimir made an agreement so favorable to the Lithuanians. Its chief weaknesses are that Lubart's conquests in Ruthenia are not mentioned in Clement VI's letter of 1345. Surely, it might be argued, Casimir would have used the conquests as an excuse for his dealings with the Lithuanians. It is possible of course that this factor is conspicuous by its absence only because the king's arguments are imperfectly reflected in the papal letter. It is more probable that Casimir chose not to mention this new humiliation, instead preferring to hold his counsel until he could return more vigorously to Halicz and Vladimir.[78]

Despite the loss of Ruthenia, which had been bound to Poland by only the loosest of connections, the acquisition of Sanok was an important gain for Casimir. It had already at this time emerged as a minor administrative and economic center. It was also an extremely sparsely settled territory which proved in following decades to be a colonization center of great importance to the

75. This whole question is complicated in some presentations. For example, Halecki, *Dzieje unii Jagiellońskiej*, 2 vols. (Cracow, 1919), I, 62, accepts Długosz's narration *sub anno* 1344 which describes a joint Ruthenian-Tatar invasion. It has been shown, however, by Paszkiewicz, *Polityka Ruska*, p. 104 n. 2, that Długosz, who sometimes left matters of chronology to assistants, here describes the events of 1341 under the wrong year.

76. Rhode, *Die Ostgrenze Polens*, I, 184–85.

77. Janko of Czarnków, *Chronicon*, p. 629.

78. Another possibility is that, as Adam Fastnacht, *Osadnictwo ziemi sanockiej w latach 1340–1650* (Wrocław, 1962), pp. 15–16, assumes, Sanok was taken by Casimir in 1340 and Polish administrative control grew up there so gradually that its origin cannot be clearly identified. Two sources do in fact suggest the conquest came in 1340: both Długosz, *Historia*, III, 198, and *Gustinskaja letopis'* in *Polnoe sobranie russkich letopisej*, 26 vols. (St. Petersburg and Moscow, 1841–), II, 349, specifically mention Sanok as one of the locations taken by Casimir in that year. Such an assertion probably reflects, however, simply the knowledge that Sanok had been taken by Casimir before 1349. For Casimir to have conquered in his 1340 campaign all the locations mentioned by the sources would have approached physical impossibility. Thus the question of when Sanok was taken is most adequately answered by Paszkiewicz.

regnum.[79] In the years after 1344, Sanok was firmly tied administratively to the kingdom (more completely than any other part of Ruthenia), and in this way Poland's boundaries were permanently extended across the San River for the first time. Even more important from a strategic point of view, this expansion gave Poland control of the Łupków pass over the Carpathians. The chief Hungarian route into Ruthenia was thus blocked, an advantage which enabled Casimir to regulate more easily the ambitions of Louis in the ancient kingdom which he claimed.

The years which preceded Casimir's successful Ruthenian invasion of 1349 were marked by the decline of Tatar and Lithuanian power. Following the death of Khan Uzbek in 1341, when there arose no strong leader to replace him, the influence of the Horde waned. In 1346 the Black Plague struck disastrously and more than decimated the Tatars.[80] The effects of the Tatar decline were not immediately apparent, especially since in 1342 they again mounted in incursion into Poland;[81] but Tatar weakness was a definite factor in Casimir's success in 1349. The decline of Lithuanian power was of shorter duration. The great founder of the Lithuanian state, Gedymin, died in 1341[82] after dividing his principality among his seven sons: Olgierd, Kiejstut, Monwid, Narymunt, Jawnut, Korjat, and Lubart. These sons quarrelled among themselves over the inheritance, and for some years the Gedyminowicze, with the exception of Lubart, focused their attention upon domestic adjustments rather than upon Ruthenia. This prevented them from taking full advantage of Casimir's involvement in his own internal affairs and in the conflict with Bohemia.[83]

Even after the emergence of Kiejstut, Olgierd, and Lubart as the most important of the Gedyminowicze, the Lithuanians were unable to resume their expansion into Ruthenia, for their power was badly shaken by the Teutonic Knights. Early in 1348 a small army of the Order, led by the later grand master, Winrich von Kniprode, invaded Lithuania. Olgierd and Kiejstut assembled a large army, which included many Muscovite Russians, and succeeded in driving the Order back to the lower reaches of the Strawa River, near its confluence with the Memel. There the Order in desperation made a last stand, and on February 2 inflicted a crushing defeat upon the Lithuanians. So unexpected

79. See Władysław Kucharski, *Sanok i sanocka ziemia w dobie Piastów i Jagiellonów* (Lwów, 1925), and Fastnacht, *Osadnictwo ziemi sanockiej*, pp. 15, 34–41, for a physical description of the territory.

80. See Spuler, *Die Goldene Horde*, pp. 99–101; Vernadsky, *The Mongols in Russia*, pp. 204–5.

81. See Prochaska, "W sprawie," p. 21.

82. There are many different dates given for his death in contemporary sources, but modern scholars have generally accepted 1341. The problem is best treated by Kazimierz Stadnicki, *Synowie Giedymina*, 2 vols. (Lwów, 1848–53), I, 81.

83. These developments may be followed in *Kronika Litewska*, in *Pomniki do dziejów litewskich*, ed. T. Narbutt (Vilno, 1846), p. 17; *Latopisiec litewski i kronika ruska*, ed. I. Daniłowicz (Vilno, 1827), p. 27. Stryjkowski, *Kronika*, pp. 370–78, has a fine narrative, though his chronology and sequences are sometimes faulty. See Caro, *Geschichte Polens*, II, 264–66.

and overwhelming was the Knights' victory, they could only attribute it to the direct intervention of the Virgin Mary.[84] The Lithuanians were damaged severely by this defeat and were slow to recover from its effects. Thus both the great powers of this area, the Tatars and the Lithuanians, found themselves in weakened positions and were unable to offer any immediate resistance to Casimir's invasion.

While the king was making preparations for this campaign he was also negotiating with the Lithuanian rulers for the conversion of their principality to Christianity. They apparently showed some willingness to discuss the topic. At least one author has suggested that the Lithuanians, still pagan and relatively unsophisticated, may have believed the Teutonic Order's explanation for the outcome of the battle on the Strawa, and that this played a role in their attitude toward Casimir.[85] Whatever the reason, Casimir felt he made enough progress to report to Pope Clement in early summer, 1349, that with his help Kiejstut and his brothers were ready to give up the error of their ways and, together with their people, to become adherents to the true Catholic faith. On the basis of this report, Clement wrote Casimir on September 16, exhorting him to do everything possible to confirm the Lithuanian prince in his plans. The pope also hinted that after Kiejstut and his people had been baptized, the papacy would raise the principality to the status of a kingdom. The same day Clement sent a letter to Archbishop Jarosław of Gniezno telling him to prepare qualified priests as missionaries to the Lithuanians; and a letter to Kiejstut informing him of the imminent arrival of the missionaries.[86]

This effort to Christianize Lithuania by peaceful means, as contrasted to the method of conquest and subjugation advocated and practiced by the Teutonic Order, died stillborn. By the time the papal letters reached their destination, Casimir had already begun his campaign. This being the case, why had he begun the negotiations in the first place and reported them to Avignon? In the light of later actions, it is impossible to deny that Casimir was in part motivated by a true missionary spirit, though it is difficult to evaluate this factor in the present instance; it is also possible to infer less altruistic designs on his part. It is probable that he saw in these actions an opportunity to neutralize the Lithuanians in the struggle over Ruthenia by subjecting them to the spiritual and moral influence of the papacy. Further, Casimir recognized that this was one means of redeeming himself in the eyes of Avignon, which had been outspokenly critical of his earlier dealings with the Lithuanians and with the Wittelsbachs, to whom

84. See Johannes Voigt, *Geschichte Preussens von den ältesten Zeiten bis zum Untergange der Herr-schaft des Deutschen Ordens*, 9 vols. (Königsberg, 1827–39), V, 60–62; Karl Lohmeyer, *Geschichte von Ost- und Westpreussen* (Gotha, 1881), I, 213.

85. Rhode, *Die Ostgrenze Polens*, I, 254. See also Kazimierz Chodynicki, "Próby zaprowadz-enia chrześcijaństwa na Litwie przed r. 1386," *P.H.*, XVIII (1921), 280 ff.

86. Theiner, *Mon. Pol.*, I, # 691, 692, 693.

he had given his daughter in marriage in 1345.[87] Yet another motive was his desire to diminish the reputation of the Teutonic Order as the most important Christianizing force in the East and to become known as a "trusted promoter and zealous worker" for the faith in his own right.[88]

The period from 1341 to 1349 may rightly be viewed as one in which no side gained a real advantage in Halicz and Vladimir. Yet the period is not unimportant, for despite the temporary loss of legal control over Ruthenia, Poland did gain sure possession of Sanok. Even more important was the virtual disappearance of the Tatars as Casimir's chief foe and the rise of Lithuania as Poland's main rival in the area. It was not against the Horde that Casimir fought from 1349 to 1366, but against the Gedyminowicze.

It was not an easy matter to prepare an invasion force, even in days when warfare was less complicated than today. One of the most important steps Casimir took was to guard against intervention from the west. On November 22, 1348, he brought to a temporary end his conflict with Bohemia over Silesia by signing the treaty of Namysłów with the newly elected emperor, Charles IV.[89] In addition to regularizing Polish-Luxemburg relations, this treaty also provided for Charles's aid against the Teutonic Order should it attack Poland. To prevent such an attack, Casimir opened negotiations with the Order itself, and in early summer, 1349, signed a boundary treaty with the Knights.[90] These two treaties assured Poland of peace in the west while it turned again to the east. There also, however, Casimir may have taken precautions to limit the foes against whom he must fight. This conclusion is inferred from the epigrammatic reference of the *Rocznik Miechowski*: "In the year 1349 representatives of the Tatars came to the king of Poland."[91] For what reason should the Horde send representatives to Casimir, and why should he in any way negotiate with them? The answer to this question is of course impossible to determine with any absolute assurance, but Gotthold Rhode has reasonably suggested that Casimir wished to obtain from the Tatars promises not to resist his advances into Ruthenia.[92] It is not impossible that, to gain such a promise, he might have had to pay the Horde a form of tribute, whether it was called this or not.

After diplomatic preparations had been made, Casimir gathered his army. Długosz informs us that it contained cavalry and infantry, and Janko of Czarnków says that the king marched *cum exercitu forti*.[93] These data have led

87. Ibid., # 628.

88. Chodynicki, "Próby zaprowadzenia chrześcijaństwa," p. 282. The quote is from Theiner, *Mon. Pol.*, I, # 691.

89. *C.D.M.P.*, II, # 1277.

90. Dogiel, *Codex*, IV, # 71; *C.D.Pol.*, II, # 500.

91. *M.P.H.*, II, 885.

92. Rhode, *Die Ostgrenze Polens*, I, 185.

93. Długosz, *Historia*, III, 234; Janko of Czarnków, *Chronicon*, p. 629.

Polish scholars to conclude that the Polish force was a large, powerful one,[94] but such a judgment must be tempered by the fact that the king's campaign lasted, at most, just over one hundred days, in which time the army covered some 800 kilometers and besieged four major defensive points. These factors suggest that we should think of an army not in the tens of thousands, but in the low thousands. Casimir's strategy was to utilize a relatively small, highly mobile force, counting on Lithuanian unpreparedness for his success.

Sometime early in September Casimir invaded Ruthenia.[95] Using Lwów as a point of departure, the army marched north, captured Bełz and continued on to Vladimir, which also fell to them. In the meantime[96] part of the Polish army had been dispatched to the east to attack Łuck. After besieging it, the whole force marched down the valley of the Bug River until they crossed into the heart of Lithuania and invested Brześć Litewski. After a siege lasting several days, during which part of the Polish army ravaged the immediate countryside and captured minor fortifications, this important stronghold fell to Casimir.[97] Following this, the army returned to the south, successfully besieging Chełm en route. The victorious king and army returned to their homeland, and on December 5 in Sandomir Casimir titled himself "By the grace of God, King of Poland and Lord of the Land of Ruthenia," and granted the merchants of Toruń the right "to go through our Land of Ruthenia and to come to our city of Vladimir and there to carry on business."[98] Casimir's use here for the first time of the phrase "Lord of the Land of Ruthenia" indicates that he had conquered not only Galicia but also Lodomeria.[99] The only frustration in the campaign had come at Lubart's stronghold of Łuck. There, according to his

94. Korzon, *Dzieje wojen*, I, 87; Kaczmarczyk and Weyman, *Reformy wojskowe*, p. 126; Olejnik, *Działalność militarna*, p. 81.

95. On September 1, 1349, Casimir was still in Cracow: *C.D.P.M.*, III, # 691. For Casimir's itinerary in this period, see Paszkiewicz, *Polityka Ruska*, p. 118 n. 1. The *Rocznik miechowski*, p. 885, simply reports: "and at the end of this year King Casimir seized the land of Ruthenia."

96. The contemporary sources for this campaign are very brief. For example, the *Novgorodskaja cetvertaja letopis'* in *Polnoe sobranie russkich letopisej*, IV, 59, simply reports that "the King of Cracow invaded with great power and seized the whole of Volhynia." The data given by Długosz is more extensive, and the text follows him closely with one exception. He speaks of a direct march from Lwów to Łuck, but it is more probable, as Kaczmarczyk and Weyman, *Reformy wojskowe*, p. 126, point out, that this attack was made by a detachment from the Polish army at Vladimir. See however, Olejnik, *Działalność militarna*, p. 81.

97. On the basis of the overall shortage of time connected with the campaign, Paszkiewicz, *Polityka Ruska*, p. 119, doubts that Brześć was actually taken. Janko of Czarnków, *Chronicon*, p. 630, reports, however, that the Lithuanians attacked and burned Brześć in 1350, which would hardly have happened had Casimir been unsuccessful the year before.

98. *Hansisches Urkundenbuch*, ed. K. Hohlbaum et al., 5 vols. (Halle and Leipzig, 1876–99), III, # 159.

99. The authenticity of three earlier documents in which Casimir had used this title has been denied by Paszkiewicz, *Polityka Ruska*, p. 111 n. 1, and Rhode, *Die Ostgrenze Polens*, I, 186 n. 79. They have been accepted by Balzer, *Królestwo*, II, 498, and Halecki, "Casimir the Great, 1333–1370," in *Camb. Hist. of Pol.*, I, 173 (but not in Halecki's "Kazimierz Wielki").

later vice-chancellor, Casimir "conceded out of his generosity the city of Łuck and its territory to Lubart."[100] Such a statement appears to be an attempt to disguise Casimir's failure to capture the fortress, and one may doubt whether this report presents an accurate picture of events there.

The ease with which Casimir conquered most of the old Kingdom of Halicz and Vladimir leads one to believe that his expedition took the Lithuanians by surprise, as indeed he had planned. For the moment, Casimir had achieved a greater military success than any of his Piast predecessors. Within the space of three months, the eastern boundaries of Poland had been extended some 150 miles southeast of Sanok into the region of Buczacz on the Strypa River (a tributary of the Dniester) and some 90 miles east from Lublin into the territory between Vladimir and Łuck. The task of conquest had only begun, however, and Casimir was to spend the next seventeen years defending and extending these gains.

100. Janko of Czarnków, *Chronicon*, p. 679.

6
AFFAIRS IN THE EAST
1349–1366

One unresolved conflict in Ruthenia was that between the Pole who claimed to be "Lord and heir to the Land of Ruthenia" and the Hungarian ruler who also bore the title "King of Halicz and Vladimir." Both Casimir and the Angevins had laid claim to Ruthenia following the death of Bolesław-George, but Louis had not been as active as the Piast in prosecuting his claims, preferring to defer to his uncle. But despite the friendship and alliance between the two dynasties, a formal agreement was necessary to delineate the rights and responsibilities which each had in Halicz and Vladimir. A first attempt to do this had come in 1338, but the Wyszegrad pact of that year had only envisioned the eventuality of contention for the succession in Ruthenia, and was therefore only a temporary arrangement. The intervening decade had brought the fulfillment of that which had been only vaguely apprehended before, and Casimir's successes in the campaign of 1349 had cast an entirely different light on the matter. A new agreement was necessary.

Immediately following the king's return from Ruthenia in December, 1349, royal representatives made the hazardous winter crossing of the Carpathians to Buda for negotiations with Louis. It was conflicting dynastic ambitions which brought about this meeting. Louis was disposed to new negotiations in order to protect his position, feeling that the Polish conquest of Halicz and Vladimir was indirectly prejudicial to Hungarian claims. Casimir was clearly aware that in the coming struggle with the Tatars and Lithuanians he would need Angevin support to be successful. He wished no misunderstanding to cost him this support.[1]

---

1. This former factor is emphasized by Henryk Paszkiewicz, *Polityka Ruska Kazimierza*

On April 4, 1350, a new agreement concerning Ruthenia was issued in Louis's capital. Louis renounced in favor of Casimir all his rights to the "Kingdom of Ruthenia, which was the possession of our predecessors and shall be ours," for the lifetime of the Polish king. He also renewed the promise of his father to grant Casimir help in all affairs concerning Ruthenia, "now and whenever it shall be necessary and opportune." There were, however, conditions attached to this agreement. Casimir was to have clear claim to Ruthenia only until his death; that is, Louis had renounced his claims, not in favor of the *corona regni Poloniae*, but in favor of Casimir personally. Ruthenia would be returned to Louis if he succeeded to the kingship of Poland. Should Casimir have a male heir who succeeded him, then Louis or his descendants were to be allowed to purchase rights to Ruthenia from the new king of Poland for 100,000 florins.[2]

At first glance this agreement appears to be an important diplomatic success for Louis. Hungary had not given up its claims to Ruthenia; it had only postponed them until after Casimir's death. In the meantime, all the responsibility and work of obtaining, defending, and consolidating the area lay upon Casimir's shoulders, with Hungary needing only to follow Poland's lead, granting men and material as they were needed. Historians have traditionally judged this seeming victory for the Angevin in one of two ways: either they have criticized the Piast for being too free with his conquests and not safeguarding Polish interests in Ruthenia; or they have attempted to defend Casimir by saying there was little else he could do without weakening the Hungarian alliance. He simply had to make the best of a bad situation.[3]

Closer examination of the agreement reveals two factors which suggest that it was not so unfavorable to Casimir as it might appear. First, the immediate advantage lay with Poland: Casimir was in control of Ruthenia, he had been recognized by Louis as the legitimate ruler there, and he had been given assurances that he would receive continued Hungarian support to maintain his position. Second, there is a definite possibility that in these negotiations Casimir was buying time. He had not gone personally to Hungary, and so the

---

Wielkiego (Warsaw, 1925), pp. 140–41; the latter attitude is characteristic of Casimir's farsighted and reasoned policy, according to Gotthold Rhode, *Die Ostgrenze Polens, Politische Entwicklung, kulturelle Bedeutung und geistige Auswirkung*, vol. I, *Im Mittelalter bis zum Jahre 1401* (Cologne and Graz, 1955), p. 187.

2. The original of this agreement is lost, and we know it only from a copy made in 1357 by a certain "Janussius doctor decretorum, decanus et cancellarius cracoviensis." (This is probably Janusz Suchywilk; see *Pol. Słow. Biog.*, X, 583–85.) The text of his copy is printed in Antoni Prochaska, "W sprawie zajęcia Rusi przez Kazimierza Wielkiego," *K.H.*, VI (1892), 30–31.

3. The best example of the former is Stanisław Smolka, *Rok 1386* (Cracow, 1886), p. 87. For the latter, see Prochaska, "W sprawie," pp. 23–24.

agreement was issued in Louis's name alone.[4] It therefore required confirmation by the other party; but there is neither a document extant from Casimir which confirms the Angevins' right to purchase Ruthenia in case they did not succeed in Poland, nor is there any evidence to suggest that Casimir issued such a document. From this one may infer that the Polish king had no intention of agreeing to this condition and simply left the matter in abeyance, hoping to alter it at some later time.[5] A final advantage of the agreement for Casimir was that it placed no restrictions upon him in Ruthenia. (The extent of the independent action he was able to exercise there was particularly important in view of the Polish-Lithuanian condominium of 1352.) Casimir's freedom was confirmed in the years following 1350, for although Louis still included the phrase "King of Halicz and Vladimir" in his title, he nevertheless considered Ruthenia to be foreign territory, totally independent of Hungary. Three documents in particular reflect this acknowledgment. In the first, dating from 1351, Louis says, "in our descent into Ruthenia near the border of Volhynia."[6] The second was issued a year later: "near that fortress called Belz, located in the Kingdom of Ruthenia."[7] The significance of these citations lies in Louis's failure to utilize the adjective "our" (*noster*), indicating that, to him, Ruthenia was a foreign land and a non-Hungarian land. This attitude is reflected also in a document issued in 1361,[8] in which Louis states "that all merchants from foreign lands, namely Ruthenia, Poland, and their provinces, come into our Hungarian kingdom." To summarize, while Louis held hope of eventually gaining Ruthenia in one way or another, for the lifetime of Casimir he fully recognized the latter's rights there and was willing to grant him a free hand.

Not long after the new Polish-Hungarian agreement had been negotiated, Casimir was suddenly faced with the necessity of defending himself at home and in the newly acquired Ruthenian territory. His enemy was the Lithuanians, who in late spring, 1350, began the first of two campaigns which wreaked havoc in Poland and Mazovia and which brought about an almost total reversal of the positions of Poland and the Gedyminowicze in Ruthenia.[9] According to

4. We do not know who Casimir's representatives were. On March 29, 1350, the king was in Kalisz (*C.D.M.P.*, III, # 1294); on April 13, in Poznań (*C.D.M.P.*, III, # 1295).

5. Rhode, *Die Ostgrenze Polens*, I, 187–88.

6. *Codex diplomaticus Hungariae ecclesiasticus et civilis*, ed. György Fejér, 11 vols. (Buda, 1829–44), IX, pt. ii, 16, 77.

7. Cited by Paszkiewicz, *Polityka Ruska*, p. 144 n. 4.

8. *Cod. Dipl. Hung.*, IX, iii, 114, 241. The date (incorrectly listed under both 1344 and 1368) was definitely established by Jan Ptaśnik in *Sprawozdanie z poszukiwań na Węgrzech dokonanych z ramienia Akademii Umiejętności przez . . . Jana Ptaśnika . . .* (Cracow, 1919), p. 14.

9. Karol Olejnik, *Działalność militarna Polski w czasach Kazimierza Wielkiego* (Poznań, 1966), p. 83, has recently reemphasized that which Tadeusz Korzon, *Dzieje wojen i wojskowości w Polsce*, 3 vols. (Lwów, Warsaw, and Cracow, 1912–14), I, 65 ff., pointed out two generations ago: that the Polish-Lithuanian conflict did not begin in 1350 (or 1340–41). Rather it stretches back into the thirteenth century. Only in the mid-fourteenth century, however, did it become something more than raiding. It became a struggle for territorial dominion.

the *Spominki sochaczewskie*,[10] "one of the Lithuanian dukes and his army" invaded Poland in the first half of May. On their march they attacked first the city of Łuków and devastated the countryside. Their army then crossed the Vistula and laid waste the region north of Sandomir and the land around Radom. As soon as he learned of the invasion, Casimir hurriedly gathered troops (probably largely from Little Poland, although retaliation from the east was not unexpected), and marched downriver to Sandomir. The king's nearness caused the Lithuanians to turn north, where they ravaged the territory of Łęczyca. They might well have been able to continue further had not Casimir been able to call for assistance from Mazovia. The king marched quickly to Sulejów, where he and Duke Ziemowit of Mazovia agreed upon common action against the Lithuanians.[11] On May 20 the allied armies marched north and trapped the Lithuanians on the south bank of the Bzura River near Sochaczew. In the ensuing battle, many of the enemy were driven into the river and drowned. The Polish victory was complete, and the remnants of the Lithuanian force returned home as best they could.[12] Casimir returned to Cracow to make preparations for the next phase of the conflict. During this period the Lithuanians were also preparing for another campaign.

That the first Lithuanian attack had come against Poland itself was not surprising. If the Gedyminowicze could weaken Casimir at home, then Ruthenia would be easier to capture. But even though they had been wholly unsuccessful in their attempt, the king had no doubt that the Lithuanians would nevertheless move against Ruthenia. To protect his holdings there, Casimir went to Lwów to direct his defense. Within two weeks his preparations were put to the test, for on August 24 the Lithuanians advanced south from Brześć. They captured Chełm, Vladimir, and Bełz in turn, then besieged Lwów itself. Casimir was able to defend the city, however, and the Lithuanians were frustrated in their

10. *M.P.H.*, III, 120.

11. On May 19 Casimir issued a document ("Given en route near the monastery of Sulejów") in which he speaks of being "in our meeting [colloquium]" *C.D.M.P.*, III, # 1299. The same day Duke Ziemowit also issued a document "en route near the monastery of Sulejów in a meeting held by the aforementioned king" *Kodeks dyplomatyczny księstwa mazowieckiego*, ed. T. Lubomirski (Warsaw, 1863), p. 341. The next day they marched successfully against the Lithuanians. It is interesting to note that in the midst of battle plans, Casimir found it necessary to look after the royal treasury: the document he issued was to one Peczek of Wrocław, selling him the position of wójt in Łęczyca "because of our needs and those of most of our kingdom." On the significance of the "colloquium" or "wiec" in Sulejów and the development of this important Polish institution, compare Franciszek Piekosiński, "Wiece, sejmiki i przywileje ziemskie w Polsce wieków średnich," *R.A.U.*, XXXIX (1899), 75 ff., and Paszkiewicz, "W sprawie zhołdowania Mazowsza przez Kazimierza Wielkiego," *P.H.*, XXIV (1924), 1 ff. Some of the most important of those present are listed by Paszkiewicz, *Polityka*, p. 121.

12. In addition to the *Spominki sochaczewskie*, important information on this campaign is given by Janko of Czarnków, *Chronicon Polonorum*, in *M.P.H.*, II, 630, and Długosz, *Historia*, III, 238. The military aspects of this campaign are best treated in Zdzisław Kaczmarczyk and Stefan Weyman, *Reformy wojskowe i organizacja siły zbrojnej za Kazimierza Wielkiego* (Warsaw, 1958), pp. 127–28, and Olejnik, *Działalność militarna*, pp. 84–86.

attempt to capture all of Ruthenia.[13] Nevertheless they had conquered important territories from Casimir. Brześć was given to Kiejstut, Łuck remained in Lubart's hands, while Narymunt's son George was given Bełz, and another George, probably the son of Korjat, received Chełm and Vladimir. The disposition of these last three lands is difficult to determine with any degree of confidence, and we shall return below to George Narymuntowicz and the Korjatowicz brothers.[14] The real significance of the events of 1350 lies not in which son or grandson got what, but in the fact that Casimir was able to retain Lwów. The issue in Halicz and Vladimir was not yet decided; the conflict would go on.

The year 1350 had very nearly undone all that Casimir had achieved the previous season in Ruthenia. Much of the territory he had gained at that time had been lost to the Gedyminowicze even before he could turn to the question of its organization and administration; only by concentrating his defense in Lwów had he retained Halicz. To complicate the situation further, by the end of the year the revived specter of an ancient threat stalked the steppes of Ruthenia: the Tatars. Casimir's probable neutralization of the Horde in 1349 had been only a very temporary arrangement, and upon the heels of their own successes in 1350 the Lithuanians dispatched representatives to the khan to request aid.[15] In retrospect, the assistance which the Tatars could have given was minimal, but it did not appear thus to Casimir, and the threat of this combination concerned him. Sometime after his return from Lwów he sent representatives to the papal court urgently requesting help from Clement VI.[16]

Casimir's letter to Avignon was a masterpiece of diplomatic supplication. He first described for Clement the great victories he had gained in 1349 and portrayed in glowing terms the opportunities of which the church could take advantage. According to him, this territory was so great that seven large bishoprics together with a metropolitan could easily be founded there. There was in addition a certain prince of this area who was willing to be converted together with all his subjects.[17] Having thus aroused hopes of the pope for the extension

13. The best source for this campaign is Janko of Czarnków, *Chronicon*, p. 630. See also Paszkiewicz, *Polityka Ruska*, pp. 122–23. The date of the Lithuanian attack is derived from *Rocznik miechowski*, in *M.P.H.*, II, 885.

14. On the disposition of these lands compare Paszkiewicz, *O genezie i wartości Krewa* (Warsaw, 1938), pp. 264–68, and Rhode, *Die Ostgrenze Polens*, I, 188.

15. It is not impossible that this deputation came in 1349, though the sequence of events makes the date given in the text more probable. That Casimir knew of it is reflected in the papal letter in *M.P.V.*, II, 80, which refers to a message from the king in late 1350. The Lithuanian delegation was probably headed by Gedymin's son Korjat. See Jozef Puzyna, "Korjat i Korjatowicze," *Ateneum Wileńskie*, VII (1930), 426–30; Berthold Spuler, *Die Goldene Horde. Die Mongolen in Russland, 1223–1502* (Leipzig, 1943), p. 105; Kazimierz Stadnicki, *Synowie Giedymina*, 2 vols. (Lwów, 1848–53), I, 105.

16. See Theiner, *Mon. Pol.*, I, # 702; *M.P.V.*, II, 80.

17. Scholars are generally agreed that Casimir was referring to Alexander Korjatowicz.

of the church into the east, and at the same time having certified the credentials of his own missionary spirit, Casimir turned to the primary reason for his letter. He modestly admitted that up to this point he had carried alone the full burden of the fight against the heathens, but he was now forced to request help from the papacy. Since May, all of his strength and resources had been expended in doing battle against his enemies. If he did not now receive aid from the church, not only Ruthenia but the whole of his kingdom would be devastated and laid waste by the Tatars and the Lithuanians, who had allied together against Poland.

This eloquent plea was not in vain. On March 14, 1351, Clement wrote to the bishops and other important clergy of Poland, beseeching them to grant their king the aid he needed. In order to show that he too was prepared to contribute to these efforts, the pope specified that the papal tenth from the whole of the kingdom was to be given over to Casimir for the next four years.[18]

In the meantime Casimir had bent his efforts to the twofold task of preparing at home for further conflict and urging his foreign ally, the Angevins, to greater participation in the affairs of Ruthenia. Despite the agreement of 1350 with Casimir, Louis's attention had been focused upon Neapolitan affairs and his dynasty's interest there, rather than upon Halicz and Vladimir. As a result, Hungarian troops and other assistance had been noticeably missing in May and September. To change this, Casimir urgently requested some tangible sign of support from his ally. The speed with which Louis returned from his Neapolitan expedition was probably not unrelated to these concerns.[19]

The material aid which Casimir was granted by the papacy came none too soon, for in the first half of 1351 the Lithuanians again invaded Ruthenia. Their goal was Lwów, which they besieged successfully, entering and sacking the old town (*antiqua civitas, stare miasto*).[20] Casimir's response to this attack is uncertain, for there is a great gap in his itinerary for this period which makes it impossible to determine his movements with any assurance of certainty. There has been considerable dispute as to the sequence of events in that year. The narration which follows provides a reasonable reconstruction, with assumptions and the details of data relegated to the notes.

When he received word of the Lithuanian attack, the king hurried to Lwów, from which he was able to drive the troops of the Gedyminowicze. His defence was vigorous enough to capture Lubart, although the details and circumstances

---

See Paszkiewicz, *Polityka Ruska*, p. 124; Rhode, *Die Ostgrenze Polens*, I, 189; Abraham, "Założenia biskupstwa," p. 5.

18. Theiner, *Mon. Pol.*, I, # 703.

19. Paszkiewicz, *Polityka Ruska*, p. 123. Hungarian troops did indeed participate in the campaigns of 1351. See, however, Dąbrowski, *Ostatnie lata*, p. 128; Prochaska, "W sprawie," p. 22.

20. *Spominki lwowskie*, in *M.P.H.*, III, 251.

of this event are difficult to determine.[21] Lubart was held in Polish bondage until later in 1351. Despite this minor success, Casimir recognized that he needed help to defend his position in Halicz and, if possible, to expand it. He turned to his nephew and heir-presumptive, Louis of Hungary, and asked him to fulfill his promise of aid. Although the Angevin had just returned from Italy where he had gone to avenge the murder of his brother Andrew, king of Naples, he responded quickly to Casimir's request. On June 19 Louis left Buda at the head of a large Hungarian army and marched to Cracow.[22] There the two kings spent several days together planning strategy, then early in July marched to Sandomir and on to Lublin. There, however, Casimir "became sick unto death," and was unable to continue. Louis was given sole command of the Polish and Hungarian forces, which he led northwestward into the territory of Kiejstut. After a two-week march "through forests," from which it may be concluded the army was in the vicinity of Brześć,[23] Louis made contact with the Lithuanian troops. He immediately sent three of his knights to request a meeting with Kiejstut, who surprisingly agreed to come to Louis's camp.

As the result of brief negotiations, Kiejstut declared that he was ready to become a Christian, together with all his brothers, and to go back to Buda with Louis to be baptized. He also promised to sign a treaty with the Hungarians and Poles and to support them against the Tatars and the Teutonic Order. In return, Louis promised to petition the papacy for a crown for Kiejstut and the erection of a Latin rite archbishopric for Lithuania. There was no mention of Halicz and Vladimir in this agreement, and Casimir's rights in Ruthenia formed no part of the negotiations. To seal these arrangements, Kiejstut took a solemn oath of allegiance to Louis on August 15 (again Casimir was not mentioned). In return, Lubart, who had been brought with the army, was set free. Only one condition was attached to his freedom. The nature of his capture was to be discussed by a joint Polish-Hungarian-Lithuanian panel the following year. If it concluded that Casimir had captured Lubart by treachery (as the Lithuanians charged), he was to remain free; if the capture had been made

21. During Louis's summer campaign, he released Lubart. It is only the *Chronicon Dubnicense*, in *K.H.*, III (1889), 205–13, which reports the capture of Lubart: "whom the king of Poland captured with the loss of many men at that strongly defended fortress." Since the *Spominki lwowskie*, p. 251, records "In 1351 the old city area of Lwów [Leopolis] was devastated by the infidel Lithuanians" and since the *Rocznik miechowski*, p. 885, adds the information that Casimir "appeared with a large army before Lwów [Liviviam—this is the Slavic form of Leopolis], I have reached the conclusion described in the text above. For different points of view, see Abraham, *Powstanie organizacyi kościoła łacińskiego na Rusi*, vol. I (Lwów, 1904), 219–20, and Mykhailo Hrushevsky, *Istoria Ukrainy Rusi*, 10 vols. (New York, 1955), IV, 440.

22. In addition to the *Chronicon Dubnicense*, described above, the *Chronicon Budense*, ed. Iosephus Podhradczky (Buda, 1838), pp. 315–22, is also useful for Hungarian participation in this campaign. For the relation between these two chronicles, see C. A. Macartney, *The Medieval Hungarian Historians, A Critical and Analytical Guide* (Cambridge, 1953), pp. 111–33. See also Dąbrowski, *Ostatnie lata*, p. 133 n. 2, for a discussion of the personnel of Louis's army.

23. Paszkiewicz, *Polityka Ruska*, p. 128.

during open military action, then Lubart was to return voluntarily to Casimir's custody.[24]

Apparently Louis had gained a bloodless triumph by diplomatic means; for the conversion of the Lithuanians had for some time been an elusive goal, but one continually sought. The Sisyphean character of this program was soon revealed. As the united army began its return trip, it became evident that Kiejstut had no intention of fulfilling his promises or abiding by his oath. Three days after his agreement with Louis, having freed his brother and averted the danger to Lithuania from the powerful united army, Kiejstut fled Louis's camp "in the middle of the night." The Hungarian king immediately set out to pursue him, and apparently found the Lithuanian army. In the ensuing battle Duke Bolesław III of Płock, legally a Bohemian vassal but in this instance an ally of Casimir, was killed on August 21 near Mielnik. This encounter was inconclusive, however, and the campaign as a whole came to naught. Louis entered Cracow and Buda empty-handed.[25]

While Louis had been expending time and energy in his fruitless campaign, Casimir had been recovering in Cracow. He was already making plans for another campaign in Ruthenia, which he undoubtedly discussed with his Angevin nephew on the latter's return from the region of Brześć. From later events we are able to conclude that Casimir requested Louis's aid and assistance, which were given. By early 1352 Casimir had assembled his military levy, the *pospolite ruszenie*, which was to fight under the banners of Greater and Little Poland, and which included also the Mazovian troops of Dukes Ziemowit III and Casimir.[26] In February he went to Lwów, and while there perhaps informed Louis of his plans before going on to besiege Bełz.[27] The Angevin with his troops joined Casimir at Bełz late in March. This fortress had been chosen to bear the brunt of the allied attack because it had been isolated as a result of the engagement of the other Lithuanian princes in a struggle with the Teutonic Knights since early February.[28] Despite this disadvantageous position, the

24. In addition to our sources, see the legal study by A. Mierzyński, "Der Eid des Keistutis im Jahre 1351," *Sitzungsberichte der Alterthums Prussia Gesellschaft*, XVIII (1893), 104–12.

25. *Spominki płockie*, in *M.P.H.*, III, 120: "On the twelfth calends of September, Duke Bolesław of Płock died ... on a campaign"; *Rodowód Xiążąt Polskich*, in *M.P.H.*, III, 284: "[Wencelaus the son of Bolesław] had one son, Bolko, who was killed in Myelnik." Mielnik was in the territory of Kiejstut. For this campaign in general, see Alfons Huber, "Ludwig I von Ungarn und die ungarischen Vasallenländer," *Archiv für Österreichische Geschichte*, LXVI (1885), 11–13, who quotes from Peter Suchenwirt to confirm the *Chronicon Dubnicense*.

26. See Kaczmarczyk and Weyman, *Reformy wojskowe*, p. 129; Olejnik, *Działalność militarna*, p. 88; Paszkiewicz, "W sprawie zhołdowania," pp. 3 ff.

27. According to Paszkiewicz, *Polityka Ruska*, p. 130, Casimir probably spent most of February in Lwów. The king's presence at Bełz is shown by the hitherto unpublished document printed by Paszkiewicz (p. 130 n. 6): "Given on our campaign, in the vicinity of the fortress of Bełz on [March 23]."

28. See Johannes Voigt, *Geschichte Preussens von den ältesten Zeiten bis zum Untergange der Herrschaft des Deutschen Ordens*, 9 vols. (Königsberg, 1827–39), V, 93–95.

castellan of Bełz succeeded in mounting an heroic defense during the six-day action. Louis was wounded, and the two rulers had to be satisfied with an oath of homage by the castellan, made meaningless because the fortress had not surrendered. The oath does not indicate any kind of Polish-Hungarian victory.[29]

Before Casimir could continue this campaign in Ruthenia, a not wholly unexpected Tatar invasion intervened. Even in decline, the Horde was always a factor with which to be reckoned in this area, and it is indicative of this that the author of the *Chronicon Dubnicense* described Bełz as a "fortress in Tatar territory." After the siege of Bełz the Tatars became an actual, rather than a potential, threat. Late in March or early April, probably at the instigation of Olgierd,[30] the Tatars moved into Podolia. From this position it was impossible to determine the direction of their next move, whether into Ruthenia and on to Poland, or into Hungary. The latter possibility forced Louis to pull back through Lwów and across the Carpathians.[31] In the meantime, Casimir made his own preparations; but too late, for the Horde swept quickly through Ruthenia and moved on to Lublin, that shield which had borne the thrust of so many invading lances. This siege resulted in the devastation of the region around Lublin and in the capture and deportation of many from the area, as well as in a great many deaths. It does not seem to have resulted in any substantial change in Ruthenia or to have inflicted any lasting result upon Poland.[32] Casimir successfully defended the city, then returned to Cracow.

The struggle which Casimir had begun in 1349 with the Lithuanians for control of Ruthenia was not one to be decided in a single campaign or a single year. By the mid-point of 1352 it was fully apparent to the king that the ultimate conquest of Halicz and Vladimir would demand a sustained effort throughout a protracted, uncertain struggle. For this, Casimir needed material resources which exceeded his normal reserves.[33] Before preparing for a renewed assault upon the Lithuanians, he attempted to strengthen his position. Even before the Tatar invasion of the spring, Casimir had written to Avignon portraying in detail the nature of the threats to Poland from the east and requesting, because of this, substantial ecclesiastical subsidies. Pope Clement responded on May 15, 1352, but not in the way the king had hoped. He simply proclaimed in an open letter to the bishops of Poland (and also of Bohemia and Hungary),

29. See the remarks of Peter Suchenwirt described in Huber, "Ludwig und die ungarischen Vasallenländer," pp. 14–15.

30. This allegation is made by Długosz, *Historia*, III, 245.

31. See A. Lewicki, "Jeszcze w sprawie zajęcia Rusi Czerwonej przez Kazimierza Wielkiego," *K.H.*, IX (1895), 480–85; Hrushevsky, *Istoria*, IV, 442–43.

32. *Rocznik miechowski*, p. 885. See also Theiner, *Mon. Pol.*, I, # 713, and the comments of Prochaska, "Dokument graniczny czerwono-ruski z r. 1352," *K.H.*, XIV (1900), 54.

33. The sources of Casimir's revenue are discussed in Rutkowski, *Historia gospodarcza*, I, 58–116, and Kaczmarczyk, *Monarchia Kazimierza Wielkiego*, 2 vols. (Poznań, 1939–46), I, 157–202.

that they should preach a crusade against the heathens. As an added incentive for support of such a movement, plenary indulgences were to be granted, not only to those who fought, but also to those who contributed money for the eventual success of the crusade.[34]

This kind of support, while always welcome, was not sufficient for the king's purposes, and Casimir was forced to resort to other ways of raising money. During the summer he mortgaged the territory of Dobrzyń to the Teutonic Knights for an indefinite period, receiving in return some 40,000 florins.[35] At the same time he pledged the principality of Płock to the Dukes of Mazovia for 2,000 Polish marks.[36] Casimir even resorted to behind-the-scene dealings with the papal collector in Poland, nuncio Arnold de Caucina. Without the knowledge of the pope, the nuncio, through the mediation of certain residents of Cracow, lent Casimir 13,211 florins for the war effort in Ruthenia.[37] From these same citizens and at the same time, Casimir borrowed 20,000 Prague groschen,[38] but even this was not sufficient. From the abbot of the monastery at Tyniec, the king borrowed 2,000 marks;[39] and, supposedly upon the advice of his nobles, he expropriated individual items of gold and pearl worth 2,000 marks from the archiepiscopal treasury at Gniezno, promising to repay by assigning annually 100 marks from the income of the salt mines at Bochnia and Wieliczka.[40] After satisfying himself that he had sufficient financial resources with which to continue the Ruthenian struggle, Casimir wrote again to Pope Clement asking him to extend the length of the indulgence the Holy See had granted for the crusade.[41] We do not know if this was done.

34. Theiner, *Mon. Pol.*, I, # 713. It is interesting to note, as Hrushevsky, *Istoria*, IV, 39 n. 2, has commented, that this letter is a verbatim repetition of a bull of Benedict XII in 1340 (see Theiner, *Mon. Hung.*, I, # 958).

35. *C.D.Pr.*, III, # 73. The good relations which existed between Poland and the Order at this time are shown by the fact that no repayment deadline was established. The document is undated, but must be placed in 1352 or, at the latest, 1353. See Voigt, *Geschichte Preussens*, V, 105.

36. *Dokumenty kujawskie i mazowieckie, przeważnie z XIII wieku*, ed. Bolesław Ulanowski (Cracow, 1888), p. 38. There is some question as to the legality of this act, since Płock was still a fief of the Bohemian crown.

37. The pope discovered this transaction only from Casimir two years later; see *M.P.V.*, II, 97, 98. Casimir was not overly prompt in returning this money, for as late as 1357 Pope Innocent was beseeching the king to pay the balance of 5,000 florins immediately (*M.P.V.*, II, 135).

38. *Kodeks dyplomatyczny miasta Krakowa 1257–1506*, ed. Franciszek Piekosiński, 2 vols. (Cracow, 1879–82,) I, # 27.

39. This fact is reflected in a document of the abbot from the year 1363. See *Kodeks dyplomatyczny klasztoru tynieckiego*, ed. Władysław Kętrzyński and Stanisław Smolka (Lwów, 1875), # 85.

40. *C.D.M.P.*, III, # 1310. The sum total of these extraordinary financial negotiations was to provide income equal to nearly one-third of the crown's normal annual revenue. See Kaczmarczyk, *Monarchia Kazimierza Wielkiego*, 2 vols. (Poznań, 1939–46), I, 196–99.

41. *M.P.V.*, III, # 347.

The preparations which Casimir had been making in the months after the repulse of the Tatars suggest only one thing: that he was planning a new campaign in Ruthenia, probably that same year. Unfortunately we hear nothing of such an expedition, either from contemporary sources or later writers, such as Długosz. There is extant an undated border treaty between Casimir and the Gedyminowicze which, by its wording and the context of events to which it refers, can only be attributed to the late summer or early fall of 1352.[42] To this can be added data which arise from a careful examination of Casimir's itinrarye for the last half of the year. This places him on August 23 in the town of Szczebrzeszyn, which lies on the border of Lithuanian territory.[43] Since there is no further record of his presence until late November, this gap provides the opportunity for the campaign which must be assumed from the border treaty described below. One Polish scholar [44] has even gone so far as to suggest that in the invasion of fall, 1352, Casimir was able to obtain a measure of support from the boyars of Ruthenia. While such a detailed assumption oversteps somewhat the limits of what we may reasonably infer about this expedition, on a more modest scale it is possible to reconstruct a probable framework of events within which to describe the border treaty.

Casimir had undoubtedly hoped to win a decisive victory over the Lithuanians in this campaign, but this was denied him. The Lithuanian forces succeeded in fighting Polish troops to an inconclusive outcome, and both sides were forced to agree to a compromise. Representatives from both met and negotiated the first formal treaty which bore directly upon the inheritance in Ruthenia. For many years, the treaty's principle of physical possession conferring title was to be the basis of Polish-Lithuanian relationships in this disputed territory. By the terms of this treaty the Gedyminowicze recognized Casimir as the legitimate ruler in the territories of Przemyśl, Sanok, Halicz, and Lwów. Casimir recognized Lithuanian possession of the *ziemie* of Vladimir, Łuck, Bełz, Chełm, and Brześć. In eastern Volhynia, the territory of Krzemieniec was granted to one of the grandsons of Gedymin. It is interesting to note, that this territory was given in the name of the Polish king and the Lithuanian princes, thus creating a condominium, a not unfamiliar feature of eastern European

---

42. Stadnicki, *Synowie*, II, 32–36, placed the date of this treaty between 1340 and 1345. Later scholars have been more precise. Caro, *Geschichte Polens*, II, 296, says 1352; Hrushevsky, *Istoria*, IV, 39, 444, suggests 1352 or, less possibly, 1353. Since Paszkiewicz, *Polityka Ruska*, p. 160, presented his argument, largely adopted in the text, for 1352, no serious scholar has disagreed with this date.

43. *A.G.Z.*, V, 3. I have here rejected the possibility that Casimir was in Lwów on August 22. See Paszkiewicz, *Polityka Ruska*, p. 134 n. 2, who argues strongly against the validity of the document which places him there, though he does not close out completely that possibility. I consider it equally unlikely, as Dąbrowski, *Ostatnie lata*, p. 132 n. 2, suggests, that there was Hungarian participation in this late summer or early fall campaign.

44. Halecki, *Dzieje unii*, I, 70, and "Kazimierz Wielki, 1333–1370," in *Encyklopedya Polska*, V, pt. i (Warsaw, Lublin, Łódź, and Cracow, 1920), p. 343.

institutional development.[45] In addition to the mutual recognition of the territories of each of the parties, a defensive alliance was also included in the treaty. The Lithuanians promised to aid Casimir should the Tatars invade Poland, and the king guaranteed his aid to the Lithuanians should Louis of Hungary attack them in their homeland. Should either side be attacked in Ruthenia, then neither party was bound to grant the other aid. Finally, the treaty was to last for two years, probably until October or November, 1354.[46]

In this treaty there is no mention of Hungary's traditional claims to Ruthenia. Casimir neglected Louis deliberately, partially because Louis had included no mention of Poland's claims in his dealings with Kiejstut the year before and partially because the treaty was to last for only two years and therefore had no bearing upon the ultimate fate of Hungarian claims. Of more concern to the Angevins would have been Casimir's agreement to support the Lithuanians against Louis should he attack them. In reality, this provision of the treaty does not mark so great a departure from the traditional Polish-Hungarian alliance as at first appears. Louis possessed no common border with the Gedyminowicze. His route of access to Lithuania lay either through Poland directly or through Polish-controlled Ruthenia. Louis would hardly act against Lithuania alone. Therefore, should a Hungarian campaign into Lithuania take place, it would undoubtedly be with Casimir's support either in breach of the treaty or after its expiration. (It should be noted also that the terms of the treaty did not include campaigning in Ruthenia in the defensive alliance.) Thus there was little possibility that Casimir would be called upon to fulfill this agreement. There was some danger that the Tatars might attack Poland, in which case the Polish king could hope for Lithuanian support. As a result of these provisions, Casimir had shrewdly gained more than he had given in his dealings with the Gedyminowicze.

While Casimir had been involved in the east, the eye of his ally Louis had been cast to the south. Louis had undertaken an expedition into the Balkan peninsula in an attempt to bring Dalmatia under Hungarian control. In his absence, his mother, Elizabeth, Casimir's older sister, acted as regent in Hungary.[47] It is therefore somewhat surprising that in October she was not in Buda but in Cracow. That her visit should come at the same time as, or shortly after,

---

45. See Abraham, *Powstanie*, p. 222; Halecki, *Dzieje Unii*, I, 71.

46. The text of this treaty is written in old Russian. It has been printed several times in a simple transliteration into Latin letters, most conveniently in K. Stronczyński, ed., *Wzory pism dawnych w przerysach wystawione* (Cracow, 1839), #90. The most complete treatment of its contents is in Paszkiewicz, *Polityka Ruska*, pp. 160–63; the best summary in the Western languages is Rhode, *Die Ostgrenze Polens*, I, 192–93. The only direct reference to this treaty in Polish sources is Janko of Czarnków, *Chronicon*, p. 630. Długosz, *Historia*, III, 246, refers indirectly to it when he remarks *sub anno* 1353 that Lubart in his campaign of 1353 "had fraudulently and unfairly broken the treaty which had been sworn between King Casimir and the Lithuanians."

47. The details of the following are based upon Dąbrowski, "Elżbieta Łokietkówna," *R.A.U.*, XXXII (1914), 366.

the Polish-Lithuanian treaty is, however, not coincidental. She either feared or had learned that her brother's dealings would be prejudicial to Louis's ambitions. Her visit was brief (by November 20 she had left), suggesting she had been reassured that nothing had been done to impair Hungarian interests.

Casimir's fortunes in Ruthenia remained in flux. His early successes in 1340 had been only ephemeral and had been largely obliterated by 1349, when the Polish border again surged to the east and southeast. Immediately thereafter, the yearly comings and goings of Gedyminowicze and Tatars had begun to erode even these gains, so that by 1352 Casimir's extensive holdings had been reduced to the southern half of the heritage of the former prince, Roman. By this time, a stasis or equilibrium had been achieved which remained nearly constant for almost a decade and a half. For the first time since discussing the death of Bolesław-George II it is now possible to trace an eastern Polish boundary which served as a temporary border.[48] Beginning at the Carpathians, the boundary ran northeast on the course of the Czeremosz River to Sniatyn, then turned north to the Dniester, which it followed upstream to the confluence of the Strypa. It in turn followed this river to a point some few miles south of Buczacz, then ran due east to the Zbrucz River, which then formed the easternmost point on the boundary. The border then turned to the northwest, crossing the Seret, briefly following the upper course of the Bug, running south of Bełz and touching the Wieprz, until it reached the Polish border proper just north of Góraj. As far as the condominium of Krzemieniec is concerned, it must have passed out of existence soon after the treaty of 1352, for there is no mention of it at a later time. This is not surprising, for it had been established only for the duration of the treaty.

Casimir might well have expected, on the basis of the treaty, that he would have peace with the Lithuanians for at least two years. Kiejstut's breach of his oath and his flight from Louis's camp in 1351 showed, however, that the Gedyminowicze were not above breaking an oath or a treaty if by so doing they might gain an advantage. Thus it was that in 1353 Lubart and his brothers three times invaded Ruthenian Poland and even the *regnum* itself. Johannes Długosz, who was not overly sympathetic to the Lithuanians of his own day, seemed to take particular delight in reporting that "Lubart . . . had fraudently and unfairly broken the treaty which had been sworn between King Casimir and the Lithuanians." There seems to be no reason to doubt his assertion.[49] The first invasion of that year came in May, when Lubart led his forces against Lwów. The *Rocznik miechowski* tells us that "the Lithuanians ravaged Lwów ['Lamburg'], killing many," from which historians have concluded that the

48. The following description is based upon Halecki, "Geografja polityczna ziem ruskich Polski i Litwy 1340–1569," *Sprawozdania z posiedzeń towarzystwa naukowego Warszawskiego, wydział I i II,* X (March 16, 1917), 8; Rhode, *Die Ostgrenze Polens,* I, 193.

49. Długosz, *Historia,* III, 246. Hrushevsky, *Istoria,* IV, 41, blames Casimir for the breach, but offers no proof of his statement.

city was not taken, though the environs suffered badly.[50] Two months later, on July 7, Lubart again invaded Polish Ruthenia, this time marching upon Halicz. He was successful in breaching the defenses of the city, which was sacked and burned, and many of its inhabitants perished. The surrounding area was also devastated before the attackers withdrew. Again two months intervened between attacks. Then on September 9 the Lithuanians swept anew onto Polish territory. This time, however, they directed their attentions toward the valley of the Vistula, reaching as far as Zawichost, north of Sandomir. Despite the tales of plunder, pillage, and devastation given us, particularly by Długosz, and despite the depth of the third incursion, these three actions in 1353 were simply raids and did not in any way change the borders between the two states or alter their relative positions in Ruthenia.[51]

It is difficult to determine in what way Casimir responded to these Lithuanian assaults. The literary sources at our disposal are completely silent in this respect, although from his itinerary we can infer that sometime between July and October he was involved in carrying out his own campaign against the Lithuanians.[52] Probably in the later stages of this period Casimir gathered an army and marched into Lithuanian Ruthenia, for on October 23 he was "encamped near Bełz in Ruthenian territory."[53] Apparently this campaign had as little effect upon the territorial division of Ruthenia as the earlier Lithuanian raids.[54]

While engaged with the Lithuanians, Casimir had not ignored the possibility of a threat from the Tatars. Hoping to obtain at the very least the neutrality of the Horde in the Polish-Lithuanian struggle, in 1353 Casimir sent an ambassador to negotiate with the Tatars. He succeeded in obtaining their recognition of his rights in the whole of Ruthenia; but a price had to be paid for this, and Casimir apparently agreed to the payment of regular tribute to the Horde.[55]

---

50. *M.P.H.*, II, 885, with the date "post festum Trinitatis." See Kaczmarczyk and Weyman, *Reformy wojskowe*, pp. 130 f.; Olejnik, *Działalność militarna*, pp. 89 f.

51. Długosz, *Historia*, III, 246. Confirmation of Długosz's account is contained in the record of the mission of Jasko of Jura and Czenko of Lipa to the emperor in 1354. See Ludewig, *Reliquiae*, V, 35, 512. See also the comments of Aleksander Semkowicz, *Krytyczny rozbiór dziejów polskich Jana Długosza* (Cracow, 1887), p. 368.

52. Casimir's whereabouts is accounted for from February through May in the itinerary given by Paszkiewicz, *Polityka Ruska*, p. 168, which would disprove Hrushevsky's assertion that it was the king who broke the peace. From July 3 to October 23 there are enough gaps to have allowed military action.

53. *C.D.P.M.*, III, #702.

54. Hrushevsky, *Istoria*, IV, 42.

55. Spuler, *Die Goldene Horde*, p. 108, says Casimir's position was recognized only in western Podolia. On the question of Podolia, see below and Appendix C. The claims of the Tatars were to the whole of Ruthenia, and it must have been for this area that Casimir obtained recognition. See Rhode, *Die Ostgrenze Polens*, I, 194 n. 127. Although Halecki, *Dzieje unii*, I, 73, says that news of Casimir's payment of tribute to the Tatars had no foundation in fact and was only a rumor spread by the Order, Casimir explicitly says, in a letter to the grand master in 1355, that seven Tatar princes are supporting him against the Lithuanians (*C.D.Pr.*, III, #83). This kind of support could probably only have been gained by the payment of tribute.

News of this agreement not surprisingly created a stir in western and central Europe, and many rumors soon circulated as to what Casimir had done. One particularly garbled version was received in Wrocław in March of the following year. There it was reported that Casimir had made an alliance with the Horde and was planning to marry a Tatar princess.[56] Outspoken criticism came also from Avignon, but not until January 24, 1357. At that time Pope Innocent VI wrote heatedly to Casimir. The pope complained that he had learned (most probably from representatives of the Teutonic Order in Avignon) that Casimir had allied with the Tatars and was paying them tribute; did the king not know what a great disservice this was, both to himself and to the church![57]

Casimir's motives in his dealings with the Tatars are easily seen. He needed assurance that there would be no Lithuanian-Tatar alliance against him while he fought the Gedyminowicze for the succession in Ruthenia. His negotiations were completely pragmatic; as a proto-*realpolitiker*, Casimir profited from these arrangements, then discarded them when they no longer served his purposes. In his policy he was successful: the Tatars were never again a real threat during his reign.

The decade from 1354 to 1364 brought no substantial change in the relative positions of the Lithuanians and Poles in Ruthenia, but it was not devoid of action or importance, for Casimir did not slacken his attempts to gain full and final possession of Ruthenia. The period is important for another reason. It witnessed the renewal of Casimir's attempts to Christianize the Lithuanians, an approach which he had briefly utilized in 1348–49. These years see military and diplomatic means being used simultaneously. We shall examine each of these in turn, for though the decade was indecisive, certain patterns in Polish-Lithuanian relations were firmly established for the future.

The year 1354 apparently passed without military action by either Poland or the Gedyminowicze. Casimir devoted his attention to mending diplomatic fences in the west and obtaining material aid for use in Ruthenia. One of the most important of the former kind of activity was an effort to regain the good will of Bohemia and Charles IV. Despite the treaty of Namysłów in 1348, relations between the Piast and Luxemburg houses had recently been strained, particularly over questions relating to Mazovia. To alter this situation, in 1354 Casimir dispatched a high Czech noble, Czenko of Lipa, and his own palatine of Sandomir, Jasko of Jura, to the court of the emperor. Though it is impossible to determine the details of their mission, the fact that it concerned matters of high state policy leads us to believe that Casimir wished to assure himself of Bohemian neutrality while he was involved in the east.[58] The king also turned

56. Colmar Grünhagen, "Die Correspondenz der Stadt Breslau mit Karl IV, in den Jahren 1347–1355," *Archiv für Österreichische Geschichte*, XXXIV (1865), 365.

57. Theiner, *Mon. Pol.*, I, # 776.

58. Ludewig, *Reliquiae*, V, 35, 512: "we had to negotiate and define clearly a great many

in this same year to Avignon to request help. On November 10 Innocent responded by publishing a bull which announced a new crusade against the Lithuanians; while a dozen days later he renewed for another four years his predecessor's grant to Casimir of the papal tenth from Poland. (Only one-half of this sum was actually released for Casimir's use.)[59]

Despite the agreement of 1339 with the Angevins that Charles Robert (and, by 1354, Louis) would succeed Casimir in Poland should he die without heir, there were still a great many details to arrange concerning this eventuality. In the winter of 1354–55 Casimir traveled to Buda to clarify the succession agreement.[60] While he was there he also raised again with Louis the question of Hungary's role in the conquest of Ruthenia. Louis promised on January 20, 1355, to participate personally in Casimir's next campaign and, if prevented from doing so, to send a sufficiently large army to serve "for the expulsion and confusion of [the Lithuanians]."[61] That Louis was willing to make such agreements shows the importance Casimir laid upon Angevin aid and the earnestness with which he importuned Louis, and also the extent to which the Angevin was willing to go to please his uncle so as to strengthen his position as Polish heir-presumptive.

Yet a fourth source of support for Casimir's eastern plans came in this same period. The Polish king in his search for aid had turned to his son-in-law, Lewis the Roman, for assistance. Sometime in 1354 or 1355,[62] the grand master of the Order was informed by the new margrave of Brandenburg that he would soon be leading a mighty army into Lithuania to lend his father-in-law auxiliary support in his struggle.[63] Lewis went on, and this surely was at Casimir's urging, to exhort the Knights of the Order to join the Polish king in his expedition. At the same time Casimir had not been remiss in approaching the Knights directly. Shortly before he left Cracow on the campaign the king wrote Grand Master Winrich von Kniprode.[64] He called attention to previous correspondence in the matter of the Lithuanians and described his plans. From this it is possible,

---

and difficult things with Charles." There is little in the record of this mission to connect it so intimately with Ruthenian affairs. The case made for this, however, and the collateral evidence adduced in support by Paszkiewicz, *Polityka Ruska*, pp. 175–80, is overwhelming. It is equally true, however, that this embassy is not unconnected with the Congress of Prague in 1356 and the formation of Polish-Bohemian peace.

59. Theiner, *Mon. Hung.*, II, # 18; *Mon. Pol.*, I, # 739, and I, # 742, dated February 12, 1355.

60. Dąbrowski, *Ostatnie lata*, p. 141.

61. Louis's declaration in a copy dated September 1, 1355, in Dogiel, *Codex*, I, 37.

62. The document is undated, but most scholars agree it should be placed late in 1354, or more probably in the spring of 1355. See Abraham, *Powstanie*, p. 223 n. 3; Halecki, "Kazimierz Wielki," p. 347; Paszkiewicz, *Polityka Ruska*, p. 182 n. 3.

63. *C.D.Pr.*, III, # 84.

64. Ibid., # 83.

despite the absence of any previous correspondence, to accept the suggestion that Casimir had requested aid from the Knights themselves for this campaign and was here renewing that request.[65] Even these repeated pleas failed to move the Order. Somewhat better results had been obtained from the Horde, for this same letter of the king's asserted that he was able to depend upon the support of seven Tatar princes against the Lithuanians. He was referring, not to the agreement of two years previous, but to the results obtained from yet another visit of his ambassador to the court of the khan.[66] The king's optimism was ill-founded, for apparently the only assistance the Horde lent was its neutrality.

By the end of July, 1355, all was in readiness for Casimir's campaign. For the details of this expedition, however, we seek in vain among the literary sources. According to the gaps in the king's itinerary, a campaign could have taken place between late July and late November.[67] In addition, two other items of indirect evidence suggest that a campaign actually took place. The first is the movement of Hungarian troops. These left Buda in July and went to Poland, returning home early in October.[68] The chronology in this instance provides reinforcement for the presumption of Casimir's campaign. It should be added that Louis did not personally lend his uncle assistance, since in this same period he undertook a campaign into Serbia to further Angevin interests in the lands surrounding the Adriatic. He had, however, fulfilled his promise to send Casimir aid if he could not personally participate in the action. A second item of evidence is the brief death-notice the following year for one Stanisław Ciołek: "He died in the Tatar wars, when the Tatars attacked Vladimir, having been sent by King Casimir to defend this fortress, in the year 1356." The fortress of Vladimir had been captured by the Lithuanians in the campaigns of 1351–52. That it in 1356 found itself in Polish hands can only have been as the result of a successful campaign in 1355.[69] This is the only evidence of Polish success in that year, for events elsewhere impinged upon Casimir's plans in Ruthenia.

The Teutonic Knights, whom Casimir had asked for help against the Gedyminowicze, not only failed to grant aid, but actually turned against Poland during this period. In the summer of 1355 the Order signed a treaty with the Lithuanians in order to gain safe passage into eastern Ruthenia for

65. This position is argued strongly by Paszkiewicz, *Polityka Ruska*, pp. 183–85.

66. Casimir wrote the pope in 1363 that a certain John Pakosławowicz had acted as his emissary to the Horde several times. *M.P.V.*, III, 421. See also Paszkiewicz, *Polityka Ruska*, p. 184 n. 5.

67. See the itinerary, including a hitherto unpublished document, in Paszkiewicz, *Polityka Ruska*, p. 186 n. 8.

68. See Dąbrowski, *Ostatnie lata*, p. 144 n. 3.

69. *Spominki o Ciołkach*, in *M.P.H.*, III, 269. Paszkiewicz, *Polityka Ruska*, p. 192 n. 3, has reasonably suggested that in the notice of Ciołek's death "Tartarorum" should be emended to "Litwanorum," since it was they who had held Vladimir until 1366.

German merchants, particularly those from Toruń. In return for this privilege, the Knights promised to lend the Gedyminowicze aid against Poland. Eventually news of this transaction reached the ears of the papacy, and on September 17, 1356, the pope issued a strongly worded protest against this action by the Order.[70] More damaging to Casimir than this promise to the Lithuanians was the actual aggression of the Knights that same summer. Shortly after the king left for the east, the Order sent troops into Mazovia, which had recently come under the control of the Polish crown. Their immediate goal was the capture of certain border fortifications, but in addition they probably wished also to force a withdrawal of Polish power in the east where their own commercial routes were threatened. This campaign should therefore be seen, not so much as indicating a desire for renewed war with Poland, but as a highly successful diversionary tactic.[71] Casimir was forced to break off his Ruthenian campaign before he achieved further success; once again his hopes for a decisive victory over the Lithuanians in Ruthenia had been frustrated.

In 1356 the Lithuanians sent an army into Ruthenia and laid siege to Vladimir. Despite the defense of the fortress by, among others, Stanisław Ciołek, it fell again into the hands of the Gedyminowicze, who retained it until Casimir's successful campaign of 1366.[72] This failure to retain Vladimir, and the generally indecisive nature of the conflict against the Lithuanians in spite of elaborate military, diplomatic, and economic preparations, effected in the next few years a subtle, though significant, change in Casimir's relations with the Gedyminowicze. Increasingly he deemphasized military action, so that a decade was to pass before he renewed the conflict. At the same time he revived a previously utilized technique for subjecting the Lithuanians to Polish influence: the Christianization of this region. A variety of factors motivated the king in this policy, besides the failure of his military action. We cannot deny to Casimir, as a Christian king in the Christian Middle Ages, the practice of pure missionary zeal; and it is not practical to exclude the possibility that Casimir hoped to apply the moral influence of the church and the papacy to the Lithuanians. Conversely, we should not disregard the role which the increasing hostility and bitterness between Poland and the Teutonic Order may have played. One manifestation of this hostility was the agitation of the Order's ambassadors in Avignon against Casimir. Their efforts were at least partially successful, for on January 24, 1357, Pope Innocent reproached Casimir for his close dealings some years before with the Tatars and the Lithuanians.[73] To counteract the activity of the Knights, to restore himself to papal favor, and to satisfy the motives

---

70. Theiner, *Mon. Pol.*, I, # 769.

71. See Paszkiewicz, *Polityka Ruska*, p. 190.

72. In addition to the *Spominki o Ciołkach*, p. 269, see also Kaczmarczyk and Weyman, *Reformy wojskowe*, pp. 132 f.; Olejnik, *Działalność militarna*, p. 91.

73. Theiner, *Mon. Pol.*, I, # 776.

mentioned above, Casimir turned again to the Christianization of the Lithuanians.

Sometime in mid-1357 Casimir wrote to Avignon suggesting the possibility and desirability of converting the Lithuanians. He urged the pope to request the cooperation of Emperor Charles IV and King Louis in this program.[74] Although the ostensible purpose for which this letter was written undoubtedly reflected sincerity on Casimir's part, at the same time the king was too intelligent not to recognize that this approach would accomplish two secondary purposes: it would restore him to the good graces of the papacy and would cut the ground from under the Order's complaints against him. In a second letter to Avignon, apparently sent about the same time, Casimir also requested the papacy to place the Lithuanian church which would arise from conversion under the jurisdiction of the archbishop of Gniezno. This would insure continued Polish influence in Lithuania, not only in spiritual matters but perhaps also in political matters.[75]

Pope Innocent responded to Casimir's first suggestion by requesting Charles IV to take an active interest in the conversion of Lithuania. As a result the emperor issued a letter to the princes of Lithuania on April 18, 1358, in which he exhorted them to be baptized, promising them imperial protection and support if they did so.[76] At the same time Casimir was active also, as he established friendly contacts with some of the Gedyminowicze. Early in June, 1358, he traveled to the border city of Lublin to carry on with the Lithuanians a series of high-level discussions. The importance the king attached to these is reflected by the fact that in his retinue he included nearly a score of the most important civil officials from Little Poland and Polish Ruthenia.[77]

The Christianization of Lithuania was the main topic discussed in Lublin, but two collateral issues were also touched upon. One was the proposal that Prince Olgierd's daughter Kenna be married to a grandson of the king, the later Duke Kaźko of Szczecin, in Pomorze Zachodnie. Despite the fact that the intended pair were related in the third degree (Kaźko's maternal grandmother had been Kenna's aunt), Casimir was able to obtain ecclesiastical dispensation for the marriage, which took place sometime in 1360, with the bride taking the Christian name Joanna.[78] Another topic of discussion was where the ecclesiastical organization of Lithuania should be concentrated. It was apparently agreed that Chełm would be the site of a Latin-rite bishopric.[79]

74. *M.P.V.*, III, 375; Abraham, *Powstanie*, p. 367.

75. *M.P.V.*, III, 375; Abraham, *Powstanie*, p. 368.

76. This hitherto unpublished letter is printed by Paszkiewicz, *Polityka Ruska*, p. 197 n. 5.

77. These officials are mentioned in documents issued on his journey. *C.D.P.M.*, III, # 721-23; *C.D.M.P.*, III, # 1280.

78. See Halecki, *Dzieje unii*, I, 74, and "Kazimierz Wielki," p. 351; *Pol. Słow. Biog.*, XII, 281.

79. See Paszkiewicz, *Polityka Ruska*, p. 200 n. 3.

These negotiations had been very successful, and at Casimir's urging the Lithuanians agreed to investigate further the matter of Christianity. In July of the same year, one of the Gedyminowicze, perhaps Olgierd, journeyed to the imperial diet at Nürnberg to meet with Charles IV.[80] There he declared his intention to become a Christian and be baptized together with all his people. He further suggested that the princes and rulers of territories in this region of Europe be convened in Wrocław at Christmas, 1358, to witness the baptism. Charles then appointed a three-man commission which was empowered to assist the Lithuanians in every way possible and to prepare the mechanics of the conversion and baptism. All of the preparations went for naught, however. When December came, Olgierd (if indeed it was he) qualified his promises by making his baptism contingent upon the return of all territory which the Teutonic Order had conquered from Lithuania. This was an embarrassing request, for since the raison d'être of the Order was the Christianization of the pagans, not its own territorial aggrandizement, it could not responsibly retain Lithuanian lands after they had become Christian. That the Order refused to return this territory reflects the transformation, during the course of the preceding century, of the Knights from a military-crusading movement into a territorially defined *Ordensstaat*. As a result of this action, hopes of Christianizing Lithuania peacefully were temporarily dashed.[81]

Despite the failure of the Lithuanians to become Christians, relations between Casimir and the Gedyminowicze remained peaceful and there was no renewed outbreak of conflict in Ruthenia. The character of these relations is partially indicated by the border treaty of 1358 between Duke Ziemowit of Mazovia, by now a vassal of Casimir, and Kiejstut. Signed in Grodno on August 8, this treaty established a clearly defined border between Mazovia and Lithuania and made provision for the adjudication of disputes by a panel of judges composed of members appointed from both sides.[82] This newly defined border now incorporated within the borders of Poland a large segment of the earlier possession of the Jadźwings, the later region of Podlachia. This land was almost surely an area very sparsely populated, for the points of reference in the treaty are overwhelmingly rivers rather than settlements. The continuation of

80. Our single source for this event, Henricus de Rebdorf, *Annales imperatorum et paparum 1294–1362*, in *Font. rer. Germ.*, IV, 544–45, says only "In July 1358, the king of the Livonians [rex liphonie gentilis] sent his brother to the aforementioned Emperor Charles." Abraham, *Powstanie*, p. 225 n. 1, and Paszkiewicz, *Polityka Ruska*, p. 201, think the visit was made by Olgierd; Emil Werunsky, *Geschichte Kaiser Karls IV. und seiner Zeit*, 3 vols. in 4 (Innsbruck, 1880–96), III, 201, says it was Kiejstut.

81. In addition to Henricus de Rebdorf, see Werunsky, *Karl IV*, III, 201–2; Voigt, *Geschichte Preussens*, V, 125–29; Kazimierz Chodynicki, "Próby zaprowadzenia chrześcijaństwa na Litwie przed r. 1386," *P.H.*, XVIII (1914), 284–95.

82. *Kod. dypl. ks. maz.*, #80. For details concerning the boundary, see *Słownik Geograficzny Królestwa Polskiego i innych krajów słowiańskich*, 15 vols. (Warsaw, 1880–1902), VIII, 411; Rhode, *Die Ostgrenze Polens*, I, 212 ff.

good relations is reflected also by an agreement to the appointment of a Latin-rite bishop of Chełm. In the discussions of 1358 a certain Franciscan named Thomas had been mentioned as *electus Chelmensis*, but it was not until May, 1359, that he was formally appointed bishop.[83] One final event shows the improved nature of Polish-Lithuanian relations during this period. On November 11, 1359, the nobility of the territory of Lublin signed a treaty of peace and friendship with the boyars of Chełm. Its main purpose was to establish clearly the boundary between the two territories, which it did in great detail.[84]

At this point in narratives dealing with Polish interests in the east during Casimir's reign, it has been traditional to consider the question of Moldavia. The dominance of Długosz as an historical source is largely responsible for this, for he records that in 1359 the king sent an army into Moldavia at the request of Hospodar Stephen.[85] On this basis, some historians have seen Casimir as an early advocate, conscious or otherwise, of a Greater Poland extending to the Black Sea.[86] Recent researches have tended to cast doubt upon the veracity of the chronicler's narrative and the validity of the traditional interpretation. For that reason, the question of Moldavia has been given separate treatment in Appendix C. Reference may be made to that section for a question which may not properly be treated as a part of Casimir's policy in the east.

There is a lull in Polish-Lithuanian relations after 1359 for some years. In none of our scanty sources is there mention of either renewed conflict or revived missionary activity. Instead a curtain of silence covers the affairs of Ruthenia. There is good reason for this. The Lithuanians were involved in expansion to the east and with defending themselves in the west from the Teutonic Knights; while Casimir was strengthening his position in the west by diplomacy and judicious marriages. Casimir was also beginning to prepare cautiously for the campaign which he eventually launched in 1366, but in so doing he was having to take into account a more powerful Lithuanian state than he had previously faced.

Under the leadership of Grand Princes Olgierd and Kiejstut, who had gradually assumed a position of greater influence and power than the rest of the Gedyminowicze, Lithuania had greatly expanded its territory and strengthened its position, both internally and externally. The greatest Lithuanian victory came in 1362 with the conquest of Kiev and its environs.[87] This concentration

---

83. Abraham, *Powstanie*, pp. 371–73; see also pp. 243–48; Paszkiewicz, *Polityka Ruska*, p. 200 n. 3. Despite his appointment, it is likely that Thomas seldom if ever set foot in his diocese, but remained in Cracow as bishop "in partibus."

84. The whole treaty is printed by Paszkiewicz, *Polityka Ruska*, p. 201 n. 6.

85. Długosz, *Historia*, III, 277–78.

86. Beginning with two articles by Aleksander Czołowski, "Początki Mołdawii i wyprawa Kazimierza Wielkiego r. 1359," *K.H.*, IV (1890), 258–85, and "Sprawy wołoskie w Polsce do roku 1412," *K.H.*, V (1891), 569–72.

87. For this expansion, see Hrushevsky, *Istoria*, IV, 73–87, and, more briefly, Paszkiewicz, *Polityka Ruska*, pp. 223–25.

upon eastern expansion had "necessarily lessened tensions with Poland, but had also increased the potential resources of the Lithuanian state, thereby strengthening it for any future conflict with Poland.

During this period of Lithuanian expansion and consolidation, two of the grandsons of Gedymin were drawn increasingly into the orbit of Polish influence, eventually becoming friends and allies of Casimir. George and Alexander Korjatowicz had received very small patrimonies upon the death of their father sometime after 1358. Dissatisfied with these, they participated in the acquisition of territory with their several brothers and uncles. George eventually gained the principalities of Chełm and Vladimir, while Alexander held land near the Polish border. Each had dealings with Casimir, and in the early 1360s events conspired to bring them even closer to him. About 1362 a controversy arose between George and Alexander on the one hand and Kiejstut and Lubart on the other. The result was the expulsion of the two Korjatowicze from their principalities. The brothers then fled for refuge to the royal court of Poland, where George witnessed two documents issued by Casimir in 1365 and 1366 and where Alexander's presence is confirmed by a reference in Janko of Czarnków.[88] While in Cracow the two undoubtedly agitated for a new Polish campaign into Ruthenia so that they might gain lands for themselves. This attitude simply reinforced the king's intentions, for as early as 1363 Casimir had begun to lay the groundwork for the campaign of 1366.

The careful and extensive preparations which Casimir made for his great expedition indicate that he hoped again for a decisive victory over the Lithuanians.[89] In the summer he sent an ambassador to Avignon. The chief petition which he bore was a request for Urban V to found a *studium generale* in Cracow,[90] but the king had also instructed him to petition the pope for spiritual and

88. The Korjatowicze have been the subject of extensive investigation. Their position was not clearly understood as late as 1925, for they appear only as fleeting shadows in Paszkiewicz, *Polityka Ruska*. In 1930, however, Count Jozef Puzyna began publishing the results of his investigations. His first two articles in the *Ateneum Wileńskie*, "Korjat i Korjatowicze," VII (1930), 425–55, and "Korjat i Korjatowicze oraz sprawa Podolska, uzupełnienia i poprawki," XI (1936), 61–97, presented the first coherent picture of the origins, activity, and significance of this family. His conclusions did not go unchallenged, however, and in 1938, as an appendix to his *Krewo*, Paszkiewicz wrote an essay entitled "Pierwsze wystąpienie Korjatowiczów na widowni dziejowej," pp. 264–99, which took issue with many of Puzyna's views. Puzyna answered in a third article, "Pierwsze wystąpienie Korjatowiczów na Rusi południowej," *Ateneum Wileńskie*, XIII (1938), 1–68. A review of this research with a few variant conclusions was given by Stefan Krakowski, "Korjatowicze i sprawa Podolsku w XIV wieku w oświetleniu najnowszej historjografji Polskiej," *Ateneum Wileńskie*, XIII (1938), 250–74. Rhode, *Die Ostgrenze Polens*, I, 199–201, 219–25, generally follows Paszkiewicz. On the closely related question of Podolia, see Appendix C.

89. Paszkiewicz, *Polityka Ruska*, pp. 227–28.

90. For his mission, see Stanisław Krzyżanowski, "Poselstwo Kazimierza Wielkiego do Awinionu i pierwsze uniwersyteckie przywileje," *Rocznik Krakowski*, IV (1900), 1–111; Kazimierz Morawski, *Historya Uniwersytetu jagiellońskiego, średnie wieki i odrodzenie*, 2 vols. (Cracow, 1900), I, 24–33; Paul W. Knoll, "Casimir the Great and the University of Cracow," *Jahrbücher für Geschichte Osteuropas*, XVI (1968), 240–41.

financial support for the king's struggle against "our mortal enemies,"[91] that is, the Lithuanians. Urban's response to this petition must have been disappointing, for he did not grant any financial support. He was content to grant plenary indulgences to all those in the following twelve years who might "provide aid for the defense of the aforementioned kingdom against the Lithuanians, Tatars, and other infidels and schismatics."[92]

The next year Casimir directed another request to the pope. He petitioned Urban to free him from all oaths which he had given to unbelievers in various treaties.[93] Though one cannot determine with certainty which oaths the king was referring to, they probably concerned Ruthenia and Lithuania. Some scholars have suggested that in connection with the proposed Christianization of Lithuania in 1358 Casimir had made promises from which he now desired to be released.[94] Probably priest and prince reached an informal agreement, for despite the absence of a papal dispensation there were no protests raised over royal successes in 1366.

In order to commit himself fully to a Ruthenian campaign, Casimir needed assurances that he would be free from interference in the west and the north, that none of his neighbors would strike while his back was turned. For this reason among others the king decided against any increased aggressiveness in Polish policy toward the Order. He also played a waiting game with Charles IV, preferring in the years before 1366 not to raise the explosive question of Polish claims in Silesia. In addition to these aspects of his policy, Casimir's diplomacy in the years before the campaign greatly strengthened Poland's international reputation and even brought territorial changes in the west favorable to the kingdom. Thus there was nothing elsewhere to distract the king, and by the summer of 1366 all was in readiness for the crowning achievement of Casimir's eastern policy.

Throughout the spring of that year covert military preparations were made within Poland. The *pospolite ruszenie* was gathered and a sizable army of cavalry and infantry prepared to march.[95] Though Johannes Długosz, who saw Casimir's campaign as the greatest achievement of the greatest Piast, says only that the army entered Ruthenia "after the feast of Saint John the Baptist" (June 24), the king's itinerary for this year allows us to establish more precisely when the campaign took place.[96] Sometime late in July, Casimir marched into Polish

91. Casimir continued to use this phrase even during the years when there was de facto peace between Poland and Lithuania. See, for example, in 1360: *C.D.P.M.*, III, # 739.

92. Theiner, *Mon. Pol.*, I, # 833.

93. *M.P.V.*, III, 458.

94. Paszkiewicz, *Polityka Ruska*, p. 227; Rhode, *Die Ostgrenze Polens*, I, 201. Halecki, "Casimir the Great," in the *Camb. Hist. of Pol.*, I, 184, says this move was directed against Bohemia and the Teutonic Order also.

95. Długosz, *Historia*, III, 307.

96. Casimir was in Cracow on July 22 (*C.D.P.M.*, I, # 284), and in Vladimir on August 28 (*A.G.Z.*, III, 16). By October 17 he had returned to Little Poland (*C.D.P.M.*, III, # 794).

Ruthenia to Lwów. From there he followed the traditional route northward toward Bełz. He apparently found it unnecessary to besiege the fortress there, for George Narjmuntowicz capitulated to Casimir and accepted his overlordship, receiving in return his principality of Bełz as a fief of the Polish crown. There may even have been preliminary agreements to this effect made through the agency of George and Alexander Korjatowicz.[97] Of this particular part of the campaign Janko of Czarnków, the only contemporary narrator, says only that George of Bełz subjected himself cleverly, in order to be later free.[98] From Bełz the royal army moved north, across the Bug River, until the fortress of Vladimir was reached. While the chief thrusts of the Polish army were directed against this fortress, other divisions of troops devastated the surrounding countryside, reaching as far east as Łuck, where Lubart fled to preserve himself. After the fall of Vladimir, Casimir enfeoffed Alexander Korjatowicz with the region and began the construction of stone fortifications for a castle there.[99] The return trip to Poland was made, not through Lwów and the valley of the San, but via the northern route; this meant the fortress of Chełm lay across Casimir's path. He did not hesitate to conquer this place also, bestowing it upon George Korjatowicz, who accepted it as a fief of the Polish crown.[100] In this short expedition Casimir gained the three chief regions of Lithuanian Ruthenia and added besides several lesser territories. The expedition is rightly regarded as a success,[101] but in order to determine the dimensions of this success it is necessary to examine the two treaties which the king negotiated in the immediate wake of the campaign.

While he was still in the field, perhaps in late September or early October, Casimir signed a treaty with the Gedyminowicze and their descendants.[102] It had as its chief purpose the stabilization of Polish-Lithuanian relations in Ruthenia. It was apparently not completely adequate for this purpose, and in

97. See Kaczmarczyk and Weyman, *Reformy wojskowe*, p. 133.

98. Janko of Czarnków, *Chronicon*, p. 631. Janko forms the basis for Długosz's later, and most frequently utilized, account. See Semkowicz, *Krytyczny rozbiór*, pp. 377–78.

99. Most of these details are based upon Długosz, *Historia*, III, 308.

100. It is impossible to determine from Janko, who reports "he gave Chełm to Duke George," whether the son of Narymunt or of Korjat is intended. Scholars have traditionally suggested the former, and even today this view is widely held: see Kaczmarczyk, *Polska czasów Kazimierza Wielkiego* (Cracow, 1964), p. 164, and Kaczmarczyk and Weyman, *Reformy wojskowe*, pp. 133–34. Paszkiewicz, *Polityka Ruska*, pp. 228–31, has shown, however, that it must have been the latter.

101. The military aspects of the campaign are treated in Kaczmarczyk and Weyman, *Reformy wojskowe*, pp. 133–34; Olejnik, *Działalność militarna*, pp. 91–92.

102. The original text of this treaty is lost. Marcin Kromer, ed., *Inventarium privilegiorum in archivo regni* (reprinted, Cracow, 1832), pp. 371–72, gave a short regest of the treaty. The text was still extant in the eighteenth century, apparently, for Adam Naruszewicz utilized it. More recently, A. Czuczyński prepared a reconstructed edition for the *K.H.*, IV (1890), 513–15, giving the Old Russian text in Latin character transcription. In 1955, Rhode published a German translation of this text in his *Die Ostgrenze Polens*, I, 381–82.

October, 1366, the king signed a second, supplemental treaty with Lubart.[103]
In the first treaty the Lithuanians were represented by Grand Princes Olgierd
and Kiejstut, together with their brothers Jawnut and Lubart and their sons.
Poland was represented by George Narjmuntowicz, King Casimir, and his
two vassals, George and Alexander Korjatowicz. Together they negotiated
an agreement by which the Ruthenian territories were partitioned between the
two states on the basis of actual possession, volosts (administration areas)
and fortresses being used as points of reference. The total effect of this partition
was to strengthen Casimir personally. In addition to those territories under
Polish control as fiefs, he also obtained some territory for himself on the right
bank of the Bug. This treaty also confirmed the feudal arrangements which
Casimir had earlier made in the field.

A second provision of this first treaty concerned the possibility of future border
disputes between the two states. A joint Polish-Lithuanian commission was
established to adjudicate such disputes. Its seat was to be at Horodło, and two
representatives from each side were originally named to it. In addition to the
disposition of the territory and the establishment of a board of adjudication,
this treaty also forced Lubart to promise he would provide military assistance
to the Polish king should he request it. In return for this aid, Casimir promised
to protect Lubart as if he were his vassal. Although this arrangement has
certain feudal characteristics which suggest suzerainty over Lubart, such is not
the case. Lubart did not do homage and swear fealty to Casimir: his responsibilities were simply specific provisions of the treaty. In addition, this relationship
was only temporary; it was to expire on October 26, 1367. After this date, a
new arrangement was to be negotiated between the two rulers. Finally, the
nature of Lubart's relation to Casimir was modified in the second treaty of
that fall. In this document the Lithuanian prince was not bound to provide
aid to the Polish king against his own brothers. Rather, in the event of a
future Polish-Lithuanian dispute, he was simply to remain neutral. This
second treaty also fixed the boundaries between Lubart and Casimir. Here,
however, the boundary was based not upon the individual volosts and cities
held by each, but upon an actual geographical course which the boundary
followed. One final agreement which was part of both these treaties indicates
the importance of commercial activity in the region. Any increases in taxes
and tolls and any harrassment of merchants by either side was forbidden, so
that "the merchant may travel his ancient routes, and he shall not be con-
strained; but wherever he wishes, there shall he go."

Casimir had not succeeded in conquering the whole of Ruthenia. Nevertheless,
he had brought under his control, either directly or through a vassal, the largest

103. This treaty is printed in *Archiwum książąt Lubartowiczów-Sanguszków w Sławucie*, ed.
Z. L. Radzimiński (Lwów, 1887–1910), I, pt. i, 1, which I have been unable to consult. It is
discussed in detail by Paszkiewicz, *Polityka Ruska*, pp. 232–36. The date assigned to the treaty
arises from the fact it was to be operative until October 26, 1367.

and perhaps the most valuable part of it. He possessed not only the left bank of the upper reaches of the Bug River, but also a considerable area on the right bank, which included a wedge-shaped projection extending to the upper reaches of the Pripet River. In addition, as the result of his campaign in 1366, he had slightly enlarged his holdings in Ruthenian Halicz. The eastern boundary of Poland had been extended further east than ever before; and though there was some further conflict with the Gedyminowicze, the boundary of 1366 remained stable until Casimir's unexpected death four years later.

The new Polish border, including Casimir's recent conquests and feudal acquisitions, was substantially altered from that of 1352–53. Its southernmost point began, as before, at the high wall of the Carpathians just east of the headwaters of the Czeremosz River. Where this stream made a great curve to the east and then to the north, border and river became identical, and continued to be so until near the latter's confluence with the Prut. From here it turned north to the Dniester, which it followed upstream to the mouth of the Strypa. It in turn followed this river to a point some four miles south of Buczacz, then ran due east to the Zbrucz River. The border followed the Zbrucz northward beyond its source, crossing the upper reaches of the Horyn River. From there it turned generally northwestward, passing to the east and north of Krzemieniec and Boreml, crossing both branches of the Styr River. North of Boreml, the border turned south for about ten miles, then again northwest until it reached almost to the Bug River north of Sokol. Without touching the Bug, it stretched to the northeast, crossed the Turja headwaters, then joined the Turja downstream above Kowel. It continued further downstream some twenty miles below Kowel, then turned east to the Stochód, which it followed a short way before turning northwest and crossing the Pripet some ten miles below the confluence of the Turja. From there it turned generally westward, briefly touching the Włodawka River, a tributary of the middle Bug. It continued in this same direction until it reached the border of the *regnum* proper, due east of Kock. The total territory under Polish rule or control in Ruthenia was now approximately 26,000 square miles. It had taken Casimir twenty-six years to finish his conquest, but with the area firmly under his control, he had, whether he was aware of it or not, firmly set the kingdom's face to the east for the next five and one-half centuries.

This account of the eastern expansion of Poland under Casimir the Great will seem to many to be incomplete. It contains no treatment of the question of Polish suzerainty over Podolia. There certainly is ample precedent for discussing this region, since a great many scholars have concluded that this territory lying to the east of Halicz was held, perhaps as early as 1349, by one or more of the Korjatowicze as feudal vassals of the Polish crown. There are, however, compelling reasons to suggest that Polish influence did not extend into Podolia during Casimir's reign; this whole question is explored in detail in Appendix C. At this point, it needs only to be said that the position of Podolia, as well as that of Moldavia, bears upon the general question of the relation between western and eastern interests during the last five decades of Piast rule in Poland. To the extent these two regions are absent from the narrative of this book, some conclusion may be drawn as to the limited role which the east played in Casimir's overall policy. Although the west will engage us fully in the next chapter, it is appropriate now to explore briefly the constitutional relationship of Ruthenia to the *regnum Poloniae*.

The starting point for any analysis of this relationship is the narrative accounts of Janko of Czarnków and Johannes Długosz[104] concerning the conquest of Ruthenia. The general tenor of both their accounts is that in 1340 Casimir conquered the whole of Ruthenia, turned it into a Polish province, and annexed it so firmly to the *regnum* that it was never really separated from this union. On the basis of the preceding text, it is possible to see that this is a highly optimistic picture, colored by knowledge of the future, and bearing only a vague resemblance to the realities of the situation of 1340. But while they may have incorrectly set the date and extent of effective Polish control in the east, it is true that after 1349, or more precisely 1352, Casimir was master of Halicz and was able to proceed with the administration of this territory. The question of how this was done and what was the nature of Polish rule there has occupied the efforts of a great many Polish scholars, but they have not always agreed in their conclusions.

Roughly two major positions emerged from these researches. One was best represented by Oswald Balzer, for a generation the dean of Polish legal historians, who devoted his entire scholarly life to a study of the legal and constitutional structure of Poland. In his magisterial *Królestwo Polskie 1295–1370*, one of the features of the structure which he attempted to demonstrate was the essentially organic and unified nature of the Polish state; and further, that Ruthenia, though perhaps some nine to twelve years after Długosz's date, was part of that organic union.[105] A second point of view is that proposed by Stanisław Kętrzyński, who was an older contemporary of Balzer and whose most important work antedates the First World War. According to Kętrzyński, there was no organic union between Poland and Ruthenia. Instead it is clear, particularly from Casimir's agreement with Louis of Hungary in 1350, that Ruthenia was bound to Poland only through a personal union under Casimir. The king clearly understood this differentiation between the two areas, for he distinguished between them in his documents by titling himself "King of Poland and Lord and heir of Ruthenia."[106] To put it more simply, Kętrzyński argues that the ruler of Poland was identical with the ruler of Ruthenia, that this was

104. Janko of Czarnków, *Chronicon*, pp. 620–22, 629–31; Długosz, *Historia*, III, 196–97.

105. Oswald Balzer, *Królestwo Polskie, 1295–1370* (Lwów, 1919–20), II, 485–514.

106. Stanisław Kętrzyński, "Zapis Kazimierza Wielkiego dla Kazimierza Bogusławowica," *P.H.*, XIV (1912), 60.

coincidental, and that the two areas were not constitutionally the same. Neither was Casimir successful in altering this situation, as reflected in the form and content of fourteen of the fifteen documents he issued concerning Ruthenia.[107] In balance it appears that Balzer's position on Ruthenia is weaker than that of Kętrzyński, though there may be yet other approaches more fruitful than either taken by these men.

There is little doubt that Casimir would have wished to bind Ruthenia more closely to the kingdom of Poland. This would have been a difficult process in the fourteenth century, however, for the work of internal unification of the *regnum* was not yet complete. Though the view of Stanisław Kutrzeba that the kingdom of Poland itself was still little more than a collection of separate territories bound together in a loose union under the rule of one person[108] can no longer be accepted today, neither is it correct to view the *regnum* as a fully realized constitutional unity.[109] Only in the last years of Casimir's reign was there the practical manifestation of this emerging unity. To be sure, with the coronation of Łokietek in 1320 the process of reunification had been completed and the concept of the *regnum Poloniae* had achieved practical concrete expression. But it was to be some years before there would take root and be reflected in the life of the kingdom the even more significant concept of the *corona Regni Poloniae* as an abstraction with a reality apart from the vagaries of political and dynastic fortune. Only half a century separated Łokietek's coronation from his son's death, and in that relatively short period not all embryonic principles could be fully elaborated.[110] How much more difficult, then, for Ruthenia to attain the same constitutional status as Little Poland or Greater Poland. Some very important legal and practical considerations underlay this fact.

First, Casimir had to combat the intentions of Louis of Hungary toward Ruthenia. The Angevin had no desire to see this region bound closely to the kingdom of Poland. He wished for it to remain united only in a personal union, for this would allow him to claim the kingdom for Hungary after Casimir's death. It was this consideration which led to the agreement of 1350 and which is reflected in Louis's consistent references to Halicz and Vladimir as the "kingdom of Ruthenia" and "kingdom of the Ruthenians," for such an appellation placed the territory on an equal footing with the *Regnum Poloniae* and made incorporation more difficult.[111] Casimir recognized Louis's strategy and its

---

107. See Paszkiewicz, *Polityka Ruska*, p. 149 n. 2.

108. Stanisław Kutrzeba, *Historja ustroju Polski: Korona*, 8th ed. (Warsaw, 1949), pp. 131–34, 135. It was the publication of the first edition of this work in 1905 which precipitated a stimulating polemic between Balzer and Kutrzeba, and resulted eventually in the publication of Balzer's *Królestwo*.

109. This is the fundamental thesis of Balzer's *Królestwo*.

110. On the question of *corona regni Poloniae*, see Dąbrowski, *Korona Królestwo Polskiego w XIV wieku* (Wrocław and Cracow, 1954), pp. 48–146.

111. See the Hungarian documents cited by Paszkiewicz, *Polityka Ruska*, p. 148 n. 4.

implications, and generally refused therefore to use the title "king" in connection with Ruthenia. There are, in fact, only five instances between 1350 and his death when Casimir spoke of himself as "King of Poland and Ruthenia."[112] He preferred the more common title, "King of Poland and Lord and heir of Ruthenia." The longer he was involved in Ruthenia the more frequent became his use of this title. From 1349 to 1360 he issued 169 documents in which he used the title 29 times, or about 17 percent; but from 1361–70 he issued 221 documents in which this title was used 169 times, or 76 percent.[113]

If Ruthenia was not an integral part of the kingdom, neither was it simply another *ziemia*, or territory, on the same level as Sandomir, Sieradz, or Kujavia. Ruthenia was itself a collection of several individual *ziemie*: Sanok, Przemyśl, Lwów, and Halicz; Vladimir, Bełz, Chełm, and perhaps Wołhyń. These collectively formed the *terra Russie*, which was then included in the list of the other territories of the *Regnum Poloniae*. In most of his documents Casimir titled himself *Rex Polonie necnon terrarum Cracovie, Sandomirie, Siradie, Lancicie, Cuiavie, Pomoranie, Russieque dominus et heres*.[114] This degree of legal distinction between Poland and Ruthenia was sometimes not wholly clear in the minds of external observers, and may suggest that the territorial extent of the *regnum* was often broadly, though loosely, defined. The best example of this is Pope Urban's letter of July 13, 1363, to Casimir in which he refers to the king's ambassador as "Lord of Rzeszów in the kingdom of Poland," even though Rzeszów was located in Ruthenia.[115]

Besides legal distinctions, there were also certain practical considerations which gave Ruthenia a unique place in the *regnum Poloniae*. The most obvious way in which Ruthenia differed from the rest of Poland was in the monies circulated there. The traditional Polish coin showed the eagle on the reverse, but in Halicz and Vladimir this symbol was usually replaced by a rampant lion, the sign of Lev Danielovicz and of his city, Leopolis (Lwów). While the obverse of a Ruthenian coin bore the traditional Polish legend *Regis Polonie*, the reverse surrounded the lion with *Moneta Do[min]i Russie*, with no mention of the *regnum Poloniae*. This coin was based upon the so-called *Kwartnik krakowski* (that is, one-half *grossus cracoviensis*), but was distinguishable from this type of money by its higher value. It maintained an assay of 87.5 percent silver, while the *Kwartnik Krakowski* dropped from 71.5 percent to near 45 percent by the end of Casimir's reign.[116] In addition, Casimir also minted in Ruthenia a copper

112. *C.D.Pr.*, III, # 65; *C.D.M.P.*, III, # 1340, 1372–73; *C.D.Pol.*, III, 120.

113. A table which shows the incidence of this title is given by Paszkiewicz, "Z dziejów rywalizacji polsko-węgierskiej na terenie Rusi halicko-włodzimierskiej w XIV wieku," *K.H.*, XXXVIII (1924), 295 n. 2, and *Polityka Ruska*, p. 149 n. 2.

114. Balzer, *Królestwo*, II, 497, gives seventeen examples of this.

115. Theiner, *Mon. Pol.*, I, # 832.

116. On these coins, see Ryszard Kiersnowski, *Wstęp do numizmatyki polskiej wieków średnich* (Warsaw, 1964), p. 126; and, in more detail, J. Stupnicki, "O monetach halicko-ruskich,"

groschen, or penny, which circulated widely, even though this coin was practically unknown in Poland itself.[117] All monies, except for foreign importations such as the *grossus Pragensis*, which circulated in Ruthenia were struck in Lwów, where the mint was under the direct control of the king.[118]

Another factor which affected the position of Ruthenia in relation to Poland was Casimir's lack of total sovereignty there. The Tatars, despite their decline after Khan Uzbek's death, were still a potential threat until bloody civil war broke out within the Horde in 1359. As we have seen, there is some reason to believe that before that date Casimir tacitly, and perhaps officially, recognized Tatar overlordship in Ruthenia while pursuing his own policy. Such a recognition technically limited the Polish king's power there. A more immediate limitation upon Casimir's sovereignty was the claim which Louis of Hungary put forth to Ruthenia. Whatever action the Piast took in Halicz and Vladimir had to be done with one eye upon the Angevin, for after Casimir's death, Ruthenia was to go to Hungary, either by inheritance or purchase.[119] Casimir was also faced with a more stubborn particularism in Ruthenia than elsewhere in his realm. The native boyars had proven in the decade 1340–48 to be particularly troublesome, but even in later years they continued to claim traditional prerogatives which hampered the king.[120]

There were also religious differences between Ruthenia and Poland. The majority of the Ruthenian population was not Roman Catholic, but belonged to the Orthodox or Armenian branches of Christendom. This situation created unique problems in the administration of the area, and Casimir was careful to respect the position of non-Catholics there.[121] In this respect he was far better than previous and subsequent Hungarian attitudes and policies in Ruthenia. Casimir's policy was early reflected in his agreement of 1341 with Diet'ko, when he promised to honor the rites of the population and protect its traditional privileges.[122] His concern for the Orthodox population is shown also in his

---

Biblioteka Ossolińskich, poczet nowy, VII (1865), 92 ff.; F. Piekosiński, *O monecie i stopie menniczej w Polsce w XIV i XV wieku* (Cracow, 1878), pp. 141 f.; K. Stronczyński, *Dawne monety polskie dynastyi Piastów i Jagiellonów*, 3 vols. (Piotrków, 1883–85), III, 31 ff.

117. See Józef Sieradzki, *Polska wieku XIV. Studium z czasów Kazimierza Wielkiego* (Warsaw, 1959), pp. 97–102, who argues strongly on a numismatic basis for the distinct character of Ruthenia.

118. On the mint in Lwów, see Stupnicki, "O monetach halicko-ruskich," pp. 85 ff.; Stronczyński, *Dawne monety polskie*, III, 37 ff., 64 ff. But see also R. Mękicki, "Mennica lwowska w latach 1656–1657," *Biblioteka Lwowska*, XXXI–XXXII (1932), 271 f.

119. See Dąbrowski, *Ostatnie lata*, pp. 103, 128, 141–42; Rhode, *Die Ostgrenze Polens*, I, 195.

120. See the remarks of Sieradzki, *Polska wieku XIV*, p. 265 n. 27.

121. See Paszkiewicz, *Polityka Ruska*, pp. 253–55; Kaczmarczyk, *Monarchia Kazimierza Wielkiego*, 2 vols. (Poznań, 1939–46), II, 115–21.

122. Theiner, *Mon. Pol.*, I, # 566. See also Stanisław Zakrzewski, "Wpływ sprawy ruskiej na państwo polskie w XIV," *P.H.*, XXIII (1921–22), p. 109.

remarkable letter of 1370 to the patriarch of Constantinople.[123] In it the king requested Patriarch Filotej to confirm the selection of Bishop Antonias as Orthodox metropolitan of Halicz. This bishop had been selected jointly by Casimir and the Ruthenian boyars. The king's concern for religious minorities in Ruthenia was not limited to the Orthodox, for it included the Armenian church also. For example, in 1363 he founded an Armenian cathedral in Lwów.[124] Nevertheless Casimir was in no way remiss in his attention to the needs of the Roman Catholic population of Ruthenia. In Lwów alone after 1340 there were founded a Dominican monastery, the Corpus Christi church, a Franciscan monastery, the Holy Cross church, a St. Catherine's chapel, and the hospital and church of the Holy Spirit.[125] In Halicz, Vladimir, and Przemyśl, similar, though less extensive, activity may be observed; while in the country-side, the parish system had begun to emerge by 1370, though it was still largely a missionary oriented development. Yet another implication of the religious and ethnic composition of Ruthenia was the fact that the language of official intercourse was neither Polish nor Latin, but Old Russian. This necessitated special linguistic accomplishments in the royal chancery, though probably on a temporary rather than a permanent basis.[126] The final complication in the ecclesiastical administration of Ruthenia lay in the fact that the Roman Catholic population was not subject directly to the archbishop of Gniezno, but to the bishop of Lubusz. Despite the pope's promise to transfer jurisdiction over Ruthenia from the latter to the former, this was never done.[127]

The nature of legal practices in Ruthenia also distinguished this area from Poland. The great codification of Polish law which Casimir had initiated in the second decade of his reign and which had been implemented in the third decade was not extended successfully to Ruthenia. There local law, or, for new colonial settlements, German law, was chiefly utilized. This made it difficult, if not impossible, for any kind of unified administrative approach to be carried out from Cracow for Poland and Ruthenia.[128]

This abbreviated discussion of the relationship of Ruthenia to Poland must suffice. Much work needs to be done on this topic, particularly upon the socio-economic aspects of the relationship. Fortunately, it is precisely these kinds of topics which now receive adequate attention among Polish historians. Upon their contributions and the researches of an earlier generation of scholars, a comprehensive, balanced synthesis may be achieved.[129]

123. Printed in Greek, with a Polish translation, in *M.P.H.*, II, 626–28.

124. The act of foundation is printed in Abraham, *Powstanie*, pp. 378–79.

125. See Kaczmarczyk, *Monarchia*, II, 113; Abraham, *Powstanie*, p. 251.

126. Kaczmarczyk, *Monarchia*, I, 136–41.

127. On the question of Lubusz and Ruthenia, see Abraham, *Powstanie*, pp. 230–37.

128. See Paszkiewicz, *Polityka Ruska*, pp. 263–69; Kaczmarczyk, *Monarchia*, I, 29 f.

129. The overwhelming orientation of older scholarship, as indeed the treatment in the

Another question concerning Ruthenia which should be included at this point is that of the significance of this region in the life of Poland. As Gotthold Rhode has recently pointed out,[130] by its expansion into Halicz and Vladimir Poland had moved out of the Vistula-Oder basin, with its northward and westward orientation, and had set foot into the Dniester basin with its orientation toward the Black Sea. Moreover, this new world was non-Roman-Catholic and to an extent non-Western. What impact did these factors have upon the life of the kingdom and the policy of the king?

In attempting to answer this question, some scholars have concluded that in the conquest of Ruthenia the king "wished to erect a defensive wall for the west against the east . . . thus forming an eastern march on the border of Christendom"[131] and that Casimir's campaigns in this area were not simply military expeditions but a defense of the Roman Catholic Church and Western civilization, and tended to acquire over the years the character of crusades.[132] Such views reflect the fact that among later generations there was indeed a conscious belief in the state of Poland (whether kingdom or republic) as a bulwark of Christendom (*antemurale Christianitatis*). To suggest, however, that this was true in the time of the last Piast is to attribute too much to Casimir's own understanding of his aims. It is possible to suggest, however, that some of these ideas were present in embryonic form in the policy of the king.

Before 1341 Casimir's primary interest in Ruthenia lay in gaining an outpost against the Tatars from which Poland could protect and defend itself more easily. Only later in his reign can one see the emergence of any idea that the Polish eastern border was a dividing point, perhaps even a barrier, between Christian Poland (whose interests were largely identical with the rest of Christendom) and an aggressively hostile, anti-Catholic world. The primary means by which Casimir sought success in the east was through military conquest. For this he was dependent not only upon his own resources and whatever help he could obtain from neighbors and allies (these two not always being synonymous), but also upon the papacy. Thus he repeatedly requested aid from Avignon.

In 1343 he wrote to the pope that his enemies, "namely the Tatars, Ruthenians and Lithuanians," were also "enemies of the Christian faith."[133] This statement is the first instance where Casimir justified the kingdom's involve-

---

present text, was toward the question of the legal relationship of Ruthenia to Poland. These considerations predominate in the work of Balzer, Paszkiewicz, and Kaczmarczyk. The more broadly based approach discussed in the text has been attempted by the late Józef Sieradzki in his *Polska wieku XIV*, in which two chapters explicitly, and much else implicitly, are devoted to Ruthenia.

130. Rhode, *Die Ostgrenze Polens*, I, 225.

131. Max Goldschneider, *Glanz und Verderb der polnischen Republik*, 2 vols. (Vienna, 1919), I, 249–50.

132. Michał Bobrzyński, *Dzieje Polski w zarysie*, 4th ed. (Warsaw, 1927–31), I, 105.

133. Theiner, *Mon. Pol.*, I, # 604.

ment in the east upon the basis of defense, not only of Poland, but also of Christendom. This same idea is reflected in another letter to Avignon later that year. Casimir requested aid from the papacy and in the process reported that he had already made, and would continue to make, great sacrifices "for the honor of the holy, Roman church, whose enemies pursue hostilely everything which it undertakes in the area."[134] Nine years later the consciousness of Poland's border position in relation to western Christendom had become even clearer. Thus in 1352, when Casimir wrote again requesting financial support, we find the following explicit expression of this idea: "The kingdom of Poland, which is inhabited by the faithful, is located on the farthest boundaries of Christians, and is therefore more open to attack from the Tatars than other catholic princes and others of the faithful." He must ask the pope for help because the inhabitants of his kingdom were particularly faithful sons of the church and dedicated to the defense, not only of the kingdom, but also of the church and its faithful everywhere, whether they be near to or remote from the adversities which the Poles were suffering.[135] One final expression of this attitude is found eleven years later when Casimir again wrote to Avignon, saying that all believers should support his campaigns, including the "fervidly zealous in the defense of the catholic faith," and that their battle "for the kingdom of Poland, which is located near these perverse infidel nations, was a defense of the faithful which deserved support."[136]

It is possible, of course, to argue that Casimir simply used these arguments with the pope because he knew they would be the most effective in obtaining the monies he desired. To accept this view of the king would be to make of him a far greater cynic than one might expect to find in fourteenth-century Poland. One may more appropriately conclude that Casimir was a faithful son of the church who honestly held the opinions outlined above so long as such a position and attitude was not inconsistent with the best interests of the Polish state.[137] It was undoubtedly Casimir's judgment that what was good for Poland in the east was good for the church, and vice versa. Without too seriously warping historical reality, one can argue that by the end of Casimir's reign, at least on the highest levels, the frontier mentality had made inroads in Poland. This later became deeply ingrained in the whole of Polish society. Because of its obvious ideological overtones, the fully elaborated idea of Poland as the defender of the West came in later centuries to occupy a dominant position in Poland's view of itself. In this way also, as well as by geographical factors already mentioned and socioeconomic factors to be discussed below, Poland's attention was

---

134. Ibid., # 605.

135. Ibid., # 713.

136. Ibid., # 833.

137. A brief description of the religious attitudes of Casimir is given by Kaczmarczyk, *Polska czasów Kazimierza,* pp. 180–85.

focused upon the east in a way that would have been quite inconsistent with Casimir's own view and understanding.[138]

Casimir's requests for aid were answered, and the papacy granted either moral and spiritual support or financial and material assistance. The former was given eight times,[139] the latter five times.[140] In the king's eyes the financial aid was the most help, for the money he received represented the papal tenth in Poland for some eleven or twelve years, a total of 13,500 to 15,000 Polish marks.[141] Even this sum was not sufficient, and as we have seen, Casimir was reduced to borrowing within Poland and from Hungary, mortgaging Dobrzyń and Płock, and even obtaining papal monies surreptitiously.

The campaigns which Casimir carried out in Ruthenia were not crusades in the traditional medieval sense, nor even in the manner in which the Teutonic Knights (sometimes accompanied by such dignitaries as King John of Bohemia) sallied forth against the Lithuanians. Yet his expeditions were more than simple attempts at military expansion. Casimir and the papal curia were fully aware that the Poles were fighting against the Tatars and that the fight was at least partially in defense of the Christian faith. Whether Casimir consciously thought he was thereby defending the whole of Christendom is more doubtful. The fact that this battle was with non-Christians led, on at least two occasions, to attempts to Christianize the Lithuanians. This was to have been done, not by conquest or missionary activity, but by direct diplomatic negotiations with the Gedyminowicze. These attempts were unsuccessful, but they provided an example and basis for the ultimate Christianization of Lithuania in 1386, when the two countries were joined in a dynastic union.[142] A variation on this theme of Christianization, with its obvious political overtones, was attempted by Casimir in 1359. He successfully proposed the marriage of his grandson Kaźko of Szczecin to Olgierd's daughter Kenna. This union further strengthened the ties between Poland and Lithuania.

In his recognition of the significance of the Polish eastern boundaries, Casimir

138. See my comments in "The Stabilization of the Polish Western Frontier under Casimir the Great, 1333–1370," *The Polish Review*, XII, iv (1967), 28–29.

139. These have been mentioned above in passing. See *Codex diplomaticus Hungariae ecclesiasticus et civilis*, ed. György Fejér, 11 vols. (Buda, 1829–44), VIII, pt. iv, 450–52; Theiner, *Mon. Hung.*, I, # 959; idem, *Mon. Pol.*, I, # 566 and # 713; *M.P.V.*, III, # 347; Theiner, *Mon. Hung.*, # 18; idem, *Mon. Pol.*, I # 770 and # 833.

140. Theiner, *Mon. Pol.*, I, # 604–5, # 702–3; # 739, # 742, # 883. Both kinds of aid are discussed in more detail by Rhode, *Die Ostgrenze Polens*, I, 252–53.

141. According to Rutkowski, *Historia gospodarcza Polski*, I, 104, the annual income of the papal tenth in Poland averaged 1,250 marks. The tenth is discussed by Kaczmarczyk, *Monarchia*, II, 318–22.

142. On this important question and the significance of Casimir's activity in this respect, see Chodynicki, "Próby," pp. 215–319, pp. 281 ff. especially: Abraham, "Polska a Chrzest Litwy," in *Polska i Litwy w dziejowym stosunku* (Warsaw, 1914), pp. 3–23; Kaczmarczyk, *Monarchia*, II, 122–26.

was in advance of his subjects and contemporaries. This is shown most clearly by the king's complaint about the lack of interest which the Polish clergy showed in the battle for Ruthenia. In 1356 the pope accused the clergy of having received great benefits from the king without at the same time supporting royal policy by word or deed, and in some instances actually opposing him.[143] This is also suggested by the fact that Janko of Czarnków, *Rocznik Traski*, and various other minor *roczniki* limit themselves to very cursory accounts of this aspect of Casimir's activity. Our knowledge of the Ruthenian policy of Casimir the Great is based largely upon nonliterary sources.

Concentration upon the eastern interests of the kingdom during Casimir's reign has forced us to refrain from tracing the king's dealings with the Luxemburgers, Wittelsbachs, and the Order in the years after the treaties of Kalisz. To obtain a fully balanced view of the whole of Piast policy in this period, let us retrace our steps to examine this aspect of Poland's external affairs up to the Congress of Cracow in 1364.

143. This is drawn from the papal answer in Theiner, *Mon. Pol.*, I, # 770.

7
AFFAIRS IN THE WEST
FROM KALISZ TO
THE CONGRESS OF CRACOW, 1343–1364

The impression one receives from reading the chief literary source for Casimir's reign, the near-contemporary chronicle of Janko of Czarnków, is that of a panegyric upon the king. One recent scholar has gone so far as to characterize the third section of this narrative as a description of "the power of the kingdom and the glory of the king."[1] While such a description may well be accurate for the last part of Casimir's reign, for an earlier period it is hardly correct. The weakness of the kingdom and the relative insignificance of its position among its more powerful neighbors in those years was best shown at the Congress of Wyszegrad in 1335. There, despite promising early successes by the young king, the responsibility for solving the external problems which beset Poland lay not upon Casimir's shoulders, but upon those of the kings of Bohemia and Hungary.

As Casimir's reign progressed, however, Poland became more and more the master of its own affairs. It was the king, together with the nation, who had brought about a settlement with the Teutonic Order and expanded the kingdom into Ruthenia.[2] Again, it was the king, together with the nation, who bound up the wounds of political fragmentation, institutional weakness, and

1. Józef Sieradzki, *Polska wieku XIV: Studium z czasów Kazimierza Wielkiego* (Warsaw, 1959), p. 59. The section of Janko of Czarnków's *Chronicon Polonorum* in *M.P.H.*, II, 623–31, briefly summarizes domestic and foreign developments during Casimir's reign and lists his achievements as a builder.

2. This concept of the partnership of the ruler and the ruled is one of the themes of Janko of Czarnków, *Chronicon*; see, for example, p. 621: "with the great power of his people." It is an idea further developed in Marian Łodyński, "Regnum Poloniae w opinii publicznej XIV wieku," *K.H.*, XXVII (1914), 38–54, and in the concluding remarks of Zdzisław Kaczmarczyk, *Polska czasów Kazimierza Wielkiego* (Cracow, 1964), pp. 186 ff.

economic underdevelopment and so strengthened the *regnum* in the twenty years following the peace of Kalisz that Poland began to emerge by the fourth decade of Casimir's reign as a central European power in its own right. This process culminated in 1363–64 with the recognition of the kingdom and its ruler as one of the chief arbiters of the affairs of its region and the host of the most magnificent congress of the fourteenth century. It is this process in its external orientation which we shall trace in this chapter.

No great national ruler willingly gives up part of his territory, and Casimir's decision in 1339 to renounce claim to Silesia rested only upon his conviction that no other reasonable course lay open to him. There is no evidence to suggest, however, that he was fully resigned to the loss of this province to Bohemia. Thus it is not surprising that, as relations with the Luxemburgers deteriorated after the zenith of Polish-Bohemian friendship in 1341, Casimir turned again to the question of Silesia. This time the focus of his immediate concern was the traditional capital of the region, Wrocław.

This episcopal city, which may have reached a population of more than 14,000 in this period, was in an ambiguous position.[3] It was traditionally a Slavic city, closely tied until the thirteenth century to the *regnum Poloniae*; but it was also a city which had been early exposed to foreign elements, particularly German and Czech, from the west. These had wrought a certain change. The nature of this change is hotly disputed to this day, with scholarly judgment largely divided along national lines. Anna Lipska has argued that even though foreign influences were concentrated more upon Wrocław than elsewhere in Silesia, the city was still predominantly Polish.[4] Its nobility still bore Polish names, the language of the city was Polish, and preaching in the churches was in Polish. Such an interpretation clashes sharply with traditional German scholarship, which argues that by the mid-fourteenth century Silesia and Wrocław were politically, economically, and culturally largely Germanized.[5] In reality, neither side is wholly correct. To be sure, Silesia, including Wrocław, was politically under the rule of Bohemia, though there were still individual princes in 1342 who held aloof from King John. Culturally and socially, however, there were two Silesias: an urban and rural aristocracy which looked increasingly to Bohemia and the empire for leadership; and the lower classes

---

3. See Karol Maleczyński, *Dzieje Wrocławia do roku 1526* (Katowice and Wrocław, 1948), pp. 169 ff.; Wacław Długoborski, Józef Gierowski, and Karol Maleczyński, *Dzieje Wrocławia do roku 1807* (Warsaw, 1958), pp. 84–85.

4. Anna Lipska, "Der polnische Hochadel im 14. und in der ersten Hälfte des 15. Jh. und das Problem der Vereinigung Schlesiens mit Polen," in Ewa Maleczyńska, ed., *Beiträge zur Geschichte Schlesiens* (Berlin, 1958), p. 190.

5. A good expression of this view is found in Joseph Klapper's article "Schlesisches Volkstum im Mittelalter," in *Geschichte Schlesiens*, vol. I, *Von der Urzeit bis zum Jahre 1526*, published by the Historische Kommission für Schlesien, ed. Hermann Aubin, et al., 3d ed. (Stuttgart, 1961), pp. 484–543.

of the city and countryside which had successfully resisted foreign influences.[6] It was this remnant of Polish character which partially motivated Casimir's interest in Wrocław, for he saw in it a means by which Polish political influence might be kept alive.

A second basis for the king's interest was the fundamental contradiction between Wrocław's political dependence upon Bohemia and its ecclesiastical subjugation to the archbishop of Gniezno. So long as the Luxemburg capital of Prague remained only an episcopal city, there was little possibility that this anomalous situation would change. The Polish church would thus be able to ensure on the one hand that Polish interests were represented in Wrocław and on the other that the substantial income of the diocese would go to Gniezno. Nevertheless the ecclesiastical position of Wrocław was precarious. The Luxemburgers had a tradition of intervention in the religious affairs of the city, and it had long been one of their goals to bring to an end the dichotomy between the political and ecclesiastical allegiances of the city. Following the election of Pope Clement VI in 1342, Margrave Charles of Moravia had begun negotiations with his former tutor to remove Prague from the archdiocese of Mainz and raise it to archiepiscopal status.[7] The threat which Prague as an archbishopric would offer to Wrocław's dependence upon Gniezno was only too apparent to Casimir, and provided him with further reason to intervene in Silesian affairs.

The financial impact of the loss of Wrocław on the Polish church was made clear in 1343, when Clement granted King John the papal tenth from the diocese of Wrocław for two years.[8] This episcopal see was a wealthy one, and its income constituted some 10 percent of the Polish total. The papal grant would thus be felt.[9] The reason why Clement granted the money to John displeased Casimir as much as the grant itself. It is clear from the papal letter that the pope was using this grant as a tool in the implementation of papal policy: he wanted John to break off negotiations for peace with Emperor Lewis of Bavaria.[10]

While this situation was developing, the Luxemburgers were taking steps to

6. This somewhat oversimplified characterization of Silesian society can be easily disputed with individual exceptions, but I think it remains generally valid. The question of the "ethnic" and "national" character of Wrocław is more fully treated by Maleczyński, *Dzieje Wrocławia do roku 1526*, pp. 162–77, and *Dzieje Wrocławia do roku 1807*, pp. 137–43.

7. For these negotiations, see Emil Werunsky, *Geschichte Kaiser Karls IV und seiner Zeit*, 3 vols. in 4 (Innsbruck, 1880–96), I, 349–50; Josef Šusta, *Karel IV, Otec a Syn* (Prague, 1946), p. 416.

8. Theiner, *Mon. Pol.*, I, # 592.

9. On the question of the tenth in Silesia, see Tadeusz Gromnicki, *Świętopietrze w Polsce* (Cracow, 1908), pp. 81–82, 94–100; Kaczmarczyk, *Monarchia Kazimierza Wielkiego*, 2 vols. (Poznań, 1939–46), II, 35–38.

10. Theiner, *Mon. Pol.*, I, # 613. See also Jacob Caro, *Geschichte Polens*, 4 vols. in 5 (Gotha, 1863–86), II, 260; Carl Müller, *Der Kampf Ludwigs des Baiern mit der römischen Curie*, 2 vols. (Tübingen, 1879–80), II, 170–74.

consolidate their position in Silesia. Beginning in 1341, and continuing for some years thereafter, King John moved to have his son recognized as holding the expectancy over the Silesian principalities already under Bohemian control. This was enough to force the Polish king to act. In the face of deteriorating Polish-Luxemburg relations, the continuing interference of the Bohemian rulers in Wrocław, the extension of John's control in the region, and by 1343 assurance of safety in the north as a result of the treaties of Kalisz, Casimir resolved to take active steps to prevent further consolidation of Bohemian influence and control in Silesia and at the same time perhaps to recover part of the area for Poland.[11]

Sometime after the treaties of Kalisz, probably at the beginning of September, he gathered the *pospolite ruszenie*, including some mercenaries in his force.[12] His goal was that part of Silesia which had earlier in the century been under the control of the duke of Greater Poland, but over which Łokietek had been unable to establish control. To obtain it he marched first against the city of Wschowa, which held out for some days before finally capitulating to Casimir's army. Since the king planned to incorporate the territory into the *regnum*, he prohibited looting by his troops and left the fortifications of the city intact. This victory did not end the year's campaigning, for Casimir immediately led the army south to the Oder River which he followed upstream to Ścinawa, which was then invested. This siege was more difficult than Wschowa, for the city was more strongly fortified—both the walls and the fortress—and its location on the Oder created further complications. Nevertheless the city was eventually stormed, the army was given free reign to plunder, the stone walls were systematically razed, and the buildings were burned. Following this success, Casimir apparently divided his troops. Part marched west into the territory of Duke Henry of Żagań, who was forced to sign a truce with the Poles. The other detachment continued east into the territory of Duke Conrad of Oleśnica. Despite considerable devastation there, the duke was able to mount a counter-offensive which halted the Polish progress. The season's campaigning ended with Poland having recovered a small portion of its lost Silesian territory.[13]

This invasion marked the beginning of five years of intermittent warfare between Casimir and King John and Charles. The Luxemburgers did not at

11. See *Historia Śląska*, general editor Karol Maleczyński, vol. I, *do roku 1763*, in four parts (Wrocław, 1960–64), pt. i, pp. 569–70; Jan Dąbrowski, "Dzieje polityczne Śląska w latach 1290–1402," in *Historja Śląska od najdawniejszych czasów do roku 1400*, ed. Stanisław Kutrzeba, et al., 3 vols. (Cracow, 1933–39), I, 449.

12. As reflected in Długosz, *Historia*, III, 209. Our other sources for this campaign, though not as full as Długosz, are Janko of Czarnków, *Chronicon*, pp. 628–29; *Rocznik Traski*, in *M.P.H.*, II, 861; *Chronica principum Polonie*, in *M.P.H.*, III, 539–40.

13. The military aspects of this campaign are treated by Kaczmarczyk and Stefan Weyman, *Reformy wojskowe i organizacja siły zbrojnej za Kazimierza Wielkiego* (Warsaw, 1958), pp. 138–40; Karol Olejnik, *Działalność militarna Polski w czasach Kazimierza Wielkiego* (Poznań, 1966), pp. 71–72. A somewhat broader treatment is provided by Dąbrowski, "Dzieje polityczne," pp. 449–51.

first respond to Polish aggression, for they were involved in the continuing conflict with Lewis the Bavarian. Nevertheless they did take note of the king's expedition, for Wschowa was subject directly to the crown of Bohemia, and Ścinawa was jointly administered by Dukes Henry and Conrad as Bohemian vassals. The following year, upon the occasion of the consecration of Arnošt of Pardubice as the first archbishop of Prague, John announced his intention to recover Wschowa. At the same time he accepted the feudal homage of Henry of Żagań for his recently inherited duchy, promising to lend him sufficient aid to defend himself against Casimir.[14]

With the formal breach between Poland and Bohemia, Casimir turned once again to the Wittelsbachs in Brandenburg. (Throughout Casimir's reign, the better the relations between Poland and Bohemia, the looser the ties of Poland with the Wittelsbachs; conversely, whenever Casimir's relationship with either John or Charles was strained, there usually was a rapprochement between Poland and Brandenburg.) Despite the vicissitudes of time, the earlier alliance between Margave Lewis and Casimir had never been repudiated. Two factors now drew the two dynasties closer together again. The first was the growing probability that Margrave Charles would be elected Holy Roman Emperor in place of Lewis IV, the head of the Wittelsbach house. Second, because Charles's elevation to the imperial dignity would greatly strengthen the Luxemburgers against Poland, Casimir naturally turned to the Bohemians' mortal foe. Margrave Lewis, on behalf of his father, welcomed the renewal of Polish friendship, for this would give the Wittelsbachs an ally in the east who could be useful against the Luxemburgers.[15]

In order to seal the Polish-Wittelsbach rapprochement, representatives opened negotiations for a military and marriage pact between Poland and Brandenburg. Late in 1344 agreement was reached, and on January 1, 1345, Casimir announced his adherence to an alliance in which he bound himself to provide Brandenburg with 400 heavy cavalry and 400 archers in case of war against anyone (that is, Bohemia) except his two nephews, King Louis of Hungary and Duke Bolko of Świdnica. Should the Luxemburgers invade Brandenburg, Casimir promised in addition to march into Silesia and not to sign a separate treaty with John or Charles without the permission of the Wittelsbachs.

14. *C.D.Mor.*, VII, # 560–61. While it is true that Casimir attacked Wschowa and Henry of Żagań at a time when the duke had ranged himself in opposition against the Bohemians over the issue of Luxemburg feudal overlordship over Żagań, I find unacceptable the thesis, implicit in Kaczmarczyk and Weyman, *Reformy wojskowe*, p. 138, and explicit in *Historia Śląska*, I, pt. i, 570, that Casimir was allied with John and Charles against Duke Henry. Casimir's campaign may in part have worked to the benefit of the Luxemburgers, but it was a unilateral action, which from the Polish point of view was directed against the Bohemians.

15. See Stanisław Zajączkowski, "Polska a Wittelsbachowie w pierwszej połowie XIV wieku," in *Prace historyczne w 30-lecie działalności profesorskiej Stanisława Zakrzewskiego* (Lwów, 1934), pp. 108–11; F. W. Taube, *Ludwig der Aeltere als Markgraf von Brandenburg, 1323–1351* (Berlin, 1900), pp. 82–83.

Lewis for his part promised Casimir equal military aid and support. At this same time, the engagement of Casimir's second daughter, Kunigunde, to the margrave's younger brother, Lewis the Roman, was announced. Each side promised a handsome dowry, and the marriage took place sometime in 1345.[16]

The previously noted special status of Duke Bolko appears again in this treaty. Since he was to play a major role in Casimir's Silesian policy for two decades, it is worth emphasizing again that he was one of the last independent Piast princes of Silesia, bitterly hostile to King John and frequently sympathetic to his uncle Casimir. Thus he was a major obstacle in the path of the Bohemians and a symbol of Casimir's ambitions in Silesia. The Polish king hoped to strengthen Bolko, so as to make him the premier power in the region, even above Wrocław. For this reason, Casimir opened the route through Cracow into Ruthenia to merchants of Świdnica, though it had been closed since 1340 to merchants of Wrocław. At the same time Bolko was embarking upon a program of territorial expansion in Silesia. In 1343 he had purchased the fortress of Sobótka, thus gaining control of the transit route from Kłodzko to Wrocław. His negotiations in 1344 with his uncle, Duke Henry of Jawór, for the expectancy to this principality were part of the same program.[17]

The emergence of Duke Bolko and Casimir's new alliance with the Wittelsbachs did not escape the attention of the Bohemian rulers. The unsettling effect which the latter event, in particular, had may be judged from a letter of King John to the pope. He complained that Casimir had allied himself with excommunicated heretics against faithful Christians. The pope recognized the point of these charges, but trusted to his influence over Casimir to bring about a resolution of the difficulties. He did nothing to chastise the Polish king, but simply wrote John on March 9, 1345, saying that he would do all in his power to reconcile Poland and Bohemia over this matter.[18]

By that time further conflict between Casimir and the Bohemians resulted in the renewal of open warfare between them. Late in December, 1344, both King John and Charles undertook a joint campaign with the Teutonic Order against the Lithuanians. In addition to fulfilling the crusading ambitions of John's wild and restless nature, the Luxemburgers hoped to achieve at least two goals in this campaign. First they wished to demonstrate to Casimir that the traditional Bohemian-Teutonic Order friendship had not in any way been altered by the peace of Kalisz; they were also reinforcing their friendship with

16. *Monumenta Wittelsbacensia: Urkundenbuch zur Geschichte des Hauses Wittelsbach*, ed. F. W. Wittmann, 2 vols. (Munich, 1857–61), II, 384. Many of the details concerning the negotiations and the marriage are obscure. Those which are available are discussed by Oswald Balzer, *Genealogia Piastów* (Cracow, 1895), pp. 398–400.

17. On Duke Bolko in general, see Erich Gospos, *Die Politik Bolkos II von Schweidnitz-Jauer 1326–1368* (Halle, 1910); Krystyna Pieradzka, "Bolko II Świdnicki na Łużycach," *Sobótka*, II (1947), 93–109; see also Dąbrowski, "Dzieje polityczne," pp. 455 ff., and *Historia Śląska*, I, pt. i, 571–73.

18. Theiner, *Mon. Pol.*, I, # 619.

the Order in case they should have to call for aid in a Polish-Bohemian conflict. Casimir fully understood the significance of this gesture, for he recognized the danger of this potential German pincer and he knew that such obvious Bohemian support might well give the Order aggressive new confidence in its long-standing hostility toward Poland. A second goal was that the Bohemians and the Order hoped to deal the Lithuanians such a defeat that they would be convinced there was no opportunity to expand to the west. The result of this would be twofold: it would allow the Order to concentrate upon its internal administration, and it would also force the aggressive Lithuanians to turn all their attention to Ruthenia. Casimir would be obliged to devote himself more completely to the defense of his own Ruthenian holdings, thereby relieving the Luxemburgers of his intervention in Silesia.[19]

Early in 1345 a Bohemian army, strengthened by adventurers from throughout northern Europe and adorned by the presence of King Louis of Hungary and as many as two hundred other princes and nobles, marched through Poland into Prussia and joined the troops of the Knights. Without wasting any time, the joint Bohemian-Order army invaded Lithuania.[20] The campaign had hardly begun, however, when news reached Grand Master Ludolf König that the Lithuanians had marched into Samogitia and were besieging Königsberg. At this news, he broke off the campaign and returned to defend the threatened city. There it was discovered that the Lithuanian attack had been only a feint and that the real target was Livonia. This territory was brutally ravaged by the Gedyminowicze, and great damage was done to the Order's position there. Ludolf König began to brood over his responsibility in the matter; his anguish ultimately became so great that he went mad. On September 14, 1345, he resigned as grand master and retired to a monastery, where he lived peacefully till his death three years later.[21]

In the meantime, King John had decided not to return immediately to Bohemia, but to go to Luxemburg and attend to family matters. Charles, however, took the most direct route back to Prague, through Kalisz and Wrocław. Even though this would take him through hostile territory, he apparently had no fear for his safety, for, according to the later chronicler Beneš of Weitmil, Casimir had granted both him and his father a letter of

19. Werunsky, *Karl IV*, I, 373–74; Šusta, *Karel IV*, pp. 435–36.

20. For the details of this campaign, see *Vita Caroli IIII*, in *Rerum Bohemicarum antiqui scriptores . . .*, ed. C. V. Marquard Freher (Hanover, 1602), p. 103; *Chronica Olivensis*, in *M.P.H.*, VI, 338; Wigand of Marburg, *Chronica nova Prutenica*, in *SS. rer. Pr.*, II, 504 f.; Beneš Krabice z Weitmil, *Chronicon ecclesiae Pragensis, 1283–1374*, in *SS. rer. Boh.*, II, 335. Secondary accounts are given in Werunsky, *Karl IV*, I, 376–77; Šusta, *Karel IV*, pp. 434–35; and Johannes Voigt, *Geschichte Preussens von den ältesten Zeiten bis zum Untergange der Herrschaft des Deutschen Ordens*, 9 vols. (Königsberg, 1827–39), V, 27–31, though he incorrectly sets the campaign in 1344.

21. *Chronica Olivensis*, p. 339. See also Voigt, *Geschichte Preussens*, V, 32–35, and Marjan Tumler, *Der Deutsche Orden im Werden, Wachsen und Wirken bis 1400* (Vienna, 1955), pp. 346–47.

safe-conduct.[22] When Charles arrived in Kalisz on his return, however, he was immediately placed under close guard by Polish officials, acting on royal orders. Detained and prevented from returning to Prague, he was in effect a prisoner, though his cell was the whole of the city. Charles later contended that Casimir had been led to this act by Duke Bolko of Świdnica, who feared that the Luxemburgers threatened his independence in Silesia. At the same time, the future emperor recognized that there were other reasons for Casimir's action, since the Polish king made Charles's release contingent upon the payment of a substantial ransom. These monies were to be, in effect, repayment of the funds which Charles had borrowed in Poland.

When Charles had again borrowed money from Casimir in 1343, he had promised to repay it within three weeks. If he did not do so, then Casimir and Louis of Hungary were to regard him as a criminal for having broken his oath. Charles had indeed defaulted upon his promised repayment, and Casimir therefore felt justified in detaining the Bohemian in Kalisz. Another minor reason for the king's actions may be inferred from one of Pope Clement's letters in which he suggests that Casimir had detained Charles in order to show good will to the Lithuanians (he had recently signed an alliance with them; see above, chapter 5); and to gain revenge for them in some small way for the recent Bohemian-Order campaign.[23]

During his detention in Kalisz, Charles was treated by Casimir's officials with the utmost respect and deference. He was allowed to go wherever he wished within the city and its immediate environs, though he was always closely watched. This relative freedom enabled him to send word to one of the civil administrators of Wrocław, informing him of the situation in Kalisz and instructing him to send aid. It was not long before the aid marched from Wrocław at the head of three hundred troops. He brought the horses and soldiers to a hiding place in the forest around the city, then sent a secret message to Charles describing a plan for escape. Shortly thereafter the margrave went for a walk on the public fields outside the walls of the city, while his rescuer sent a horse and rider into Kalisz. At a prearranged signal, the rider jumped off, Charles outraced his guards to the horse, sprang into the saddle, and galloped into the woods surrounding the city, where he fled immediately to safety in Wrocław. Charles's astounded guards could do no more than imprison the rider and the remainder of Charles's retinue, but the king soon ordered them to be set free.[24]

---

22. Beneš, *Chronicon*, p. 335. Charles says nothing of any such safe-conduct in *Vita Caroli*.

23. The document in Ludewig, *Reliquiae*, V, 510, contains both Charles's promise and Casimir's dispensation from that promise under the date 1343. The second half of this document should, however, be dated in 1346. See Caro, *Geschichte Polens*, II, 242 n. 1. The papal letter is in Theiner, *Mon. Pol.*, I, # 628.

24. The above account is drawn from *Vita Caroli*, pp. 104–5, and Beneš, *Chronicon*, p. 336. The latter bases his narrative upon the former, but has expanded his treatment into a more

The events in Kalisz, much as they appear to have been a comedy of errors, were in reality the prologue to a multi-act revival of the drama of Polish-Bohemian conflict which ran, with pauses, from April 1345 to November 1348. From the Polish point of view, the conflict had two purposes: the first, related to Poland's position as a member of an anti-Luxemburg coalition, aimed at the reduction of Luxemburg power and influence in Europe; the second, more narrowly limited in its scope, focused upon the possibility of reversing the political situation in Silesia.[25] It was not, however, Poland which initiated hostilities, but Bohemia.

When news of the Kalisz outrage to the dignity of the House of Luxemburg reached him in the west, John hurried to Bohemia to prepare his revenge against the individual he held responsible for Casimir's actions and who was also the greatest threat to Bohemian control in Silesia: Duke Bolko of Świdnica. Early in April John appeared in Wrocław, where he borrowed money for his war effort and assembled an army. Then he marched south into the duke's territory and besieged the fortress of Świdnica. Despite repeated stormings, he was unable to capture it and had to content himself with burning the outskirts of the city. From Świdnica, John continued through Bolko's territory, devastating the countryside and capturing the city of Kamienna Góra, near the Czech border. In the meantime, Bolko sought in vain for help from Casimir. Finally, almost in desperation, he opened negotiations for a truce with the Bohemians. To his surprise, it was granted. The Luxemburgers suddenly realized that a formidable coalition had been formed against them. They needed peace with Bolko in order to devote their attention to this greater threat.[26]

The chief architect of this coalition was the House of Wittelsbach, whose motives are obvious. They had succeeded in drawing Poland, Hungary, and Duke Bolko into their camp, and may also have won over Dukes Frederick of Meissen and Albert of Austria.[27] (Louis of Hungary adhered to the Wittelsbach cause, despite the fact he was by now Charles's son-in-law, because he wished to have his brother Andrew crowned king of Sicily. Pope Clement had hitherto been hesitant to fulfill this desire, and Louis hoped to gain imperial support by aiding the Wittelsbachs.[28]) The Luxemburgers' first assault upon

---

dramatic account. The *Vita's* further account of Casimir's attack upon Ścinawa actually refers to the campaign of 1343.

25. See *Historia Śląska*, I, pt. i, 572.

26. *Vita Caroli*, p. 105; Beneš, *Chronicon*, p. 337; *Chronica principum Polonie*, p. 510. See also Dąbrowski, "Dzieje polityczne," pp. 437–39; Werunsky, *Karl IV*, I, 380; Šusta, *Karel IV*, p. 437.

27. According to *Vita Caroli*, p. 105. See also Caro, *Geschichte Polens*, II, 268. Charles's assertion is questioned by Werunsky, *Karl IV*, I, 382 n. 1; Jan Dąbrowski, *Ostatnie lata Ludwika Wielkiego, 1370–1382* (Cracow, 1918), p. 119 n. 5.

28. See Johannes de Thurócz, *Chronica Hungarorum*, in *Scriptores rerum Hungaricarum veteres ac genuini . . .* , ed. J. G. Schwandtner, 3 vols. (Vienna, 1746–48), I, 177; Dąbrowski, *Ostatnie lata*, p. 119.

the coalition was led by Duke Conrad of Oleśnica and Margrave Charles. The former attempted to recover Wschowa from Poland, but his attack failed; the latter invaded lower Lusatia, which was held by the Wittelsbachs, but a spirited defense by local forces repulsed him, and he gave up the campaign.[29]

Faced with this lack of early success and the formidable nature of the coalition, King John suffered an uncharacteristic lapse of courage. He sent emissaries to Emperor Lewis to negotiate either a truce or a peace; but Lewis, confident of his strength, refused to discuss the issue. Thus rebuffed, John recovered his usual aggressive bravado, and Charles reported that he cried, "In the name of God, the more enemies we have, the more spoils and booty we shall take; and I swear by the Lord Jesus Christ that whoever of them first invades me, I shall so overwhelm him that all the others will take fright."

The first to test the King's boast was the Polish king. Following John's campaign of revenge against Bolko of Świdnica, Casimir invaded Silesia, supported by Hungarian and perhaps Lithuanian troops.[30] His goal was the district of Racibórz, which had been given to Duke Nicholas of Opawa by the Bohemians not long before. He quickly laid siege to, and captured, several important fortresses, and with much of the district in Casimir's hands, the Polish army ranged almost to Racibórz itself. There the beleaguered duke appealed to his suzerain for aid. John confidently promised that he would personally lead a large army to relieve him within four days. He then turned to the knights and nobles of Bohemia for support, but they refused, replying that Racibórz was not within the boundaries of Bohemia and Moravia, and by ancient law they were not required to fight outside those boundaries. John then appealed to their knightly honor, and by leaving the meeting immediately at the head of a small army, largely supplied by Archbishop Arnošt of Prague, he succeeded in forcing them to follow him. By the time John's army saw military action, it numbered some two thousand cavalry and an unspecified number of infantry.

By the end of June, John had brought his troops to the relief of the duchy of Racibórz. When an expected Wittelsbach offensive into Bohemia did not materialize, Casimir deemed retreat the better part of valor and began a rapid return to Cracow. The Czech army followed close behind and even won a substantial victory en route. Hungarian support forces were cut off from the main Polish army, and John inflicted serious losses upon them on the Vistula west of Cracow. The way to the capital then lay open for John and Charles, and by July 12, they had invested the city. The outskirts were captured and

29. Johannes Vitoduranus, *Chronicon a Friderico II imperatore ad annum 1348*, in J. G. Eccardus, ed., *Corpus Historicum Medii Aevi* . . . , 2 vols. (Leipzig, 1723), I, 1911, says he invaded Brandenburg itself. See, however, Werunsky, *Karl IV*, I, 381 n. 1, and Johannes Schultz, *Die Mark Brandenburg*, 4 vols. (Berlin, 1961–), II, 65.

30. Details of this campaign are drawn from Johannes Thurócz, *Chronica*, p. 177; Beneš, *Chronicon*, p. 281; Franciscus Pragensis, *Chronica Pragensis, 1125–1353*, in *Font. rer. Aust.*, VIII, 580; Długosz, *Historia*, III, 215–17. See also Pope Clement's letter in Theiner, *Mon. Pol.*, I, # 628, in which there is mention of "schismatic Lithuanians."

burned, the surrounding countryside was devastated by Bohemian troops, but the walls of Cracow and the fortifications on Wawel Hill withstood several attacks during the siege.

During this period, Casimir was finally driven by desperation to seek radical means of shortening the war and bringing the devastation to an end. According to Charles,[31] the young Polish king suggested trial by combat to the aging Luxemburger. Casimir proposed that the two monarchs be locked in a room, and that the identity of the one who emerged would determine the victor in the war! John replied he was willing, but only provided the combatants were evenly matched: because he was blind, Casimir should put out his own eyes to make the combat more fair. After this, nothing more was heard of the Polish proposal. Instead, Casimir proposed a truce, which John eventually accepted because of the growing lack of supplies and food for his troops.

This truce did not last, however, because Polish fortunes revived. Just as the Czech army began its return to Silesia, Hungarian reinforcements arrived for Casimir. The allies then pursued the Bohemian army, which had been divided into two detachments to find supplies and provisions. In a few days, heavy losses were inflicted upon both detachments. Late in July, John led the battered remnants of his army to safety in Silesia.[32]

Elsewhere, the conflict had not gone so badly for the Luxemburgers, and John was able to persuade the Wittelsbachs to sign a three-month peace in Gubiń on August 15.[33] Left suddenly without an ally, Casimir was loath to renew the conflict alone, despite his partial successes against John. He therefore agreed at Pyzdry in early September to sign a truce with the Bohemian to last until November 11.[34] Mutual exhaustion on both sides, however, prevented resumption of conflict that winter. There remained only the question of future Wittelsbach-Polish relationships. Lewis had broken his alliance with Casimir by signing a separate peace with John (the Wittelsbachs had, in fact, brought very little to the alliance), and the apparently successful negotiations which he undertook with Poland in the fall were designed to placate the Polish ruler.

Although physically far removed from the events of the preceding months, the papacy had watched with concern the growing estrangement of, and ultimate breach between, Poland and Bohemia and the concomitant reconciliation of Casimir with the Wittelsbachs. Such a development might undermine,

---

31. *Vita Caroli*, p. 106.

32. The most complete modern account of the year's conflict is given by Dąbrowski, "Dzieje polityczne," pp. 454–66. The more strictly military aspects are treated by Kaczmarczyk and Weyman, *Reformy wojskowe*, pp. 140–42, and Olejnik, *Działalność militarna*, pp. 72–74.

33. Older scholars, such as Caro, *Geschichte Polens*, II, 271, and Werunsky, *Karl IV*, I, 386, place this truce in Spremberg on August 11. This has now been shown to be incorrect. See Taube, *Ludwig der Aeltere*, p. 84 n. 2; Dąbrowski, "Dzieje polityczne," p. 464; Schultz, *Die Mark Brandenburg*, II, 65.

34. Dogiel, *Codex*, I, 5, though with the incorrect date of September 6, 1346.

and perhaps wreck, the papal plans to put an end to its own struggle with Lewis the Bavarian by replacing him as emperor with Charles of Bohemia. By harrassing the Luxemburgers and supporting the Wittelsbachs, Casimir was acting counter to papal policy. Thus the pope undertook the task of mediating peace between Casimir and John and Charles.

As the date for the expiration of the Polish-Bohemian truce neared, it seemed in Avignon, where the extent of mutual exhaustion in the two countries was perhaps not fully recognized, that fighting would again break out between the two kings. Clement therefore commissioned his nuncio in Hungary, William of Pusterla, to exhort John and Casimir to conclude a more durable peace, or at the very least to prolong the truce. If they would not accept William's mediation, then he was to instruct them to send representatives to Avignon empowered to decide the dispute between the two states. In case this effort was in vain, then William was authorized to use the full force of papal power to prevent the revival of conflict.[35]

The same day he wrote to William, Clement also sent letters to Bohemia and Poland. To John and Charles he expressed his deep desire that they prolong their truce with Casimir so that a definitive peace might be worked out. He further requested them to send representatives to Avignon who would entrust to the papal see the responsibility of mediating a peace between Poland and Bohemia.[36] To Casimir, Clement wrote that he hoped the Polish king would not further tarnish the dignity of his royal person by continuing to deal with the condemned and rejected house of a heretic emperor. The pope recognized that certain practical considerations had forced Casimir to carry on these dealings, but he was confident that in the future there would be no need for such action.[37] Clement made one further effort this same day to bring about peace. He wrote to King Louis of Hungary urging him to persuade Casimir and John to abstain from further conflict and to entrust the mediation of their differences to the pope.[38] Unfortunately for papal policy, Louis was little inclined at this point to follow advice and direction from Avignon, because of papal-Angevin conflict over the crown of the Kingdom of Naples. Louis, in fact, had gone so far as to support Lewis of Bavaria against the pope in hopes of gaining his own end in Italy. Still not satisfied with these efforts, Clement wrote to John and Casimir again on October 29, warning them to undertake no further hostile action after the expiration of the truce.[39]

It is difficult to evaluate the influence which the papal peace initiative

35. Theiner, *Mon. Hung.*, I, # 1046, 1048.

36. Theiner, *Mon. Pol.*, I, # 626–27.

37. Ibid., # 628.

38. Theiner, *Mon. Hung.*, I, # 1049–50. See also Eugen Csuday, *Die Geschichte der Ungarn*, 2 vols. (Vienna, 1900), I, 347–57; Dąbrowski, *Ostatnie lata*, pp. 121–23.

39. Theiner, *Mon. Pol.*, I, # 632–33.

exercised. The first group of letters, which were dated September 18, would perhaps have arrived at their destinations by the expiration of the truce of Pyzdry on November 11, but those sent in October would still have been in transit. Though they certainly reflected the sincere concern of the pope for peace, it is not too much to suggest that these letters had their greatest influence in reinforcing the intentions of the two rulers. John desired the extension of peace to have a free hand against the Wittelsbachs in his efforts to gain the imperial dignity for his son; while Casimir was acutely aware of the economic and military weaknesses of his kingdom and of how dangerous a resumption of conflict might be at this time.[40] Thus there was no war after November 11. Neither was there peace; there were still unresolved problems over Silesia and financial relations between Luxemburger and Piast. These had to be dealt with before permanent peace could be established between Poland and Bohemia.

The year 1346 brought the strengthening of the Polish position in Silesia, the extension of the Polish-Bohemian peace, resolution of some of the extant problems between the two kingdoms, and a change in Bohemian rule which had an important effect on Casimir's relations with the Luxemburg house.

One place where Casimir's hand was strengthened in Silesia was the territory of Duke Władysław of Koźle-Bytom. This prince of Upper Silesia had never had the close relations with the rulers of Bohemia that many of his peers had had. Instead he had managed to retain a relative independence, even showing some sympathy toward the Polish rulers.[41] Because his duchies were strategically located between Cracow and Bohemia's allies in Silesia, Czech troops had attacked Duke Władysław in 1345, and it was only with some difficulty that he succeeded in driving them off. Now he sought protection from Casimir. On February 15, 1346, the two signed a treaty whereby the king promised to grant military aid to the prince in case of attack. Władysław for his part promised not to grant access to his territory to any enemy of Casimir's, specifically King

40. One of the themes which underlies Oskar Halecki's writing on Casimir is the king's great desire to maintain peace. This appears throughout Halecki's "Kazimierz Wielki," but is more clearly evident in his shorter "Casimir the Great, 1333–1370," in *The Cambridge History of Poland*, ed. W. F. Reddaway, et al., 2 vols. (Cambridge, 1941–50), I, 167–87, and his treatment of Casimir in "Medieval Poland," in L. I. Strakhovsky, ed., *A Handbook of Slavic Studies* (Cambridge, Mass., 1950), pp. 86–88. He suggests that this theme is well illustrated by the king's refusal to resume the war with Bohemia after November 11. In overall terms, Halecki's thesis is correct, and it is certainly true that Casimir pursued a far more peaceful policy than had his father, Władysław Łokietek. Two things should, however, be pointed out. First, in addition to more altruistic motives, certain practical considerations such as the strength of the kingdom caused Casimir's policy to be more pacific. Second, Casimir resorted to war rather more frequently than might be inferred at first from Halecki's generalization. This conclusion arises clearly from the study of Olejnik, *Działalność militarna*, pp. 3–4, 167–69 especially. War was for Casimir, not surprisingly, an instrument of state policy.

41. He had in 1316 and after been an ally of Władysław Łokietek in the latter's attempts to resist Bohemian encroachments in Silesia. See Edmund Długopolski, *Władysław Łokietek na tle swoich czasów* (Wrocław, 1951), p. 266; and *Historia Śląska*, I, i, 547.

John, his sons, or Duke Nicholas of Opawa-Racibórz. This important territory was thus neutralized in the Polish-Bohemian conflict; at the same time it became another obstacle in the path of Luxemburg consolidation in Silesia.[42]

Several months later, Casimir's position was further strengthened when Duke Henry of Jawór died in May without direct heir. On the basis of a previous inheritance agreement, his Lower Silesian duchy went to his nephew, Duke Bolko of Świdnica. According to feudal practice, Jawór should have escheated to Henry's suzerain, King John of Bohemia. But the Luxemburgers were involved in the west, and chose not to contest Duke Bolko. His aggrandizement made him the most powerful independent ruler in Silesia.[43]

By 1346 the attention of the Luxemburgers was drawn not so much to Silesia as to the crown of the Holy Roman Empire. The long, bitter contest between Emperor Lewis IV and the papacy was drawing to a close, and for some time Clement had been resolved to see that the Wittelsbach was deposed and the pope's former pupil, Charles, elected in his place. The prospect of this honor for the house of Luxemburg disposed John and Charles to follow papal policy in many matters. Thus they informed Clement early in 1346 that they would let the papacy mediate the Polish-Bohemian conflict. This news encouraged the pope to send a representative to Casimir with instructions to dispatch representatives to Avignon to sign a peace with Bohemia.[44] Though all the circumstances of this settlement are impossible to determine, on June 4, 1346, an extension of the truce was agreed upon, and the Luxemburgers jointly renounced in Casimir's favor all claims to the city and territory of Wschowa, thus confirming the Polish conquest of 1343.[45]

One of the events of 1346 which augured well for future Polish-Bohemian relations was the death of King John. For many years he had been unremittingly hostile to Poland, showing only very infrequently any softening toward Casimir. In contrast, Margrave Charles and the Polish king had developed strong ties of friendship, despite the occasional strain of events. This difference between the two Luxemburgers assumes significance as the result of John's heroic death on the field of battle at Crécy on August 26, 1346. The restless, wandering spirit of this blind, chivalric knight-errant was forever stilled. No longer would coronations, weddings, funerals, battles, and crusades throughout the whole of Europe be able to count upon his presence. A man who had outlived his time was dead. In a narrower sense, one of Poland's greatest foes was gone. Casimir can hardly have shared the grief of Edward of England, who was reported to

---

42. Dogiel, *Codex*, I, 538, # 3. See also Dąbrowski, "Dzieje polityczne," p. 466.

43. Charles was later to use this failure to follow feudal custom as the basis for his annexation of Jawór to Bohemia. See Colmar Grünhagen and E. Markgraf, eds., *Lehns- und Besitzurkunden Schlesiens und seiner einzelnen Fürstentümer im Mittelalter*, 2 vols. (Leipzig, 1881–83), I, 89.

44. Theiner, *Mon. Pol.*, I, # 640.

45. Ludewig, *Reliquiae*, V, 510; Dąbrowski, "Dzieje polityczne," p. 467 n. 2.

have cried, with tears in his eyes, "The crown of chivalry has fallen today. Never was anyone equal to this king of Bohemia."[46]

By the end of 1347, relations between Casimir and Charles, for a year king and emperor, had become strained to the point of war. Two factors had been involved in this: Charles's continued attempts to bring Wrocław under the ecclesiastical jurisdiction of Prague[47] and the efforts of Casimir's nephew Bolko of Świdnica to expand his territory in Silesia. Early in January, 1348, Bolko invaded Kamienna Góra, which John had wrested from him three years before. A short time later, in concert with the duke, a Polish army led by Casimir invaded Silesia and marched directly toward Wrocław. At the same time Bolko advanced on the city from the southwest. The citizenry appealed in vain to Charles for aid, and only by mounting a hasty counteroffensive against Wschowa were they able to negotiate short truces with Bolko and Casimir. One interesting aspect of this conflict was that the cathedral chapter and bishop of Wrocław failed to grant the city any financial or material aid and even expressed a certain sympathy with Duke Bolko.[48]

Charles's eventual response to these attacks was to issue a decree which incorporated Luxemburg holdings in Silesia into the Bohemian crown and formally granted Wrocław the right of self-defense.[49] In so doing he forced the city to break the truces with Bolko and Casimir, and in response the Polish king renewed his campaign. He marched into the area devastating the countryside and capturing a few small towns. Only in midsummer was Charles able to send any aid into Silesia, by which time Casimir and Bolko had consolidated their gains and strengthened their strategic positions. Charles recognized that recourse to arms would result in a long, bitter conflict in which he might not be successful. He therefore signed truces with Casimir and Bolko and arranged for a peace conference.[50]

The preliminaries of peace were negotiated in October by Czenko of Lipa. This Czech nobleman and adviser to the Luxemburgers had been captured

---

46. Šusta, *Karel IV*, pp. 505–12, has closely analyzed the traditions which surround John's death, and has concluded that most of them are nonhistorical, particularly the tradition concerning "Ich dien'." Werunsky, *Karl IV*, II, 65–67, gives a sympathetic account of John's death. See also Franz Palacky, *Geschichte von Böhmen*, 5 vols. in 10 (Prague, 1836–67), II, pt. ii, 252–56; and, more briefly, Adolf Bachmann, *Geschichte Böhmens*, 2 vols. (Gotha, 1899–1905), I, 802–3.

47. This action was based upon a papal agreement with Charles in 1344. See Palacky, *Literarische Reise nach Italien im Jahre 1837 zur Aufsuchung von Quellen der böhmischen und mährischen Geschichte* (Prague, 1838), p. 86, # 180.

48. This is clearly shown in a somewhat later declaration. See Georg Korn, ed., *Breslauer Urkundenbuch* (Wrocław, 1870), # 189.

49. See Dąbrowski, "Dzieje polityczne," pp. 477–81.

50. Extensive details concerning this war are reflected in the documents printed in Colmar Grünhagen, "Die Correspondenz der Stadt Breslau mit Karl IV. in den Jahren 1347–1355," *Archiv für Österreichische Geschichte*, XXXIV (1865), 353–59, and represented in Korn, *Bres. U.B.*, # 189, 190. See also Dąbrowski, "Dzieje polityczne," pp. 468–70; *Historia Śląska*, I, pt. i, 573–74.

in battle in 1345, and had developed very close relations with Casimir during the months of his confinement.[51] We find him acting as Charles's representative in Cracow and at the same time designated as Casimir's plenipotentiary in the later peace negotiations. These were based upon tentative agreements made in the Polish capital and confirmed on November 22, 1348, in the Silesian town of Namysłów, where Casimir's representatives met with Charles. The emperor's first act was to inform the Polish representatives that on October 14 he had signed a treaty with Duke Bogusław V of Pomorze-Wołogosz, Casimir's son-in-law, and with his brothers, Barnim and Warcisław. These princes had promised to provide the emperor with aid against his enemies, while Charles had made similar promises to them.[52] Charles was careful to explain that this treaty was not directed against Poland but against the Wittelsbachs in Brandenburg. After this, the peace treaty between the two rulers was signed. In its form, the treaty of Namysłów was a renewal of the pact signed in 1341 between Casimir and John and Charles, and of the agreements made in 1345. Casimir again renounced all claims for repayment of his loans to Charles, while the emperor confirmed Poland in its possession of Wschowa and other minor gains in Silesia. In addition Charles promised to assist Casimir in regaining those territories which had been taken from the kingdom by the Teutonic Order and the rulers of Brandenburg. When this had been accomplished (and it required considerable optimism to believe that this part of the treaty was anything more than window-dressing), Casimir agreed to protect the emperor and lend him aid against all his enemies, except King Louis of Hungary and the cosigner of the treaty, Duke Bolko. A final provision of the treaty bound Bolko to submit his conflict with Charles to Duke Albert of Austria for arbitration. On November 25, Charles and Bolko signed a separate treaty.[53]

It is difficult to overestimate the significance of this treaty. It brought to an end five years of intermittent Polish-Bohemian strife over Silesia. At the same time it left Casimir in possession of his hard-won gains in the region and protected the independence of his strongest ally there, Duke Bolko. In the future, disputes between the two rulers over Silesia were to be infrequent and would not result in armed hostility. Equally important was the fact that the peace of Namysłów established a durable personal peace between Charles and Casimir. Conflicting dynastic interests would sometimes strain this relationship, but on the whole it was from this time forward a permanent feature of Casimir's policy. Casimir sought peace with Charles at this time because he recognized the temporary

51. See Beneš, *Chronicon*, p. 289.

52. See Stanisław Nowogrodzki, "Pomorze zachodnie a Polska w latach 1323–1370," *Rocznik Gdański*, IX–X (1935–36), 37–39; Wiktor Fenrych, *Nowa Marchia w dziejach politycznych Polski w XIII i XIV wieku* (Zielona Góra and Poznań, 1959), pp. 59–60.

53. The Polish text of the treaty is in *C.D.M.P.*, II, # 1277, and in *Archivum coronae regni Bohemiae*, ed. V. Hrubý, 2 vols. (Prague, 1928–35), II, # 84. The Bohemian text has not survived. For Bolko's treaty with Charles, see Werunsky, *Karl IV*, II, 141.

inadequacy of his kingdom's resources for the regaining of Silesia. In addition, he needed to stabilize affairs in the west in order to return to the question of Ruthenia.[54]

One of the most important gains which Casimir made in Silesia in this period was unrelated to his military action or the peace of Namysłów. It came, rather, from his persistent diplomacy at the papal court in Avignon. Casimir was only too aware that Charles and Archbishop Arnošt of Prague sought to have Wrocław removed from the ecclesiastical jurisdiction of Gniezno and made subject to the Bohemian capital. To prevent this, Casimir wrote heatedly to Clement to inform him again of the harm such an act would cause to the church in Poland. The pope was moved by the appeal and replied to Casimir that he would not heed the emperor's entreaties and would preserve the relationship between Gniezno and Wrocław.[55] Charles was never able to change this.

Despite the treaties of Kalisz in 1343 and the peace which had followed between Poland and the Teutonic Order, Casimir never felt entirely safe from the power of the Knights. He recognized the need to maintain sufficient defensive strength so that the Order might be deterred from renewed expansion, and he seized every opportunity to ally himself with rulers who might be able to provide aid against the Knights. Even while preparing for the treaties of Kalisz, he had signed a treaty with Duke Bogusław V of Pomorze-Wołogoszcz that was obviously directed against the Order. It was this same concern in 1348, during the height of the Polish-Bohemian conflict, which drove him to strengthen himself in the north. He opened negotiations with another prince of Pomorze Zachodnie, and on March 24 signed a formal treaty at Poznań with Duke Barnim III of Pomorze-Szczecin. Casimir promised to provide the duke with aid should he be attacked, and Barnim made similar promises. While the terms of this treaty are not as explicit as that of 1343, it is likely that in this instance also aid consisting of some four hundred heavy cavalry was envisioned.[56]

Though this treaty, like its predecessor, was directed against the Knights, its provisions were never implemented. Casimir was too realistic to call upon the emperor to fulfill the promises made at Namysłów, for Charles had no real desire to see Poland strengthened by the acquisition of more territory. Charles rightly feared that should Poland regain Pomorze and other lost western territories, it might well turn next to the recovery of Silesia. At the same time,

54. On the significance of the treaty in general, see Dąbrowski, "Dzieje polityczne," pp. 470–73; *Historia Śląska*, I, pt. i, 574–75; *Geschichte Schlesiens*, I, p. 214; Caro, *Geschichte Polens*, II, 279–81; Kaczmarczyk, *Polska czasów Kazimierza*, pp. 58–59.

55. Theiner, *Mon. Pol.*, I, # 695.

56. The text of the treaty and a brief commentary is given by Otto Heinemann, "Die Bündnisse zwischen Polen und Pommern von 1348 und 1466," *Zeitschrift der historischen Gesellschaft für die Provinz Posen*, XIV (1899), 323–26. Fenrych, *Nowa Marchia*, pp. 58–59, points out that this alliance was also designed to counteract Bohemian influence. This is true, but it was a secondary consideration.

despite the alliance with Barnim, Casimir had little desire to become involved in a protracted war in the west. His immediate need was for peace there, since he was already preparing for another Ruthenian campaign.

To assure himself of this peace, Casimir turned to the Knights directly. Late in the spring of 1349 he traveled into Kujavia to investigate the administration of his kingdom there. During his stay he informed Grand Master Heinrich Dusmer that he wished to put to rest all rumors of hostility between the Order and Poland, and at the same time establish a clear boundary between the two states. The grand master willingly responded to this request and began negotiations with the Poles in the Kujavian city of Trzesącz, where on June 14 a treaty was signed which for the first time clearly described the border between Kujavia and Chełmno and Pomorze.[57] Only slightly modified from 1343, the border began on the west bank of the Vistula River about half-way between Świecie to the north and Wyszogród to the south and ran northwestward till it touched the Brda River at its confluence with the Zempolna. From there it turned north to the Kamionka River, then ran due west and followed the north bank of this stream to its source south of the village of Grunau. From here westward to the upper reaches of the Dobrzyńka River the frontier was marked out with boundary stones. It then followed the south bank of the Dobrzyńka to the confluence with the Gwda, where the border ended with the beginning of Pomorze Zachodnie. With only minor modifications, this boundary remained unchanged until the beginning of the Thirteen Years War in 1454. At this same time, a tariff was established which was fair and equitable to merchants of both states, and a panel of arbiters was appointed to adjudicate disputes which might arise over the boundary. With the resolution of this problem, the peace between Poland and the Order which had been established at Kalisz was confirmed.[58]

These good relations did not lull Casimir into a false sense of security, and he continually sought to strengthen his system of alliances. After he returned from his victorious Ruthenian campaign in 1349 and before he returned to defend his gains against the Lithuanians, he received King Waldemar IV of Denmark in Poland.[59] Not all the reasons for this visit are entirely clear, but Waldemar was closely connected with opposition to the Wittelsbachs in Brandenburg, and, as the result of conflicting territorial and economic interests, was also

57. The boundary is described in detail by Voigt, *Geschichte Preussens*, V, 74 n. 1, and Erich Sandow, *Die polnisch-pommerellische Grenze, 1309–1454 (Beihefte zum Jahrbuch der Albertus-Universität, Königsberg, Pr.,* VI) (Kitzingen/Main, 1954), pp. 7–10, 24.

58. The Polish copy, dated June 14, 1349, in *C.D.Pol.*, II, pt. ii, # 500; *C.D.M.P.*, II, # 1286, and *Pr. U.B.*, IV, # 423. The grand master's confirmation, dated June 23, in Dogiel, *Codex*, IV, # 67; *C.D.M.P.*, II, # 1290; *Pr. U.B.*, IV, # 425. Stanisław Kętrzyński, "Zapis Kazimierza Wielkiego dla Kazimierza Bogusławowica," *P.H.*, XIV (1912), 65 n. 1, has suggested that this treaty was the final act of the Peace of Kalisz whereby the Knights made definitive renunciation of Kujavia to Poland. I find nothing in the sources to support such a view.

59. See Karol Maleczyński, "Przymierze Kazimierza Wielkiego z Danją z r. 1350," in *Prace Historyczne w 30-lecie działalności profesorskiej Stanisława Zakrzewskiego* (Lwów, 1934), pp. 194–95.

identified with the enemies of the Order. He was undoubtedly trying to rally northern European support for both aspects of his policy. He was only partially successful. Casimir did agree to enter an anti-Order alliance. On May 13, 1350, the kings signed a treaty in which Casimir promised to lend Waldemar aid against all his enemies, except Charles IV, Louis of Hungary, Margrave Lewis of Brandenburg and Lewis the Roman, Bolko of Świdnica, Władysław of Dobrzyń, Bolesław III of Płock, Ziemowit III and Casimir I of Mazovia, and the princes of Pomorze Zachodnie! The only candidate against whom the treaty could be directed was the Order. Although the Danish copy of this treaty has not survived, Waldemar apparently promised Casimir the same aid against Poland's enemies. The actual extent of mutual support involved in this treaty was modest: only one hundred armored troops; but the diplomatic significance was a far more substantial gain for Poland.[60]

Despite the king's treaty with Denmark, good relations between Poland and the Order were not disrupted. While in Lwów in June, 1350, Casimir wrote the grand master to assure him that, even though commercial routes through Ruthenia had been temporarily closed as a result of the Polish-Lithuanian struggle, resulting in losses to merchants from Toruń and the other cities of the *Ordensstaat*, there was nothing which he desired more than to maintain close ties between Poland and the Order. Above all, he did not want conflict to break out between the two states.[61] This attitude was in marked contrast to that which existed during the reign of Łokietek, or even in the early days of Casimir's reign. It even enabled Casimir to turn in 1352 to the Order for financial support in his battle for Ruthenia, something which would have been unthinkable before. Part of the explanation for this is that Casimir was fighting one of the Order's most dangerous enemies, the Lithuanians. By forcing the Gedyminowicze to concentrate upon Ruthenia, Casimir was indirectly aiding the Order. But it was an arrangement which was more directly satisfactory to both sides: Casimir received the money he needed immediately and ran no risk of losing his territory; the Knights were able to enjoy the usufruct from Dobrzyń while Casimir fought their mortal enemies.

Although Casimir allied himself at various times with the Luxemburgers, Wittelsbachs, Knights of the Teutonic Order, Lithuanians, and even Tatars, his foreign policy was not predicated upon any of these alliances. He recognized that in every instance these were marriages of convenience, temporary in nature and not to be relied upon permanently. With only one state and ruler were his relations always good, and upon one country only did he rely constantly as his strongest supporter in the prosecution of his policy. That country was Hungary.

60. The text is printed in Maleczyński, "Dwa niedrukowane akty przymierza Kazimierza Wielkiego z Danją z r. 1350 i 1363," *K.H.*, XLV (1931), 256–57. See also Maleczyński, "Przymierze z Danją," pp. 196–209.

61. *C.D.Pr.*, III, # 65; *Pr. U.B.*, IV, # 610.

The Polish-Hungarian alliance was predicated upon several factors. It had originally arisen in Łokietek's time out of common opposition to the ambitions of the Přemyslid dynasty, and opposition to Bohemia was still an important consideration. Only the dynastic opponent had changed: it was now Luxemburg power which made allies of Casimir and Louis. The alliance sprang also from mutual interests in Ruthenia. While these might in some instances cause momentarily strained relations between the two, in general the concord between Piast and Angevin was maintained. Geographical considerations also were part of the Polish-Hungarian friendship. The two states were neighbors and had frequent economic and cultural contact, but the rugged Carpathians prevented the kind of easy contact which might have encouraged invasion. But by far the most important factor in the Polish-Hungarian alliance was the dynastic tie. It was this which had led Casimir's brother-in-law, King Charles Robert, to hope for eventual Angevin succession in Poland. This had been granted in principle in 1339, but the agreement was incomplete and required amplification and more precise definition. The details connected with the question of Angevin succession in Poland constitute one of the more important aspects of Casimir's reign.[62]

Since the early researches of Jan Dąbrowski, scholars have generally accepted that the first discussion of the succession problem after 1339 did not come until 1351.[63] That was the occasion for Louis and Casimir to lead a joint campaign against the Lithuanians. In July the armies were in Lublin, where the Polish King became "sick unto death." Louis was forced by necessity to take over command of the united forces. Seeing in this an opportunity to insure his accession in Poland should Casimir die, he was able to obtain from the civil and military dignitaries gathered in Lublin a promise to recognize him as king. Before they agreed, they in turn demanded from Louis an oath with far-reaching implications. The Angevin first promised he would not let his brother Stephen interfere in Polish affairs, then guaranteed not to appoint Germans as castellans or civil officials in Poland. If he broke his oath, the knights and nobles swore they would renounce their allegiance to him. In addition the Poles forced Louis to agree that the only money he would take from the kingdom would be amounts sufficient to maintain himself and his family. Related to this stipulation was a promise not to use Polish monies to support Hungarian policies and

62. The problem of Angevin succession has been studied most thoroughly by Jan Dąbrowski, *Ostatnie lata Ludwika Wielkiego*. Some of his conclusions were challenged by Halecki, "O genezie i znaczeniu rządów andegaweńskich w Polsce," *K.H.*, XXXV (1921), 31–68. Dąbrowski answered in "Polityka andegaweńska Kazimierza Wielkiego," *K.H.*, XXXVI (1922), 11–40. His views are best summarized in his *Dzieje Polski od r. 1333 do r. 1506*, vol. II of Roman Grodecki, Stanisław Zachorowski, and Jan Dąbrowski, *Dzieje Polski średniowiecznej* (Cracow, 1926). I have in general followed Dąbrowski.

63. See Halecki, "Kazimierz Wielki," pp. 339–40; *Historia Polski*, general editor Tadeusz Manteuffel, vol. I, *do roku 1764*, in three parts, ed. Henryk Łowmiański (Warsaw, 1958–61), pt. i, 500; Kaczmarczyk, *Polska czasów Kazimierza*, p. 66.

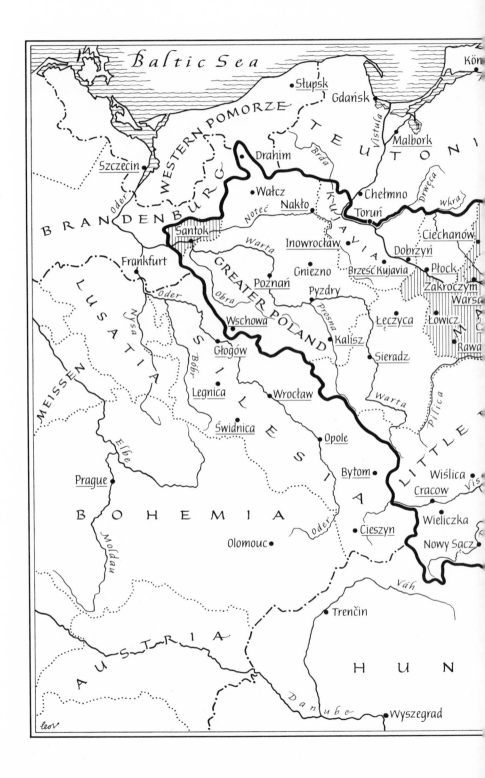

• Vilno

Poland in 1370

— Boundaries of The Kingdom of Poland
including Vassal States

|||||||| Vassal States of The Kingdom

<u>Lwów</u> State, provincial and land capitals

0   50   100   150 Miles

GRAND

Neman

DER

<u>Wizna</u>

Narew

<u>Drohiczyn</u>

Bug

<u>Brześć</u>

Pripet

Pripet

D U C H Y

Goryn

Styr

O F

L I T H U A N I A

uków

prz

Lublin

<u>Chełm</u>

V L A D I M I R

•<u>Vladimir</u>

•<u>Łuck</u>

domierz

San

<u>Bełz</u>•

• <u>Krzemieniec</u>

• Jarosław

•<u>Lwów</u>

<u>Przemyśl</u>

<u>Sanok</u>

H   A   L   I   C   Z

• Halicz

P O D O L I A

•<u>Kamieniec Podolski</u>

R   Y

Prut

Dniester

M   O   L   D   A   V   I   A

programs. Only because the illness of Casimir was so serious, and only after Louis had sworn to keep these promises, did the Poles give him their allegiance.[64]

Specific as this agreement was, it did not fully clarify all points concerning Louis's succession in Poland. In particular, the events of 1351 raised the question of whether those in Lublin could speak for the whole of the kingdom. As a result, in 1355, while making plans for a new Ruthenian campaign, Casimir went to Hungary to request Louis's aid. He arrived in Buda early in January, accompanied by many important Polish nobles and officials, and the question of the Angevin succession was immediately raised. Agreement was quickly reached, and on January 23 the two kings issued a joint renewal and amplification of earlier royal documents concerning the succession. Specifically, Casimir confirmed Louis in his right to succeed him should he die without legitimate male heir.[65]

The next day Louis negotiated a separate agreement with four of the officials whom Casimir had brought with him. These individuals, though they were all from Little Poland, spoke officially "on the part of all the inhabitants of the Kingdom of Poland."[66] To them, Louis promised that after he succeeded Casimir he would levy no new taxes without the consent of those affected, that in his travels through the kingdom he would maintain his entourage at his own expense, and that in case of war he would not require his Polish subjects to fight outside the boundaries of their own kingdom. He also declared that the right of Angevin succession in Poland extended only to him and to his nephew John and their male descendants. Finally, he promised to honor all pacts, agreements, and treaties issued by Casimir which affected his future subjects.[67] In return, the four representatives of the nation signified their acceptance of Louis and invited him to receive the homage of his future subjects in person on Polish soil. This same day the Angevin monarch issued two documents which promised his help to Casimir in the Ruthenian campaign.[68]

Three more documents were issued this same year which concerned Hungarian succession in Poland. On April 13 Louis empowered his mother, Elizabeth, Casimir's sister, to go to Poland to accept formally the allegiance promised in Buda, since he was prevented from going in person by Angevin ambitions in

---

64. Our knowledge of the incident is based upon the *Chronicon Dubnicense*, in *K.H.*, III (1889), 205–13. I judge it to be highly probable that a veiled description of this event is given by Janko of Czarnków, *Chronicon*, pp. 638–39. Dąbrowski, *Ostatnie lata*, p. 135 n. 1, is more cautious. Oswald Balzer, *Królestwo Polskie, 1295–1370*, 3 vols. (Lwów, 1919–20), apparently makes no mention of this agreement as a precedent for the limitations of royal authority in Poland.

65. The original is lost. Dąbrowski, *Ostatnie lata*, pp. 141–42, has reconstructed it from a similar document in Antoni Prochaska, "W sprawie zajęcia Rusi przez Kazimierza Wielkiego," *K.H.*, VI (1892), 31–33. For the constitutional significance, see Balzer, *Królestwo*, III, 99–117.

66. See Dąbrowski, *Ostatnie lata*, p. 142 n. 4.

67. *C.D.M.P.*, III, # 1328.

68. Dogiel, *Codex*, I, 37–38.

Serbia.[69] Elizabeth was accompanied on this trip by several of the leading ecclesiastic and civil officials of the Hungarian kingdom. When the party reached Nowy Sącz, they were met by a delegation of Polish nobles and officials. On April 30, the Hungarian representatives promised in Louis's name to abide by the conditions of the Angevin succession in Poland,[70] and the Polish estates granted Elizabeth, as Louis's plenipotentiary, their homage and swore allegiance to their future king.[71]

These agreements of 1339, 1351, and 1355 firmly established the right of the Angevins to succeed Casimir and set forth the conditions under which they might do so. It was argued above that Długosz's description of the accession of Casimir in 1333 as an election was anachronistic. With the question of Angevin succession, such a description would not be so wide of the mark, for Louis did have to gain the approval of the knights and nobility of Poland. The way in which he did this contained the germ of constitutional developments which came full flower two centuries later. The agreements to which Louis bound himself mark the beginnings of the limitation of royal authority. This process was to culminate in the *pacta conventa* of the sixteenth century, ironically with another Angevin, Henry of Valois. Beyond this, it is possible to see in the events of the 1350s the seeds of the abuses which were a part of the Polish trauma in the eighteenth century.[72] These seeds were planted at the very time when the authority and control of the monarchy were being augmented by Casimir to an extent that the growth of royal centralization is one of the great themes of his thirty-seven-year reign.

The same year that Louis was formally accepted as royal heir-apparent, Casimir completed a process which marks one of the most important successes of his reign: the feudal acquisition of Mazovia. Since this region had long been considered Polish territory, the king's success there can be viewed in much the same light as, for example, his policy toward Greater Poland: the breaking down of regional barriers within the *regnum*. More accurately, he was dealing with an area which since the thirteenth century had been an independent principality whose position was analogous to that of Silesia. Its princes had even carried out policies which ran counter to those of the ruler of the *regnum*. This had been especially true during the reign of Władysław Łokietek, when the Piast princes of Mazovia had at times been closely associated with the Teutonic Order.[73] Even in the midpoint of Casimir's reign, at least one part of the region

69. Prochaska, "W sprawie," pp. 31–32; see also Dąbrowski, *Ostatnie lata*, p. 146.

70. Dogiel, *Codex*, I, 38–39; Prochaska, "W sprawie," pp. 31–32.

71. The record of this has not been preserved, and we do not know who participated from the Polish side. See Dąbrowski, *Ostatnie lata*, p. 146 n. 2.

72. On the relation of the agreements of 1355 to the *pacta conventa* and the *pacta* in general, the authoritative work is still Władysław Sobociński, *Pakta Konwenta: Studium z Historii prawa polskiego* (Cracow, 1939), pp. 34–89 especially.

73. For Mazovia in this period, see Stanisław Zachorowski, "Wiek XIII i panowanie

was still subject to divided loyalties: Duke Bolesław III held Płock as a fief of the king of Bohemia.[74]

In 1340 the province of Mazovia was a geographically defined unit with traditionally established boundaries. Within these borders, however, there was no political unity, for the principality was divided into several districts ruled by members of a collateral branch of the Piast family. Duke Ziemowit II ruled Rawa, Sochaczew, and Wiżna; his brother Trojden I controlled Czersk, Warsaw, Ciechanów, Łomża, Rożań, Nursk, and Liw; and their nephew Bolesław III was lord of Wyszogród, Zakroczym, Gostynin, and held Płock as a fief of the king of Bohemia. This territorial disposition was further fragmented in 1341, for on March 13 Duke Trojden I died leaving his holdings to his sons Ziemowit III and Casimir I, brothers of the ill-fated Bolesław-George II of Halicz and Vladimir. Four years later, on February 18, 1345, Duke Ziemowit II of Rawa, Sochaczew, and Wiżna died without direct heir, leaving Rawa jointly to his nephews Ziemowit III and Casimir, and the territories of Sochaczew and Wiżna to his other nephew, Bolesław III of Płock.

Although the Mazovian princes remained independent, they were often closely allied with Casimir, especially in his Ruthenian campaigns. Dukes Ziemowit III and Casimir I had claims to the succession in Ruthenia through their brother Bolesław-George, but they apparently renounced that claim in favor of Casimir. In addition, it was probably they whom *Rocznik Traski* mentioned as having participated in Casimir's Ruthenian campaign in 1340.[75] Mazovian troops apparently took part also in the king's Ruthenian expedition of 1349, for Mazovia was one of the targets of the Lithuanians' campaign of revenge in the following year.[76] This Mazovian support for Casimir laid the foundation for the eventual aquisition of the province by the kingdom of Poland.

The process was completed and confirmed de jure by 1355, but when it began and when de facto Polish control may be said to have existed is a more difficult question which we must examine in some detail. Three hints at an early relationship are contained in documents dating from 1350, 1351, and

---

Władysława," in Grodecki, Zachorowski, and Dąbrowski, *Dzieje Polski średniowiecznej*, I, 286–87, 370–71, 408–9; Stanisław Russocki, "Region mazowiecki w Polsce średniowiecznej," *P.H.*, LIV (1963), 388–417.

74. As a result of the recognition of Bohemian suzerainty in 1329 by Wacław of Płock. See *Kodeks dyplomatyczny księstwa mazowieckiego*, ed. T. Lubomirski (Warsaw, 1863), # 59; and above, chap. 2.

75. *Rocznik Traski* in *M.P.H.*, II, 861. This idea has been criticized, though unsuccessfully in my judgment, by Ewa Maleczyńska, *Książęce lenno Mazowieckie, 1351–1526* (Lwów, 1929), p. 35.

76. Długosz, *Historia*, III, 237–38. See also Gotthold Rhode, *Die Ostgrenze Polens, Politische Entwicklung, kulturelle Bedeutung und geistige Auswirkung*, vol. I, *Im Mittelalter bis zum Jahre 1401* (Cologne and Graz, 1955), p. 207.

1352. In the first, Duke Ziemowit III described the king on May 19 as "our illustrious prince Lord Casimir, King of Poland."[77] This phrase suggests some kind of formal tie between the two, though not necessarily of a feudal nature.[78] The second document arose from events the following year. On August 20 the ruler of Płock, Duke Bolesław III, died without direct heir.[79] According to the traditions of feudal tenure, Płock should have escheated to its overlord. For this reason, on September 7 of that year Emperor Charles IV, the successor to King John as suzerain, enfeoffed Bolesław's brother-in-law, Duke Henry V of Żagań and Głogów, with Płock.[80] King Casimir refused to accept this disposition, despite its undeniable legality. He and Bolesław had previously agreed that Płock would go to the king of Poland upon the death of the duke.[81] On September 18, in the key document in this welter of events, Casimir claimed Płock, Wiżna, and Zakroczym as crown lands, and enfeoffed Ziemowit III and Casimir I with Sochoczew.[82] (The territories of Wyszogród and Gostynin were to go to Bolesław's mother, Elizabeth, for her lifetime, with the former escheating to the *regnum* and the latter going as a royal fief to Ziemowit III and Casimir I upon her death.)[83]

The final document which provides us with a helpful hint is the Polish-Lithuanian treaty of 1352. Here the Gedyminowicze state they signed it "with Casimir the King of Poland and with Ziemowit and his brother Casimir and with his [the king's] territories of Płock, Mazovia. . . ." This wording has been interpreted as implying more than a casual connection between the king and the Mazovians.[84]

With so few details, it is not surprising that scholars have differed widely, and often heatedly, on the nature and date of Polish control over Mazovia.

77. *Kod. dypl. ks. maz.*, p. 341, # 6.

78. Paszkiewicz, "Zhołdowanie Mazowsza," p. 3, argues for de facto control on this basis. His interpretations were challenged by Maleczyńska in a Note in *K.H.*, XXXIX (1925), 534–39, and in *Książęce lenno*, pp. 33–34. She argues that Ziemowit's statement is too vague to admit of any such interpretation.

79. *Spominki płockie*, in *M.P.H.*, III, 120; *Rodowód Xiążąt polskich*, in *M.P.H.*, III, 284. Duke Bolesław's death is undoubtedly connected with the treachery of Kiejstut and Lubart. See above, chap. 6.

80. Grünhagen-Markgraf, *Lehns- und Besitzurkunden*, II, 174. See also Halecki, "Kazimierz Wielki," p. 344; Dąbrowski, "Dzieje polityczne," pp. 474–75, 495.

81. This is inferred from Casimir's statement in 1355: "the fortress of Płock with all its territory which we now hold . . . by virtue of the donation made . . . by Duke Bolesław." *Kod. dypl. ks. maz.*, # 77.

82. *Kod. dypl. ks. maz.*, # 72. Caro, *Geschichte Polens*, II, 290, misread the document and stated that the king gave the two brothers the whole of their uncle's inheritance.

83. Bolesław had previously provided that Wyszogród would go to his mother. *Kod. dypl. ks. maz.*, # 70.

84. The treaty printed in Latin letter transliteration in K. Stronczyński, ed., *Wzory pism dawnych w przerysach wystawione* (Cracow, 1839), # 90. The interpretation is in Maleczyńska, *Książęce lenno*, p. 35.

Henryk Paszkiewicz contended that the beginnings of de jure control came as early as 1349 and that Bolesław III had been Casimir's vassal before his death.[85] He based his reasoning on three points: that the language used by Duke Ziemowit III in 1351 in his treaty with the king implied previous feudal relations between the crown and Bolesław; that the duke lent his support to Casimir's Ruthenian campaign of 1351; and that Casimir must have been feudal overlord of Płock by 1349, because on June 10 of that year he granted merchants from Toruń free passage through the region. This argument for a feudal connection at this early date has appeared vulnerable, especially to Ewa Maleczyńska and Gotthold Rhode.[86]

One thrust of their argument is against the document of June 10, 1349, whose authenticity has been sharply questioned. Nine days after the date of that document Casimir granted to the same merchants rights of transit through the kingdom, but made no mention of Płock.[87] Since it is doubtful that Casimir would have issued two such similar documents in such a short period of time, Maleczyńska especially has dismissed the former document and effectively disputed the rest of Paszkiewicz's theory by arguing that the relationship between Bolesław and Casimir can be explained by a treaty or alliance between them without the suggestion of feudal ties. In general, an argument for a later date, probably 1351, for the establishment of feudal ties between Mazovia and Casimir is more correct.

With the death of Bolesław and the Lithuanian treaty of 1352 with Dukes Ziemowit and Casimir, there can be little doubt that there was a great deal of de facto control exercised by the king in Mazovia. The use of such phrases in the treaty as "by virtue of dependency" and "faithful dependency" are clear indications.[88] The extent to which Casimir felt himself to be lord of Płock is shown by the fact that in 1352, when he was badly in need of money for his Ruthenian policy, he mortgaged Płock to Ziemowit III and Casimir I.[89]

The position of Płock was such that its fortunes had implications for both Mazovia and Silesia. It is in this latter context that we must now view it before returning to conclude the question of Polish control in Mazovia. The interest which Charles IV showed in Płock was minimal, for because of its position, isolated from the rest of the Bohemian holdings, it could offer him no direct advantage. He nevertheless continued to regard himself as its legal lord. His first opportunity to regulate its position vis-à-vis Poland came in 1353 on the

85. Paszkiewicz, "Zhołdowanie Mazowsze," p. 12.

86. Maleczyńska, note in *K.H.*, XXXIX (1925), 534–39, and *Książęce lenno*, pp. 35–36; Rhode, *Die Ostgrenze Polens*, I, 208–9.

87. *Hansisches Urkundenbuch*, ed. K. Hohlbaum, et al., 5 vols. (Halle and Leipzig, 1876–99), III, # 147; *Pr. U.B.*, IV, # 424.

88. A good treatment of this general question is given by Kaczmarczyk, *Monarchia*, I, 38–40.

89. *Dokumenty kujawskie i mazowieckie, przeważnie z XIII wieku*, ed. B. Ulanowski (Cracow, 1888), # 38.

occasion of the emperor's marriage to Anna of Świdnica, Duke Bolko's niece and King Casimir's grandniece. This marriage marked also the resolution of Charles's problems with Bolko.

The duke, who had no male heir to succeed him, had already begun to compose his differences with the emperor in the months following the treaty of Namysłów. This process had proceeded so far that in December, 1350, he had gone to Prague to negotiate a treaty with Charles concerning the succession in Świdnica and Jawór. There it was agreed that Bolko's niece, the heiress of the two duchies, was to be married to Charles's infant son, Václav. This arrangement preserved the independence of Bolko while at the same time assuring that the Luxemburgers would eventually inherit these two important Silesian territories.[90] These plans seemed to have been for naught, however, for Václav died in 1351. Not long after, on February 2, 1353, Charles's second wife died, and although profoundly grieved by this misfortune, the emperor did not hesitate to request Anna's hand. Bolko agreed in a meeting in Vienna the next month, and after suitable, though rapid, preparations, the marriage was held in May of the same year in Buda, where Anna had been raised and educated. According to the treaties signed at that time, Bolko was to remain independent, and so long as his wife lived there was to be no final disposition of Świdnica and Jawór. When she died, however, thus removing any hope of an heir for Bolko, Charles's wife and her children were to receive the expectancy to the territories, that is, they were to pass to Bohemian hands. In other areas also the future of Świdnica and Jawór was clarified on the occasion of this wedding. King Louis of Hungary, as heir-presumptive in Poland, renounced all future claims which he might have to Świdnica and Jawór. As Casimir's personal representative, he also renounced all Polish claims to the cities of Byczyna and Kluczborek, which Casimir had gained from Duke Władysław of Legnica in 1341. In return, Charles renounced all claim to the territory of Płock in favor of Casimir.[91]

According to the terms of this renunciation, Casimir was given four months within which to ratify the commitments made for him by King Louis. He failed to do this, however, and Charles IV continued to call himself lord of Płock. His concern was more in the inheritance to Świdnica and Jawór and in gaining title to Byczyna and Kluczborek, not in Płock itself. It would serve, however, as the perfect lever to force Casimir to agree to the conditions which had been established at Buda. Therefore on October 9, 1355, Charles announced that he was incorporating all his varied holdings into the Bohemian crown

90. *Archivum coronae regni Bohemiae*, II, # 166–68; Grünhagen-Markgraf, *Lehns- und Besitzur-kunden*, I, 493–94. See also Grünhagen, *Geschichte Schlesiens*, 2 vols. (Gotha, 1884–86), I, 181–82.

91. The general background surrounding these events is discussed by Werunsky, *Karl IV*, II, 348–51; Dąbrowski, "Dzieje polityczne," pp. 487–94; *Historia Śląska*, I, pt. ii, 205–8. Louis's renunciation in *Archivum coronae regni Bohemia*, II, # 238–39; Grünhagen-Markgraf, *Lehns- und Besitzurkunden*, I, 331, 496. On the question of Byczyna and Kluczborek, see Dąbrowski, "Dzieje polityczne," pp. 445–48; *Kod. dypl. ks. maz.*, # 74. Charles's renunciation has apparently not survived.

lands and that they would henceforth be ruled by royal administrators.[92] This threat was partially responsible for convincing Casimir that he should make an end to the confusion over Płock. His task was easier because the situation in Mazovia had suddenly altered.

The death on November 26, 1355, of Duke Casimir I resulted in the final absorption of Mazovia by the crown. It was quickly agreed what should be done with the duke's inheritance. On December 27 of the same year, Duke Ziemowit III received the lands of his dead brother and then promptly became a vassal of King Casimir. At Kalisz he transferred all his own holdings, including now those of his brother, to the ruler, then received them back as a fief.[93] The territory of Płock was thus returned to the *regnum* without the repayment of the mortgage loan. By the terms of this agreement, if Casimir were to have a male heir who succeeded him, Płock was to be given to Ziemowit or his heirs as a fief, following the king's death. The territories of Wiżna and Zakroczym were to remain in Ziemowit's possession for three years, until the beginning of 1359, then were to go to Casimir personally for the rest of his lifetime. Following the king's death, they, like Płock, were to be given as a fief to Ziemowit or his heirs, but only if Casimir were succeeded by a male heir. Should anyone else succeed him (that is, Louis of Hungary), then all feudal ties between Mazovia and Poland were to be ended, and the province would again become an independent principality.

This agreement of 1355 is the first formal record of the feudal relationship of Mazovia to Poland. From the contents and wording of the documents issued in connection with this agreement, it is clear that some kind of feudal ties had existed previously. According to Casimir's statement, Duke Casimir I had been his vassal before his death: "by feudal arrangement, which we had arranged during his lifetime." Similarly, in Ziemowit's declaration there is evidence to suggest the same thing, for he says, "moreover, we renew the feudal arrangement previously established for our territories and castles . . . which we received as fiefs from this same overlord." When these previous ties had been formed is difficult to determine. To summarize, the date 1349 or before has less to commend it than 1351 or shortly thereafter.

In the matter of Płock, Casimir recognized that in order to obtain this title, he must agree to the conditions set forth in the agreement of 1353. It cannot have been an easy decision for him to make, for two reasons: Bolko of Świdnica had long been friendly to him and was a staunch ally; in addition, because of the family relationship between the two,[94] Casimir had held out the not un-

---

92. Grünhagen-Markgraf, *Lehns- und Besitzurkunden*, I, 8–13. Charles listed the individual principalities he held. The last named is "principatus Mazovie et ducatus in Ploczk."

93. Casimir's declaration in *Kod. dypl. ks. maz.*, # 77; Ziemowit's oath as vassal in Stronczyński, *Wzory pism dawnych*, # 36. See also Długosz, *Historia*, III, 250–51.

94. Bolko's mother had been Casimir's aunt. Balzer, *Genealogia*, pp. 374 ff.

reasonable hope of gaining Świdnica following Bolko's death. The marriage of Bolko's niece and heir to the emperor in 1353 effectively dashed Casimir's hopes, however, and he decided after the feudal incorporation of Mazovia that the formal acquisition of Płock was worth renouncing his claim to Świdnica and Jawór. Thus early in the spring of 1356 he traveled to the Bohemian capital to meet with Charles IV.

The so-called Congress of Prague in May, 1356, resulted first in a formal renewal of the peace of Namysłów of 1348.[95] In addition, Casimir renounced all claims for himself and his heirs to the territories of Świdnica and Jawór, and all claims to Byczyna and Kluczborek.[96] For his part, Charles repeated his three-year-old renunciation of Płock in Casimir's favor.[97] This agreement resolved all outstanding points of controversy and brought to an end a period of Polish-Bohemian conflict (sometimes armed, sometimes verbal) over Silesia. Despite the simplicity of this meeting, the agreements made in Prague, rather than the peace of Namysłów, mark the end of an era in Polish-Bohemian relations. Casimir was not wholly resigned to the loss of this province and the eclipse of his hopes there (events in 1369–70 demonstrate this clearly), but he recognized that for the moment Poland must acquiesce in the loss.[98]

Although Casimir's stay in Prague solved one of the problems confronting him, it brought him another, this one with both personal and dynastic implications. Casimir had never shown himself to be a model of conjugal fidelity. The high spirits he had manifested in Hungary in 1329 revealed themselves continually during his reign. For example, in 1347 (if not earlier) Cudka, the beautiful daughter of one of his castellans, drew his attention. Despite the fact that she was already married, Casimir established an enduring liaison with her from which were born three natural sons: Niemierz, Jan, and Pełka. Ironically, after the death of Cudka's husband in 1352, Casimir's interest in the affair waned and he broke off the relationship. It was during this same time that yet another romantic attachment of the king was supposed to have occurred: that with the Cracow Jewess, Esterka. The details of this relationship are vague. Even though the tourist of today is regularly shown the *Szara Kamienica* (Gray House) where she was supposed to have lived and told a variety of tales about her relationship to the king, she was probably a legendary figure only.[99]

---

95. Ludewig, *Reliquiae*, V, 469–70; *Regesta diplomatica Bohemiae et Moraviae*, VI, # 326.

96. Grünhagen-Markgraf, *Lehns- und Besitzurkunden*, I, 332, 507; *Regesta diplomatica Bohemiae et Moraviae*, V, # 327, 328.

97. Ludewig, *Reliquiae*, X, 217. See Dąbrowski, "Dzieje polityczne," p. 499 n. 3.

98. See in general on this question, *Historia Śląska*, I, pt. ii, 216–18. The background to the congress is described from the Czech side by Josef Šusta, *Karel IV, za císařskou korunou 1346–1355* (Prague, 1948), pp. 334–37.

99. See, in brief, Kaczmarczyk, *Polska czasów Kazimierza*, p. 74. We shall have more to say on Casimir's marital problems.

These previous attachments are merely background to events in Prague in 1356. There, while negotiating the agreements of the congress, Casimir's ever-watchful eye was struck with the beauty of Christina Rokiczana, the widow of a rich Prague merchant and at that time one of the ladies-in-waiting at the Bohemian court. Blinded by her grace and all-too-obvious charms, Casimir impetuously attached her to himself. When he returned from Prague, he brought her with him. Sometime in 1356 or 1357, Casimir persuaded the abbot of the Monastery of Tyniec to marry them in a secret ceremony.[100] This romantic episode would ordinarily be of only passing interest were it not for the fact that Casimir was still married to Adelheid of Hesse!

At the instigation of the then Margrave Charles, Casimir had married Adelheid in 1341, but the union had never been a successful one. Eventually Casimir had sent her away from the court to an isolated castle to live; he never visited her. The ostensible reason which he gave for his action was that Adelheid's father, Duke Henry of Hesse, had refused to pay the dowry which he had promised. He further contended that Adelheid had failed to be a wife to him (that is, she had not borne him a male heir). The king's complaints eventually reached papal ears, and in 1353 Pope Innocent VI decided to intervene. On March 17 he wrote to Adelheid telling her to be reconciled with Casimir, to be a faithful wife to him, and to urge her father to fulfill his promise of a dowry.[101]

Adelheid had borne her lonely exile in a foreign land with patience and dignity, but she felt this papal letter did her a grave injustice. She therefore replied, giving her side of the story. She claimed that her husband was using Duke Henry's failure to pay the dowry only as an excuse, that it was not she, but he, who had been unfaithful, and that in all instances Casimir was at fault. She demanded a thorough papal investigation and justice for herself.[102] Sometime later Innocent wrote to Louis of Hungary requesting him to effect some kind of solution for Casimir's marital difficulties.[103] During his pontificate, however, he did nothing else to resolve this problem.

Casimir's excuse that he had not been paid Adelheid's dowry was no longer valid after the congress in Prague. At that time, perhaps at the suggestion of his advisors or some prince of the empire, Charles IV declared that he himself would

100. Our chief source for this is Długosz, *Historia*, III, 262. He should, however, be supplemented by Aleksander Semkowicz, "Adelajda, Krystyna i Jadwiga, żony Kazimierza Wielkiego," *K.H.*, XII (1898), 561–66; Balzer, *Genealogia*, pp. 388 ff., and "Z prywatnego życia Kazimierza Wielkiego," *K.H.*, IX (1895), 193.

101. Theiner, *Mon. Pol.*, I, # 723.

102. This is inferred from the papal letter to Louis of Hungary in Theiner, *Mon. Pol.*, I # 745; and in the *Libellus in causa matrimoniali illustrissime domine Alheidis regine Polonie contra illustrem dominum Kaczmirum regem Polonie*, printed by Semkowicz, "Żony Kazimierza," pp. 562 ff.

103. On the correct order and significance of the papal letters, see Caro, *Geschichte Polens* II, 309 n. 2, 333 n. 1; Zofia Kozłowska-Budkowa, "Z ostatnich lat Kazimierza Wielkiego," *Małopolskie Studia Historyczne*, VI, pts. iii/iv (1963), 15–21.

pay Casimir the dowry.[104] This act might have provided a basis for the resolution of the problem had not Casimir exacerbated an already difficult situation by his alliance with Christina Rokiczana. When Adelheid heard of this outrage to her honor, the unhappy queen requested her father to take her back home. She left Poland, never to return to the land which had brought her so much grief and misery. To compound the insult, Casimir then confiscated her holdings and possessions in Poland.[105] The marriage continued technically in force, and some years later Pope Urban V was to attempt unsuccessfully to reconcile the two. In all these dealings the royal concern which underlay all else was the possibility of gaining a legitimate heir.

When Casimir returned to Poland from Prague in 1356 one of the concerns which immediately engaged his attention was the state of the kingdom's northern border. The good relations which the king had enjoyed with the Order in recent years had begun to deteriorate. Much of this was due to the king himself. Although he had explicitly renounced all claim to Pomorze at Kalisz in 1343, Casimir still continued to use the title "Lord and heir of Pomorze."[106] In addition, the Order was well aware that in 1355 one of the promises which Louis of Hungary had confirmed was that he would attempt to regain Pomorze for the *regnum*. It was all too clear to the Knights that Casimir was not in any way attempting, as he had promised in 1343, to obtain from the Angevins a renunciation of their claims to Pomorze. Yet a third element in the attitude of the Order was the promises which the emperor had made in 1348 and 1356 to aid Casimir in his efforts to recover lands taken by the Knights. While it assumed that such statements possessed more show than substance, the Order could not be entirely sure. The final source of friction, and in fact the decisive one, was to be found in the uncertain border which separated Mazovia and the Order.

Minor boundary disputes between the two finally resulted in 1355 in a punitive incursion into Mazovia by the Knights during Casimir's Ruthenian campaign.[107] This invasion led Casimir to complain bitterly to the pope that not only had the Order denied him aid against the Lithuanians, it had even allied secretly with them and had hampered the Polish effort in Ruthenia by invading Mazovia. The papal response was to chastise the Order and exhort the Knights

---

104. J. F. Böhmer, *Regesta imperii*, vol. VIII: *Die Regesten des Kaiserreichs unter Kaiser Karl IV, 1346–1378*, ed. A. Huber (Innsbruck, 1877), #2449.

105. Beneš minorita, *Chronicon*, in *Mon. Hist. Boem.*, IV, 41; *Kalendarz Władysławski*, in *M.P.H.*, II, 944. See also Kaczmarczyk, *Polska czasów Kazimierza*, p. 99.

106. See, for example, *C.D.M.P.*, III, #1299, 1310, 1317–18.

107. Theiner, *Mon. Pol.*, I, #769: "guerre tempore, cum Rex ipse circa illa occupatus existeret, vos ducatum Mazovie . . . absque ulla rationabili causa violenter invadere, et nonnulla ipsius castra occupare non veriti, illa detinetis adhuc contra iustitiam occupata." See also Henryk Paszkiewicz, *Polityka Ruska Kazimierza Wielkiego* (Warsaw, 1925), pp. 187–90. It was possibly this invasion which was decisive in Duke Ziemowit's decision not long after to seek the feudal protection of King Casimir.

to abandon their divisive activity and support Casimir with all their resources. The Order responded in turn by complaining to Avignon that Casimir had allied himself with heathens (the Tatars) and completely disregarded the welfare of other Christian princes (that is, of the Order).[108] The only tangible result of these mutual recriminations was to heighten the ill-feeling between the two states.

When Archbishop Arnošt of Prague was commissioned in 1358 by the emperor to make preparations for the possible conversion of the Lithuanians, he also undertook to investigate the dispute between the Order and Poland. He found that relations had become so strained that Casimir had apparently given up completely the peaceful, conciliatory policy of the last few years, and had adopted an uncompromisingly aggressive attitude. He was again raising claim to all the territories which the Order had taken from Poland. Arnošt also learned that the Poles claimed the Order was totally responsible for all the difficulty and that the Knights contended Casimir was completely at fault! He reported all this to the pope, who replied that Arnošt should attempt to mediate a peace between Poland and the Order by using all the tools of his ecclesiastical position. Should he find the situation impossible, he was to transfer the whole matter to the papal court, which would then propose some new solution.[109]

As Arnošt continued his investigations, he learned eventually that the real point of conflict between the Order and Casimir rested upon the definition of the border between Ziemowit III of Mazovia and the Teutonic Order and upon Polish attempts to fortify this border against the Knights. Ziemowit and Casimir had both recently entered into a period of rapprochement with the Gedyminowicze and were using this respite from danger in the east to strengthen themselves in the north. On August 13, 1358, the duke had signed a boundary treaty with the Lithuanians which established the border between him and Grand Prince Kiejstut and his son for the first time.[110] This treaty extended the rule of Mazovia, and therefore of Poland, over territory which the Order had claimed and which had in fact been recognized as belonging to the Knights in a pact signed by the late Duke Casimir in 1343 as a part of the treaties of Kalisz.[111] There existed a certain inconsistency between the two versions of the border defined in these treaties and nowhere was this more evident than in the area of the headwaters of the Netta River near the village of Rajgród. This location had

---

108. Reflected in the papal letter in Theiner, *Mon. Pol.*, I, # 776. See also Caro, *Geschichte Polens*, II, 313 f.; Voigt, *Geschichte Preussens*, V, 120–22; Karol Górski, *Państwo Krzyżackie w Prusach* (Gdańsk and Bydgoszcz, 1946), pp. 108 f.

109. Theiner, *Mon. Pol.*, I, # 789.

110. *Kod. dypl. ks. maz.*, # 80. For a detailed description of the boundary, see *Słownik Geograficzny Królestwa Polskiego i innych krajów słowiańskich*, 15 vols. (Warsaw, 1880–1902), VIII, 411; and, with slight corrections and modifications, Rhode, *Die Ostgrenze Polens*, I, 212–18.

111. *C.D.Pr.*, III, # 39.

in the past been claimed by both the Order and the Lithuanians; and since it was not mentioned in the decisions of 1358, Ziemowit apparently decided to assume the Lithuanians had given up their rights and would allow him a free hand there. He and his overlord reckoned without the Knights.

To protect this territory from the Order, Duke Ziemowit began, either with the approval or more probably at the command of King Casimir, the building of a stone fortress in or near Rajgród. Work on this project was well advanced in 1360, when news of what was considered to be a violation of the territory of the Order reached Grand Master Winrich von Kniprode. He immediately sent what might today be called a "reconaissance in force" to Rajgród. It was led by a quartet of the most prominent military personalities of the Order; when these troops reached Rajgród and saw how far the construction had progressed, their commander demanded that the work be ceased immediately and that the workmen leave the area, for they were building in the territory of the Order. To demonstrate this, he then produced documents to substantiate his position. In response, the Polish foreman declared that he had no authority to discuss legal questions. He and his crew had been sent by the king and were responsible only for finishing the work. After further discussions it was agreed that the foreman would consult with the nearest civil administrator. The workmen withdrew and never returned. After an appropriate interval, the Knights razed the half-finished fortress and burned it to the ground.[112] This whole affair at first increased the tension between Poland and the Order, but eventually, because no new points of conflict developed, affairs returned to normal. Casimir recognized anew, as he had in 1333 and 1343, that the Polish position was not yet sufficiently secure to challenge the Knights. The Rajgród episode marked the zenith of Polish-Order hostility in the years after Kalisz.

While Casimir had been involved in dealings with the Order, events elsewhere in central Europe had been leading to the formation of a great anti-Luxemburg coalition. The House of Habsburg, which had emerged from relative obscurity in the thirteenth century to gain the imperial crown, was led at this time by Duke Rudolf IV of Austria, Charles IV's son-in-law. Having accustomed themselves to the purple under an earlier Rudolf, it was not surprising that the Habsburgs should envy the more recent ascendancy of the Luxemburgers. Moreover, there were sharp differences over territorial ambitions between the two dynasties, and the ambitions of Rudolf were well known to Charles. He recognized that the family was a potential threat to his own position, particularly since it could draw upon a considerable reservoir of anti-Luxemburg hostility

---

112. The notarial instrument which was prepared by the Knights over this incident is printed in *C.D.Pr.*, III, # 87. See also the comments of Wigand of Marburg, *Chronica*, p. 525. The account in Voigt, *Geschichte Preussens*, V, 135–37, which speaks of the Poles fleeing from the Knights, is overly imaginative, since all that the sources say is "and thus the aforementioned Poles left there."

elsewhere in the region. These are the factors which lay behind the gossip which swept through the empire in 1359–60 to the effect that Charles was to be deposed as emperor and either Rudolf IV or Louis of Hungary elected in his place.[113] Charles took immediate steps to prevent rumor from becoming reality.

In May, 1360, the emperor traveled to the Hungarian city of Nagyszombat to meet personally with Louis and Rudolf. There the three dynasts solemnly declared that none had believed the evil innuendoes about the honor, reputation, and intentions of the others in the past, nor would they do so in the future. Then Rudolf and Charles agreed to let Louis mediate any dispute which might arise between them. Finally, Charles and Louis swore eternal friendship for one another. In order to avoid offending Casimir in any way by these acts, Charles also issued on this occasion the most strongly worded declaration yet concerning his intentions toward Wrocław: he promised that neither he nor any of his successors would ever undertake any diplomatic maneuverings in Avignon for the purpose of separating Wrocław from the archdiocese of Gniezno. He also reaffirmed his renunciation of all claims to Płock.[114]

With the agreements of Nagyszombat, it appeared that the status quo had been restored and the outbreak of hostilities narrowly averted. In reality, this gathering of rulers in Hungary was only the prelude to open conflict. Some near-contemporaries believed that it was an offhand remark by the emperor which brought about war in central Europe.[115] He is reported to have said that Elizabeth, Louis's mother and Casimir's sister, did not behave in a virtuous manner. Though this incident was unknown to contemporary chroniclers, this assertion is reflected in at least one of the letters sent between Charles and Louis. Louis's response to this insult was immediate and in kind. He dispatched a heated letter to Charles claiming that the canard was a typical phenomenon, for the emperor always lost control of his senses and his tongue when he had drunk too much. He demanded an apology.[116]

It was not forthcoming, and Louis resolved to punish Charles by joining Rudolf of Austria in the coalition he was forming against the emperor. Charles's insult was the ostensible reason for Louis's action, but the creation of the anti-Luxemburg coalition was based upon more profound reasons of dynastic

113. For these developments in general, see Werunsky, *Karl IV*, III, 190–220; Adam Wandruszka, *Das Haus Habsburg* (Stuttgart, 1956), pp. 68–82; E. K. Winter, *Rudolf IV. von Österreich*, 2 vols. (Vienna, 1934–36), I, 290–99; and, more briefly, Dvornik, *The Slavs*, pp. 76–77.

114. Dogiel, *Codex*, I, 538. See also Werunsky, *Karl IV*, III, 221–22; Dąbrowski, *Ostatnie lata*, pp. 151–52; Caro, *Geschichte Polens*, II, 322.

115. Długosz, *Historia*, III, 290–91, merely dates this "sometime before 1363." In reality the events he described probably took place in 1361. His account is somewhat embellished.

116. The details of the incident are found in S. Steinherz, "Die Beziehungen Ludwigs I. von Ungarn zu Karl IV.," *Mittheilung des Instituts für oesterreichische Geschichtsforschung*, IX (1888), 604 n. 3; Franz Palacky, *Über Formelbücher, zunächst in Bezug auf böhmische Geschichte* (Prague, 1847), p. 261; Palacky, *Geschichte von Böhmen*, II, pt. ii, 343 n. 191.

rivalry, in which Rudolf IV was the driving force.[117] Late in December, 1361, Rudolf and Louis signed a formal alliance against Charles in Pozsony; three months later this alliance was enlarged by the adherence of Duke Meinhard of the Tyrol and of Casimir, who entered partially to defend the honor of his sister and partially out of hope of gaining some advantage in Silesia.[118] The strategy of the alliance was to attack Charles from all sides in the summer of 1362. When the appointed time came, however, Louis alone took the field. Rudolf and Meinhard failed to grant the support which they had promised, and Casimir at first hesitated to enter a fight in which the dynastic rivalries involved offered him only the possibility of benefit. Only belatedly did he send troops.

The two monarchs united forces, but before they could enter Bohemian territory Duke Bolko of Świdnica arrived with a message from Charles requesting a truce and negotiations for peace. At Casimir's urging, Louis agreed, and sent representatives to the emperor, who was at Brno. Beyond the simple truce, an agreement could not be reached, and Louis's representatives returned without success to Trenčín. In the meantime, the Hungarian troops had dispersed, and Casimir was unwilling to continue the fight. The campaign which in 1361 had looked so promising for the coalition had been a total failure.[119] By calling for a truce, Charles had successfully avoided attack. The anti-Luxemburg coalition was further weakened in succeeding months by the death without heir of Duke Meinhard on January 13, 1363. In an attempt to gain the Duke's Tyrolean lands, Rudolf IV turned his attention away from Charles, thus removing one of the initiators of the coalition.

On January 24 Pope Urban V, who had succeeded Innocent VI in the fall of 1362, intervened, sending a special legate to central Europe to attempt to obtain a peaceful settlement between Charles IV and Louis, who by now was the emperor's only enemy.[120] Despite good intentions, the papal representative was unable to solve the problem. Another mediator had to be found.

This person was King Casimir of Poland. As suggested above, he had no real

---

117. See Winter, *Rudolf IV*, I, 294–98. This excellent work is only incidently concerned with matters of foreign or dynastic policy. In this section, however, Winter does treat the duke's dynastic ambitions.

118. Dogiel, *Codex*, I, 152; Ludewig, *Reliquiae*, IV, 294. The date of the formation of this alliance is difficult to determine. I have followed Kaczmarczyk, *Polska czasów Kazimierza*, pp. 108–9, whose work, though only sparsely documented, rests upon a comprehensive knowledge of the sources and the secondary materials. For other interpretations of these events, see Caro, *Geschichte Polens*, II, 324; Steinherz, "Die Beziehungen," pp. 604–9; Werunsky, *Karl IV*, III, 262–65; Csuday, *Geschichte der Ungarn*, I, 360–61.

119. Certain details of this narrative are drawn from Johannes de Thurócz, *Chronica*, p. 191.

120. This was true because by the time the legate took up his work, Charles had persuaded the Wittelsbachs to agree to a succession treaty. On March 18, 1363, Margraves Lewis and Otto agreed that if they died without direct heir, Brandenburg and Lusatia were to pass to Charles's son Václav. This finally took place in 1373. See *Codex diplomaticus Brandenburgensis*, ed. Adolph Friedrich Riedel, 41 vols. (Berlin, 1838–69), II, 445 ff. See also Werunsky, *Karl IV*, III, 267 ff.; Schulz, *Die Mark Brandenburg*, II, 136–37.

reason to become involved in the anti-Luxemburg coalition, for the insult to his sister was in reality only a minor unpleasantry. Actually, it was far more important to the Polish king to see that peace was preserved in central Europe, so that nothing there would upset the plans he was already formulating for another Ruthenian campaign; and Charles was the key to peace in the region. Casimir had also been influenced by the efforts of the papacy to preserve peace between Louis and Charles, and so he offered his good offices as a mediator of the conflict. That his offer was accepted by both sides is one indication of the new respect which the kingdom of Poland was able to command; that he was successful in bringing about peace is a tribute to his diplomatic skill and personal integrity.[121]

Casimir chose to accomplish his goal by proposing a marriage alliance to the recently widowed emperor. He suggested that Charles marry his granddaughter Elizabeth, daughter of Duke Bogusław V of Pomorze-Wołogoszcz and Casimir's oldest daughter. The emperor was willing to do this, for it offered him the opportunity of extending Luxemburg control to the mouth of the Oder.[122] He agreed, however, only on condition that Louis, who was also a relative of Elizabeth, would agree to a lasting peace. Casimir obtained the required promises for the Angevin, and by April, 1363, Charles and Louis had been reconciled.[123] The first tangible result of Casimir's mediation came on May 8 when Charles met with Louis and Rudolf at Hradiště in Moravia. There the preliminaries of peace were signed between Charles, his brother the Margrave of Moravia, Louis, and Rudolf. This was an agreement which became the basis for the later treaty of Brno (see below), but which for the present could be terminated upon four months' notice.[124]

Immediately after this agreement had been signed, Charles hurried to Cracow to meet Casimir, and on May 21 he was married to the King's granddaughter. Several difficulties are connected with describing this marriage, however, and for many years accounts by modern scholars seemed hopelessly garbled. Some sources record that the marriage was the occasion for a great gathering of rulers and princes. According to the *Rocznik świętokrzyski*: "Charles ... came to Cracow and married Elizabeth ... there were present these kings: Louis of Hungary, Casimir of Poland, Václav of Bohemia, the king of Cyprus, Sigismund of Denmark, and a great many other princes."[125] Other sources, particularly Janko of Czarnków, Casimir's later vice-chancellor, also report a great gather-

121. This kind of tribute is the theme of Janko of Czarnków, *Chronicon*, pp. 628–31. It is reflected equally in the short biography by Jan Kochanowski, *Kazimierz Wielki* (Warsaw, 1900), p. 120 especially.

122. See Fenrych, *Nowa Marchia*, pp. 69–70.

123. Charles referred to Louis as his "most beloved brother" on April 4, 1363. See Werunsky, *Karl IV*, III, 271.

124. Böhmer-Huber, *Regesten des Kaiserreichs*, # 7104, 7114. See also Werunsky, *Karl IV*, III, 272; Dąbrowski, *Ostatnie lata*, pp. 154–55.

125. *M.P.H.*, III, 80. A somewhat less clear text (*Annales sanctae crucis Polonici*) is available in *M.G.H. SS.*, XIX, 684.

ing of princes and rulers, but make no mention of Charles's marriage.[126] Besides this basic contradiction, two added difficulties may be noted: first, according to the itineraries of these rulers, it would have been impossible for them to have been in Cracow at the same time in 1363; and, second, the title applied to Václav by the *Rocznik świętokrzyski* was not bestowed until the following year. In the face of these problems, small wonder that older accounts of this marriage are confused![127] Only through the researches of S. Steinherz in 1888 was it first established that two separate events had been confused in the reports given by our sources: the marriage in 1363 of Charles to Elizabeth, at which only Charles, Casimir, and the princes of Pomorze Zachodnie were present; and the great Congress of Cracow of 1364 at which there foregathered the most brilliant collection of crowned heads seen in the fourteenth century.[128]

The marriage alliance of May established Casimir's position as a successful mediator. In the next months he was able to extend thi; reputation by further resolving the conflicts in central Europe. By December 12, 1363, he was able to announce to all concerned that the emperor and his brother on the one side and King Louis and Duke Rudolf on the other had settled all differences between them and that henceforth they would live in peace and friendship with one another.[129] On that occasion it was agreed that the several parties which had been involved in the recent conflict would meet early the following year to sign a definitive peace treaty. On February 10, 1364, Charles, together with a retinue of the highest nobles and prelates of his kingdom, signed the Peace of Brno with Louis and Rudolf.[130] On this same occasion the Luxemburgers and Habsburgs signed a mutual inheritance agreement whereby each would inherit the other's lands should either dynasty fail. Though little to the benefit of either came from this particular arrangement, its approach foreshadowed that which brought the Habsburgs the hegemony of Europe in the sixteenth century.

Although Casimir's attention had in recent months been largely focused upon the Bohemian-Austrian-Hungarian strife, he had not neglected other aspects of his policy. Late in 1363 he received a visit from King Waldemar IV of Denmark.[131] On December 13 he renewed his thirteen-year-old treaty with this monarch, promising to grant him aid against all his enemies, except Charles IV

126. Janko of Czarnków, *Chronicon*, pp. 630–31: "In 1363 there was a great feast in Cracow, which included Charles, the King of Hungary, the King of Dacia [that is, Denmark—the Latin has been miscopied]."

127. See, for example, Długosz, *Historia*, III, 295; Marcin Kromer, *Kronika Polska* (Warsaw, 1767), pp. 362–63; Adam Naruszewicz, *Historya narodu polskiego od początku chrześciaństwa*, 8 vols. (Warsaw, 1780–1806), VI, 309–11; Palacky, *Geschichte von Böhmen*, II, ii, 346–47; Caro, *Geschichte Polens*, II, 326–29.

128. Steinherz, "Die Beziehungen," pp. 609–10.

129. *C.D.Mor.*, IX, # 326.

130. Ibid., IX, # 337; Böhmer-Huber, *Regesten des Kaiserreichs*, # 4010.

131. Though Maleczyński, "Dwa niedrukowane akty," p. 255, suggests that events in

and Louis of Hungary, whom Casimir called "his dearest brothers."[132] As in the case of the earlier treaty, there is little doubt that this alliance was directed against the Order. It was characteristic of Casimir to keep his defensive system against the Knights strong at all times, and Denmark was still deeply involved in continuing dispute with the Hanseatic League and the Knights. Not surprising, then, that the two rulers should be drawn closer together.

If one were to single out a specific event which symbolized the emergence of Poland as an important central European power, it would be difficult to make a better choice than Janko of Czarnków's *convivium maximum*, the great Congress of Cracow in 1364.[133] That the meeting was held in Cracow was the result of the perigrinations of King Peter Lusignan of Cyprus.

Peter, whose island kingdom was directly threatened by the Turks, had been traveling throughout Europe seeking support for a crusade against the Ottomans. He had found a sympathetic ear in France, but the death of King John II had cost him that support. He continued his journeys, including in his entourage the great French poet-musician, Guillaume de Machaut.[134] Peter went to Avignon, then traveled through Germany to Bohemia, where he visited Charles, who suggested that because of Poland's interests in Ruthenia it would be wise to consult with Casimir in the matter of defense against the Turks. The Polish ruler proposed a general congress of the rulers and princes of central Europe, and early in September Charles and Peter proceeded to Cracow.[135]

The personages assembled in the Polish capital were truly an impressive group. In addition to the kings already mentioned, there were in attendance Kings Wenzel of Bohemia, Louis of Hungary, and Waldemar of Denmark; plus Dukes Otto of Bavaria, Bolko of Świdnica, Władysław of Opole, Ziemowit of Mazovia, Bogusław V of Pomorze-Wołogoszcz, who had been partially responsible for the presence of King Waldemar, and other lesser princes. In addition, each ruler brought with him large retinues of nobles and civil

---

Sweden prevented Waldemar from coming personally to Cracow, Roman Grodecki, *Kongres Krakowski w roku 1364* (Warsaw, 1939), pp. 95–96, has shown him in the Polish capital en route to Bohemia.

132. The text, of which only the Polish copy is extant, is printed by Maleczyński, "Dwa niedrukowane akty," pp. 258–59.

133. The standard treatment of the congress is Grodecki, *Kongres Krakowski*, which treats all aspects of the gathering in detail against the background of Polish development and the general central European situation. It is a work which deserves to be better known. That it is not, is partially the result of the destruction of nearly all copies of the newly printed book in the warehouse of Gebethner and Wolff during the siege of Warsaw in 1939.

134. Guillaume has left us a record of Peter's wanderings, including some comments on the Congress of Cracow, in his poem *La prise d'Alexandrie*, ed. M. L. de Mas Latrie, *Guillaume de Machaut* (Geneva, 1877).

135. Mas Latrie, *Guillaume de Machaut*, pp. 27–32. See also K. Herquet, "Beiträge zum Itinerar Karl IV und zu seinem Aufenthalt in Schlesien mit dem König von Cypren im Jahre 1364," *Zeitschrift des Vereins für Geschichte Schlesiens*, XIV (1878), 521–27.

officials. The rulers were Casimir's guests in the royal castle on Wawel Hill, while the others found lodgings in the city. The festivities connected with the congress were magnificent indeed. Casimir liberally distributed gifts to his guests, numerous tourneys and games were held, and Mikołaj Wierzynek, a municipal councillor and reputedly the richest man in Cracow, sumptuously entertained the whole congress in his private quarters on the central market square. For nearly three weeks the guests enjoyed themselves and passed the time amid the spectacular results of Casimir's program of building within the city. The business of the congress fared less well, however, for only Louis, as the only ruler directly threatened by the Turks, showed any interest in Peter's plan for a crusade. Charles IV, recognizing that the time for crusades had passed, limited himself to a simple promise to commend the crusade to the estates of the empire. Casimir, as host, made no promises at all, because he was so deeply involved in Ruthenia.[136]

There were some positive results of the congress, though admittedly unrelated to King Peter's concerns. On September 22, Louis confirmed and renewed with Charles the Peace of Brno as a sign of his good will. Five days later Louis also negotiated a new agreement with Casimir concerning his succession in Poland.[137] Yet another result was the extent to which Poland's progress and development were revealed. In no area was this as clearly shown as in education, symbolized by the celebration of the founding of a *studium generale* in Cracow. On September 1, after extensive preliminary negotiations, Pope Urban V had issued a bull of foundation for a university "in canon and civil law, as well as all other legitimate faculties (except in theology)."[138] Among Casimir's guests, only Charles IV could claim a university in his lands.

Although the stated purpose of the Congress of Cracow had not fared well, the congress marked one of the high points in Casimir's reign. Modern writers have seldom summarized the event as well as the brief characterization of the externals of the congress given by Janko of Czarnków:[139]

> It is not possible to describe the extent of delight, magnificence, glory, and abundance that there was in this "convivium," not even if it were given to everyone to report as much as they wished. The kings and princes promised and affirmed great friendship for one another, and were given many gifts for themselves by King Casimir of Poland.

136. The foregoing details of the congress are derived from *Rocznik świętokrzyski*, p. 80; Janko of Czarnków, *Chronicon*, p. 630; and particularly Długosz, *Historia*, III, 290–98. The story of Wierzynek's hospitality, which comes from Długosz, may have been somewhat exaggerated in the fifteenth century; but it has taken on legendary proportions in the contemporary restaurant Wierzynek House in Cracow. There is, however, no reason to disbelieve the core of the story.

137. See Dąbrowski, *Ostatnie lata*, p. 155; Steinherz, "Die Beziehungen," p. 610.

138. *Codex diplomaticus universitatis studii generalis Cracoviensis*, 5 vols. (Cracow, 1870–1900), I, 6. On the question of the founding of the university in 1364, see my study, "Casimir the Great and the University of Cracow," *Jahrbücher für Geschichte Osteuropas*, XVI, ii (1968), 237–43.

139. Janko of Czarnków, *Chronicon*, p. 631.

8
THE END OF THE REIGN
1364–1370

The emergence of Poland as one of the major powers of central Europe was heralded by the events of 1363–64, symbolized by the Congress of Cracow and confirmed by the stunning royal triumphs in Ruthenia in 1366. In the twilight years of his reign, Casimir was able to reap the benefits of more than four decades of Piast rule over a *Polonia restaurata*. At the same time, the king dealt in this period with the continuing problems whose threads we have been following in preceding chapters. This interplay between culmination and continuation is the theme of the following pages; it is revealed particularly in the letter which Casimir dispatched to Avignon on the eve of the *convivium maximum* described above.

In this letter, the king stated his renewed vision of successfully achieving that which had earlier lain beyond the total resources of the kingdom.[1] He described to Urban how in the past he had been forced by circumstances to renounce all claims to territories which had from time immemorial belonged to the kingdom of Poland. Frequently he had done this without first obtaining the permission or approval of the Holy See, since he recognized that his actions were prejudicial to the interests of the papacy. He regretted now the impropriety of such decisions, and he humbly requested the pope to dispense him of all responsibility for the oaths he had taken in connection with these territorial renunciations. Casimir had reference in this supplication to both Pomorze and Silesia.[2] He now felt the resources at his disposal were more adequate for

1. *M.P.V.*, III, #427, dated April 20, 1364.

2. See Jan Dąbrowski, "Dzieje polityczne Śląska w latach 1290–1402," in *Historja Śląska od najdawniejszych czasów do roku 1400*, ed. Stanisław Kutrzeba, et al., 3 vols. (Cracow, 1933–39),

regaining these lands; much of Polish policy in the next years was devoted to finding the best means to accomplish this aim.

One of Casimir's approaches was dynastic in character. His own reign had been, despite some differences in tactics and some important variations in emphases, a continuation of that of his father, Łokietek. He still hoped that this dynastic continuity would not be broken after his death and that his successor would continue his own policies. But despite two legal marriages, Casimir had no legitimate male heir. Although he had already turned to his nephew Louis of Hungary to provide the kingdom with a successor, he decided upon yet another marriage, hoping that from this union would come the son he desired.

The king's choice for a new bride fell upon Jadwiga, the young daughter of Duke Henry of Żagań. Casimir saw a twofold advantage to this proposed union: the possibility of an heir and family ties to Jadwiga's father. After Bolko of Świdnica, Duke Henry was the most powerful individual ruler in Silesia. He was also a close associate of Emperor Charles IV, having assisted him in the imperial coronation ceremony and having been sent as imperial ambassador to Constantinople.[3] Moreover, his daughter Jadwiga was heir to a part of his territorial holdings. Casimir hoped eventually to inherit Henry's lands and regain thereby a foothold in Silesia which could ultimately result in the return of this region to Poland.

Despite these obvious advantages, two major obstacles confronted Casimir. First, he and Jadwiga were related in the fourth degree, so that their marriage was prohibited by the church;[4] second, and more serious, the king was still married to his second wife, Adelheid of Hesse. Casimir would therefore have to obtain dissolution of his union with Adelheid and a special dispensation from Avignon to marry Jadwiga. Two contradictory historical traditions tell the story of Casimir's activity.

According to Queen Adelheid,[5] her marriage to Casimir had continued until September, 1357. At that time, the king confiscated her goods and expelled her from the kingdom. Casimir then contracted an illegal marriage, performed by Abbot John of Tyniec, with Christina Rokiczana of Prague. Six years later, on February 25, 1363, he then was married a second time; in Wschowa, the bishop of Poznań, on the basis of a falsified papal dispensation, united him with Anna, the daughter of Duke Henry of Żagań.

I, 524–25; *Historia Śląska*, general editor Karol Maleczyński, vol I, *do roku 1763*, in four parts (Wrocław, 1960–64), pt. ii, 218; Zdzisław Kaczmarczyk, *Polska czasów Kazimierza Wielkiego* (Cracow, 1964), p. 111.

3. For Henry and his career see Oswald Balzer, *Genealogia Piastów* (Cracow, 1895), p. 448; Halecki, *Un empereur de Byzance à Rome* (Warsaw, 1930), pp. 46–47; *Pol. Słow. Biog.*, IX, 412–13.

4. Balzer, *Genealogia*, p. 388.

5. In a tract entitled *Libellus in causa matrimoniali illustrissimi domine Alheidis regine Polonie contra illustrem dominum Kaczmarum regem Polonie*, printed by Aleksander Semkowicz, "Adelajda, Krystyna i Jadwiga, żony Kazimierza Wielkiego," *K.H.*, XII (1898), 562–66.

The queen's details of chronology are somewhat confused. Thus, while she did indeed leave the kingdom in 1357, the formal marriage continued after that.[6] The resolution of the marriage problem did not come until after the Congress of Cracow. A second error is the date given for the marriage of Casimir with Jadwiga (not Anna). It came not in 1363, but two years later. Roman Grodecki and Zofia Kozłowska-Budkowa have correctly dated the marriage in the spring or summer of 1365.[7] Before the ceremony was performed, however, there had been almost frantic attempts by the king to gain approval for this step.

Casimir was unwilling to approach the pope personally to resolve his marital problems, undoubtedly recognizing that his behavior had somewhat compromised him in papal eyes. He turned instead to his staunchest ally, the king of Hungary. Louis had been informed of Casimir's plans for a new marriage[8] and was understandably concerned lest they affect his right of succession in Poland. He therefore raised the matter with his uncle as early as the Congress of Cracow in 1364, and on September 17 the two monarchs reached an agreement. Louis agreed grudgingly to plead Casimir's cause to the papal court, in order to obtain the dissolution of the marriage with Adelheid and the dispensation necessary for the marriage to Jadwiga. He also agreed that should Casimir gain an heir from the proposed marriage, this son would succeed him and all Hungarian claims to the throne of Poland would be declared null and void. Should no heir be forthcoming, then Louis would succeed Casimir under the conditions agreed upon prior to 1355. Casimir's persuasive powers were impressive indeed, for Louis gained nothing from this arrangement.[9]

6. See *Kalendarz i Spominki Włocławskie*, in *M.P.H.*, *Series Nova*, VI, 83; Zofia Kozłowska-Budkowa, "Z ostatnich lat Kazimierza Wielkiego," *Małopolskie Studia Historyczne*, VI, pts. iii/iv (1963), 16–17.

7. Roman Grodecki, *Kongres Krakowski w roku 1364* (Warsaw, 1939), pp. 65–68; Kozłowska-Budkowa, "Z ostatnich lat," pp. 17–19. The date 1365 was originally suggested by Balzer, *Genealogia*, pp. 390–92, on the basis of the itinerary of Jadwiga's father. After the publication of Adelheid's *Libellus* by Semkowicz in 1898, however, scholars have generally accepted the date 1363. The date of 1357, given by Długosz, *Historia*, III, 265, has never been seriously considered.

8. It had been no great secret for some years that Casimir wished to end his marriage to Adelheid and contract a new union. As early as 1354, Mikołaj Wierzynek (see above, chap. 7) had intimated that the king was even considering marrying a Tatar princess. See Colmar Grünhagen, "Die Correspondenz der Stadt Breslau mit Karl IV in den Jahren 1347–1355," *Archiv für Österreichische Geschichte*, XXXIV (1865), 365. Such an intent may also be seen in his "marriage" to Christina Rokiczany, which is described by the *Wspominek o Ciołkach*, in *M.P.H.*, III, 269.

9. This agreement is printed by Antoni Prochaska, "W sprawie zajęcia Rusi przez Kazimierza Wielkiego," *K.H.*, VI (1892), 33. This document is dated "in festo beati Stanislai martiris" which can be either May 8 or September 27. Most Polish scholars have incorrectly chosen the former, but see Kozłowska-Budkowa, "Z ostatnich lat," p. 19, and *Chronologia Polska*, ed. Bronisław Włodarski (Warsaw, 1957), p. 257. The extent of Louis's role is partially inferred from the fact that the papal letters are directed to him. See Dąbrowski, *Ostatnie lata Ludwika Wielkiego, 1370–1382* (Cracow, 1918), p. 160.

Nevertheless, Pope Urban was not immediately receptive to these requests on Casimir's behalf. To one of Louis's early letters, he replied that, instead of making these efforts for Casimir, the Angevin should exert all the influence he could to see that Adelheid and Casimir were reconciled.[10] This same letter reveals that Urban had also written to Casimir exhorting him to give up his plans for a new marriage and to take Adelheid back. Casimir did not respond. He had become impatient with the delay, recognizing that at the age of fifty-five time was growing short for him if he were to father an heir. He therefore decided to take matters into his own hands. He obtained a forged papal dispensation, and on this basis persuaded the bishop of Poznań to marry him and Jadwiga, probably in the summer of 1365.[11]

This rash step nearly cost Casimir the formal dissolution of his former marriage and the legitimization of his new union. When Adelheid heard of Casimir's marriage, she again took up her suit with the papacy. Louis and his mother in turn intensified their own efforts, sending a representative to Avignon to plead their case on Casimir's behalf. Urban recognized that Louis's support of the church deserved reward, but he refused to grant the Angevin's request regarding the king of Poland. In effect, he said that where principles of justice had been disregarded, there would be no exceptions made.[12]

Not until 1368 was this matter partially resolved. Although there was no reconciliation between Casimir and Adelheid, and despite his previously adamant attitude, when faced with the fait accompli of Casimir's new marriage, Pope Urban was inclined to end the king's difficulties by granting his request. The factor which finally convinced him to do so was Polish support of papal policy in Italy. Urban had for some time been considering the return of the papacy to Rome, but before he could do so he had to break the power of the Visconti family in Italy. This meant military intervention, and at various times between 1363 and 1368 Polish troops fought under papal auspices against Bernabo Visconti.[13] As a direct result of this aid, Urban tacitly approved Casimir's union with Jadwiga, though he steadfastly refused to annul explicitly the marriage to Adelheid.

In the months after the king's marriage to Jadwiga, rumors about the forged papal dispensation circulated widely and the complicity of the king was commonly assumed. It was to squelch such charges that Urban wrote Casimir

10. Theiner, *Mon. Hung.*, II, # 135.

11. On the question of the forgery and the date of the marriage, see Kozłowska-Budkowa, "Z ostatnich lat," p. 20.

12. Theiner, *Mon. Hung.*, II, # 147–48.

13. See the papal comments in Theiner, *Mon. Pol.*, I, # 830–32; see also L. A. Muratori, *Annales d'Italia . . .*, 18 vols. (Milan, 1753–56), XII, 227, and Stanisław Krzyżanowski, "Poselstwo Kazimierza Wielkiego do Awinionu i pierwsze uniwersyteckie przywileje," *Rocznik Krakowski*, IV (1900), 1–5. For papal policy in Italy against the Visconti, see Emil Werunsky, *Geschichte Kaiser Karls IV. und seiner Zeit*, 3 vols. in 4 (Innsbruck, 1880–96), III, 238 ff.; G. Mollat, *The Popes at Avignon, 1305–1378* (London, 1963), pp. 146–60.

on May 28, 1368, telling the king that he did not in any way consider him to have been guilty of misconduct and that he considered the matter closed.[14] Two days before, however, when Urban had issued a general declaration that Casimir had had no responsibility in the preparation of the forged dispensation and was therefore free of infamy and blame, he had also explicitly denied papal approval of the standing royal petition for annulment. He had concluded his letter, "we do not, however, intend with this letter to approve. . . ."[15]

Thus the matter remained until Casimir's death. The papacy tolerated a situation which it was powerless to change. Ironically, despite the efforts to which Casimir had gone to obtain an heir, his hopes were not fulfilled. Jadwiga bore him only daughters. To compound the irony of failure, although Duke Henry died before the Polish king, Casimir did not inherit Żagań. Although this dynastic policy had remained barren, the question of Silesia was by no means dropped.

It was, however, other areas of Charles IV's activity which first drew Casimir's attention. The emperor, ever anxious to strengthen and expand the power of his dynasty, had long desired to obtain the Mark of Brandenburg. During the early 1360s when the Wittelsbachs had been involved in the formulation of anti-Luxemburg coalitions, Charles had succeeded in negotiating an inheritance treaty with them which laid the foundation for his eventual acquisition of Brandenburg. On March 18, 1363, he and Margrave Lewis the Roman had agreed that should Lewis and his younger brother Otto die without heir, Wittelsbach holdings in Brandenburg and Lower Lusatia would go to Charles's oldest son Václav.[16] Further negotiations in 1364 resulted in the immediate cession of Lower Lusatia to Václav, with Duke Bolko of Świdnica receiving the territory as a fief of the crown of Bohemia.[17]

It was clear to Casimir that this Luxemburg expansion would result in semiencirclement of Poland and that the position of the kingdom would be correspondingly precarious should Polish-Luxemburg relations weaken. He took steps to strengthen his western flank against such an eventuality. His first object of attention was the region in the area of the confluence of the Noteć and Warta rivers, where many cities owed their allegiance not to the margrave of Brandenburg, but to his wife Kunegunde, Casimir's second daughter.

Upon this basis the king claimed the territory for the crown of Poland in

14. Theiner, *Mon. Pol.*, I, # 877.

15. Ibid., # 876.

16. J. F. Böhmer, *Regesta imperii*, vol. VIII: *Die Regesten des Kaiserreichs unter Kaiser Karl IV, 1346–1378*, ed. A. Huber (Innsbruck, 1877), # 3939, 3940, 3943; *Codex diplomaticus Brandenburgensis*, ed. Adolph Friedrich Riedel, 41 vols. (Berlin, 1838–69), II, 445 ff. See also Werunsky, *Karl IV*, III, 269–70; Johannes Schulz, *Die Mark Brandenburg*, 4 vols. (Berlin, 1961–).

17. Böhmer-Huber, *Regesten des Kaiserreichs*, # 4024, 7117; *C.D.Pr.*, II, 459–60. See also Dąbrowski, "Dzieje polityczne," pp. 514–15.

his daughter's name. Then, to legitimize his actions, Casimir opened negotiations with other rulers who had interests there. These included the Knights of the Teutonic Order and the Knights of the Hospital of St. John in Jerusalem. Each eventually agreed to recognize Polish claims in the area in return for certain concessions by Casimir. On July 2, 1364, the three parties signed an agreement which established a boundary upon the basis of a similar pact in 1251 between the two crusading orders and Duke Bolesław of Cracow. As a result of this treaty, the Polish western border was effectively extended west and north along the sixteenth meridian, thus returning to Poland the territory of Wałcz.[18] Not until 1368, however, did the margraves of Brandenburg recognize and confirm what had been a reality for some four years.[19]

Even before this, Casimir had gained another territorial success. In 1365 he had obtained feudal overlordship over the strategically located territories of Drezdenko and Santok, which in the earlier part of the century had been disputed between Poland and Brandenburg. Following the death of Margrave Lewis in May of that year, the rulers of these two areas refused to give their allegiance to Margrave Otto. They preferred instead to become part of the kingdom of Poland, fearing particularly the extension of Luxemburg power and the recent aggressive growth of Duke Barnim III of Szczecin. In July, 1365, four brothers from the families of Ost and Wedel came to Cracow to swear feudal allegiance to Casimir for Drezdenko and Santok. They declared that by law and custom they should obey the natural ruler of their territories rather than the foreign Wittelsbachs. Then they swore solemnly that Drezdenko and Santok rightfully belonged to the king of Poland.[20]

The acquisition of Wałcz, Drezdenko, and Santok was a major diplomatic success for Casimir. In total area these districts did not mark a large gain; but geopolitically they were of the highest importance. Their union to Poland cut off the last direct access route from the empire into the territory of the Teutonic Order. This meant that the supply and reinforcement of the Knights would be an increasingly difficult task. It also severed the connection between the *Ordensstaat* and Brandenburg. Should Luxemburg control be extended to the latter territory, such a territorial disruption would hamper the revival of the old Bohemian-Order pincer around Poland. Finally, Casimir's achievement brought Poland into direct contact with the princes of Pomorze Zachodnie, who were being increasingly drawn toward Poland as the great powers of the

18. *C.D.M.P.*, III, # 1527. See Dąbrowski, *Dzieje Polski od r. 1333 do r. 1506*, vol. II of Roman Grodecki, Stanisław Zachorowski, and Jan Dąbrowski, *Dzieje Polski średniowiecznej* (Cracow, 1926), pp. 82–83.

19. For the details of this stage in the acquisition of Wałcz, see Stanisław Nowogrodzki, "Pomorze zachodnie a Polska w latach 1323–1370," *Rocznik Gdański*, IX–X (1935–36), 63 ff.

20. Dogiel, *Codex*, I, 593, and his *Limites regni Poloniae et magni Ducatus Lithuaniae* . . . (Vilno, 1758), pp. 1–2; *C.D.M.P.*, III, # 1545. See Caro, *Geschichte Polens*, II, 339; Kaczmarczyk, *Polska czasów Kazimierza*, pp. 162–63.

region exerted pressure upon the mouth of the Oder. For his part, Casimir hoped to turn this new territorial connection to Poland's advantage as it sought ways to recover Pomorze from the Knights. Though Casimir was unable to exploit these newly created advantages fully in his lifetime, they were of primary importance in later Polish struggles with the Order.[21]

Another region where Casimir had to contend with the influence of the Order in these last years was in the eastern Baltic, where he and his kingdom were temporarily involved by virtue of their heightened international importance. Here Casimir was named Protector of the Archdiocese of Riga. The archbishop there had been continually confronted with efforts by the Teutonic Order to encroach upon his ecclesiastical holdings.[22] The pressure became so intense in 1365–66 that the archbishop appealed to the pope and emperor for aid. Charles IV responded on April 23, 1366, by confirming all the privileges and rights of the archdiocese, and by appointing several of the rulers of the area to act as protectors and defenders of the church there: Kings Waldemar of Denmark, Haakon of Sweden, and Casimir of Poland, plus Dukes Bogusław of Pomorze-Wołogoszcz and Albert of Mecklenburg. This position was largely an honorary one, and Casimir had little contact with the affairs of Riga. It was Duke Albert who took the initiative in protesting to the Order its actions. Grand Master Winrich von Kniprode then wisely decided to liquidate the Order's quarrel in this region. In May, 1366, he negotiated an agreement in Gdańsk by which the rule of the archbishop and his successors over Rigan territory was confirmed.[23]

Of more immediate concern than this peripheral involvement was the continued presence of the Knights on the northern border of the *regnum* and in Pomorze. In the fall of 1366 Casimir undertook to review completely his policy toward the Knights, focusing upon the question of whether, having strengthened the kingdom and consolidated his rule in the past three decades, and having added the resources of men and material which Ruthenia provided, he was now sufficiently strong to attempt to recover Pomorze.

There was from the Polish point of view much to explain why such a question might be raised. Despite his acceptance of the treaties of Kalisz, Casimir had not resigned himself to the permanent loss of Pomorze any more than he had to the loss of Silesia. In the eyes of the Polish church and the Polish nation, Pomorze

21. See Wiktor Fenrych, *Nowa Marchia w dziejach politycznych Polski w XIII i XIV wieku* (Zielona Góra and Poznań, 1959), pp. 71–72; and the remarks of Stefan M. Kuczyński, *Wielka wojna z Zakonem Krzyżackim w latach 1409–1411*, 3rd ed. (Warsaw, 1966), pp. 78–79.

22. On the background of the Order's expansion and its goals under Winrich von Kniprode, see Johannes Voigt, *Geschichte Preussens von den ältesten Zeiten bis zum Untergange der Herrschaft des Deutschen Ordens*, 9 vols. (Königsberg, 1827–39), V, 178–84.

23. The best modern discussion of this is Henryk Paszkiewicz, *Polityka Ruska Kazimierza Wielkiego* (Warsaw, 1925), pp. 222–23. Older accounts, such as Voigt, *Geschichte Preussens*, V, 188–90, and Feliks Koneczny, "Kazimierz Wielki, protektorem kościoła ryskiego," *Pamiętnik uczniów Uniwersytetu Jagiellońskiego* (Cracow, 1887), pp. 554–69, have been completely superseded.

was *Polonia irredenta*.[24] There was in addition some sentiment in the native population of Pomorze for a return to Poland. Casimir was only too aware of the significance of the popular uprising in Gdańsk some years earlier. In 1361, as the result of a long series of repressive measures directed by the Order against the Slavic population of the city, there broke out, apparently quite spontaneously, popular agitation against the rule of the Knights. For some days there was street fighting in which the cry of the rebels was "Cracow, Cracow!"[25] It was upon this slender reed that Casimir could perhaps hope for local support in any campaign against the Order.

The king was too judicious to rely only upon sentiment, however, and decided to determine more directly what the chances of Polish attempts to recover Pomorze would be. In the fall of 1366[26] he audaciously traveled to Marienburg to meet with Grand Master Winrich. He was received with the respect befitting his rank; and in a demonstration of supreme confidence by his hosts, during the three days of his visit he was given a complete tour of the fortifications of the Order. It was apparent to all that Casimir had come with hopes and expectations of finding the Knights weakened and unprepared for military activity.[27] In this he was disappointed, for the power of the Order had never been greater. Under Winrich, the Order stood in what would later be fondly remembered as its *goldene Blütezeit*. This was the time when "Prussia shone with honor, peace, sternness, law, justice and discipline," and when "under Grand Master Winrich, Prussia stood amid great honor and praise."[28] The Order was not vulnerable enough for Poland to commit itself to the waging of what could be a long war for the reconquest of Pomorze. That task would have to be

24. The Polish church still claimed ecclesiastical jurisdiction over Pomorze and demanded that Peter's Pence be collected there; while the testimony of the witnesses of 1339 suggests the strong commitment which the laity—noble and non-noble—had to the view of Pomorze as Polish territory. Among the extensive literature on these subjects, see particularly Marian Łodyński, "Regnum Poloniae w opinii publicznej XIV wieku," *K.H.*, XXVIII (1914), 38–54; Kaczmarczyk, *Monarchia Kazimierza Wielkiego*, 2 vols. (Poznań, 1939–46), II, 39–47, 51–61; Helena Chłopocka, "Tradycje o Pomorzu Gdańskim w zeznaniu świadków na procesach polsko-krzyżackich w XIV i XV wieku," *Roczniki Historyczne*, XXV, i (1959), 65–142.

25. On the revolt in Gdańsk in 1361, see Halecki, "Kazimierz Wielki," p. 353; Kazimierz Piwarski, *Dzieje Gdańska w zarysie* (Gdańsk, Bydgoszcz, and Szczecin, 1946), pp. 41–42; Kaczmarczyk, *Polska czasów Kazimierza*, pp. 107–8.

26. Both Caro, *Geschichte Polens*, II, 343, and Voigt, *Geschichte Preussens*, V, 185, incorrectly date this visit in 1365. The correct date is to be found in Hermannus de Wartberge, *Chronicon Livoniae, 1200–1378*, in *SS. rer. Pr.*, II, 556, and Johannes of Posilge, *Chronik des Landes Preussen*, in *SS. rer. Pr.*, III, 119. For Casimir's itinerary in this period, see Paszkiewicz, *Polityka Ruska*, p. 238 nn. 1, 2.

27. This, at least, is what the chroniclers of the Order reported. See Wigand of Marburg, *Chronica nova Prutenica*, in *SS. rer. Pr.*, II, 613; Hermannus de Wartberge, *Chronicon*, p. 556; Johannes of Posilge, *Chronik*, p. 119. Their view is partially confirmed by Długosz, *Historia*, III, 308 f.

28. *Codex epistolaris Vitoldi*, cited in Marjan Tumler, *Der Deutsche Orden im Werden, Wachsen und Wirken bis 1400* (Vienna, 1955), p. 350, and Wigand of Marburg, *Chronica*, p. 613.

accomplished at a later date. Casimir returned to Cracow to concentrate upon the dynastic and territorial ambitions of Charles IV.

Throughout Casimir's reign, one of the touchstones for determining the status of Polish-Bohemian relations was the position of Wrocław. When Czech interest in the ecclesiastical position of the Silesian center waned, Casimir's dealings with the Luxemburgers improved. Conversely, evidence of Bohemian plans to detach Wrocław from Gniezno was sufficient to bring the two dynasties to the point of conflict. In this latter respect, the record of Charles IV left much to be desired from Casimir's point of view, for the emperor had been zealous in his attempts to rectify the anomaly of Wrocław's ecclesiastically and politically divided allegiance. Following the Congress of Cracow in 1364, Casimir received reports that Charles had intensified his efforts over Wrocław. The Polish king wrote again to Pope Urban protesting these actions and beseeching him to retain Wrocław's present ecclesiastical position. The pope replied on February 24, 1365, with an outright denial of Casimir's charges. He asserted that during his pontificate, Charles had never in any way, directly or indirectly, attempted to alter Wrocław's status. Certain slanderers must have misled the king. Nevertheless he assured Casimir that the papacy had no intention of transferring Wrocław to the jurisdiction of Prague.[29]

This papal declaration was definitive. It marked the ultimate failure of Luxemburg ambitions in the diocese. Charles was forced to content himself with less substantial gains there. Sometime in this period, a Bohemian apparently was elected dean of the cathedral chapter in Wrocław, for Janko of Czarnków mentions in passing that "a Bohemian was forced in, obtaining the deanship."[30] In addition, Charles's relations with the bishop and his court were increasingly close in the last years of his reign. But the bishopric itself remained outside his grasp. Nevertheless, the fact that Casimir had been able to complain again about Bohemian designs suggests that relations between Poland and the Luxemburgers were again becoming strained.

The event which precipitated new friction was the death without heir of the Duke of Świdnica on July 28, 1368. According to the treaty signed between Bolko and Charles in 1353 and modified in 1364, the duke's lands were to escheat to the Bohemian crown and his rule in Lower Lusatia was to be transferred to Charles's son Václav. Thus on September 24 the emperor enfeoffed his son with the territories of Świdnica and Jawór plus the remainder of Bolko's holdings.[31] It was not long before Casimir made formal protest of this settlement. He argued that Bolko owed him a debt of 3,000 marks which had not been repaid, and that until he received payment he would not recognize Bohemian

29. Theiner, *Mon. Pol.*, I, # 848. See also Dąbrowski, "Dzieje polityczne," pp. 484–85.

30. Janko of Czarnków, *Chronicon Polonorum*, in *M.P.H.*, II, 667. See also Dąbrowski, "Dzieje polityczne," pp. 485–87.

31. Colmar Grünhagen and E. Markgraf, eds., *Lehns- und Besitzurkunden Schlesiens und seiner einzelnen Fürstentümer im Mittelalter*, 2 vols. (Leipzig, 1881–83), I, 185–86.

rights to Bolko's Silesian territory.[32] It is not difficult to see that this was merely a pretext, and that Casimir was really interested in frustrating Charles's attempts to expand Bohemian control in Silesia. This same motive underlay his announcement at this same time that he had not actually renounced his claims to Bolko's territory in 1356 or his claim to the cities of Byczyna, Kluczborek, and Wołczyń.[33] One senses in these actions a certain air of desperation on Casimir's part, as if he were clutching at any straw which might enable him to regain a foothold in Silesia. The petty character of his pretexts and the volatile topic of Silesia as a point of contention between Poland and Bohemia almost ensured open conflict with Charles. That it did not come at this point was due in large measure to the emperor's involvement in a sharp internal dispute in Wrocław.[34] This potential for conflict was heightened in these years by Luxemburg expansion elsewhere.

In Brandenburg, Casimir sought to combat Charles's ambitions and to strengthen and expand his western border. On May 10, 1368, in Poznań he confirmed the rights granted to the citizens of Wałcz in 1303 by the last Ascanian margraves; and on November 30 he confirmed certain of the privileges in the region which Duke Przemysł II had granted to the Knights of the Hospital of St. John in Jerusalem in 1286.[35] He then turned to Margrave Otto of Brandenburg. By holding out to him the possibility of a formal alliance, Casimir persuaded him to recognize the earlier Polish acquisition of Wałcz. Otto also agreed, in order to establish more clearly the border between Poland and the Mark, to cede to Casimir the minor territories of Czaplinek and Drahim. Representatives of the two rulers then negotiated an alliance, which was signed on December 24, 1368. Each ruler promised to support the other militarily, while the treaty also established a panel of arbiters to adjudicate any disputes which might arise between the subjects of the two rulers.[36]

This minor rectification of Poland's western border was of great importance to Casimir's program of defense against the ambitions of Charles IV. By the

32. Beneš Krabice z Weitmil, *Chronicon Ecclesiae Pragensis*, in *SS. rer. Boh.*, II, 402.

33. These claims involved him not only in a dispute with Charles, but also in one with Duke Louis of Brzeg. The chief sources for this conflict are Beneš, *Chronicon*, pp. 402–3; *Chronica principum Poloniae*, in *M.P.H.*, III, 533–34. This latter is, however, a highly fragmentary and inaccurate source and must be supplemented by the evidence assembled by Dąbrowski, "Dzieje polityczne," pp. 528 n. 2, 529, who also gives a good secondary account on pp. 527–30. See also *Geschichte Schlesiens*, vol. I, *Von der Urzeit bis zum Jahre 1526*, published by the Historische Kommission für Schlesien, ed. Hermann Aubin, et al., 3d ed. (Stuttgart, 1961).

34. This dispute involved the emperor and the municipal government of Wrocław with Bishop Přeslav of Pohořelce and his cathedral chapter. Of an unusually bitter nature and involving the use of both interdict and excommunication, the dispute was fundamentally over jurisdictional issues. It was not settled until 1370. See Dąbrowski, "Dzieje polityczne," pp. 530–34; *Historia Śląska*, I, pt. ii, 181.

35. For the first, *C.D.M.P.*, III, # 1596; see also idem, II, # 865. For the second, idem, III, # 1603; see also idem, I, # 570.

36. *C.D.M.P.*, III, # 1592 and 1607.

acquisition of Czaplinek and Drahim, just as with Wałcz, Drezdenko, and Santok, a stronger, deeper wedge had been driven between Brandenburg and the Order, and between the Order and the empire. Poland's border with Pomorze Zachodnie had also been extended.[37]

While affairs in the west certainly absorbed most of Casimir's attention in his last years, the king did not neglect his hard-won Ruthenian holdings. Much of his activity there after 1366 was connected with attempts to introduce the organs and instruments of the *regnum Poloniae* into Ruthenia. His success in this respect was modest, but he did manage to strengthen and consolidate his position. This is particularly clear in the case of Vladimir, part of the territory given as a fief to Alexander Korjatowicz in 1366, where it is possible to see the gradual eclipse of Alexander's power by Casimir. The king began the construction of a stone fortress for the city sometime in 1368 in order to replace the older wooden structure.[38] The work progressed rapidly, but despite the fact that more than three hundred workers and many horses and yoke of oxen worked uninterruptedly for two years, the fortress remained unfinished at Casimir's death. The project was of sufficient concern to the king that, in addition to the 3,000 marks which had already been expended in construction, he appropriated an additional 600 marks for this purpose only four days before he died.[39] Another indication of the extension of royal power in Ruthenia came late in Casimir's reign when he placed all civil administration in the hands of a citizen of Łęczyca, who was subordinate only to the king. His position soon overshadowed that of Alexander.[40]

Elsewhere in the east, the peace which Casimir had established in 1366 with the Gedyminowicze was broken two years later when Kiejstut invaded Polish territory. The details which have survived concerning this incursion are fragmentary at best, and it has been difficult for scholars to determine even the location of the invasion.[41] According to the papal regest of the letter which Casimir sent Urban requesting aid, the Lithuanians had destroyed the cities of "Wrucz, Plonee, Rotemburch, and Polcolsko in the diocese of Cracow."[42]

---

37. On the question of Czaplinek and Drahim, see Nowogrodzki, "Pomorze zachodnie a Polska," pp. 63–65; Kaczmarczyk, *Polska czasów Kazimierza*, p. 170. Their place in the larger question of Polish conflict with the Order may be seen in Adam Vetulani, *Walka Polski w wiekach średnich o dostęp do Bałtyku* (Warsaw, 1954), pp. 53–54.

38. Janko of Czarnków, *Chronicon*, p. 643.

39. Ibid., p. 644.

40. Ibid., p. 643. This is one of the few names which seems to have escaped the meticulous eye of Zdzisław Kaczmarczyk in the lists of Casimir's officials which he prepared for his *Monarchia*. He does mention him, however, in *Polska czasów Kazimierza*, p. 169.

41. Some helpful remarks on the historiography of this problem are made by Kaczmarczyk, *Monarchia*, I, 225–27, and Gotthold Rhode, *Die Ostgrenze Polens, Politische Entwicklung, kulturelle Bedeutung und geistige Auswirkung*, vol. I, *Im Mittelalter bis zum Jahre 1401* (Cologne and Graz, 1955), p. 205 n. 177.

42. *M.P.V.*, II, 226.

These names have been badly corrupted, however, and establishing their modern equivalents is difficult. The great Ukrainian historian Hrushevsky identified these cities as locations in Podolia and Halicz; other evidence led Henryk Paskiewicz to look elsewhere, however, with convincing results.[43] He pointed out that, according to Janko of Czarnków, in 1368 Kiejstut led a Lithuanian force into Mazovia and captured "Poltowsk," that is, Pułtusk. His testimony is confirmed by Franciscus Thorunensis, who also reported a Lithuanian incursion in Mazovia in 1368.[44] These data led Paszkiewicz to look to Mazovia, and he identified "Wrucz, Plonee, Rotemburch, and Polcolsko," with Łowicz, Płonsk, Czerwinsk on the Vistula, and Pułtusk.

News of this invasion reached Casimir while he was en route to Hungary; upon his arrival, he and Louis discussed what action to take. They decided to send a letter to Avignon describing the effects of this wanton incursion and to request aid. The papal response on May 15, 1369, granted Casimir substantial support. Urban provided the Polish king with the papal tenth in Poland for two years, specifically for reconstruction of devastated areas, strengthening of existing fortification and initiation of new building to improve and extend Poland's eastern defenses against the "schismatics and treacherous unbelievers."[45] Despite these concerns, there was no substantive change in the Polish position in the east.

In the west, Casimir was pursuing a complicated dynastic arrangement. After three years of marriage to Jadwiga, he was resigned to the probability he would remain without heir and that Louis would succeed him as king of Poland. Louis, however, had also remained without male heir; and Casimir recognized that the direct Angevin line could also die out. In view of this, Casimir conceived the plan of providing for the return of Poland to the rule of one of his own descendants. Sometime during the second half of 1368 he officially adopted Duke Casimir of Szczecin as his son. This youth, who was born in 1351 to Duke Bogusław of Pomorze-Wołogoszcz and Elizabeth of Poland, was therefore the king's grandson.[46]

The young Kaźko, as Duke Casimir is most commonly known in Polish historiography, had already, by his marriage in 1359 to Grand Prince Olgierd's daughter, played a role in the king's policy. He had furthered Polish Ruthenian

43. Hrushevsky, *Istoria Ukrainy Rusy*, 10 vols. (reprinted, New York, 1955), IV, 49 n. 1; Paszkiewicz, *Polityka Ruska*, pp. 243–44.

44. Janko of Czarnków, *Chronicon*, p. 631; Franciscus Thorunensis, *Annales Prussici, 941–1410*, in *SS. rer. Pr.*, III, 87.

45. The documents in *M.P.V.*, II, 226, and Theiner, *Mon. Pol.*, I, # 883. See also Rhode, *Die Ostgrenze Polens*, I, 205–6, 252; Kaczmarczyk, *Polska czasów Kazimierza*, p. 169. The construction of the above-mentioned fortification at Vladimir and the Lithuanian expedition of 1368 are not unrelated.

46. Janko of Czarnków, *Chronicon*, p. 641. For the dates and genealogy, see Balzer, *Genealogia*, pp. 471–73.

ambitions, while at the same time this union had brought together three of the chief foes of the Teutonic Order. This latter consideration was involved also in the events of 1368. Late in April of that year, Każko's wife had died, and Casimir had arranged a second marriage, this one with the teenage daughter of Duke Ziemowit III of Mazovia. In connection with this marriage, the king adopted his grandson. He did more, however; he promised Każko overlordship of the territories of Sieradz and Łęczyca and recognized him as part of the line of succession to the Polish crown. It is doubtful that the king expected that Każko would succeed him upon his death, for he recognized that the right of Louis of Hungary was too firmly established to be challenged. He did hope that Louis would be succeeded by Każko; he even went so far as to attempt to persuade the Angevin to declare Każko his heir in a meeting in February, 1369.

Quite apart from the question of succession, the significance of the adoption of Każko is integrally connected with Casimir's concern over Luxemburg expansion into Brandenburg and toward the mouth of the Oder as well as with his stubborn refusal to forget that Pomorze had once been Polish territory and that a substantial portion of his kingdom would still agree with those who three decades before had argued for the recovery of Pomorze. By attempting to make Każko a powerful Polish prince and eventual ruler of the kingdom, Casimir was preparing the way for Poland's return to the Baltic coast. At the death of his father, Bogusław, Każko would inherit most of Pomorze Zachodnie, which, when combined with the kingdom of Poland, would again give Poland a coastline. In addition, it was hoped, Każko would be powerful enough to wrest the remainder of Pomorze from the Order. Had these plans been fulfilled, Casimir would be justly regarded as the architect of one of his kingdom's greatest triumphs. That they were not, was the result of Louis's modification of part of Casimir's will and his success in advocating the candidacy of one of his daughters as his successor.[47]

Casimir's visit to Louis of Hungary in February, 1369, has been mentioned; but neither the question of the succession in Poland nor the renewed threat of the Lithuanians was the prime purpose for the trip. Instead it was the king's growing alarm over the rise of Luxemburg power in central Europe which sent

47. The territorial considerations are best discussed, if briefly, by Nowogrodzki, "Polska a Pomorze zachodnie," pp. 73–74, and Vetulani, *Walka Polski o dostęp do Bałtyku*, p. 54. The adoption of Każko, and Casimir's policy toward him, raised several constitutional issues about the nature of the *regnum Poloniae*. These are discussed authoritatively and exhaustively from two fundamentally different viewpoints by Stanisław Kętrzyński, "Zapis Kazimierza Wielkiego dla Kazimierza Bogusławowica," *P.H.*, XIV (1912), 26–47, 164–94, 295–316, and Oswald Balzer, *Królestwo Polskie, 1295–1370*, 3 vols. (Lwów, 1919–20), 119–42. A short biographical sketch is provided by Józef Mitkowski in *Pol. Słow. Biog.*, XII, 281–82. More detailed is Krystyna Pieradzka, *Każko Szczecinski na tle polityki pomorskiej Kazimierza Wielkiego* (Warsaw, 1947). In the west European languages, the comments of Michał Sczaniecki, "Political Ties Between Western Pomerania and Poland, Up to the 16th Century," in *Poland at the XIth International Congress of Historical Sciences in Stockholm* (Warsaw, 1960), p. 97, are helpful, although he sets the date of Każko's adoption in 1360.

him to his closest ally. Casimir was fully aware that the growth of this dynasty had upset the regional balance of power and presented a threat to the peace and stability of the whole area. Thus he crossed the Carpathians in winter to formulate an anti-Luxemburg coalition which from the immediate Polish point of view had as its purpose to regain Silesia for the kingdom. On February 14, 1369, Louis and Casimir signed a treaty in Buda promising to aid one another against all enemies, especially Emperor Charles IV.[48] They further agreed that in case of war they would sign no separate treaty with the emperor and would not under any circumstances agree to a marriage pact with the Luxemburgers.[49] Casimir's plans were further developed on April 12, 1369, when he and some of his more important civil officials met with Dukes Ziemowit of Mazovia, Wacław of Niemodlin, Henry the Younger of Żagań, and Kaźko of Szczecin. At this meeting, both Lithuanian and Silesian affairs were discussed, and the Silesian princes agreed to support Casimir against Charles.[50] The anti-Luxemburg coalition was further strengthened in October, 1369, when representatives of the Wittelsbachs signed a treaty with Louis in Pozsony, agreeing to forbid entrance to the Mark by any member of the Luxemburg house.[51] Casimir also attempted to block Charles's plans in Brandenburg by reconciling himself with the bishop of Lubusz. The conflict between these two had concerned ecclesiastical jurisdiction in Ruthenia, but was finally settled on June 25, 1369, when the bishop and the king agreed to let the clergy of Poland arbitrate their dispute. As a result of this agreement, Casimir was able to depend upon the support and friendship of Lubusz, which was in territory held by Brandenburg.[52] Finally Casimir hoped that these diplomatic efforts, if translated into actual warfare, would be supported by the papacy. Echoes of this hope are reflected in Beneš of Weitmil's comment[53] that "Urban ... similarly conceived a great displeasure against the emperor two years before his death. Those responsible for this were King Casimir of Poland, [the duke] of Nassau, and the archbishop of Mainz ... the major enemies of the emperor."

When Charles IV learned of the formation of a coalition directed against him he turned to Avignon, hoping to neutralize either Louis or Casimir, thus breaking the alliance. The most that Urban was willing to do, however, was to

48. Dogiel, *Codex*, I, I, 39. See also Dąbrowski, *Ostatnie lata*, pp. 163 f.

49. This last provision was directed against Charles's designs upon the right of succession in Poland, which were already known. See S. Steinherz, "Die Beziehungen Ludwigs I. von Ungarn zu Karl IV.," *Mittheilungen des Instituts für oesterreichische Geschichtsforschung*, IX (1888), 574.

50. Paszkiewicz, *Polityka Ruska*, p. 250. The evidence for this meeting rests upon inferences drawn from the document in *Kodeks dyplomatyczny księstwa mazowieckiego*, ed. T. Lubomirski (Warsaw, 1863), # 86. Paszkiewicz's interpretation is accepted by Kaczmarczyk, *Polska czasów Kazimierza*, p. 170.

51. See Steinherz, "Die Beziehungen," p. 574; Dąbrowski, *Ostatnie lata*, pp. 164–65.

52. The documents in *C.D.M.P.*, III, # 1613, 1623; Dogiel, *Codex*, I, 594. See also Władysław Abraham, *Powstanie organizacya kościoła łacińskiego na Rusi*, vol. I (Lwów, 1904), 255–59.

53. Beneš, *Chronicon*, p. 413.

232 THE END OF THE REIGN

investigate the emperor's charges and offer to mediate any conflict. The pope sent a representative, who had, however, no success.[54] Charles then recognized he must take the initiative in his own behalf. He hurriedly returned to Bohemia from Italy and attempted to arrange a marriage pact. First he suggested that his son Václav should marry Louis's niece Elizabeth. The Angevin refused, and Charles turned next to Casimir. This time he suggested the marriage of Václav to any one of Casimir's daughters. In addition to ending the coalition against him by this arrangement, Charles hoped also to gain the right of succession in Poland for Václav. The emperor even went so far as to obtain papal permission for this. This attempt also failed, but in a third effort Charles was successful. On June 13, 1370, he engaged Václav to Joanna, daughter of Duke Albert of Bavaria, and on September 29 the two were married. As a result, the emperor was able to remove the Wittelsbachs from the anti-Luxemburg coalition.[55]

While Charles had been following the time-honored policy of *divide et impera*, Casimir had been actively prosecuting his claims in Silesia. Throughout 1369 and 1370 he continued to claim Byczyna and Kluczborek and the Silesian lands of the late Bolko of Świdnica. Charles's response was to obtain from all Bolko's relatives formal recognition of Václav as the new ruler of these territories and to transfer rule over Świdnica and Jawór to the hands of Václav. He also undercut the ostensible grounds for Casimir's claims by paying him 3,000 marks on October 12 as the amount owed by Bolko.[56] In two other areas, Charles demonstrated his diplomatic adroitness and defensive skill. In February, 1370, he purchased the village of Fürstenberg on the Oder. Its importance lay in its strategic location on the route to Poznań, its extensive fortifications, and the bridge over the Oder which it controlled. It was a perfect base for military operations against Poland. He also succeeded in signing a treaty with some of the princes of Pomorze Zachodnie in May, providing for their neutrality in any Polish-Bohemian conflict.[57] All of these things represented a substantial deterioration in Casimir's position vis-à-vis Charles. Thus thwarted, the Polish king began to prepare for war. In turn, the emperor also made ready for conflict. Had this trend continued, hostilities would surely have broken out between Charles and Casimir over Silesia.[58] The entire situation was suddenly changed, however, by the unexpected death of Casimir.

54. See Dąbrowski, "Dzieje polityczne," p. 535.

55. The foregoing details are in Theiner, *Mon. Hung.*, II, # 171 and 172, and *Annales Matseenses*, in *M.G.H.* SS., IX, 834.

56. Grünhagen-Markgraf, *Lehns- und Besitzurkunden*, I, 511–12; Beneš, *Chronicon*, p. 402. See also Dąbrowski, "Dzieje polityczne," p. 537 n. 1.

57. Beneš, *Chronicon*, p. 405; Böhmer-Huber, *Regesta imperii*, # 4822a–28. See also Nowogrodzki, "Polska a Pomorze zachodnie," p. 70; Fenrych, *Nowa Marchia*, pp. 72–73.

58. The Hungarians also recognized the possibility of war and during the winter of 1369–70 made preparations for defense on their western border. See Steinherz, "Die Beziehungen," pp. 577, 614.

For most of the period treated in this study, the historian is dependent upon diplomatic documents, rough inferences drawn from papal correspondence in the absence of royal originals, and upon fragments of information in a variety of annals and chronicles. This frequently means that precious facts are hidden or unrecorded and that the figures of Łokietek and Casimir are nowhere fully revealed. But for the king's last days, the situation is quite different. Here the historian is confronted by a narrative of unusually full detail which possesses also significant literary value. This is the account of Janko of Czarnków, Casimir's vice-chancellor and an eyewitness to the events he here describes. Upon his testimony rest all later narratives of the king's death.[59]

Casimir spent the summer of 1370 in Greater Poland reviewing affairs there and attending to the administration of the kingdom. Early in September he decided to return to Cracow in order to watch more closely events in Silesia. His route took him through Sieradz, and when he reached the village of Przedbórz near Pilica he interrupted his journey to visit his recently completed residence there. On September 8, the feast of the Nativity of the Virgin Mary, Casimir was invited to participate in a hunt. Although already past sixty, he was still strong and vigorous, and he agreed. As he was about to mount his horse, certain members of his entourage gently reminded him of what day it was and suggested that it would be appropriate to refrain from sport on this holy day. Casimir was inclined at first to agree, but someone else described in glowing details the enjoyment to be had on the hunt. Convinced, the king swung into the saddle and rode off.

The hunt took place without incident, and the next day another hunt was held. Again Casimir took part; but while he was riding at full gallop through the forest, his horse stumbled, throwing him heavily to the ground. He was unable to rise, and it was discovered that he had seriously injured his left leg.[60] Immediately a fever set in, but it soon diminished to the point where the return journey to Cracow could be resumed. These events ended the first phase of the king's final illness, though the complications which were to come were undoubtedly connected with the injury. The trip from Przedbórz to Sandomir followed a route of some 135 kilometers through the region of Radom and the heavy forests of the Holy Cross Mountains. In Sandomir the entourage halted,

59. Janko of Czarnków, *Chronicon*, pp. 631–36. He was followed by Długosz, *Historia*, III, 319–27, who is the basis for Marcin Kromer, *Kronika Polska* (Warsaw, 1767), pp. 365–69, and Maciej Stryjkowski, *Kronika Polska, Litewska, Żmodzka . . .* (Warsaw, 1766), p. 412. Since Jacob Caro, *Geschichte Polens*, II, 354–55, all modern writers generally follow Janko of Czarnków.

60. ". . . vulnus non modicum in tybia sinistra suscepit." This may have been a broken leg, as Kaczmarczyk, *Polska czasów Kazimierza*, p. 174, asserts. Caro, *Geschichte Polens*, II, 354, says somewhat inaccurately, "der König . . . erhielt eine schwere Verletzung an der linken Seite des Körpers." In the most recent study of the king's death by Roman Grodecki, "Zgon Kazimierza Wielkiego (1370)," in *Mediaevalia, w 50 rocznicę pracy naukowej Jana Dąbrowskiego* (Warsaw, 1960), pp. 151–57, the suggestion of a broken leg is not made. The progression of the king's final illness as described above and by Janko of Czarnków does not exclude such a possibility, however, and in fact would correspond well with Grodecki's hypothesis.

and the king felt well enough to take a bath, despite the explicit prohibitions of his doctor, Henry of Cologne. As the physician had predicted, Casimir regretted his action, for his fever returned. It was not so serious, however, that he could not travel, and the journey was resumed. En route, Casimir again exercised his royal prerogative and disregarded the instructions of his physician. He indulged himself in a great feast of fruits, nuts, and various kinds of mushrooms, and again bathed. When he emerged from the water his fever worsened, and grew so bad that further travel was impossible. The nearby residence of the castellan of Lublin provided convenient overnight shelter. At first Casimir did not improve, and his doctor and other members of his retinue began to despair for his life. By morning, however, he had rallied somewhat, and it was decided to move him to a Cistercian monastery some fifteen kilometers away. By carrying the weakened monarch in a litter, they came safely to the cloister.

The constitution of the king had always been strong, despite several serious illnesses; and in the eight days spent there, while prayers were constantly directed to God and St. Sigismund for Casimir's recovery, the condition of the monarch gradually improved. Great was the rejoicing when it was apparent that the king was out of danger. To give thanks for his recovery, Casimir commanded the renovation of the Romanesque cathedral of Płock, which reportedly contained the relics of St. Sigismund.[61] The next day it was decided to continue on, and from the monastery, the retinue carried Casimir to Osiek. There another physician, named Matthias, encouraged Casimir to drink some mead, against the advice of Henry of Cologne. As a result, according to Janko, the fever returned and Matthias successfully agitated for an immediate return to Cracow, saying he could better care for the king there. The retinue, now in danger of becoming a cortege, continued only slowly on its way, passing through Korczyń and Opatów, where it halted for a day to enable Casimir to rest. Not until October 30, after seven weeks and a journey of over 300 kilometers, did the party reach Cracow. Casimir had been so thoroughly exhausted by the trip that he was near death.

On November 1 Casimir recovered sufficiently to ask his doctors through the intermediary of Janko whether he was truly in Cracow. Matthias misunderstood the king's question and asked scornfully "whether he was delirious, or whether he was mad, that he was asking whether he was in Cracow." With obvious relish, Janko snapped back that Casimir knew perfectly well where he was, but that he had been told on the road he would be better cared for in Cracow. He had thus far failed to note any efforts to save his life! Casimir later

61. Janko of Czarnków, as vice-chancellor and a member of the king's entourage, was given the responsibility of seeing that the ruins of the church at Płock were investigated: "post quod votum, prout me accersito, mane mihi et aliis audientibus retulit, statim se sensit aliqualiter a febri relevatum, mandans mihi ut ad Plocensem civitatem mitterem, ut ruinae ecclesiae conspicerentur. . . ."

indicated that he doubted both the possibility of his recovery and the intentions of his physicians, for he commanded them not to conceal from him any information concerning his condition, since he had important affairs of state to deal with.

Two days later Casimir called Bishop Florian of Cracow, who had served him so well;[62] Duke Władysław of Opole, as the representative of Angevin interests; and several notables of his kingdom to his bedside.[63] He received the last rites of his church, reiterated his reliance upon the Christian faith, and made his will. To Duke Kaźko of Szczecin he left the duchies of Sieradz, Łęczyca, and Dobrzyń, the castellanies of Kruszwica and Bydogoszcz in Kujavia, as well as other fortifications in Złotów and Wałcz in Greater Poland. Thus did he fulfill his promise to make Kaźko the most powerful Polish prince.[64] To knights Zbigniew and Przedbórz he left the villages of Niekłan and Nieczda. Other close associates were also remembered by the King. To Jasiek Żerawski went the village of Podgaje, to another, Jan, went the castle of Międzygórze and the wojtship of Sobota in Zawichost, while Peter Brun of Żmigród received part of the village of Szczytnik near Proszowice. For his natural sons, Niemierz and Jan, Casimir provided the villages of Bogucice, Chomętów, Brugnia, and Pierzchnica in the region of Stopnica.[65] To the cathedral of Cracow, he left a beautiful golden cross worth some ten thousand florins; for the church in Poznań, he provided an arm of St. Cosmas encased in a golden reliquary box; and to the metropolitan church in Gniezno, he presented an ornamented Bible and an ostensory containing many relics. To his two daughters from his marriage to Jadwiga of Żagań, he gave many precious jewels, ornamented clothes, and fine works of art. Half the royal plate was given to his daughters, with the other half going to his wife, Jadwiga. During this period, Casimir also took care of the final details of the administration of the kingdom. This included the granting of 600 marks for the completion of the fortifications in Vladimir, for the king was well aware that this area would come under Lithuanian attack upon his death.

Following these exertions, Casimir's condition grew rapidly worse. On

62. As early as October 19, 1350, Casimir could say "consideratis fidelibus serviciis nobis per ... dominum Florianum prepositum Cracoviensem et cancellarium Lanciciensem a multis retroactis temporibus constanter exhibitis et imposterum dante deo exhibendis," *Kodeks dyplomatyczny katedry krakowskiej ś. Wacława*, ed. Franciszek Piekosiński, 2 vols. (Cracow, 1874–83), I, 243. In the next two decades, he served also as bishop of Cracow and chancellor of the University of Cracow.

63. Długosz, *Historia*, III, 321.

64. See Marcin Dragan, "Testament Kazimierza Wielkiego," in *Sprawozdanie Dyrekcyi c. k. Gimnazyum V we Lwowie za rok szkolny 1911* (Lwów, 1911), pp. 3–23.

65. At least one of these sons was thought to be an issue from the king's Jewish mistress, Esterka. See Długosz, *Historia*, 321: "Nyemerzae, quem ex Iudaea susceperat." See also *Historia*, III, 263.

November 5, at about sunrise, the great king died at the age of sixty, apparently from pneumonia and its complications.[66] Two days later, with great honor and respect, he was buried on the right-hand side of the choir in the cathedral of Cracow he had helped to renovate. Archbishop Jarosław of Gniezno, Bishop Florian of Cracow, and Bishop Peter of Lubusz presided at the interment, concerning which Janko later wrote in his terse manner:

> It is impossible for the human tongue to describe the extent of the clamor, lamentation, and outcries of the princes, nobles, prelates, canons and ecclesiastics, as well as the populace, at his burial.

Even as Casimir lay dying, the storm clouds of party strife gathered around the kingdom. Louis of Hungary immediately began his trip to Poland, but on November 7 he stopped in Wieliczka and was not present for the king's burial. This was by design, for those who presided in Cracow were all bitter opponents of the Angevin. They represented the interests of Greater Poland as over against Louis's supporters, who came chiefly from Little Poland. This factionalism was to be a constant feature of the next fifteen years.[67] Louis was responsible, however, for erecting a handsome monument to his uncle. The tomb of Casimir was completed about 1380 and is constructed of the same red marble that Wit Stowsz was to use so effectively on the tomb of another King Casimir a century later. The tomb of Casimir the Great bears a reclining figure of the king, somewhat idealized; at his feet rests a lion. On the frieze around the massive block of marble are examples of Gothic sculpture which depict anonymous figures of the fourteenth century and also illustrate the high level of artistic development in this period.[68]

The death of Casimir brought to an end the direct line of the Piast dynasty which had ruled Poland since its appearance on the historical scene in the tenth century. It is somehow fitting that he should have died "early in the morning, about sunrise," for although the sun of his life was setting, his reign had been the dawning of Poland's golden age. To be sure, some early clouds during the reign of Louis of Hungary cast passing shadows; but it was not long before Poland's position as a great central European power was assured.

---

66. Recognizing the difficulties of diagnosing an illness after six hundred years, Professors Grodecki and Tochowicz, correctly, I think, identify three stages to Casimir's final days: (1) the king's injury and resulting fever as something largely independent of what followed; (2) the onset of pneumonia in the days from the departure from Sandomir until the arrival in Kordzyń; and (3) complications in the form of "purulenty" in the lungs in the last stages of the trip and in Cracow. See Grodecki, "Zgon Kazimierza," p. 157, for a concise summary of these conclusions. Minor disagreement is voiced by Kaczmarczyk, *Polska czasów Kazimierza*, p. 174 n. 2. It should be remembered that pneumonia is not an unusual complication in older patients confined to bed as Casimir may have been.

67. See Kaczmarczyk, *Polska czasów Kazimierza*, pp. 178–79.

68. The tomb is described by Józef Muczkowski, "Pomnik Kazimierza Wielkiego w katedrze na Wawelu," *Rocznik Krakowski*, XIX (1922), 134–57.

APPENDIX A
GLOSSARY
OF POLISH PLACE NAMES

For the sake of clarity and reasonable uniformity, the text has utilized the Polish version of place names, except when there is a familiar English form (Cracow, Warsaw) or when the use of the Polish form would have created unnecessary confusion (Królewiec for Königsberg, for example).

The following is a table of the chief equivalents, German unless noted, arranged alphabetically.

Brzeg	Brieg	Gubiń	Guben
Byczyna	Pitschen	Inowrocław	Hohensalza
Bydgoszcz	Bromberg	Jawór	Jauer
Bytom	Beuten	Kalisz	Kalisch
Chełmno	Kulm	Kamień	Kammin
Cieszyń	Teschen	Kluczborek	Kreuzberg
Czaplinek	Templeburg	Kłodzko	Glatz
Darłowo	Rügenwalde	Kościan	Kosten
Drahim	Draheim	Kożel	Kosel
Drezdenko	Driesen	Krzywiń	Kriewen
Drwęca	Drewenz	Legnica	Liegnitz
Gdańsk	Danzig	Lubusz	Lebus
Głogów	Glogau	Lwów	Lemberg
Gniewa	Mewa	Międzyrzecz	Meseritz
Gniezno	Gnesen	Michałowo	Michalau

Milicz	Militsch	Sławno	Schlawe
Murzyń	Gross Morin	Słupsk	Stolp
Namysłów	Namslau	Stary Sącz	Alt Sandecz
Nieszawa	Nessau	Strzelin	Strehlen
Nowe	Neuenburg am Weichsel	Sychów	Wartenberg
		Szczecin	Stettin
Nysa	Neisse	Ścinawa	Steinau
Oleśnica	Oels	Środa	Schroda
Opawa	Troppau	Świecie	Schwetz
Opole	Oppeln	Świdnica	Schweidnitz
Ostrzeszów	Schildberg	Tczew	Dirschau
Oświęcim	Auschwitz	Toruń	Thorn
Pełczysk	Bernstein	Tuchoło	Tuchel
Polnowo	Polnow	Ujście	Usch
Poznań	Posen	Wałcz	Deutsch Krone
Pozsony (Hung.)	Pressburg (German)	Wieleń	Wildenberg
	Bratislava (Czech)	Włocławek	Leslau
Pszczyna	Pless	Wołczyń	Konstadt
Pyzdry	Peisern	Wołogoszcz	Wolgast
Racibórz	Ratibor	Wschowa	Fraustadt
Santok	Zantoch	Wrocław	Breslau
Skwierzyna	Schwerin	Żagań	Sagan

APPENDIX B
GENEALOGICAL TABLES

I THE LAST PIASTS (*simplified listing*)

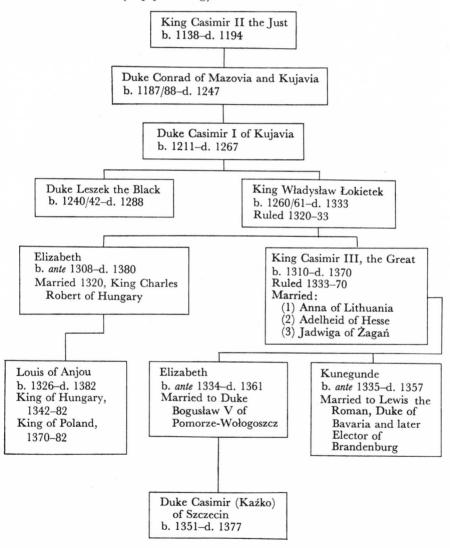

King Casimir II the Just
b. 1138–d. 1194

Duke Conrad of Mazovia and Kujavia
b. 1187/88–d. 1247

Duke Casimir I of Kujavia
b. 1211–d. 1267

Duke Leszek the Black
b. 1240/42–d. 1288

King Władysław Łokietek
b. 1260/61–d. 1333
Ruled 1320–33

Elizabeth
b. *ante* 1308–d. 1380
Married 1320, King Charles
   Robert of Hungary

King Casimir III, the Great
b. 1310–d. 1370
Ruled 1333–70
Married:
   (1) Anna of Lithuania
   (2) Adelheid of Hesse
   (3) Jadwiga of Żagań

Louis of Anjou
b. 1326–d. 1382
King of Hungary,
   1342–82
King of Poland,
   1370–82

Elizabeth
b. *ante* 1334–d. 1361
Married to Duke
   Bogusław V of
   Pomorze-Wołogoszcz

Kunegunde
b. *ante* 1335–d. 1357
Married to Lewis the
   Roman, Duke of
   Bavaria and later
   Elector of
   Brandenburg

Duke Casimir (Kaźko)
   of Szczecin
b. 1351–d. 1377

II The Piasts of Mazovia (*simplified listing*)

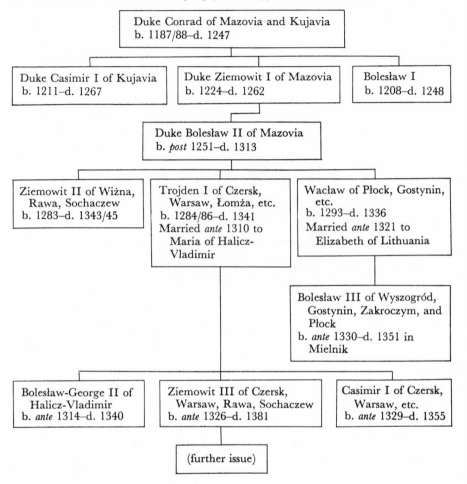

Duke Conrad of Mazovia and Kujavia
b. 1187/88–d. 1247

Duke Casimir I of Kujavia
b. 1211–d. 1267

Duke Ziemowit I of Mazovia
b. 1224–d. 1262

Bolesław I
b. 1208–d. 1248

Duke Bolesław II of Mazovia
b. *post* 1251–d. 1313

Ziemowit II of Wiżna,
Rawa, Sochaczew
b. 1283–d. 1343/45

Trojden I of Czersk,
Warsaw, Łomża, etc.
b. 1284/86–d. 1341
Married *ante* 1310 to
Maria of Halicz-
Vladimir

Wacław of Płock, Gostynin,
etc.
b. 1293–d. 1336
Married *ante* 1321 to
Elizabeth of Lithuania

Bolesław III of Wyszogród,
Gostynin, Zakroczym, and
Płock
b. *ante* 1330–d. 1351 in
Mielnik

Bolesław-George II of
Halicz-Vladimir
b. *ante* 1314–d. 1340

Ziemowit III of Czersk,
Warsaw, Rawa, Sochaczew
b. *ante* 1326–d. 1381

Casimir I of Czersk,
Warsaw, etc.
b. *ante* 1329–d. 1355

(further issue)

APPENDIX C
MOLDAVIA AND PODOLIA
IN THE REIGN OF CASIMIR

The role which Moldavia played in the eastern policy of Casimir the Great was for many years the subject of considerable misunderstanding. Much the same is true for the region of Podolia, except that even today there are sharply divergent conclusions drawn. In this appendix we shall examine the basis for the judgments made in the text about these two areas.

According to Joannes Długosz, a dispute broke out in 1359 between the two palatines of Moldavia, Stephen and Peter, over the right to rule. Stephen turned to Poland for aid, and promised to submit to Polish overlordship if Casimir would lend him assistance. In response, the Polish king conferred with his advisors, who apparently proposed that substantial aid be sent. The *pospolite ruszenie* was assembled, with contingents from both Little Poland and Ruthenia, and in June it departed from Cracow. Soon after it entered Moldavia, however, it encountered difficulties. Despite some preliminary conquests, it was increasingly subject to guerrilla attacks by Peter's adherents; and when the Polish army finally met the enemy in open battle, the encounter was a disaster! The flags of twelve Polish divisions (nine knightly and three territorial) fell into Moldavian hands, and many Polish knights were captured, forcing Casimir to ransom them later at great expense.[1]

The prestige of Długosz, the detailed information he gives, and the gap in Casimir's itinerary from June 11 to September 30 of that year[2] have led many historians to accept this campaign as fact. Thus in the two most authoritative studies of the military policy of the king, there are explicit descriptions of this expedition. One suggests that "much better known [than the Ruthenian campaigns] is the expedition of the Polish army to Moldavia in 1359";[3] while the other argues that "the expedition . . . of 1359 requires special discussion."[4] This is indeed correct, but not for the reasons given. In reality, in

1. Długosz, *Historia*, III, 277–78.

2. Henryk Paszkiewicz, *Polityka Ruska Kazimierza Wielkiego* (Warsaw, 1925), p. 204 n. 4.

3. Zdzisław Kaczmarczyk and Stefan Weyman, *Reformy wojskowe i organizacja siły zbrojnej za Kazimierza Wielkiego* (Warsaw, 1958), p. 136.

4. Karol Olejnik, *Działalność militarna Polski w czasach Kazimierza Wielkiego* (Poznań, 1966), p. 95. There is no evidence that Olejnik made any use of the researches of Spieralski or Rhode.

the words of Zdzisław Spieralski, "Casimir never carried out an expedition to Moldavia."[5]

Although Długosz's account is not confirmed by any other source, the fact of a Polish expedition to Moldavia should not automatically be regarded as a fiction. Aleksander Semkowicz pointed out nearly a century ago that Długosz was probably relying upon the family tradition of one of his contemporaries and that this should be considered a real basis for acceptance.[6] Nawój Tęczyński and Zbigniew Oleśnicki are specifically mentioned by Długosz as participants in the 1359 campaign, and this led Semkowicz to conclude that the historian based his narrative upon information given him by his friend and associate Zbigniew Cardinal Oleśnicki, chancellor of Poland, the grandson of the individual mentioned in the text.

The narrative of the fifteenth-century annalist provided the foundation for one of the most influential ideas in Polish history. Beginning with Adam Naruszewicz in the eighteenth century,[7] and expressed in a more fully developed form by Aleksander Czołowski a century later,[8] Polish historians have traditionally seen Casimir's campaign in Moldavia and conquests there[9] as the beginning of Poland's drive to the Black Sea, with Casimir the first advocate of a "Poland from Sea to Sea."[10] Within the last generation, however, three voices have arisen to question the existence of Casimir's campaign in 1359 and to challenge the interpretation of "Poland from Sea to Sea."[11] To understand the full force of the arguments by Górka, Rhode, and Spieralski, it is necessary to sketch briefly the development of Moldavia in the fourteenth century.

During the eleventh and twelfth centuries Moldavia had occasionally been ruled by the prince of Halicz, but with the Tatar invasion it had fallen under the control of the Golden Horde. As the Tatar power began in turn to wane in the late thirteenth and early fourteenth centuries, Hungarian influences had begun to flow through the passes of the Carpathians into Moldavia. By the mid-fourteenth century, a state-like organization had

5. Zdzisław Spieralski, "W sprawie rzekomej wyprawy Kazimierza Wielkiego do Mołdawii," *P.H.*, LII (1961), 147. There is no mention in this article of Rhode's work.

6. Aleksander Semkowicz, *Krytyczny rozbiór dziejów polskich Jana Długosza (do roku 1384)* (Cracow, 1887), p. 371.

7. Adam Naruszewicz, *Historya narodu polskiego od początku chrześciaństwa*, 8 vols. (Warsaw, 1780–1806), VI, 288–95. The idea had been present in embryo in previous historians. See Spieralski, "W sprawie," p. 147 n. 2.

8. Aleksander Czołowski, "Początki mołdawii i wyprawa Kazimierza Wielkiego r. 1359," *K.H.*, IV (1890), 258–85. See also his "Sprawy wołoskie w Polsce do roku 1412," *K.H.*, V (1891), 569–72.

9. Długosz mentions the territory of Șipinț but makes no assertion that the Polish army conquered it.

10. See Oskar Halecki, "Kazimierz Wielki, 1333–1370," in *Encyklopedya Polska*, V, i (Warsaw, Lublin, Łódź, and Cracow, 1920), 352; Jan Dąbrowski, *Dzieje Polski od r. 1333 do r. 1506*, vol. II of Roman Grodecki, Stanisław Zachorowski, and Jan Dąbrowski, *Dzieje Polski średniowiecznej*, 2 vols. (Cracow, 1926), p. 75; Paszkiewicz, *Polityka Ruska*, pp. 204–6 (with reservations); *Historia Polski*, general editor Tadeusz Manteuffel, vol. I, *do roku 1764*, in three parts, ed. Henryk Łowmiański (Warsaw, 1958–61), pt. i, 502; Paweł Jasienica, *Polska Piastów* (Warsaw, 1966), p. 364; Kaczmarczyk, *Kazimierz Wielki, 1333–1370* (Warsaw, 1948), pp. 175–76, but not in his *Polska czasów Kazimierza Wielkiego* (Cracow, 1964). Jacob Caro, *Geschichte Polens*, 4 vols. in 5 (Gotha, 1863–86), II, 321, is inclined to doubt Długosz's word.

11. Olgierd Górka, "Zagadnienia czarnomorskie w polityce polskiego średniowiecza," *P.H.*, XXX (1932–33), 325–91; Gotthold Rhode, *Die Ostgrenze Polens, Politische Entwicklung, kulturelle Bedeutung und geistige Auswirkung*, vol. I, *Im Mittelalter bis zum Jahre 1401* (Cologne and Graz, 1955), pp. 225–28; Spieralski, "W sprawie," pp. 147–52.

developed among the native peoples, headed by a certain Bogdan, who styled himself, in the Hungarian manner, *voevoda Moldaviensis*. This first ruler was succeeded by one named Latzko; after his death, his sons Stephen and Peter quarrelled over the inheritance. It was this which presumably occasioned Stephen's request for aid from Casimir.[12]

When the chronology of these rulers is worked out, Długosz is shown to have been somewhere in error, and the comments of the critics take on special significance. According to N. Iorga, one of the first and perhaps the greatest of Rumanian national historians, Wojewoda Bogdan lived until 1364, that is, five years after the date given in Długosz's narrative.[13] His successor, Latzko, appears in documents as late as 1372.[14] Finally, according to Rumanian sources, it was not until 1377 that Stephen and Peter quarrelled over the succession in Moldavia.[15] On the basis of this chronology it is apparent that Casimir could not have sent aid to Stephen in 1359, or in fact at any time during his reign. How then is it possible to understand the error of the Jagiellonian historian? In one manner or another, Górka, Rhode, and Spieralski all suggest that Długosz simply confused the chronology, either in an attempt to show another proof of Casimir's greatness, or (more probably) misled by a faulty collective memory of the Oleśnicki family tradition.[16]

Though it has been shown that Casimir did not send an expedition to Moldavia in 1359, two further questions remain to be answered: when we may date the expedition described by Długosz; and whether there were any Polish-Moldavian contacts in the reign of Casimir.

Stephen and Peter emerged as rulers of Moldavia in 1376, and any Polish intervention must be dated after this.[17] That it came in the next year, when the quarrel began, is strongly suggested by the fact that Johannes von Posilge records a Lithuanian expedition to Moldavia in 1377[18] and by our knowledge that the Polish overlord of Ruthenia at this time, Władysław of Opole, had very close contacts with the Gedyminowicze.[19] A final piece of evidence is Długosz's passing statement that, right after the campaign, Nawój Tęczyński went to Rome to become installed as a priest.[20] From other sources we know that Nawój became canon of Cracow in 1379.[21] A date of about 1377 has become increasingly accepted.

---

12. This brief discussion is based upon A. D. Xénopol, *Histoire des Roumains de la Dacie Trájane*, 2 vols. (Paris, 1896), I, 193–219; N. Iorga, *Histoire des Roumains et de la Romanité oriental* (Bucharest, 1937), III, 145–269; R. W. Seton-Watson, *History of the Roumanians* (Cambridge, 1934), pp. 17–32; Georg Stadtmüller, *Geschichte Südosteuropas* (Munich, 1950), pp. 206–10.

13. Iorga, *Histoire des Roumains*, III, 257–58.

14. Górka, "Zagadnienia czarnomorskie," pp. 344 f.; see also Stadtmüller, *Geschichte Südosteuropas*, p. 495.

15. Górka, "Zagadnienia czarnomorskie," pp. 345 ff.; Rhode, *Die Ostgrenze Polens*, I, 228.

16. Górka, "Zagadnienia czarnomorskie," pp. 347 f.; Rhode, *Die Ostgrenze Polens*, I, 228; 238–39; Spieralski, "W sprawie," pp. 151–52.

17. For the date of this accession to power, see P. P. Panaitescu, "Din istoria luptei pentru independentă Moldovei in veacul al XIV-lea," *Studi Revilistà de istorie*, IV (1956), 110.

18. Johannes of Posilge, *Chronik des Landes Preussen*, in *SS. rer. Pr.*, III, 106–7.

19. These connections are convincingly made by Panaitescu, "Din istoria," pp. 110–13. See also A. Sacerdoțeanu, "Lupta moldovenilor cu litvanii în 1377," in *Omagiu fraților Lapedatu* (Bucharest, 1936), pp. 773–76.

20. Długosz, *Historia*, III, 278.

21. Ludwik Łętowski, ed., *Katalog biskupów, prałatów i kanoników krakowskich*, 4 vols. (Cracow, 1852–53), IV, 153.

Even though the Polish expedition to Moldavia did not come until after Casimir's death, there were contacts between the two regions in his lifetime. During the rule of Latzko after 1365, there was an informal arrangement made with Poland to keep Hungarian ecclesiastical influences out of Moldavia.[22] As a result, Polish churchmen were sent into the region, even founding a short-lived Catholic bishopric in the Seret region.[23] In addition, it is quite probable that before 1370 the money which was used in circulation in Moldavia was struck in the royal mint in Lwów.[24]

The question of Podolia during Casimir's reign is a more difficult one. This area lies to the east of Halicz. During the first waves of the Tatar invasions, it and its chief city, Kamieniec, had come under the domination of the Golden Horde and had regularly thereafter paid tribute to the khan.[25] During the reign of Khan Ğambek, however, the Tatar yoke had gradually disappeared from Podolia, and by the time of the great civil war within the Horde after 1359, there was little Tatar influence there.[26] Had no other authority taken control in Podolia, there would have been a power vacuum in a region geographically athwart the east-west trade routes and *Wanderungwege*. According to Joannes Długosz, this did not happen, for before 1352 Casimir had intervened in this area and subjected it to Polish authority.

Using a source which modern scholars have been unable to identify, Długosz reports for the year 1352 that "the Tatars, gathered into a great force, ravaged the land of Podolia, which was subject to the Kingdom of Poland."[27] Since there is no reference to a Polish conquest of Podolia in contemporary sources, since no other source confirms Długosz's statement, and since the Jagiellonian historian was fully capable of reading later developments back into the past,[28] one might be inclined to disregard his statement. Yet his reference, parenthetical as it may be, was not lightly or unconsciously written. On two other occasions he repeated his original assertion. For the year 1396 he speaks of "Podolia, which Casimir the Second [that is, Casimir the Great], the best king of Poland, had acquired by weapons and sword from the power and control of the Tatars";[29] for 1448 he records that during the discussion of Podolia, the Polish magnates said "that it is well known Casimir the second, King of Poland, conquered this afore-mentioned territory of Podolia from the Tatars."[30]

Długosz's statement that by 1352 Podolia was under Polish control has been accepted by many Polish scholars. In 1895 Antoni Prochaska, one of the greatest and most highly respected scholars of prewar Poland, wrote a brilliant essay elaborating upon Długosz's assertion.[31] His basic conclusion that Długosz was correct was widely accepted for many

22. *Istorija Moldavii*, ed. A. D. Udalcov and L. V. Čerepnin, vol. I (Kišinev, 1951), 89.

23. See Władysław Abraham, *Powstanie organizacyi kościoła łacińskiego na Rusi* (Lwów, 1904), I, 282–87.

24. Rhode, *Die Ostgrenze Polens*, I, 227.

25. Berthold Spuler, *Die Goldene Horde. Die Mongolen in Russland, 1223–1502* (Leipzig, 1943), pp. 20, 91, 117.

26. George Vernadsky, *The Mongols and Russia* (New Haven, Conn., 1953), pp. 245–63.

27. Długosz, *Historia*, III, 245.

28. See Heinrich Zeissberg, *Die Polnische Geschichtsschreibung des Mittelalters* (Leipzig, 1873), pp. 334–35, and the comments of Janina Hoskins in the *American Historical Review*, LXXIII (1967–68), 682. Długosz was writing during the fifteenth-century dispute between Poland and Lithuania, and since he was no great friend of the latter, he might well have had reason to proclaim prior Polish rights to Podolia.

29. Długosz, *Historia*, III, 519.

30. Ibid., V, 48.

31. Antoni Prochaska, "Podole lennem Korony 1352–1430," *R.A.U.*, XXXII (1895), 256–79.

years, even though there was disagreement among scholars as to the date of the beginning of Polish suzerainty in Podolia. All were agreed, however, that it came during Casimir's reign. This position still finds important representatives today.

The semiofficial *Historia Polski*, published by the Historical Institute of the Polish Academy of Sciences, places the origins of Polish overlordship in Podolia in 1349, with the Korjatowicze as Casimir's vassals.[32] This cooperative effort represents the best of contemporary Polish scholarship. Another collective work takes essentially the same view. The volume *Polska i jej dorobek dziejowy* was prepared by several emigré scholars and was published in London in 1956. Although Leon Koczy, who wrote the historical section on the Piast dynasty, mentions neither Podolia nor its relationship to the Kingdom, the map *Polska Kazimierza Wielkiego—1370* clearly shows this area as a Polish fief.[33] Three more recent works on the Piasts and Casimir have done nothing to alter Prochaska's original conclusion. Józef Sieradzki, Paweł Jasienica, and Zdisław Kaczmarczyk all accept Polish suzerainty over Podolia. The first simply assumes it;[34] the second makes a flat, undocumented statement, placing the beginning of this relationship in 1349;[35] and the last, who is the most careful student of Casimir's reign, argues for the capture of Podolia on the expedition of 1349 and its subsequent transfer to the Korjatowicze as a Polish fief.[36]

One of the elements which provides a strong argument in favor of these views is the close relationship of George and Alexander Korjatowicz to Casimir.[37] In 1365 the former is mentioned as a witness to a document by the king,[38] while in the next year both appear in Casimir's treaty with the Lithuanians as Ruthenian allies and vassals of the Polish king.[39] In addition, Janko of Czarnków, when describing events of 1366, spoke of Alexander as Casimir's *fidelissimus princeps*.[40] Prochaska, Stefan Kuczyński, and Zygmunt Wojciechowski have combined these facts with Długosz's statement and concluded that the two Korjatowicze also held Podolia as a fief from Casimir.[41] Other scholars have essentially agreed.[42]

32. *Historia Polski*, I, i, 500. See also map 4 in the *Atlas* (I, iii) which shows Podolia as a Polish fief.

33. *Polska i jej dorobek dziejowy w ciągu tysiąca lat istnienia*, ed. Henryk Paszkiewicz, vol. I (London, 1956), 113. The views of the editor are somewhat different. See below.

34. Józef Sieradzki, *Polska wieku XIV. Studium z czasów Kazimierza Wielkiego* (Warsaw, 1959), map 3.

35. Jasienica, *Polska Piastów*, p. 330.

36. Kaczmarczyk, *Polska czasów Kazimierza*, pp. 63, 66. In his earlier *Monarchia Kazimierza Wielkiego*, 2 vols. (Poznań, 1939–46), I, 41, Kaczmarczyk was less certain: "Of the Korjatowicze, Prince Alexander may have been Casimir's vassal in Podolia . . . however, the feudal status of Podolia is not certain, and neither is the date of its acquisition by the Korjatowicze." In his article on Casimir for the *Pol. Słow. Biog.*, XII, 266, Kaczmarczyk simply says, "On his expedition to the east in 1366, Casimir also added to his Kingdom . . . Podolia as a Polish fief."

37. On the Korjatowicze, see above, chap. 6.

38. Paszkiewicz, *O genezie i wartości Krewa* (Warsaw, 1938), p. 280.

39. See A. Czuczyński, "Traktat książąt Litewskich z Kazimierzem Wielkim z roku 1366," *K.H.*, (1890), 513–15, and the German translation in Rhode, *Die Ostgrenze Polens*, I, 381–82.

40. Janko of Czarnków, *Chronicon Polonorum*, in *M.P.H.*, II, 631.

41. Prochaska, "Podole lennem Korony," p. 259; Stefan Kuczyński, "Sine Wody. Rzecz o wyprawie Olgierdowej 1362 r.," in *Księga ku czci Oskara Haleckiego* (Warsaw, 1936), p. 89; Zygmunt Wojciechowski, *L'Etat Polonais au Moyen-age* (Paris, 1949), p. 133.

42. For example, Jozef Puzyna, "Korjat i Korjatowicze oraz sprawa Podolska," *Ateneum Wileńskie*, XI (1936), 71, and "Pierwsze wystąpienie Korjatowiczów na Rusi południowej," *Ateneum Wileńskie*, XIII (1938), 53; Spuler, *Die Goldene Horde*, pp. 107–8.

Not all, however, have been willing to accept these conclusions. The most recent criticism of these views has come from Gotthold Rhode, who suggests that there are two fundamental weaknesses to the reasoning expressed above.[43] First, the Lithuanian-Ruthenian chronicle says that the Korjatowicze gained their territory in Podolia with Lithuanian help after the battle in 1362 or 1363 of *Sine wody* (The Blue Waters); and second, there is no extant document issued by the Korjatowicze which prove they were in Podolia before 1370.

According to the Lithuanian-Ruthenian chronicle,[44]

> When Grand Prince Olgierd was Lord of the Ruthenian land, he went into the steppes with the Lithuanian army, and at the "Blue Waters"[45] he defeated the Tatars, which included three brothers, Chaczibej, Kotlobug, and Demetrius.[46] These three brothers were the heirs of the land of Podolia. From them the collectors [of the Tatars] took tribute. The brother of the Grand Prince, however, Korjat, had four sons: George, Alexander, Constantine, and Theodore. Of them, with the permission of Olgierd and the help of the Lithuanians, three were set up to rule in Podolia. And when they were come, they signed a treaty of friendship with the Hetmen and stopped giving tribute to the collectors.[47]

The battle of the Blue Waters was thus, according to this account, decisive in Podolian affairs.

The followers of Prochaska do not deny the evidence of the Lithuanian-Ruthenian chronicle, but do dispute some of its details. They argue that Casimir had conquered the western part of Podolia on his campaign in 1349 before the Lithuanians came into the area. At the same time, or perhaps even slightly before, the Korjatowicze seized the northeastern part of Podolia and at some later time, probably 1366, accepted Polish suzerainty in return for rule over the rest of the region. If this view is accepted, the battle of *Sine wody* in 1362 or 1363 becomes an encounter of only local significance that had nothing at all to do with the fate of Podolia.[48] These same scholars attack the problem of lack of documentation for the presence of the Korjatowicze by pointing out the general paucity of records for this era of eastern European history.[49]

43. Rhode, *Die Ostgrenze Polens*, I, 221. To the best of my knowledge, Polish historians have totally ignored this aspect of Rhode's work.

44. This chronicle, printed in a Latin-letter transliteration by I. Daniłowicz, *Latopisiec litewski i Kronika ruska* (Vilno, 1827), is actually based on only one of five manuscripts which bear this title. The *Codex suprasliensis* formed the basis of Daniłowicz's edition, but the other four (Akademia, Krasinski, Raczynski, and Bychova codices) are very similar, and for this period almost identical. The best modern edition of all is the Cyrillic one in *Polnoe sobranie Russkich letopisej*, 26 vols. (St. Petersburg and Moscow, 1841–), XVII, ed. S. L. Ptashichij and A. A. Schachmatov.

45. The "Blue Waters" is either Sinjucha, a tributary of the Bug River which flows to the Black Sea, or Sinwodji on the border of Podolia and Volhynia. See Mykhailo Hrushevsky, *Istoria Ukrainy Rusi*, 10 vols. (reprinted, New York, 1955), IV, 82, who prefers the latter, and Spuler, *Die Goldene Horde*, p. 116, who prefers the former.

46. For these princes, see Spuler, *Die Goldene Horde*, pp. 116–17.

47. The details of this campaign are also reflected in sources associated with the Teutonic Order. See *SS. rer. Pr.*, III, 144.

48. Kuczyński, "Sine Wody," p. 132; Puzyna, "Korjat i Korjatowicze oraz sprawa Podolska," p. 71; and, though less definitely, Spuler, *Die Goldene Horde*, pp. 106–8, 117.

49. Even Rhode, *Die Ostgrenze Polens*, I, 201 n. 158, who is otherwise critical of the conclusions reached by many concerning Podolia, is forced to admit that "In kaum einem Zeitab-

In reply to these explanations, Rhode has remarked that our sources offer no proof whatsoever for an expedition by Casimir into Podolia in 1349, and that such a campaign is highly improbable.[50] Even though Casimir's campaign in 1349 was extremely successful, it took at the most one hundred days, for the king's presence in Poland on September 1 and December 5 can be demonstrated.[51] Had he gone into Podolia to Kamieniec, his route of march, including the cities he besieged and conquered, would have taken him through Sandomir-Lwów-Halicz-Kamieniec-Lwów-Bełz-Vladimir-Brześć-Chełm-Sandomir· in some three months, a distance of over a thousand miles.[52] This would have been an impossible pace, even with his light, mobile troops. Rhode also dismisses, again with good reason, the possibility that Casimir sent a separate army to take Podolia. Though the king might send a detachment to some nearby target (such as Łuck during the siege of Vladimir), he never dispatched troops on an extended mission. He had seen too clearly at Płowce in 1331 the danger an army ran when it divided its forces. Finally, according to Rhode, there could have been no conquest of Podolia before 1352, since Casimir's presence is accounted for in 1350, 1351, and 1352; and Podolia is not mentioned in the Polish-Lithuanian treaty of 1352, which would certainly have been the case had it been subject to Poland.

Another possibility for the entrance of the Korjatowicze into Podolia has been suggested by Jozef Puzyna, who feels that Casimir may have lent Alexander Korjatowicz aid in 1350 which led to the conquest of Podolia by him and his brother George in that year.[53] Rhode correctly points out that this suggestion is pure hypothesis, unsupported by facts, and does not correspond to what could be considered probable in that year of constant hostilities against the aggressive Lithuanians.[54]

An examination of the ages of the Korjatowicze reveals further difficulties in arguing for their early entrance into Podolia. Korjat was born about the same time as Casimir, in 1310.[55] Thus he was barely of age when he received Nowogródek in 1329. His oldest sons could not have been born much before 1330. The others, with whom we are concerned, were born much later,[56] and were still teenagers in 1349–50. Although it would not have been impossible for them to have conquered territory at this age, it is highly unlikely. They were not sons of an important and powerful prince who could easily supply them with men and material. They had to depend, as in the case of *Sine wody*, upon the support of others. During the 1350s they probably held minor territories in Volhynia, but their adventures and conquests had to come later, when they received aid from their uncle. It is only in 1366 that we meet them as vassals of Casimir in Ruthenia.

There is thus no evidence to support Długosz's statement that Podolia belonged to Poland as early as 1352 and little reason to believe that the Korjatowicze were there until the aftermath of *Sine wody*. When the Korjatowicze became Casimir's vassals in

---

schnitt ist die Quellenlage für die Entwicklung im polnisch-reussischen Grenzraum so ungünstig wie um die Mitte des 14. Jh."

50. Ibid., 221–22.

51. See Paszkiewicz, *Polityka Ruska*, p. 118 n. 1.

52. I differ here with Rhode on the route of march. See Kaczmarczyk and Weyman, *Reformy wojskowe*, pp. 126–27 and map.

53. Puzyna, "Korjat i Korjatowicze oraz sprawa Podolska," p. 71.

54. Rhode, *Die Ostgrenze Polens*, I, 222–23.

55. Kazimierz Stadnicki, *Synowie Giedymina*, 2 vols. (Lwów, 1848–51), I, 140.

56. Puzyna, "Korjat i Korjatowicze," p. 453.

Ruthenia in 1366, they did not also accept Polish suzerainty over Podolia. This territory they ruled as independent Lithuanian princes. Neither is there any evidence to indicate that between 1366 and 1370 this situation was in any way altered. Finally, there is no real basis to speak of Podolia as a Polish fief before 1370.

Gotthold Rhode has been the sharpest critic of the traditional view on Podolia, but he has not been the only scholar to question Długosz's statement and the position taken by Antoni Prochaska. Both Oskar Halecki and Henryk Paszkiewicz have also been reluctant to accept these assertions. Of the two, Halecki is the more cautious, preferring to say only that whatever holdings the Korjatowicz had in Podolia came through the aid of Olgierd.[57] Paszkiewicz is more definite. In his early *Polityka Ruska Kazimierza Wielkiego*,[58] he avoided dealing with the question directly, though he did lean slightly toward Prochaska's traditional view. In the following decade his understanding of the role of the Korjatowicze began to change, and in 1938 he published an appendix to his *O genezie i wartości Krewa* which presented his mature opinion. Here he denied that the Korjatowicze had held Podolia before 1370. He reasoned, first, that they issued no known documents from there before 1370, and, second, that the only source which places them there, the Lithuanian-Ruthenian chronicle, is unreliable. It was written in the fifteenth century at the height of the Polish-Lithuanian conflict over Podolia, and much of its information has a partisan character which casts doubt on its validity. Paszkiewicz also categorically denied any Polish suzerainty over Podolia before 1370.[59] On the whole, the balance weighs more heavily on the side of Halecki, Paszkiewicz, and Rhode.[60]

57. Oskar Halecki, *Dzieje unii jagiellońskiej*, 2 vols. (Cracow, 1919), I, 70–71. The question of Podolia is not really touched upon in his "Kazimierz Wielki."

58. Paszkiewicz, *Polityka Ruska*, pp. 228–31, 248.

59. Paszkiewicz, *Krewo*, p. 298. See also his contribution to *Polska i jej dorobek dziejowy*, I, 118.

60. An excellent survey of research on the Korjatowicze to 1938 is given by Stefan Krakowski, "Korjatowicze i sprawa Podolska w XIV wieku w oświetleniu najnowszej historjografji Polskiej," *Ateneum Wileńskie*, XIII (1938), 250–74.

BIBLIOGRAPHY

Bibliographies, Handbooks, and Historiographical Studies

Adamus, Jan, "O syntezach historycznych Szujskiego Szkic z dziejów polskiej myśli historycznej," in *Studia historyczne ku czci Stanisława Kutrzeby*, 2 vols. (Cracow, 1938), II, 1–27.

Arnold, Stanisław, *Geografia historyczna Polski* (Warsaw, 1951).

Balzer, Oswald, *Genealogia Piastów* (Cracow, 1895).

Baszkiewicz, Jan, "Poglądy Stanisława Kutrzeby na państwo," *Państwo i Prawo*, V, pt. x (1950), 60–75.

Baumgart, Jan, ed., *Bibliografia historii polskiej*. Volumes for 1948 (Cracow, 1952), 1949, 1950–51, 1952–53 (Wrocław, 1954, 1955, 1956), 1954, 1955 (Wrocław and Cracow, 1957, 1958).

Baumgart, Jan, and Anna Malcówna, eds., *Bibliografia historii polskiej*. Volumes for 1956–57, 1958, 1959 (Wroclaw and Cracow, 1960, 1961), 1960, 1961, 1962, 1963, 1964, 1965, 1966 (Wrocław, Warsaw, and Cracow, 1962, 1963, 1964, 1965, 1966, 1967, 1968).

Baumgart, Jan, and Stanisław Głuszek, eds., *Bibliografia historii Polskiej za lata 1944–1947*. (Wrocław, Warsaw, and Cracow, 1962).

Bibliografia Historii Polski, general editor Helena Madurowicz-Urbańskiej, vol. I, *do roku 1795*, in three parts (Warsaw, 1965).

Čapek, T., and A. V. Čapek, *Bohemian (Čech) Bibliography* (New York, Chicago, London, and Edinburgh, 1918).

Chevalier, Ulysse, ed., *Répertoire des Sources historiques du Moyen-Age: Bio-bibliographie*, 2 vols. (Paris, 1905–7).

———, ed., *Répertoire des Sources historiques du Moyen-Age: Topo-bibliographie*, 2 vols. in 1 (Montbéliard, 1894).

Cottineau, L. H., *Répertoire topo-bibliographique des Abbayes et Prieurés*, 2 vols. (Macon, 1939).

Dahlmann, F. C., and G. Waitz, *Quellenkunde der Deutschen Geschichte*, editor-in-chief Hermann Haering, 2 vols., 9th ed. (Leipzig, 1931–32).

Daniłowicz, Ignacy, "Wiadomość o właściwych litewskich latopiscach," in Maciej Stryjkowski, *Kronika Polska . . .*, 2 vols. (Warsaw, 1846), I, 31–63.

David, Pierre, *Les sources de l'histoire de Pologne à l'époque des Piasts, 963–1386* (Paris, 1934).

Dąbrowski, Jan, *Dawne Dziejopisarstwo Polskie* (Wrocław, Warsaw, and Cracow, 1964).

———, "Stanisław Kutrzeba," *Nowa Polska*, VI (1946), 185–92.

Eubel, Conrad, ed., *Hierarchia Catholica Medii Aevi*, 2 vols. (Regensburg, 1913–14).

Finkel, Ludwik, *Bibliografia historii Polskiej*, 3 vols. (reprinted, Warsaw, 1955).

————, "Karol Szajnocha, Próba ujęcia syntezy i genezy poglądów historjograficznych wielkiego pisarza," *Ziemia Czerwieńska*, I (1935), 1–17.

————, "Marcin Kromer, Historyk polski XVI wieku. Rozbiór krytyczny," *R.A.U.*, XVI (1883), 302–508.

Gams, Pius Bonifacius, ed., *Series Episcoporum ecclesiae catholicae* (Leipzig, 1931).

Gebhardt, Bruno, *Handbuch der Deutschen Geschichte*, 4 vols., ed. Herbert Grundmann, et al., 8th ed. (Stuttgart, 1954).

Graesse, J. G. T., *Orbis Latinus, oder Verzeichnis der wichtigsten lateinischen Orts- und Ländernamen* (Berlin, 1922).

Hahn, Wiktor, "Karol Szajnocha jako autor dramatyczny. W 80-rocznicę śmierci 1868–1948," *Roczniki Zakładu Narodowego im. Ossolińskich*, III (1948), 471–528.

Halecki, Oskar, "Potrzeby nauki polskiej w dziedzinie historji," *Nauka Polska*, X (1929), 259–65.

Herbst, Stanisław, and Irena Pietrzak-Pawłowska, eds., *Polskie Towarzystwo Historyczne 1886–1956. Księga pamiątkowa z okazji Zjazdu Jubileuszowego PTH w Warszawie 19–21 X 1956* (Warsaw, 1956).

Howe, George Frederick, et al., eds., *The American Historical Association's Guide to Historical Literature* (New York, 1961).

Hulewicz, Jan, *Polska Akademia Umiejętności 1873–1948, Zarys dziejów* (Cracow, 1948).

Jasiński, Kazimierz, "Uzupełnienia do genealogii Piastów," *Studia Źródłoznawcze*, III (1958), 199–212; V (1960), 89–111.

"Jubileusz 50-lecia P.T.H. i Kwartalnika Historycznego," *K.H.*, LI (1937), 643–53.

Kerner, Robert J., *The Foundations of Slavic Bibliography* (Chicago, 1916).

Kieniewicz, Stefan, "Tło historyczne 'Dziejów Polski' M. Bobrzyńskiego," *P.H.*, XXXVII (1947), 343–56.

Kirmis, Max, *Handbuch der polnischen Münzkunde* (Poznań, 1892).

Klauser, R., and O. Meyer, *Clavis Mediaevalis: Kleines Wörterbuch der Mittelalterforschung* (Wiesbaden, 1962).

Korzon, Tadeusz, "Pogląd na działalność J. Lelewela," *K.H.*, XI (1897), 257–309.

Kubala, Ludwik, "Jan Czarnkowski i jego kronika," *Biblioteka Warszawska*, XXXI (1871), pt. iii, 348–65; pt. iv, 59–75.

Kürbisówna, Brygida, *Dziejopisarstwo Wielkopolskie XIII i XIV wieku* (Warsaw, 1959).

Kutrzeba, Stanisław, *Polska Akademia Umiejętności 1872–1937* (Cracow, 1938).

Libiszowska, Zofia, "Tendencje społeczne i polityczne dramatów Józefa Szujskiego," *Prace Polonistyczne*, X (1952), 285–301.

Łętowski, Ludwik, ed., *Katalog biskupów, prałatów i kanoników krakowskich*, 4 vols. (Cracow, 1852–53).

Łowmiański, Henryk, "Les recherches sur l'histoire du moyen age jusqu'à la fin du XVe s. au cours vingt années de la République Populaire de Pologne," *La Pologne au XIIe Congrès International des sciences historiques à Vienne* (Warsaw, 1965), pp. 165–202.

Macartney, C. A., *The Medieval Hungarian Historians, A Critical and Analytical Guide* (Cambridge, 1953).

Malinowski, Mikołaj, "Wiadomość o życiu i pismach Macieja Stryjkowskiego," in Maciej Stryjkowski, *Kronika Polska . . .*, 2 vols. (Warsaw, 1846), I, 1–30.

Moszczeńska, Wanda, "O interpretację Janka z Czarnkowa," *K.H.*, XL (1926), 400–8.

Osborne, R. H., *East Central Europe, An Introductory Geography* (New York, 1967).

Paetow, John L., *A Guide to the Study of Medieval History*, rev. ed., (New York, 1931).

Pamięci Oswalda Balzera, Przemówienia na uroczystej Akademji urządzonej staraniem Towarzystwa Naukowego 22 Stycznia 1934 (Lwów, 1934).

Polski Słownik biograficzny (Cracow [later, also Warsaw and Wrocław], 1935–).

Potthast, August, ed., *Bibliotheca Historica Medii Aevi: Wegweiser durch die Geschichtswerke des europäischen Mittelalters bis 1500*, 2 vols., 2d ed. (Berlin, 1896).

Pounds, Norman, *Poland Between East and West* (New York, 1964).

Quirin, Heinz, *Einführung in das Studium der mittelalterlichen Geschichte* (Braunschweig, 1961).

Rautenberg, Otto, *Ost- und Westpreussen: Ein Wegweiser durch die Zeitschriftenliteratur* (Leipzig, 1897).

Repertorium fontium historiae Medii Aevi ..., edited by Walther Holtzmann and Raffaello Morghen, vols. I-II (Rome, 1962–).

Rutkowska, Neomisia, *Bishop A. Naruszewicz and His History of the Polish Nation. A Critical Study* (Washington, D.C., 1941).

Semkowicz, A., *Krytyczny rozbiór Dziejów polskich Jana Długosza (do roku 1384)* (Cracow, 1887).

Semkowicz-Zarembina, Wanda, *Powstanie i dzieje autografu Annalium Jana Długosza* (Cracow, 1952).

Serejski, M. H., "Wstęp," in *Joachim Lelewel, Wybór pism politycznych* (Warsaw, 1954), pp. v-xlix.

Sieradzki, Józef, "Sprawa Janka z Czarnkowa i jego utwór," *Studia Źródłoznawcze*, IV (1959), 33–57.

Słownik Geograficzny Królestwa Polskiego i innych krajów słowiańskich, 15 vols. (Warsaw, 1880–1902).

Smolenski, Władysław, *Szkoły historyczne w Polsce*, 4th ed. (Wrocław, 1952).

Ślaski, Kazimierz, *Wątki historyczne w podaniach o początkach Polski* (Poznań, 1968).

Ten Haaf, Rudolf, *Kurze Bibliographie zur Geschichte des Deutschen Ordens 1198–1561* (Kitzingen am Main, 1949).

Więckowska, Helena, "Wstęp," in *Joachim Lelewel, Wybór pism historycznych* (Wrocław, 1950), pp. iii-lix.

Wielka Encyklopedya Powszechna Illustrowana, series I, 48 vols. (Warsaw, 1890–1912); series II, 5 vols. (Warsaw, 1903–7).

Włodarski, Bronisław, ed., *Chronologia Polska* (Warsaw, 1957).

Zeissberg, Heinrich, *Die polnische Geschichtsschreibung des Mittelalters* (Leipzig, 1873).

Zíbrt, Čeněk, *Bibliografie české historie*, 5 vols. (Prague, 1900–1912).

Ziffer, Bernard, *Poland, History and Historians, Three Bibliographical Essays* (New York, 1952).

SOURCES

A. Collections of Sources

Akta grodzkie i ziemskie z czasów Rzeczypospolitej Polskiej z Archiwum tak zwanego Bernardyńskiego w Lwowie ..., 25 vols. (Lwów, 1868–1935).

Eccardus, J. G., ed., *Corpus Historicum Medii Aevi ...*, 2 vols. (Leipzig, 1723).

Fontes rerum Austriacarum: Österreichische Geschichtsquellen, Erste Abtheilung: *Scriptores*, 9 vols. (Vienna, 1855–75).

Fontes rerum Bohemicarum, edited by F. Palacký and J. Emler, 7 vols. (Prague, 1873–1932).

Fontes rerum Germanicarum, edited by J. F. Böhmer, 4 vols, (Stuttgart, 1843–68).

Historiae Hungaricae fontes domestici, edited by M. Florianus, 4 vols. (Fünfkirchen and Leipzig, 1881–85).

Joannis Długossii Senioris Canonici Cracoviensis Opera Omnia, edited by A. Przezdziecki, 14 vols. (Cracow, 1863–87).

Monumenta Germaniae Historica, Scriptores, 32 vols. (Hanover, Leipzig, and Hahn, 1826–1934).

Monumenta Germaniæ Historica, Scriptores rerum Germanicarum nova Series, vols. I-XII (Berlin and Weimar, 1922–).

Monumenta Historica Boemiae, edited by G. Dobner, 6 vols. (Prague, 1764–85).

Monumenta Medii Aevi historica res gestas Poloniae illustrantia: Pomniki dziejowe wieków średnich do objaśnienia rzeczy polskich służące, 19 vols. (Cracow, 1874–1927).

Monumenta Poloniae historica: Pomniki dziejowe Polski, edited by A. Bielowski and the Akademia Umiejętności w Krakowie, 6 vols. (Lwów 1864–93 [vol. VI, Cracow], reprinted Warsaw, 1960–61); *Nova series*, vols. I–IV, VI–VII (Cracow and Warsaw, 1946–).

Monumenta Poloniae Vaticana (Cracow, 1913–), vols. I, II, *Acta Camerae Apostolicae*, edited by J. Ptaśnik (Cracow, 1913); vol. III, *Analecta Vaticana*, edited by J. Ptaśnik (Cracow, 1914).

Polnoe sobranie russkich letopisej, 26 vols. (St. Petersburg and Moscow, 1841–).

Pomniki do dziejów litewskich, edited by T. Narbutt (Vilno, 1846).

Rerum Bohemicarum antiqui scriptores, edited by C. V. Marquard Freher (Hanover, 1602).

Rerum Italicarum Scriptores, edited by L. A. Muratori, 25 vols. plus indexes (Milan, 1723–51).

Scriptores rerum Austriacarum veteres ac genuini . . ., edited by Hieronymus Pez, 3 vols. (Leipzig and Ratisbon, 1721–45).

Scriptores rerum Bohemicarum, edited by F. M. Pelzel, J. Dobrovský, and F. Palacký, 3 vols. (Prague, 1783–1829).

Scriptores rerum Hungaricarum veteres ac genuini . . ., edited by J. G. Schwandtner, 3 vols. (Vienna, 1746–48).

Scriptores rerum Prussicarum: Die Geschichtsquellen der preussischen Vorzeit bis zum Untergange der Ordensherrschaft, edited by Theodore Hirsch, Max Töppen, and Ernst Strehlke, 5 vols. (Leipzig, 1861–74).

Silesiacarum rerum Scriptores aliquot adhuc inediti, edited by Wilhelm Sommersberg, 3 vols. (Leipzig, 1729–32).

Urstisius, Christian, ed., *Germaniae Historicorum illustrium* . . ., 2 vols. (Frankfurt, 1585).

B. Individual Sources

Albertus Argentinus, *Chronicon integrum* . . ., in Christian Urstisius, ed., *Germaniae Historicorum illustrium* . . ., 2 vols. (Frankfurt, 1585), II, 97–166.

Annales ecclesiastici . . ., compiled by Caesar Baronius, Odericus Raynaldus, and Jacob Laderchius, new edition by Augustin Theiner, vols. I–XXVII (Bar-le-Duc, 1864–74); vols. XXVIII–XXXVII (Paris and Bar-le-Duc, 1887).

Annales Matseenses, in *M.G.H. SS.*, IX, 823–37.

Annales Mechoviensis, in *M.G.H. SS.*, XIX, 666–77 (see *Rocznik miechowski*).

Annales Posnanienses, in *M.P.H.*, V, 874–84.

Archivum coronae regni Bohemiae, edited by V. Hrubý, 2 vols. (Prague, 1928–35).

Beneš Krabice z Weitmil, *Chronicon Ecclesiae Pragensis, 1283–1374*, in *SS. rer. Boh.*, II, 199–424; and *Font. rer. Boh.*, IV, 460–548.

Beneš minorita, *Chronicon*, in *Mon. Hist. Boem.*, IV, 23–78.

Böhmer, J. F. *Regesta imperii*, vol. VIII, *Die Regesten des Kaiserreichs unter Kaiser Karl IV, 1346–1378*, edited by A. Huber (Innsbruck, 1887).

Breslauer Urkundenbuch, edited by Georg Korn (Wrocław, 1870).

Chronica Cracoviae, in *Silesiacarum rerum Scriptores aliquot adhuc inediti*, edited by Wilhelm Sommersberg, 3 vols. (Leipzig, 1729–32), II, 78–155.

Chronica Olivensis, in *M.P.H.*, VI, 310–50.

Chronica principum Poloniae, in *M.P.H.*, III, 423–578.

Chronica terrae Prussiae, in *M.P.H.*, IV, 31–40.

Chronicon aule regiae, in *Font. rer. Boh.*, IV, 3–337; *Mon. Hist. Boem.*, V, 19–501; *Rerum Bohemicarum . . .*, pp. 21–85.

Chronicon Budense, edited by Iosephus Podhradczky (Buda, 1838).

Chronicon Dubnicense, in *Historiae Hungaricae fontes domestici*, edited by M. Florianus, 4 vols. (Fünfkirchen and Leipzig, 1881–85), III; and (fragment) in *K.H.*, III (1889), 205–13.

Codex diplomaticus Brandenburgensis, edited by Adolph Friedrich Riedel, 41 vols. (Berlin, 1838–69).

Codex diplomaticus et epistolaris Moraviae, edited by A. Boczek, et al., 15 vols. (Olomouc and Brno, 1836–1903).

Codex diplomaticus Hungariae ecclesiasticus et civilis, edited by György Fejer, 11 vols. (Buda, 1829–44).

Codex diplomaticus Majoris Poloniae, edited by Ignacy Zakrzewski and Franciszek Piekosiński, 5 vols. (Poznań, 1877–1908).

Codex diplomaticus Poloniae Minoris, edited by Franciszek Piekosiński, 4 vols. (Cracow, 1876–1905) (vols. III, IX, X, and XVII of *Monumenta medii Aevi historica res gestas Poloniae illustrantia*).

Codex diplomaticus Poloniae, quo continentur privilegia . . . ad annum 1506, edited by Leon Rzyszczewski, Antoni Muczkowski, et al., 4 vols. in 6 (Warsaw, 1847–87).

Codex diplomaticus Prussicus, edited by Johannes Voigt, 6 vols. (Königsberg, 1836–61).

Codex diplomaticus universitatis studii generalis Cracoviensis, 5 vols. (Cracow, 1870–1900).

Czuczyński, A., "Traktat książąt Litewskich z Kazimierzem Wielkim z roku 1366," *K.H.*, IV (1890), 513–15.

Dogiel, Matthias, ed., *Codex diplomaticus regni Poloniae et magni ducatas Lithuaniae . . .*, 3 vols. (I, IV, and V) (Vilno, 1758–64).

———, ed., *Limites regni Poloniae et magni Ducatus Lithuaniae . . .* (Vilno, 1758).

Dokumenty kujawskie i mazowieckie, przeważnie z XIII wieku, edited by Bolesław Ulanowski (Cracow, 1888).

Dumont, J., ed., *Corps universel diplomatique du droit des gens . . .*, 8 vols. (Amsterdam and The Hague, 1726–31).

Fransiscus Pragensis, *Chronica Pragensis 1125–1353*, in *SS. rer. Boh.*, II, 1–196; *Mon. Hist. Boem.*, VI, 253 ff.; *Font. rer. Boh.*, II, 199–424; *Font. rer. Aust.*, VIII, 535–606.

Franciscus Thorunensis, *Annales Prussici, 941–1410*, in *SS. rer. Pr.*, III, 57–316.

Galvaneus Flamma, *Opusculum de rebus gestis ab Azone Luchino et Johanne vicecomitatibus ab anno 1328–1342*, in *Rerum Italicarum Scriptores*, XII, 997–1050.

Grünhagen, Colmar, and E. Markgraf, eds., *Lehns- und Besitzurkunden Schlesiens und seiner einzelnen Fürstentümer im Mittelalter*, 2 vols. (Leipzig, 1881–83).

Gustinskaja letopis' in *Pol. sob. rus. letop.*, II.

Hansisches Urkundenbuch, edited by K. Hohlbaum, et al., 5 vols. (Halle and Leipzig, 1876–99).

Henricus de Rebdorf, *Annales imperatorum et paparum 1294–1362*, in *Font. rer. Germ.*, IV, 507–68; *M.G.H. SS.*, *n.S.*, I.

Hermannus de Wartberge, *Chronicon Livoniae, 1200–1378*, in *SS. rer. Pr.*, II, 1–116.

Janko of Czarnków, *Chronicon Polonorum*, in *M.P.H.*, II, 619–756.

Johannes Długosz, *Annales seu Cronicae incliti regni Poloniae*, vol. I (Warsaw, 1964).

—————, *Historia Polonica*, 5 vols. (Cracow, 1873–78) (vols. X–XIV of *Joannis Dlugossii . . . Opera Omnia*).

Johannes de Cornazanis, *Chronica abbreviata (Parmensis) ab a. 1085 ad. a. 1355*, in *Rerum Italicarum Scriptores*, XII, 729–50.

Johannes de Thurócz, *Chronica Hungarorum*, in *Scriptores rerum Hungaricarum veteres ac genuini . . .*, edited by J. G. Schwandtner, 3 vols. (Vienna, 1746–48), I, 39–291.

Johannes of Posilge, *Chronik des Landes Preussen*, in *SS. rer. Pr.*, III, 79–388.

Johannes Victoriensis, *Chronicon Carinthiae 1211–1343*, in *Font. rer. Germ.*, I, 271–450; *SS. rer. Aust.*, I, 751–966.

Johannes Vitoduranus, *Chronicon a Friderico imperatore ad annum 1348*, in J. G. Eccardus, ed., *Corpus Historicum Medii Aevi . . .*, 2 vols. (Leipzig, 1723), I, 1793–1930; *M.G.H. SS.*, *n.S.*, III.

Kalendarz i Spominki włocławskie, in *M.P.H.*, *Nova Series*, VII, 79–91.

Kalendarz władysławski, in *M.P.H.*, II, 941–944.

Kodeks dyplomatyczny katedry krakowskiej ś. Wacława, edited by Franciszek Piekosiński, 2 vols. (Cracow, 1874–83) (vols. I and VIII of *Monumenta Medii Aevi historica res gestas Poloniae illustrantia*).

Kodeks dyplomatyczny klasztory tynieckiego, edited by Władysław Kętryński and Stanisław Smolka (Lwów, 1875).

Kodeks dyplomatyczny księstwa mazowieckiego, edited by T. Lubomirski (Warsaw, 1863).

Kodeks dyplomatyczny miasta Krakowa 1257–1506, edited by Franciszek Piekosiński, 2 vols. (Cracow, 1879–82) (vols. V and VII of *Monumenta Medii Aevi historica res gestas Poloniae illustrantia*).

Krabbo, Hermann, and Georg Winter, eds., *Regesten der Markgrafen von Brandenburg aus askanischem Hause*, 12 vols. (Berlin, 1910–55).

Kromer, Marcin, ed., *Inventarium privilegiorum in archivo regni* (reprinted, Cracow, 1832).

Kronika Litewska, in *Pomniki do dziejów litewskich*, edited by T. Narbutt (Vilno, 1846).

Kuraś, Stanisław, ed., *Zbiór dokumentów małopolskich*, vols, I–II (Wrocław, 1962–).

Latopisiec litewski i Kronika ruska, edited by I. Daniłowicz (Vilno, 1827).

Libri antiquissimi civitatis Cracoviensis 1300–1400, edited by Franciszek Piekosiński (Cracow, 1878) (vol. IV of *Monumenta Medii Aevi historica res gestas Poloniae illustrantia*).

Lites ac res gestae inter Polonos Ordinemque Cruciferorum, editio altera by Ignacy Zakrzewski and J. Karwasińka, 3 vols. (Poznań and Warsaw, 1890–1935).

Liv-, Est-, und Kurländisches Urkundenbuch nebst Regesten, edited by F. G. Bunge, et al., 10 vols. (Reval, Riga, and Moscow, 1853–1910).

Ludewig, Johann Peter, ed., *Reliquiae manuscriptorum omnis aevi diplomatum ac monumentorum ineditorum adhuc . . .*, 12 vols. (Frankfurt, Leipzig, and Halle, 1720–41).

Matthias Nuewenburgenis, *Chronica 1272–1350*, in *Font. rer. Germ.*, 149–276.

Monumenta Vaticana historiam regni Hungariae illustrantia, Series prima, 6 vols. (Budapest, 1887–91).

Monumenta Wittelsbacensia: Urkundenbuch zur Geschichte des Hauses Wittelsbach, edited by F. W. Wittmann, 2 vols. (Munich, 1857–61).

Novogrodskaja četvetaja letopis', in *Pol. sob. rus. letop.,* IV.

Palacky, Franz, *Literarische Reise nach Italien im Jahre 1837 zur Aufsuchung von Quellen der böhmischen und mährischen Geschichte* (Prague, 1838).

———, *Über Formelbücher, zunächst in Bezug auf böhmische Geschichte* (Prague, 1847).

Peter of Dusberg, *Chronica terre Prussie* in *SS. rer. Pr.,* I, 3–219.

Poczet królów polskich, in *M.P.H.,* III, 289–96.

Pommerellisches Urkundenbuch, edited by Max Perlbach (Danzig, 1882).

Pommersches Urkundenbuch, 7 vols. (Szczecin, 1868–1958).

Pray, György, ed., *Annales regum Hungariae ab anno Christi CMXCVII ad annum MDLXIV...,* 5 vols. (Vienna, 1764–70).

Preussische Sammlung allerley bisher ungedruckten Urkunden ..., edited by M. C. Hanov, et al., 3 vols. (Gdańsk, 1747–50).

Preussische Urkundenbuch, edited by R. Philippi, et al., vols. I–IV (Königsberg and Marburg, 1882–1964).

Raczyński, Kazimierz, ed., *Codex diplomaticus Maioris Poloniae* (Poznań, 1840).

Regesta diplomatica nec non epistolaria Bohemiae et Moraviae, vols. I–VII (Prague, 1855–1961).

Regesten zur schlesischen Geschichte, edited by Colmar Grünhagen, et al., 8 vols. (Wrocław, 1875–1925).

Rocznik Krasińskich, in *M.P.H.,* III, 128–33.

Rocznik małopolski, in *M.P.H.,* III, 135–202.

Rocznik miechowski, in *M.P.H.,* II, 880–96.

Rocznik świętokrzyski, in *M.P.H.,* III, 53–118.

Rocznik Traski, in *M.P.H.,* II, 826–61.

Rodowód Xiążąt polskich, in *M.P.H.,* III, 280–84.

Spominki lwowskie, in *M.P.H.,* III, 250–51.

Spominki o Ciołkach, in *M.P.H.,* III, 267–71.

Spominki płockie, in *M.P.H.,* III, 118–24.

Spominki sochaczewskie, in *M.P.H.,* III, 118–24.

Stronczyński, K., ed., *Wzory pism dawnych w przerysach wystawione* (Cracow, 1839).

Theiner, Augustin, ed., *Vetera Monumenta historica Hungariam sacram illustrantia ...,* 2 vols. (Rome, 1859–60).

———, ed., *Vetera Monumenta Poloniae et Lithuaniae gentiumque finitimarum historiam illustrantia ...,* 4 vols. (Rome, 1860–64).

Urkundenbuch des Bistums Culm, edited by K. P. Wölky, 2 vols. (Gdańsk, 1884–87).

Vita Caroli IIII, in *Rerum Bohemicarum antiqui scriptores ...,* edited by C. V. Marquard Freher (Hanover, 1602), pp. 86–107.

Wigand of Marburg, *Chronica nova Prutenica,* in *SS. rer. Pr.,* II, 429–662.

Wspominki władysławskie, in *M.P.H.,* II, 944–45.

SECONDARY WORKS

A. Books

Abraham, Władysław, *Powstanie organizacyi kościoła łacińskiego na Rusi,* vol. I (Lwów, 1904).

Bachmann, Adolf, *Geschichte Böhmens,* 2 vols. (Gotha, 1899–1905).

Bardach, Juliusz, *Historia państwa i prawa Polski do połowy XV wieku*, 2d ed. (Warsaw, 1964).

Bartels, Karl, *Deutsche Krieger in polnischen Diensten von Miska I. bis Kasimir dem Grossen, ca. 963–1370* (Berlin, 1922).

Baszkiewicz, Jan, *Polska czasów Łokietka* (Warsaw, 1968).

——, *Powstanie zjednoczonego państwa polskiego (na przełomie XIII i XIV w.)* (Warsaw, 1954).

Balzer, Oswald, *Królestwo Polskie, 1295–1370*, 3 vols. (Lwów, 1919–20).

Bobrzyński, Michał, *Dzieje Polski w zarysie*, 3 vols., 4th ed. (Warsaw, 1927–31).

Borawska, Danuta, *Z dziejów jednej legendy* (Warsaw, 1950).

Buczek, Karol, *Targi i Miasta na prawie polskim (okres wczesnośredniowieczny)* (Wrocław, Warsaw, and Cracow, 1964).

The Cambridge History of Poland, edited by W. F. Reddaway, et al., 2 vols. (Cambridge, 1941–50).

Caro, Jacob, *Geschichte Polens*, 4 vols. in 5 (Gotha, 1863–86) (continuation of R. Röpell, *Geschichte Polens*, vol. 1 [Gotha, 1840]).

Carsten, F. L., *The Origins of Prussia* (Oxford, 1954).

Castelin, K., *Česká drobna mince doby předhusitské a husitské 1300–1411* (Prague, 1953).

Charewiczowa, L., *Handel średniowiecznego Lwówa* (Lwów, 1925).

Chłopocka, Helena, *Procesy Polski z Zakonem krzyżackim w XIV wieku* (Poznań, 1967).

Csuday, Eugen, *Die Geschichte der Ungarn*, 2 vols. (Vienna, 1900).

Dąbrowski, Jan, *Dzieje Polski od r. 1333 do r. 1506*, vol. II of Roman Grodecki, Stanisław Zachorowski, and Jan Dąbrowski, *Dzieje Polski średniowiecznej*, 2 vols. (Cracow, 1926).

——, *Jean de Czarnków et sa chronique (Extrait du Bulletin de l'Académie Polonaise des Sciences et de Lettres, Classes d'histoire et de philosophie—année 1928)* (Cracow, 1928).

——, *Korona Królestwo Polskiego w XIV wieku* (Wrocław and Cracow, 1954).

——, *Ostatnie lata Ludwika Wielkiego 1370–1382* (Cracow, 1918).

——, ed., *Kraków, Studia nad rozwojem miasta* (Cracow, 1957).

Długopolski, Edmund, *Władysław Łokietek na tle swoich czasów* (Wrocław, 1951).

Dobrzeniecki, Tadeusz, *Wrocławski Pomnik Henryka IV* (Warsaw, 1964).

Dvornik, Francis, *The Making of Central and Eastern Europe* (London, 1949).

——, *The Slavs in European History and Civilization* (New Brunswick, N.J., 1962).

Dzieje Szczecina wiek X–1805 (Warsaw, 1963).

Dzieje Wrocławie do roku 1807, edited by Wacław Długoborski, Józef Gierowski, and Karol Maleczyński (Warsaw, 1958).

Dziesięć wieków Płocka (Płock, 1966).

Fastnacht, Adam, *Osadnictwo ziemi sanockiej w latach 1340–1650* (Wrocław, 1962).

Fenrych, Wiktor, *Nowa Marchia w dziejach politycznych Polski w XIII i XIV wieku* (Zielona Góra and Poznań, 1959).

Fischer, S., *Kazimierz Wielki i jego stosunek do Bochni i Bochenszczyzny* (Bochnia, 1934).

Forstreuter, Kurt, *Preussen und Russland von den Anfängen des Deutschen Ordens bis zu Peter dem Grossen* (Göttingen, Berlin, and Frankfurt, 1955).

Friedrich, Walter, *Der Deutsche Ritterorden und die Kurie in den Jahren 1300–1330* (Königsberg, 1912).

Gawęda, Stanisław, *Możnowładztwo małopolskie w XIV i w pierwszej połowie XV wieku* (Cracow, 1966).

257 BIBLIOGRAPHY

Geschichte Schlesiens, vol. I, *Von der Urzeit bis zum Jahre 1526*, published by the Historische Kommission für Schlesien, edited by Hermann Aubin, et al., 3d ed. (Stuttgart, 1961).

Goldschneider, Max, *Glanz und Verderb der polnischen Republik*, 2 vols. (Vienna, 1900).

Göller, Emil, *Die Einnahmen der apostolischen Kammer unter Johann XXII* (Paderborn, 1910).

Górski, Karol, *Państwo Krzyżackie w Prusach* (Gdańsk and Bydgoszcz, 1946).

Gospos, Erich, *Die Politik Bolkos II von Schweidnitz-Jauer 1326–1368* (Halle, 1910).

Grodecki, Roman, *Kongres Krakowski w roku 1364* (Warsaw, 1939).

———, *Rozstanie się Śląska z Polską* (Katowice, 1938).

———, Stanisław Zachorowski, and Jan Dąbrowski, *Dzieje Polski średniowiecznej*, 2 vols. (Cracow, 1926).

Gromnicki, Tadeusz, *Świętopietrze w Polsce* (Cracow, 1908).

Halecki, Oskar, *Dzieje unii Jagiellońskiej*, 2 vols. (Cracow, 1919).

———, *Un empereur de Byzance à Rome* (Warsaw, 1930).

———, *A History of Poland* (reprinted, New York, 1966).

Historia Polski, general editor Tadeusz Manteuffel, vol. I, *do roku 1764*, in three parts, edited by Henryk Łowmiański (Warsaw, 1958–61).

Historia Śląska, general editor Karol Maleczyński, vol. I, *do roku 1763*, in four parts (Wrocław, 1960–64).

Historja Śląska od najdawniejszych czasów do roku 1400, edited by Stanisław Kutrzeba, et al., 3 vols. (Cracow, 1933–39).

Hóman, Bálint, *Geschichte des Ungarischen Mittelalters*, 2 vols. (Berlin, 1940–43).

Hrushevsky, Mykhailo, *Istoria Ukrainy Rusy*, 10 vols. (reprinted, New York, 1955).

Iorga, N., *Historie des Roumains et de la Romanité oriental*, 4 vols. in 5 (Bucharest, 1937).

Istoria Moldavii, edited by A. D. Udalcov and L. V. Čerepnin, vol. I (Kišinev, 1951).

Jasienica, Paweł, *Polska Piastów* (Warsaw, 1966).

Kaczmarczyk, Zdzisław, *Kazimierz Wielki (1333–1370)* (Warsaw, 1948).

———, *Monarchia Kazimierza Wielkiego*, 2 vols. (Poznań, 1939–46).

———, *Polska czasów Kazimierza Wielkiego* (Cracow, 1964).

Kaczmarczyk, Zdzisław and Stefan Weyman, *Reformy wojskowe i organizacja siły zbrojnej za Kazimierza Wielkiego* (Warsaw, 1958).

Kiersnowski, Ryszard, *Wstęp do numizmatyki polskiej wieków średnich* (Warsaw, 1964).

Kochanowski, Jan, *Kazimierz Wielki* (Warsaw, 1900).

Köhler, G., *Die Entwicklung des Kriegswesens und der Kriegsführung in der Ritterzeit*, 3 vols. (Wrocław, 1886–93).

Korzon, Tadeusz, *Dzieje wojen i wojskowości w Polsce*, 3 vols. (Cracow, 1912–14).

Kromer, Marcin, *Kronika Polska* (Warsaw, 1767).

Kucharski, Władysław, *Sanok i sanocka ziemia w dobie Piastów i Jagiellonów* (Lwów, 1925).

Kuczyński, Stefan M., *Wielka Wojna z Zakonem Krzyżackim w latach 1409–1411*, 3d ed. (Warsaw, 1966).

Kujot, Stanisław, *Dzieje Prus Królewskich*, 2 vols. (Toruń, 1924).

Kutrzeba, Stanisław, *Historia ustroju Polski: Korona*, 8th ed. (Warsaw, 1949).

Ladenberger, Tadeusz, *Zaludnienie Polski na początku panowania Kazimierza Wielkiego* (Lwów, 1930).

Lelewel, Joachim, *Polska, dzieje i rzeczy jej rozpatrywane*, 20 vols. (Warsaw, 1851–68).

Lohmeyer, Karl, *Geschichte von Ost- und Westpreussen*, vol. I (Gotha, 1881).

Luck, K., *Deutsche Aufbaukräfte in der Entwicklung Polens* (Plauen, 1934).

Lunt, William E., *Papal Revenues in the Middle Ages* (New York, 1934).

Lviv, A Symposium on its 700th Anniversary (New York, 1962).

Ładogórski, Tadeusz, *Studia nad zaludnieniem Polski XIV wieku* (Wrocław, 1958).

Macartney, C. A., *Hungary, A Short History* (Edinburgh, 1962).

Maleczyńska, Ewa, *Książęce lenno mazowieckie 1351–1526* (Lwów, 1929).

Maleczyński, Karol, *Dzieje Wrocławia do roku 1526* (Katowice and Wrocław, 1948).

————, *Polska a Pomorze Zachodnie w walce z Niemcami w wieku XIV i XV* (Gdańsk, Bygdoszcz, and Szczecin, 1947).

Maschke, Erich, *Der Peterspfennig in Polen und dem deutschen Osten* (Leipzig, 1933).

Mas Latrie, M. L. de, *Guillaume de Machaut* (Geneva, 1877).

Mollat, G., *The Popes at Avignon, 1305–1378* (London, 1963).

Morawski, Kazimierz, *Historya Uniwersytetu jagiellońskiego, średnie wieki i odrodzenie*, 2 vols. (Cracow, 1900).

Müller, Carl, *Der Kampf Ludwig des Baiern mit der römischen Kurie*, 2 vols. (Tübingen, 1879–80).

Muratori, L. A., *Annales d'Italia . . .*, 18 vols. (Milan, 1753–56).

Naruszewicz, Adam, *Historya narodu polskiego od początku chrześciaństwa*, 8 vols. (Warsaw, 1780–1806).

Nowak, Tadeusz, *Walki z agresją Zakonu Krzyżackiego w okresie jednoczenia Państwa Polskiego* (Warsaw, 1952).

Olejnik, Karol, *Działalność militarna polski w czasach Kazimierza Wielkiego* (Poznań, 1966).

Palacky, Franz, *Geschichte von Böhmen*, 5 vols. in 10 (Prague, 1836–67).

Paszkiewicz, Henryk, *O genezie i wartości Krewa* (Warsaw, 1938).

————, *Polityka Ruska Kazimierza Wielkiego* (Warsaw, 1925).

Pazyra, Stanisław, *Geneza i rozwój miast mazowieckich* (Warsaw, 1959).

Piekosiński, Franciszek, *O monecie i stopie menniczej w Polsce w XIV i XV wieku* (Cracow, 1878).

Pieradzka, Krystyna, *Kaźko Szczeciński na tle polityki pomorskiej Kazimierza Wielkiego* (Warsaw, 1947).

Piwarski, Kazimierz, *Dzieje Gdańska w zarysie* (Gdańsk, Bydgoszcz, and Szczecin, 1946).

Polska i jej dorobek dziejowy w ciągu tysiąca lat istnienia, edited by Henryk Paszkiewicz, vol. I (London, 1956).

Rhode, Gotthold, *Geschichte Polens, Ein Überblick* (Darmstadt, 1966).

————, *Die Ostgrenze Polens, Politische Entwicklung, kulturelle Bedeutung und geistige Auswirkung*, vol. I, *Im Mittelalter bis zum Jahre 1401* (Cologne and Graz, 1955).

Rutkowski, Jan, *Historia Gospodarcza Polski*, 2 vols. (Poznań, 1946–50).

Sandow, Erich, *Die Polnische-pommerellische Grenze 1309–1454* (*Beihefte zum Jahrbuch der Albertus-Universität, Königsberg, Pr.*, VI) (Kitzingen/Main, 1954).

Schiemann, Theodore, *Russland, Polen und Livland bis ins 17. Jahrhundert*, 2 vols. (Berlin, 1886–87).

Schulz, Johannes, *Die Mark Brandenberg*, vols. I–IV (Berlin, 1961–).

Schumacher, Bruno, *Geschichte Ost- und Westpreussen* (Königsberg, 1937).

Seraphim, A., *Das Zeugenverhör des Franciscus de Moliano 1312* (Königsberg, 1912).

Seton-Watson, R. W., *History of the Roumanians* (Cambridge, 1934).

Sieradzki, Józef, *Polska wieku XIV. Studium z czasów Kazimierza Wielkiego* (Warsaw, 1959).

Silnicki, Tadeusz, *Biskup Nanker* (Warsaw, 1953).

Sinor, Denis, *History of Hungary* (New York, 1959).

Smolka, Stanisław, *Die reussische Welt. Historisch-politische Studien, Vergangenheit und Gegenwart* (Vienna, 1916).

——, *Rok 1386* (Cracow, 1886).

Sobociński, Władysław, *Pakta Konwenta: Studium z Historii prawa polskiego* (Cracow, 1939).

Sprawozdanie z poszukiwań na Węgrzech dokonanych z ramięnia Akademii Umiejętności przez ... Jana Ptaśnika (Cracow, 1919).

Spuler, Berthold, *Die Goldene Horde. Die Mongolen in Russland, 1223–1502* (Leipzig, 1943).

Stadnicki, Kazimierz, *Synowie Giedymina*, 2 vols. (Lwów, 1848–53).

Stadtmüller, Georg, *Geschichte Südosteuropas* (Munich, 1950).

Stavrianos, L. S., *The Balkans Since 1453* (New York, 1958).

Stronczyński, K., *Dawne monety dynastyi Piastów i Jagiellonów*, 3 vols. (Piotrków, 1883–85).

Stryjkowski, Maciej, *Kronika Polska, litewska, zmudzka, i wszystkiej Rusi* (Warsaw, 1766; in 2 vols., 1846).

Šusta, Josef, *Dvě knihy českich dějin*, 2 vols. (Prague, 1917–19; vol. II, 2d ed., 1935).

——, *Karel IV, Otec a Syn 1333–1346* (Prague, 1946).

——, *Karel IV, za císařskou korunou 1346–1355* (Prague, 1948).

——, *Král cizinec* (Prague, 1939).

Szajnocha, Karol, *Odrodzenie się Polski za Władysława Łokietka* (Cracow, 1887).

——, *Wiek Kazimierza Wielkiego* (Lwów, 1854).

Taube, F. W., *Ludwig der Aeltere als Markgraf von Brandenburg 1323–1351* (Berlin, 1900).

Thomson, S. Harrison, *Czechoslovakia in European History*, 2d ed. (Princeton, N.J., 1953).

Treitschke, Heinrich von, *Das Deutsche Ordensland Preussen* (reprinted Göttingen, 1955).

Tumler, Marjan, *Der Deutsche Orden im Werden, Wachsen und Wirkung bis 1400* (Vienna, 1955).

Vernadsky, George, *The Mongols and Russia* (New Haven, Conn., 1953).

Vetulani, Adam, *Walka Polski w wiekach średnich o dostęp do Bałtyku* (Warsaw, 1954).

Voigt, Johannes, *Geschichte Preussens von den ältesten Zeiten bis zum Untergange der Herrschaft des Deutschen Ordens*, 9 vols. (Königsberg, 1827–39).

Wandruszka, Adam, *Das Haus Habsburg* (Stuttgart, 1956).

Werunsky, Emil, *Geschichte Kaiser Karls IV. und seine Zeit*, 3 vols. in 4 (Innsbruck, 1880–96).

Weyman, Stefan, *Cła i drogi handlowe w Polsce piastowskiej* (Poznań, 1938).

Winter, E. K., *Rudolf IV. von Österreich*, 2 vols. (Vienna, 1934–36).

Wojciechowski, Zygmunt, *L'Etat Polonais au Moyen-age* (Paris, 1949).

——, *Studia Historyczne* (Warsaw, 1955).

——, *W sprawie Regnum Poloniae za Władysława Łokietka* (Lwów, 1924).

Wyrobisz, Andrzej, *Budownictwo murowane w Małopolsce w XIV i XV wieku* (Wrocław, Warsaw, and Cracow, 1963).

Xenopol, A. D. *Histoire des Roumains de la Dacie Trájane*, 2 vols. (Paris, 1896).

Zajączkowski, Stanisław, *Polska a Zakon Krzyżacki w ostatnich latach Władysława Łokietka* (Lwów, 1929).

Zakrzewski, Stanisław, *Zagadnienia Historyczne*, 2 vols. (Lwów, 1936).

Ziekursch, Irene, *Der Prozess zwischen König Kasimir von Polen und dem Deutschen Orden im Jahre 1339* (Berlin, 1934).

B. Articles and Periodical Literature

Abraham, Władysław, "Polska a Chrzest Litwy," in *Polska i Litwy w dziejowym stosunku* (Warsaw, 1914), pp. 3–23.

———, "Sprawa Muskaty," *R.A.U.*, XXX (1894), 122–80.

———, "Stanowisko Kurii papieskiej wobec koronacji Łokietka," *Księga pamiątkowa wydana przez Uniwersytet lwowski ku uczczeniu 500-letniego jubileuszu Uniwersytetu krakowskiego* (Lwów, 1900), pp. 1–34.

———, "Założenie biskupstwa łacińskiego w Kamieńcu Podolskim," in *Księga pamiątkowa ku uczczeniu 250-tej rocznicy założenia Uniwersytetu Lwowskiego przez Króla Jana Kazimierza r. 1661* (Lwów, 1912), I, 1–39.

Balzer, Oswald, "O następstwie tronu w Polsce. Studya historycznoprawne," *R.A.U.*, XXXVI (1897), 289–431.

———, (letters), *K.H.*, XX (1906), 1–57, 397–441; XXI (1907), 1–58, 193–291.

———, "Polonia, Poloni, gens Polonica," in *Księga pamiątkowa ku czci Bolesława Orzechowicza* (Lwów, 1916), I, 71–93.

———, "Z prywatnego życia Kazimierza Wielkiego," *K.H.*, IX (1895), 193.

Bauer, Otakar, "Poznámky k mírovým smlouvám českopolským z roku 1335," in *Sborník prací venovaných prof. dru. Gustavu Friedrichovi k šedesátým narozeninám 1871–1931* (Prague, 1931), pp. 9–22.

Biskup, Marian, "Analiza bitwy pod Płowcami i jej dziejowego znaczenia," *Ziemia Kujawska*, I (1963), 73–104.

Bobrzyński, Michał, "Bunt wójta krakowskiego Alberta z r. 1311," *Biblioteka Warszawska*, XXXVII, pt. iii (1877), 329–48.

Boswell, Alexander Bruce, "Poland and Lithuania in the Fourteenth and Fifteenth Centuries," in *The Cambridge Medieval History*, vol. VIII (Cambridge, 1936), 556–86.

———, "Territorial Division and the Mongol Invasion, 1202–1300," in *The Cambridge History of Poland*, edited by W. F. Reddaway, et al., 2 vols. (Cambridge, 1941–50), I, 85–107.

———, "The Teutonic Order," in *The Cambridge Medieval History*, vol. VII (Cambridge, 1932), 248–69.

———, "The Twelfth Century: From Growth to Division, 1079–1202," in *The Cambridge History of Poland*, edited by W. F. Reddaway, 2 vols. (Cambridge, 1941–50), I, 43–59.

Buczek, D. S., "Archbishop Jakub Swinka (1283–1314), An Assessment," in *Studies in Polish Civilization*, ed. D. S. Wandycz (New York, n.d. [1971?]), pp. 54–65.

Buxbaum, M., "Stosunki polsko-ruskie w latach 1288–1323," *Sprawozdanie Dyrekcji Państw. Gimnazjum w Końskich za r. 1931–1932* (Końskie, 1932).

Castelin, K., "Pražske groše v cizině," *Numismatické Listy*, XI (1956).

Chłopocka, Helena, "Dotychczasowe edycje Lites ac res gestae w świetle krytyki," *Studia Źródłoznawcze*, X (1965), 109–15.

———, "Tradycje o Pomorzu Gdańskim w zeznaniu świadków na procesach polsko-krzyżackich w XIV i XV wieku," *Roczniki Historyczne*, XXV, i (1959), 65–142.

Chodynicki, Kazimierz, "Próby zaprowadzenia Chrześcijaństwa na Litwie przed r. 1386," *P.H.*, XVIII (1914), 215–319.

Czołowski, Aleksander, "Początki Moldawii i wyprawa Kazimierza Wielkiego r. 1359," *K.H.*, IV (1890), 258–85.

———, "Sprawy wołoskie w Polsce do roku 1412," *K.H.*, V (1890), 569–72.

Dąbrowski, Jan, "Dzieje polityczne Śląska w latach 1290–1402," in *Historja Śląska od najdawniejszych czasów do roku 1400*, edited by Stanisław Kutrzeba, et al., 3 vols. (Cracow, 1933–39). I, 327–562.

———, "Elżbieta Łokietkówna," *R.A.U.*, LVII (1914), 302–430.

———, "Polityka andegaweńska Kazimierza Wielkiego," *K.H.*, XXXVI (1922), 11–40.

———, "Z czasów Łokietka, Studya nad stosunkami polsko-węgierskimi w XIV w.," *R.A.U.*, Series II, XXXIV (1916), 278–326.

Długopolski, Edmund, "Bunt wójta Alberta," *Rocznik Krakowski*, VII (1905), 135–86.

Doebner, Richard, "Ueber Schlesiens auswartige Beziehungen vom Tode Herzog Heinrich IV, bis zum Aussterben der Přemysliden in Böhmen, 1290–1306," *Zeitschrift für Geschichte und Alterthums Schlesiens*, XIII (1876), 343–67.

———, "Polityczny testament ostatniego z książąt Pomorza Gdańskiego," *Rocznik Gdański*, V (1932), 5–50.

Dragan, Marcin, "Testament Kazimierza Wielkiego," in *Sprawozdanie Dyrekcyi c. k. Gimnazyum V we Lwowie za rok szkolny 1911* (Lwów, 1911), pp. 3–23.

Droba, Ludwik, "Stosunki Leszka Białego z Rusią i Węgrami," *R.A.U.*, XIII (1881), 361–426.

Fiedler, Joseph, "Böhmens Herrschaft in Polen. Ein urkundlicher Beitrag," *Archiv für Kunde österreichischer Geschichtsquellen*, XIV (1855), 161–88.

Fijałek, Jan, "Średniowieczne biskupstwa kościoła wschodniego na Rusi i Litwie na podstawie źródeł greckich," *K.H.*, X (1896), 487–521.

Forstreuter, Kurt, "Die Bekehrung Gedimins," in *Deutschland und Litauen im Mittelalter* (Cologne and Graz, 1962), pp. 43–60.

———, "Die Bekehrung Gedimins und der Deutsche Orden," *Altpreussische Forschungen*, V (1928), 239–61.

———, "Briefe aus Preussen nach Köln um 1330," *Jahrbuch der Kölnischen Geschichtsvereins*, XXVI (1951), 85–99.

Górka, Olgierd, "Zagadnienia czarnomorskie w polityce polskiego średniowiecza," *P.H.*, XXX (1932–33), 325–91.

Górski, Karol, "Śmierć Przemysława II," *Roczniki Historyczne*, V (1929), 170–200.

Górski, Kazimierz, "Stosunki Kazimierza Sprawiedliwego z Rusią." *Przewodnik Naukowy i Literacki*, III (1875), 572–84, 649–56, 750–57.

Gorzycki, Kazimierz, "Wpływ stolicy apostolskiej na rokowania pokojowe Kazimierza Wielkiego z Czechami i Zakonem niemieckim," *Przewodnik Naukowy i Literacki*, XXI (1893), 78–87, 170–77, 266–74, 366–70, 448–55.

Grodecki, Roman, "Dzieje Polski do r. 1194," in Roman Grodecki, Stanisław Zachorowski, and Jan Dąbrowski, *Dzieje Polski średniowiecznej*, 2 vols. (Cracow, 1926), I, 1–194.

———, "Pojawienie się groszy czeskich w Polsce," *Wiadomości Numizmatyczno-Archeologiczne*, XVIII (1936), 76–87.

———, "Zgon Kazimierza Wielkiego (1370)," in *Mediaevalia w 50 rocznicę pracy naukowej Jana Dąbrowskiego* (Warsaw, 1960), pp. 151–57.

Grünhagen, Colmar, "Die Correspondenz der Stadt Breslau mit Karl IV in den Jahren 1347–1355," *Archiv für Österreichische Geschichte*, XXXIV (1865), 345–70.

————, "König Johann von Böhmen und Bischof Nanker von Breslau," *Sitzungsberichte der Kaiserlichen Akademie der Wissenschaften, Philosophisch-historische Classe* (Vienna), XLVII, pt. vii (1864), 4–102.

Gumowski, Marian, "Grobowiec Henryka IV," *Zaranie Śląskie*, XI (1935), 155–59, 229–31.

————, "Szczerbiec polski, miecz koronacyjny," *Małopolskie Studia Historyczne*, II, pts. ii/iii (1959), 5–18.

Halecki, Oskar, "Casimir the Great," in *The Cambridge History of Poland*, edited by W. F. Reddaway, et al., 2 vols. (Cambridge, 1941–1950). I, 167–87.

————, "Geografja polityczna ziem ruskich Polski i Litwy 1340–1569," *Sprawozdania z posiedzeń towarzystwa naukowego Warszawskiego, wydział I i II*, X (March 16, 1917), 5–23.

————, "Kazimierz Wielki, 1333–1370," *Encyklopedya Polska*, V, pt. i (Warsaw, Lublin, Łódź, and Cracow, 1920), pp. 310–409.

————, "Medieval Poland," in L. I. Strakhovsky, ed., *A Handbook of Slavic Studies* (Cambridge, Mass., 1950), pp. 77–96.

————, "O genezie i znaczeniu rządów andegaweńskich w Polsce," *K.H.*, XXXV (1921), 31–68.

Heinemann, Otto, "Das Bundniss zwischen Polen und Pommern vom Jahre 1325," *Zeitschrift der Historischen Gesellschaft für die Provinz Posen*, XIII (1898), 341–45.

————, "Die Bündnisse zwischen Polen und Pommern von 1348 und 1466," *Zeitschrift der Historischen Gesellschaft für die Provinz Posen*, XIV (1899), 323–30.

Herquet, K., "Beiträge zum Itinerar Karl IV und zu seinem Aufenthalt in Schlesien mit dem König von Cypren im Jahre 1364," *Zeitschrift des Vereins für Geschichte Schlesiens*, XIV (1878), 521–27.

Hóman, Bálint, "Hungary, 1301–1490," in *The Cambridge Medieval History*, vol. VIII (Cambridge, 1936), 587–619.

Huber, Alfons, "Ludwig I. von Ungarn und die ungarischen Vasallenländer," *Archiv für Österreichische Geschichte*, LXVI (1885), 1–44.

Jasiński, Kazimierz, "Zapis Pomorza gdańskiego przez Mszczuja w roku 1282," *Przegląd Zachodni*, VIII, ii (1952), 176–89.

Jedlicki, M. Z., "German Settlement in Poland and the Rise of the Teutonic Order," in *The Cambridge History of Poland*, edited by W. F. Reddaway, et al., 2 vols. (Cambridge 1941–50), I, 125–47.

Kaliski, Tadeusz, "Obchody 630 rocznicy bitwy pod Płowcami," *Ziemia Kujawska*, I (1963), 253–57.

Kaniowski, Stanislaw, "Przyczynki do dziejów wojny polsko-krzyżackiej z r. 1331," *P.H.*, XII (1911), 128–48.

————, "Uwagi krytyczne o bitwie pod Płowcami," *P.H.*, XVIII (1914), 24–38, 203–14.

Kętrzyski, Stanisław, "The Introduction of Christianity and the Early Kings of Poland," in *The Cambridge History of Poland*, edited by W. F. Reddaway, et al., 2 vols. (Cambridge, 1941–50), I, 16–42.

————, "Zapis Kazimierza Wielkiego dla Kazimierza Bogusławowica," *P.H.*, XIV (1912), 26–47, 164–94, 295–316.

————, "O przywileju księcia Mściwoja, nadającym Pomorze Przemysławowi księciu Wielkopolskiemu 1282," *Przewodnik Naukowy i Literacki*, V (1877), 1133–38.

Keyser, Erich, "Der bürgerliche Grundbesitz der Rechtstadt Danzig im 14. Jahrhundert," *Zeitschrift des westpreussischen Geschichtsvereins*, LVIII (1918), 1–70.

———, "Die Legende von der Zerstörung Danzigs im Jahre 1308," *Zeitschrift des westpreussischen Geschichtsvereins*, LIX (1919), 163–82.

Kłodziński, Adam, "Jeden czy dwa bunty wójta Alberta," *S.A.U.*, XLIII (1938), 47–51.

———, "Małżeństwo Władysława Łokietka," *S.A.U.*, XLIII (1938), 326–29.

———, "Polityka Muskaty (1304–1306)," *S.A.U.*, XLI (1936), 334–38.

———, "Problem węgierskiej pomocy dla Łokietka w r. 1304–1306," *S.A.U.*, XLI (1936), 132–34.

———, "Rokowanie polsko-brandenburskie w roku 1329," *R.A.U.*, XLVII (1905), 57–124.

———, "W obozie Cesarskim, 1331–1332," *Przegląd Polski*, CLIII (1904), 286–314.

———, "W obronie zdrajcy," *S.A.U.*, VI, vii (1901), 18–19.

———, "Z dziejów pierwszego krakowskiego buntu wójta Alberta," *Zapiski Towarzystwa Naukowego w Toruniu*, XIV (1948), 45–56.

———, "Ze studjów krytycznych nad rokiem 1331," *K.H.*, XIX (1905), 30–42.

Knoll, Paul W., "Casimir the Great and the University of Cracow," *Jahrbücher für Geschichte Osteuropas*, XVI (1968), 232–49.

———, "The Stabilization of the Polish Western Frontier Under Casimir the Great, 1333–1370," *The Polish Review*, XII, pt. iv (1967), 3–29.

———, "Władysław Łokietek and the Restoration of the *Regnum Poloniae*," *Medievalia et Humanistica*, XVII (1966), 51–78.

Koczy, Leon, "Przymierze polsko-duńskie w roku 1315 na tle stosunków polsko-brandenburskich," *Roczniki Historyczne*, VIII (1931), 31–81.

Kozłowska-Budkowa, Zofia, "Z ostatnich lat Kazimierza Wielkiego," *Małopolskie Studia Historyczne*, VI, iii/iv (1963), 11–21.

Krakowski, Stefan, "Korjatowicze i sprawa Podolska w XIV wieku w oświetleniu najnowszej historjografji Polskiej," *Ateneum Wileńskie*, XIII (1938), 250–74.

Krofta, Kamil, "Bohemia in the Fourteenth Century," in *The Cambridge Medieval History*, vol. VII (Cambridge, 1932), 155–82.

Krzyżanowski, Stanisław, "Poselstwo Kazimierza Wielkiego do Awinionu i pierwsze uniwersyteckie przywileje," *Rocznik Krakowski*, IV (1900), 1–111.

———, "Regnum Poloniae," *S.A.U.*, XIV (1909), v, 14–16, and XVIII (1913), ix, 20–26.

Kuczyński, Stefan, "Sine Wody, Rzecz o wyprawie Olgierdowej 1362 r.," in *Księga ku czci Oskara Haleckiego* (Warsaw, 1935), pp. 81–141.

Kutrzeba, Stanisław, "Handel Krakowa w wiekach średnich na tle stosunków handlowych Polski, *R.A.U.*, XLIV (1903), 1–196.

———, "Handel Polski ze Wschodem w wiekach średnich," *Przegląd Polski*, XXXVIII (1903), cxlvii, 189–219, 462–96; cxlix, 512–37; cl, 115–45.

———, (letters), *K.H.*, XX (1906), 581–626.

———, "Starostowie, ich początki i rozwój do końca XIV wieku," *R.A.U.*, XLV (1903), 231–348.

Lepiarczyk, Józef, "Fazy budowy kościoła mariackiego w Krakowie, wieki XIII–XV," *Rocznik Krakowski*, XXXIV, pt. iii (1959), 181–251.

Leniek, Jan, "Kongres Wyszegradzki w roku 1335," *Przewodnik Naukowy i Literacki*, XII (1884), 177–184, 247–71, 356–66.

Lewicki, A., "Jeszcze w sprawie zajęcia Rusi czerwonej przez Kazimierza Wielkiego," *K.H.*, IX (1895), 480–85.

Lipska, Anna, "Der polnische Hochadel in 14. und in der ersten Hälfte des 15. Jh. und das Problem der Vereinigung Schlesiens mit Polen," in Ewa Maleczyńska, ed., *Beiträge zur Geschichte Schlesiens* (Berlin, 1958), pp. 187–212.

Łodyński, Marian, "Regnum Poloniae w opinii publicznej XIV wieku," *K.H.*, XXVII (1914), 38–54.

Maleczyński, Karol, "Dwa niedrukowane akty przymierza Kazimierza Wielkiego z Danją z roku 1350 i 1363," *K.H.*, XLV (1931), 254–59.

———, "Przymierze Kazimierza Wielkiego z Danją z r. 1350," in *Prace Historyczne w 30-lecie działalności profesorskiej Stanisława Zakrzewskiego* (Lwów, 1934), pp. 187–210.

Małuszyński, Marjan, "Próba analizy bitwy pod Płowcami," *Przegląd Historyczno-wojskowy*, I (1929), 61–84.

———, "Zabór Pomorza przez Krzyżaków (1308–1309)," *Rocznik Gdański*, VII–VIII (1933–34), 44–80.

Maydorn, B., "Der Peterspfennig in Schlesien bis in die Mitte des XIV Jahrhunderts," *Zeitschrift des Vereins für Geschichte und Alterthum Schlesiens*, XVII (1883), 44–62.

Marczali, Henri, "Le procès de Félicien Záh," *Revue Historique*, CVII (1911), 43–58.

Mękicki, R., "Mennica lwowska w latach 1656–1657," *Biblioteka Lwowska*, XXXI–XXXII (1932), 271–89.

Mierzyński, A., "Der Eid des Keistutis im Jahre 1351," *Sitzungsberichte der Alterthums-Prussia Gesellschaft*, XVIII (1893), 104–12.

Mitkowski, J., "Uwagi o zaludnieniu Polski na początku panowania Kazimierza Wielkiego," *Roczniki Dziejów Społecznych i Gospodarczych*, X (1948), 121–31.

Muczkowski, Józef, "Pomnik Kazimierza Wielkiego w katedrze na Wawelu," *Rocznik Krakowski*, XIX (1922), 134–57.

Niwiński, Mieczysław, "Biskup krakowski Jan Grotowic i zatargi jego z Włodzisławem Łokietkiem i Kazimierzem Wielkim. Ustęp z dziejów stosunku Kościoła do Państwa w Polsce w w. XIV," *Nova Polonia Sacra*, III (1939), 57–99.

Nowogrodzki, Stanisław, "Pomorze Zachodnie a Polska 1323–1370," *Rocznik Gdański*, IX–X (1935–36), 2–80.

Panaitescu, P. P., "Din istoria luptei pentru independeută Moldovei in veacul al XIV-lea," *Studi Revilistà de istoria*, IV (1956).

Paszkiewicz, Henryk, "Sprawa najazdu tatarskiego na Lublin w roku 1337," *Teka Zamojskiego* (1920).

———, "W sprawie zhołdowania Mazowsza przez Kazimierza Wielkiego," *P.H.*, XXIV (1924), 1–14.

———, "Z dziejów Podlasia w XIV wieku," *K.H.*, XLII (1928), 229–45.

———, "Z dziejów rywalizacji polsko-węgierskiej na terenie Rusi halicko-włodzimier-skiej w XIV wieku," *K.H.*, XXXVIII (1924), 281–310.

———, "Ze studjów nad polityką krzyżacką Kazimierza Wielkiego," *P.H.*, XXV (1925), 187–221.

———, "Ze studjów nad polityką Polską, Litewską i Krzyżacką Bolesława Jerzego, ostatniego księcia Rusi halicko-włodzimierskiej," *Ateneum Wileńskie*, II (1924), 31–67.

Piekosiński, Franciszek, "Wiece, Sejmiki i przywileje ziemskie w polsce wieków średnich," *R.A.U.*, XXXIX (1899), 171–251.

Pieradzka, Krystyna, "Bolka II Świdnicki na Łużycach," *Sobótka* II (1949), 93–109.

Pošvář, Jaroslav, "Česká grošová reforma a Polsko," *Studia z dziejów Polskich i Czechosłowackich*, I (1960), 125–39.

Potkański, Karol, "Walka o Poznań (1306–1312)," *R.A.U.*, XXXVIII (1899), 275–94.

———, "Zajęcie Wielkopolski (rok 1313 i 1314)," *R.A.U.*, XLVII (1905), 158–71.

———, "Zdrada Wincentego z Szamotuł. Studya nad XIV wiekiem," *R.A.U.*, XXXVIII (1899), 374–95.

Prochaska, Antoni, "Dokument graniczny czerwono-ruski z r. 1352," *K.H.*, XIV (1900), 51–54.

———, "Od Mendoga do Jagiełły," *Litwa i Ruś*, IV i (1912).

———, "Podole lennem Korony 1352–1430," *R.A.U.*, XXXII (1895), 256–79.

———, "Stosunki Krzyżaków z Gedyminem i Łokietkiem," *K.H.*, X (1896), 1–66.

———, "W sprawie zajęcie Rusi przez Kazimierza Wielkiego," *K.H.*, VI (1892), 1–33.

Ptaśnik, Jan, "Denar świętego Piotra obrońcą jedności politycznej i kościelnej w Polsce," *R.A.U.*, LI (1908), 133–218.

Puymaigre, T., "Une campagne de Jean de Luxembourg, roi de Bohème," *Revue des questions historiques*, XLII (1887), 168–80.

Puzyna, Jozef, "Korjat i Korjatowicze," *Ateneum Wileńskie*, VII (1930), 425–55.

———, "Korjat i Korjatowicze oraz sprawa Podolska, uzupełnienia i poprawski," *Ateneum Wileńskie*, XI (1936), 61–97.

———, "Pierwsze wystąpienie Korjatowiczów na Rusi południowej," *Ateneum Wileńskie*, XIII (1938), 1–68.

Řežabek, Jan, "Jiří II, poslední kníže veškeré Malé Rusi," *Časopis Musea království Českého*, LVII (1883), 120–218.

Russocki, Stanisław, "Region mazowiecki w Polsce średniowiecznej," *P.H.*, LIV (1963), 388–417.

Sacerdoțeanu, A., "Lupta moldovenilor cu litvanii în 1377," in *Omagiu fraților Lapedatu* (Bucharest, 1936).

Sczaniecki, Michał, "Political Ties Between Western Pomerania and Poland, Up to the 16th Century," in *Poland at the XIth International Congress of Historical Sciences in Stockholm* (Warsaw, 1960), pp. 81–101.

Semkowicz, Aleksander, "Adelajda, Krystyna i Jadwiga, żony Kazimierza Wielkiego," *K.H.*, XII (1898), 561–66.

Sieradzki, Józef and Rafał Łąkowski, "Traktat kaliski z roku 1343," in *Osiemnaście Wieków Kalisza*, 2 vols. (Kalisz, 1960–61), II, 41–53.

Skalský, G., "Mincovni reforma Václava II," *Český Časopis Historický*, XL (1934).

Spieralski, Zdzisław, "W sprawie rzekomej wyprawy Kazimierza Wielkiego do Mołdawii," *P.H.*, LII (1961), 147–52.

Steinherz, S., "Die Beziehungen Ludwigs I. von Ungarn zu Karl IV.," *Mittheilung des Instituts für oesterreichische Geschichtsforschung*, VIII (1887), 219–57, IX (1888), 529–637.

Stupnicki, J., "O monetach halicko-ruskich," *Biblioteka Ossolińskich, poczet nowy*, VII (1865), 92 ff.

Szostkiewicz, Zbigniew, "Katalog biskupów ob. łac. przedrozbiorowej Polski," *Sacrum Poloniae Millennium* (Rome, 1954–62), I.

Szujski, Józef, "Warunki traktatu kaliskiego r. 1343," *Opowiadania i roztrząsania historyczne* (Warsaw, 1882), pp. 52–66.

Šusta, Josef, "Václav II a koruna polská," *Český Časopis Historický*, XXI (1915), 313–46.

Thomson, S. Harrison, "Medieval Bohemia," in L. I. Strakhovsky, ed., *A Handbook of Slavic Studies* (Cambridge, Mass., 1947), pp. 97–121.

Tymieniecki, Kazimierz, "Odnowienie dawnego Królestwa Polskiego," *K.H.*, XXXIV (1920), 30–87.

———, "The Reunion of the Kingdom, 1295–1333," in *The Cambridge History of Poland*, edited by W. F. Reddaway, et al., 2 vols. (Cambridge, 1941–50), I, 108–24.

———, "Studya nad XIV wiekiem: Proces polsko-krzyżacki z lat 1320–1321," *P.H.*, XXI (1917–18), 77–148.

Vielrose, Egon, "Ludność Polski od X do XVIII wieku," *Kwartalnik Historii Kultury Materialnej*, V, i (1957), 1–49.

Waugh, W. T., "Germany: Charles IV," in *The Cambridge Medieval History*, vol. VII (Cambridge, 1932), 137–54.

———, "Germany: Lewis the Barvarian," in *The Cambridge Medieval History*, vol. VII (Cambridge, 1932), 113–36.

Włodarski, Bronisław, "Polityka Jana Luksemburczyka wobec Polski za czasów Władysława Łokietka," *Archiwum Towarzystwa Naukowego we Lwowie*, XI, pt. iii (1933), 17–60.

Wojciechowski, Zygmunt, "Z dziejów pośmiertnych Bolesława Chrobrego," *Studia Historyczne* (Warsaw, 1955), pp. 194–222.

Zachorowski, Stanisław, "Wiek XIII i panowanie Władysława Łokietka," in *Encyklopedya Polska*, V, pt. i (Warsaw, Lublin, Łódź, and Cracow, 1920), pp. 134–309; and in Roman Grodecki, Stanisław Zachorowski, and Jan Dąbrowski, *Dzieje Polski średniowiecznej*, 2 vols. (Cracow, 1926), I, 195–410.

Zajączkowski, Stanisław, "Polska a Wittelsbachowie w pierwszej połowie XIV wieku," in *Prace Historyczne w 30-lecie działalności profesorskiej Stanisława Zakrzewskiego* (Lwów, 1934), pp. 41–111.

———, "Przymierze polsko-litewskie 1325 r.," *K.H.*, XL (1930), 469–93.

Zakrzewski, Stanisław, "Wpływ sprawy ruskiej na państwo polskie w XIV wieku," *P.H.*, XXIII (1921–22), 86–121.

INDEX

Wieprz River, 155
Wierzbiczan, 119. *See also* Kalisz, treaties of
William of Pusterla, papal nuncio, 189
Winrich von Kniprode, Grand Master of Teutonic Order, 138, 224; and Casimir, 158, 225; and Rajgród episode, 211
Witago, Bishop of Meissen, 75
Wittelsbach dynasty, 5, 124, 193; and Casimir, 42, 116, 136, 182; and Luxemburgers, 186, 188; and Silesia, 60. *See also* Brandenburg; Lewis, Margrave of Brandenburg
Wiżna, 202, 203, 206
Władysław, Duke of Koźle-Bytom, 61, 190–91
Władysław, Duke of Łęczyca and Dobrzyń, 68, 72, 196; attitude of, to Wyszegrad congress, 75, 83, 91; and Dobrzyń, 81, 91; peace of, with Teutonic Order, 119
Władysław, Duke of Opole, 216, 235
Władysław Łokietek, King of Poland: and Casimir, 47, 55–56, 87, 196, 219; career of, to coronation, 15–18, 21, 23–25, 26–28, 32–35; coronation of, 37–38, 39–40, 170; death of, 14, 62; evaluation of policy and reign of, 1, 6–12, 62–64, 104; policy of, character, 3, 41–42, 82, 196, 219; relations of, with Bohemia, 48, 61–62; relations of, with Brandenburg, 35, 48–49; relations of, with Lithuania, 44, 46–47; relations of, with Pomorze, 21–22, 28, 32, 49; relations of, with Ruthenia, 45, 122–23; relations of, with Teutonic Order, 29, 43–44, 49–51, 54–55, 57–58; use of Process of 1320 by, 44
Włocławek, 54
Włodawka River, 168

Wołczyn, 113, 227
Woldemar, Margrave of Brandenburg, 28–29, 31. *See also* Brandenburg
Wołhyń, 132, 171
Wrocław, diocese of, 94; dispute over, between Gniezno and Prague, 113, 179, 194, 212, 226
Wrocław, Silesian duchy and city of, 72, 157, 185; attack on, by Casimir, 192; control of, disputed between Poland and Bohemia, 81, 93, 97, 192; as part of *Regnum Poloniae*, 41; role of, in Lithuanian affairs, 51, 162
Wschowa, 93; dispute over, by Casimir and Bohemia, 181–82, 187, 191–92; treaty of Namysłów and, 193
Wyszegrad, 74, 125; Congress of, 75–82, 88, 97, 108, 143, 178
Wyszogród, 54, 195, 202

Żagań, Silesian duchy of, 61, 222. *See also* Henry V, Duke of Żagań
Zakroczym, Mazovian duchy of, 202, 203, 206
Zawichost, 156
Zbigniew, canon and chancellor of Cracow, 43, 97–98
Zbrucz River, 155, 168
Zempolna River, 195
Ziemowit II, Duke of Mazovia, 50, 68, 91, 202
Ziemowit III, Duke of Mazovia: and Casimir, 203, 233; and Lithuania, 162, 210; in Mazovia, 202, 206; mentioned, 127, 196, 216, 230; and Ruthenia, 146, 150; and Teutonic Order, 211